THE ECONOMICS

OF THE

CHEMICAL INDUSTRY

by

Jules Backman

Research Professor of Economics

New York University

Published by
MANUFACTURING CHEMISTS ASSOCIATION
1825 Connecticut Avenue, N.W.
Washington, D.C. 20009
February 1970

Preface

This book is a continuation of the series entitled *Studies in Chemical Economics* written in 1964 and 1965 for Manufacturing Chemists Association by Dr. Jules Backman, Research Professor of Economics at New York University.

The four original studies were:
- *Competition in the Chemical Industry*
- *Chemical Prices, Productivity, Wages, and Profits*
- *Chemicals in the National Economy*
- *Foreign Competition in Chemicals and Allied Products*

This new volume entitled *The Economics of the Chemical Industry* revises, updates and consolidates the subject matter of the four previous studies and provides new data where available. The format has been rearranged into one volume by chapter sequence and all appendix tables appear in numerical order at the back of the book for ready reference.

As in the case of the four original studies, this is an independent work of the author and the views expressed do not necessarily represent those of the Association or its members.

—Manufacturing Chemists Association
February 1970

Table of Contents

Chapter		Page

Table of Tables

Table of Tables (cont'd.)

Table of Tables (cont'd.)

Table of Charts

Appendix Tables

Appendix Tables (cont'd.)

Appendix Tables (cont'd.)

Appendix B: Statistical Tables (cont'd.)

Chapter I

The Chemical Industry—
Size and Scope

The size and scope of the chemical industry usually depends on the definition used.[1] There are no sharp lines of distinction between the chemical industry and a number of related industries. One observer has concluded:

> "It cannot be defined like the steel and copper industries, as a group of companies making a common product. Nor can it be defined, like the office equipment, and building materials industries, as a group of companies serving a common market. The only bond tying chemical firms together is a common use of manufacturing processes that are chemical. The result is the least homogeneous of all industries."[2]

According to Webster, chemistry is "The science that treats of the composition of substances and of the transformation which they undergo." The key word is transformation since the change of basic matter from one form to another is the essence of chemical manufacturing.

The chemical industry broadly defined embraces a complex of subindustries. The borders of the industry and of its subindustries generally are indistinct. Large expenditures for research and development create new products and new technological processes which continually alter the product mix of the industry and create opportunities for companies already in the industry as well as for those in other industries.

There is a great deal of crossing of industry lines into and out of chemicals. The outstanding illustration is the petroleum industry. Because of these developments any system of classification which attempts to separate chemical companies into special compartments must be arbitrary to some extent.

One observer has suggested that the chemical industry "is really 35-40 different businesses."[3] As will be noted at various places in this volume there are significant differences in trends between organics and inorganics, between basic petrochemicals and synthetic fibers, between dyes and plastics, etc.

The Bureau of the Census statistics combine establishments producing chemicals and those producing finished chemicals (called allied products) in one group, namely, Chemicals and Allied Products (SIC 28). According to the Bureau of the Budget's definition:

> "This major group includes establishments producing basic chemicals, and establishments manufacturing products by predominantly chemical processes. Establishments classified in this major group manufacture three general classes of products: (1) basic chemicals such as

Note: The author wishes to express his appreciation to Marvin Levine for his invaluable contributions in assembling much of the data, to Dr. Robert Winter of New York University for preparing the charts, to Mrs. Catherine Ferfoglia for her excellent handling of the typing and secretarial work, to Marjorie Campbell of The Manufacturing Chemists' Association for obtaining many helpful materials, to Martin R. Gainsbrugh, chief economist of The National Industrial Conference Board for helpful criticisms of the manuscript, and to the large number of chemical company officials who made available materials and reviewed parts of the manuscript.

acids, alkalies, salts, and organic chemicals; (2) chemical products to be used in further manufacture such as synthetic fibers, plastics, materials, dry colors, and pigments; (3) finished chemical products to be used for ultimate consumption such as drugs, cosmetics, and soaps; or to be used as materials or supplies in other industries such as paints, fertilizers, and explosives."[4]

Thus, this major group includes raw materials, intermediate products, and products which have reached various finished stages. Generally the products produced by the chemical industry are not sold directly to the final consumer.[5] A large proportion is sold to other chemical companies for further processing, the balance is sold to producers of allied products such as drugs, paints, detergents, etc. and to industry generally.

The major categories of products included in the Census classification are the following:

SIC	Subgroup
281	Industrial inorganic and organic chemicals
282	Plastics materials and synthetic resins, synthetic rubber, synthetic and other man-made fibers, except glass
283	Drugs
284	Soap, detergents, and cleaning preparations, perfumes, cosmetics and other toilet preparations
285	Paints, varnishes, lacquers, enamels, and allied products
286	Gum and wood chemicals
287	Agricultural chemicals
289	Miscellaneous chemical products

It is evident that the broad classification includes a number of different industries. Chemical companies generally produce basic chemicals and/or various synthetic products. While they sometimes produce what is defined as "finished chemical products," (e.g. Du Pont produces paints), generally those products are made by other companies which are not popularly regarded as chemical companies (for example, soaps and detergents by Procter & Gamble, paints by Sherwin-Williams, cosmetics by Revlon).

The present study is confined largely to chemical products which are equivalent to SIC 281 and 282. However, where data are available only for the broad group, chemicals and allied products, they are used. SIC 281 includes organic and inorganic chemicals. Organic chemicals are defined as "compounds containing carbon atoms in a form sim''ar to those in plant and animal matter" while inorganic chemicals "usually do not contain carbon [and] are derived from atmospheric gases, minerals, water and other matter that was never of itself, a part of living organisms."[6] SIC 282 covers synthetic products as well as other organics.

Total shipments for the entire chemicals and allied products industry in 1967 were $42.2 billion of which $14.1 billion was accounted for by SIC 281 and $7.4 billion by SIC 282. Thus, the two broad groups given main emphasis in this study accounted for 50.9% of the entire grouping.

It must be emphasized that SIC 281 and 282 each contain products with widely differing characteristics. For example, SIC 281 includes such inorganics as sulfuric acid, chlorine, acetylene, carbon dioxide, titanium pigments, nitric acid, synthetic ammonia, and potassium and sodium compounds. It also includes such organics as cyclic (coal tar) crudes, acyclic chemicals and cyclic intermediates.

2

SIC 282 covers only organics and embraces such widely different products as thermoplastic and thermosetting resins, synthetic rubber, cellulosic and other man-made organic fibers. Clearly, composite trends shown by SIC 281 and 282 will conceal many diverse changes among these products. These products or product groups each have achieved different stages of maturity, have different growth rates, are subject to different combinations of competitive and cost pressures, reflect varying degrees of new technological development, are subject to different supply-demand conditions, and respond differently to broad changes in the economy. As a result each product could merit a complete economic study covering all of the phases of the industry developed in the following chapters.[7] And in fact when new additions to capacity or new entry into a product market are being considered detailed analyses of markets, growth trends, price trends, costs and related factors are evaluated in depth by a company.

However, the comprehensive aggregates do indicate the broad trends of the industry and they are obtainable for many important economic variables such as employment, production, wages, productivity, profits, prices, investment, etc. so that they can be related. Although the main emphasis is given to these broad categories of economic variables, illustrations also are drawn from their components where data are available for subgroups (four or five digit categories contained in SIC 281 and 282) and are helpful in interpreting the broad trends. This procedure clearly demonstrates the diversity and complexity of this industry.

Economic Characteristics of the Chemical Industry

To understand the economics of the chemical industry requires a review of its economic characteristics with particular emphasis upon the role of (1) changing products and processes, (2) by-products and joint products, (3) standardized products, (4) derived demand, (5) multiple product companies, (6) structure of the chemical industry, (7) intensity and diversity of competition, (8) high rate of innovation, (9) relative ease of entry, (10) intensive use of capital, and (11) cost structure. It is the combination of these economic characteristics that helps to explain the performance of the chemical industry.

The multiplicity of products manufactured by the chemical industry makes it difficult to draw a simple profile of their characteristics. Exceptions will be found to almost any generalization about the industry's products.

A distinction may be made between heavy or bulk chemicals and fine chemicals. Bulk chemicals are produced in quantities of at least half a million tons annually and usually sell at a low price per unit. These products, which include sulfuric acid, alkalies and chlorine, ethylene, benzene, phenol, and vinyl chloride, are basic for many other industries and are key raw materials or intermediates for other chemical products; there is considerable captive use by the initial producer. "End-use distribution is usually quite broad. Freight costs represent an important part of the delivered cost to the customer. A high percentage of the volume of the products is consumed by users requiring frequent bulk deliveries in tank cars, barges, hopper cars, box cars, and trucks."[8] These bulk products become "market oriented."[9] In recent years, the volume of many chemical products has increased to the point where they have become bulk products.

Fine chemicals " . . . include nearly all elements or compounds refined to high purity, or reagent grade; or frequently complex compounds made in relatively small volume to specification for specialized use."[10] In terms of numbers, the

3

overwhelming proportion of chemicals fall into this category. They are not affected by the full economies of mass production and sell at much higher prices per unit than the bulk chemicals.

Changing Products and Processes

Change is the outstanding characteristic of the chemical industry. There is probably no other industry which experiences changes in processes, methods, and products to the same extent. The major shift from coal to petroleum and natural gas as a source of raw material is illustrative. The research laboratories yield a steady flow of new products and a continual development of by-products. This dynamic pattern makes it difficult for any company to obtain a monopoly position because substitutes are readily developed. It makes difficult the measurement of growth because the product mix changes so significantly that the numbers apply to different combinations of products whose qualitative usefulness or contribution vary widely. How does one measure the relative contribution of rayon and of acrylic fibers? Of neoprene and of "natural" synthetic rubber? Of vinyl plastic and of polyethylene plastic? Under these conditions, data showing dollars or physical tonnage can give only a partial and incomplete picture.

The laboratories are steadily developing new processes for making a product. For example, before 1960 acrylonitrile generally was produced from acetylene and hydrogen cyanide. In more recent years, it has been derived by "improved new processes, based on the reaction of propylene and ammonia." Similarly, ethylene oxide is now produced by direct oxidation of ethylene instead of "from ethylene *via* ethylene chlorohydrin."[11] The continuing development of new products and new processes results in a high rate of obsolescence. Today's plant and equipment often is obsolete tomorrow as new technology leads to ever increasing size of the most efficient plant and as products and processes are superseded.

By-Products and Joint Products

A significant proportion of chemicals are produced as by-products or as joint products because the production processes of many products are interrelated. It has been said about the meatpacking industry that its use of an animal is so complete that only the "squeal of a pig" is not converted into some product. The chemical industry also has developed an ability to utilize raw materials fully. As Hempel has pointed out "fumes, liquors, scraps, gases, sludges, and other substances created during the main process can now be turned into something useful."[12]

Because of the large expenditures for research and development, the chemical industry has steadily improved its ability to convert former waste materials into economically useful and profitable products. The process has been succinctly illustrated by an official of the Monsanto Company as follows: "We take waste natural gases, make acetylene to be used for other chemical products, take a waste by-product of acetylene and make methanol which is used in making formaldehyde which in turn goes into a host of other products."[13]

In some instances the by-product has become more important than the main product. For example, phosphoric acid originally was recovered from the waste gas formed when ferrophosphorus was made. Now the position has been completely reversed with phosphoric acid and its salts as the principal product and ferrophosphorus as the by-product.

Companies in other industries, such as meat packing, distilling, and paper also convert into chemicals what formerly were waste products. The result has been an intensification of competitive pressures as those companies enter chemical production.

Many products are produced jointly in the chemical industry. However, demand for each of the products does not increase at the same rate thus creating problems in some markets. For example, caustic soda and chlorine usually are produced together in a relatively fixed ratio. However, consumption of chlorine has tended to grow more rapidly than that of caustic soda. Thus, at times when chlorine output has been increased to meet the expanding demand, excess supplies of caustic soda have become available and created pressures in that market.

The determination of costs and their use in connection with pricing is difficult for joint products. For Union Carbide, for example, it has been reported that "The many joint products emerging from any given process, piece of equipment, or research laboratory tend to make allocation of fixed costs a difficult procedure."[14] This problem prevails for most chemical products.

Standardized Products

Most chemicals are produced according to rigid specifications established by the companies, by standards organizations, or by the government. Thus, many products manufactured by different companies or by different processes are identical and interchangeable. This is particularly true for the major inorganics such as sulfuric acid, ammonia, nitric acid, soda ash, chlorine, and caustic soda, for some organics such as benzene, ethanol, phenol, and phthalic anhydride, and for fine chemicals. Such quality is not a factor in selling these products and there are limited opportunities to emphasize effectively non-price factors.[15] Such standardization is not as significant for the vigorously expanding plastics and non-cellulosic textile fibers.

Derived Demand

Chemical products are raw materials or intermediate products which are used in further production. The requirements for these products depends upon the demand for the end-products. Thus, the demand for these raw materials and intermediates is derived. Most users of the end-products are never aware of the role of chemicals in their production. For some chemicals, such as the widely used sulfuric acid, changes in total demand tend to parallel fluctuations in the business cycle. In fact, sulfuric acid usually is considered to be a significant barometer of industrial activity. To some extent, because of the ability to substitute among chemical products price may influence the effective demand for specific products. Nevertheless, the total demand for chemicals is derived and therefore tends to be inelastic for most products.

Multiple Product Companies

Chemical companies generally manufacture many products, which may include basic raw materials, semi-finished goods, and sometimes consumer goods.[16] The larger chemical companies usually have some degree of vertical integration since they manufacture products used at different stages of production. Until recently there has been a reluctance to produce consumer items because they involve different marketing problems and often competition with important customers of the company. Chemical companies have produced paints, detergents,[17] antifreeze and other consumer goods. However, such products usually have accounted for a relatively small proportion of their total sales.

CHART I-1

PATTERN OF PROGRESS

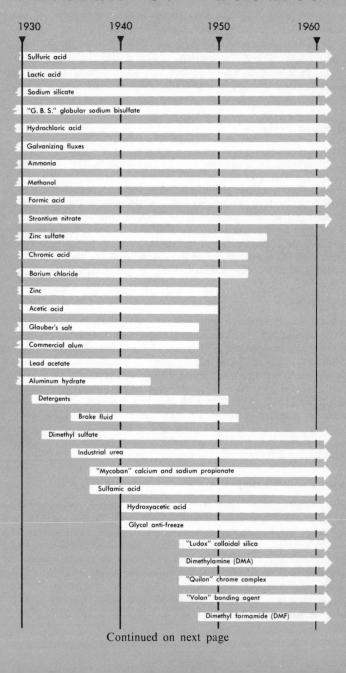

1930	1940	1950	1960

Sulfuric acid

Lactic acid

Sodium silicate

"G. B. S." globular sodium bisulfate

Hydrochloric acid

Galvanizing fluxes

Ammonia

Methanol

Formic acid

Strontium nitrate

Zinc sulfate

Chromic acid

Barium chloride

Zinc

Acetic acid

Glauber's salt

Commercial alum

Lead acetate

Aluminum hydrate

Detergents

Brake fluid

Dimethyl sulfate

Industrial urea

"Mycoban" calcium and sodium propionate

Sulfamic acid

Hydroxyacetic acid

Glycol anti-freeze

"Ludox" colloidal silica

Dimethylamine (DMA)

"Quilon" chrome complex

"Volan" bonding agent

Dimethyl formamide (DMF)

Continued on next page

CHART I-1 (Continued)

PATTERN OF PROGRESS

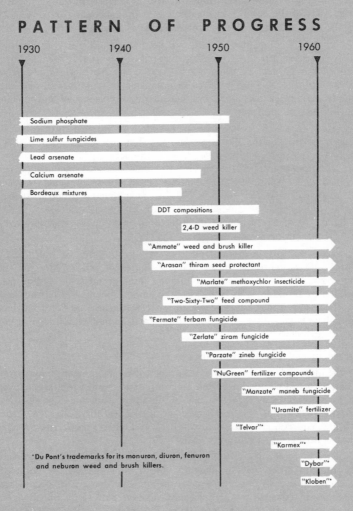

1930   1940   1950   1960

Sodium phosphate

Lime sulfur fungicides

Lead arsenate

Calcium arsenate

Bordeaux mixtures

DDT compositions

2,4-D weed killer

"Ammate" weed and brush killer

"Arasan" thiram seed protectant

"Marlate" methoxychlor insecticide

"Two-Sixty-Two" feed compound

"Fermate" ferbam fungicide

"Zerlate" ziram fungicide

"Parzate" zineb fungicide

"NuGreen" fertilizer compounds

"Manzate" maneb fungicide

"Uramite" fertilizer

"Telvar"*

"Karmex"*

"Dybar"*

"Kloben"*

*Du Pont's trademarks for its monuron, diuron, fenuron and neburon weed and brush killers.

COMINGS AND GOINGS of typical I & B products, shown by arrows in chart above, reflect impact of organic research program. Department's traditional line of industrial chemicals (top) now shares spotlight with new farm and industrial specialties. Obsolete or marginal items have been dropped.

Source: Better Living, E. I. du Pont de Nemours & Company, Sept.-Oct. 1962, p. 20.

Few companies manufacture only one or a few products. Extensive research and development is accompanied by unexpected discoveries because the search to develop one product often leads to the discovery of others. Moreover, companies have know-how in connection with chemical processes and thus are able to develop other products—sometimes to produce their own raw materials and often to develop by-products as noted above. Michael Gort has concluded that, "On the basis of the number of manufactured products per company in 1954," chemicals are among "the more diversified companies."[18]

Most chemical companies usually can readily extend their product lines so that they provide a threat of potential competition whenever demand increases markedly for a product or whenever it appears to offer a profitable outlet for capital investment. This has resulted in a considerable number of new entrants into many chemical markets and in a considerable replacement and realignment among the largest producers.

The extent to which products may be added or dropped by a multiple line company is shown for the Industrial and Biochemicals Department of Du Pont in Chart I-1. Out of 24 typical products manufactured by that department in 1930, 10 had been dropped (e.g. acetic acid, lead acetate, calcium arsenate) by 1950 and 4 others before 1960 (e.g. sodium phosphate, chromic acid). According to the company, between 1949 and 1956 it "abandoned a group of older farm chemicals which once accounted for half of its agricultural sales."[19] On the other hand, 19 of the products manufactured in 1960 were introduced after 1940; 6 in this group were introduced after 1950.

For these multiple line companies, overall profitability is much easier to determine and is more significant than estimates of profitability for specific products. The allocation of all costs among joint products or among primary and related by-products is difficult to make on any meaningful basis. Similarly, costs to be assigned to products destined for intrafirm use are not always readily determinable. Under these conditions, total costs cannot play a significant role in price determination.

Structure of the Chemical Industry

The chemical industry consists of a number of large companies, many smaller ones, and a host of competitors from other industries. When capital requirements are high and significant benefits can be obtained from mass production, the big company becomes the most efficient instrumentality. Size is needed to finance and undertake extensive research as well as to produce new items that may not contribute to profits for years.

The share of total volume accounted for by the large chemical companies is smaller than in other mass production industries. However, the largest firms in the chemical industry occupy a more prominent position in specific product markets than is indicated by their share of the aggregate volume of the industry.

The composition of the four largest companies in the chemical industry and for specific products has changed over time. As a result, the relative share of total shipments accounted for by a constant group of large companies has declined more than indicated by the data for unidentified Big Fours. (See Chapter IV) The published data obscure the full effects of competitive forces which have resulted in significant changes in the position of individual competitors.

Intensity and Diversity of Competition

The chemical industry is intensely competitive and that competition has many dimensions. For example, there exists competition among chemical products (polyethylene and polypropylene), competition with products of other industries (natural fibers and synthetic fibers), competition in research, competition from new competitors with a base in other industries or by extension of product lines by chemical companies, and non-price competition including technical services, emphasis upon quality, improvement of products through research and development, and to a limited extent (for example, antifreeze and textile fibers) the development of brand names. Product differentiation is not important for many products although it does play a role. For the various plastics and synthetic fibers, chemical characteristics have been improved to increase their attractiveness for specific end uses.[20] Such changes can alter the product considerably. It was reported in 1961, for example, that "Dow's polystyrene . . . is far different from the polystyrene it first made in 1937. Dow is now working on a 'high impact' variety that will represent the twenty-ninth improvement it has made on the one product."[21] There also have been considerable improvements for many other products.

Foreign competition also affects the American market in varying degrees. That tariffs have not permitted American producers to avoid intense competition is evident from the experience with plastics, resins, and synthetic fibers where appreciable foreign competition has been felt. For many products (e.g. chlorinated solvents) tariffs have not been restrictive and imports have affected both prices and volume of domestic producers. For other products, American producers have built excessive capacity with intensive domestic competitive pressures resulting in recent years.

High Rate of Innovation

The chemical industry has been among the largest investors in research and development. These expenditures have resulted in a flow of new products and processes which has contributed significantly to the above average growth of the chemical industry and to major changes in its product mix over the years. Synthetic fibers, plastics, gases, synthetic rubbers and many other products have been developed and expanded in relative importance. Change is the important constant in this industry.[22] For example, Stauffer Chemical estimated that one-third of its sales in 1968 was in products added during the preceding five to ten years.[23]

The rapid rate of innovation has had dramatic impacts on competitive patterns within the industry, has created enormous investment requirements and opportunities, and has fed on itself by stimulating an intensification of research efforts by many companies in order to remain competitive. It also has contributed importantly to making chemicals one of the great growth industries in the United States.

Relative Ease of Entry

There are many potential competitors who can produce chemical products. Conrad Berenson has stated: "The multitude of products, processes and raw materials which can substitute for each other, together with the availability of trained manpower and the large number of expertly qualified vendors of processes and plants, make it relatively easy to enter the chemical industry."[24]

Three unique aspects of this industry should be noted: (1) many products and processes are substitutable thus encouraging entry either to produce an existing product or by use of an existing process or by the development of substitute products or by production through alternate processes; (2) these opportunities actually are exercised by many chemical companies, and (3) there is active entry into the industry by companies whose base is in other industries. (See Chapter IV) As was noted earlier, other industries have technological know-how concerning chemical processes. This is particularly true of petroleum and rubber companies. In the past decade, invasion of the chemical industry by petroleum companies has been a major force.

Many of the new entrants into chemical markets have been large companies and hence the ability to obtain capital has been a less important factor than in many other industries despite the large amount of capital required per employee in the chemical industry. The new producers often have become important competitors in terms of volume. The result has been persistent pressures upon existing producers, both large and small, to improve their products and services and to expand their own capacity in order to meet these competitive threats. Ease of entry has been a potent competitive force in the chemical industry.

The competitive impact of ease of entry has been especially evident in connection with many organic chemicals whose prices often have been reduced drastically as excess capacity has developed because a number of companies simultaneously and independently have decided to produce certain key products, particularly among the petrochemicals. In some instances, joint ventures have been formed to produce chemicals when individual firms were reluctant to undertake such expansions on their own.

Intensive Use of Capital

The chemical industry is one of the most intensive users of capital. Both for basic chemicals and for fibers, plastics and rubber the ratio of new capital expenditures to the total for all manufacturing industries is over five times as large as the ratio for employment. In 1967, the chemicals and allied products industries accounted for 14% of the new capital investment but only 4.4% of the total employment in manufacturing industries.

In 1964, the average invested capital per employee was $29,500 for chemicals as compared with $17,100 for all manufacturing. Only the petroleum and tobacco industries reported a greater capital investment per employee[25] (See Table VIII-6).

These high capital costs reflect the large capacity required to obtain maximum efficiency in the production of many chemicals, the state of technology which permits production to be achieved with a relatively high capital input and a low labor input, the intricate nature of the equipment which makes it expensive to produce, the continuous processes utilized and the large volume of equipment required, and the rapid obsolescence and depreciation of the equipment used as new techniques and new products emerge from the research laboratory. Equipment wears out quickly because of high temperatures, pressures, and corrosion.[26]

Cost Structure

The chemical industry is largely a continuous process industry which requires a very heavy initial investment. Added output usually involves relatively small incremental costs. Thus, as volume increases unit costs decline sharply. This situation places a premium on volume - even if prices must be shaded to obtain it.

Industries differ as to their cost structures. Unfortunately, detailed cost data are not available for industries generally nor for chemicals and allied products. However, a rough picture of relative costs for the chemicals and allied products industries as compared with all manufacturing can be obtained by combining data compiled by the U.S. Department of Commerce in the national income accounts, the Census Bureau's Annual Survey of Manufactures, and the Internal Revenue Service. Similar data are not available for chemicals alone.

The total sales or value of shipments reported in these sources for chemicals and allied products appear to be close enough to suggest that the detailed data may be combined to obtain a rough picture of the structure costs. For this purpose, Commerce data are used where available (wages and salaries, wage supplements, depreciation, federal and state income taxes, and profits); the cost of materials is trom the Census of Manufactures and interest costs, advertising and executive compensation are from the Internal Revenue Service. None of these sources report data for administrative and selling costs other than advertising and hence the picture shown is incomplete.[27]

It must be recognized that the data from these separate sources cannot be added together because they are not always comparable (for example, Census data are based on *shipments of establishments* while national income and IRS data are *sales of companies*) and they may involve overlapping costs (for example, where a company produces its own materials, their cost may be included in part in the compensation for labor). Nevertheless, the data for all manufacturing and for chemicals and allied products are comparable for each component of costs because both are derived from the same source. Since the main emphasis is placed on the relationship between chemicals and all manufacturing industries, the significance of the defects in the data is minimized.

The relative importance of each of these major categories of expenses as a percentage of sales for chemicals and allied products and for all manufacturing in 1965[28] is shown in Table I-1.

TABLE I-1

Relative Costs: All Manufacturing and Chemicals And Allied Products, 1965

	All Manufacturing	Chemicals and Allied Products
	(per cent of sales)	
Compensation of labor	25.9	19.5
Wages and salaries	23.0	17.1
Wage supplements	2.9	2.4
(Compensation of Officers)	(1.2)*	(1.0)*
Cost of materials	54.4	44.9
Advertising	1.4*	4.1*
Depreciation, etc.	3.3	4.7
Interest	0.7*	0.8*
Income taxes	3.4	5.3
Profits	4.6	6.2

*From Internal Revenue Service.

Note: Sales for chemicals and allied products were $40.2 billion (Commerce), and $41.3 billion (IRS), and shipments were $37.4 billion (Census).

Sources: U.S. Department of Commerce, Office of Business Economics, *Survey of Current Business,* July 1968, pp. 41, 44, 45, 46; U.S. Treasury Department, Internal Revenue Service, *Statistics of Income—1965, Business Income Tax Returns,* Washington, D.C., 1968, pp. 243, 244; U.S. Department of Commerce, Bureau of the Census, *Annual Survey of Manufactures: 1964 and 1965,* Washington, D.C., 1968, p. 14.

As compared with all manufacturing industries, chemicals and allied products generally appear to require a smaller relative input of labor and materials and larger relative expenditures for advertising, depreciation, and income taxes. The larger proportion shown for advertising reflects the heavy role of such expenditures in the cosmetics, soap, and drug industries.[29] Research and development costs also are higher for chemicals than for all manufacturing.

In light of the relationships noted above, changes in total labor costs appear to have a relatively smaller impact on total costs for chemicals and allied products than for all manufacturing industries. However, for products made by batch processes — dyes, pigments, cosmetics, pharmaceuticals and others — labor costs are relatively much higher than shown by the aggregate data.[30]

On the other hand, changes in construction costs, in prices of equipment, in corporate income tax rates and in depreciation policy can have a relatively greater impact on chemicals and allied products. These relationships also suggest that direct costs are relatively lower for the chemical industries and hence together with the nature of continuous operations explain why it is an industry of sharply declining unit costs.

[1]For example, M. J. Rathbone, former Chairman of the Board of Standard Oil of New Jersey, has observed that " . . . it would not be much of an exaggeration to describe oil refining as a specialized chemical industry." "Oil, Chemistry and Man's Future," the International Palladium Medal Award Lecture, Hotel Pierre, New York, April 13, 1964, p. 4. (mimeo).

[2]Roland P. Soule, "Chemical Industry's Problems Slowing Profits," *Chemical and Engineering News,* August 14, p. 102.

[3]Frank Sciancalepore, "Basic Characteristics of the Chemical Industry," in *Chemical Marketing Research,* edited by N. H. Giragosian, Reinhold Publishing Corp., New York, 1957, p. 2.

[4]*Standard Industrial Classification Manual,* Executive Office of the President, Bureau of the Budget, prepared by the Office of Statistical Standards, Washington, D.C., 1967, p. 94.

[5]Exceptions are found in products such as alcohol and chlorine, a small part of whose output is in a form that can be used by final consumers.

[6]*The Chemical Industry Facts Book,* Manufacturing Chemists' Association, Inc., Washington, D.C., 1962, 5th edition, p. 11.

[7]Some such comprehensive studies have been published. See, for example, Theodore J. Kreps, *The Economics of the Sulfuric Acid Industry,* Stanford University Press, Stanford, California, 1938; Charles F. Phillips, Jr., *Competition in the Synthetic Rubber Industry,* University of North Carolina Press, Chapel Hill, N.C., 1963; and Jesse W. Markham, *Competition in the Rayon Industry,* Harvard University Press, Cambridge, Mass., 1952.

[8]W. F. Newton "The Challenge in Marketing for Inorganic and Heavy Chemicals," in *Chemical Marketing: The Challenge of the Seventies,* American Chemical Society, Washington, D.C., September 1968, p. 15.

[9]J. P. Cunningham, "The Challenges In Marketing For Organic Chemicals," *Ibid.,* p. 26.

[10]*The Chemical Industry Facts Book, op. cit.,* pp. 12-13.

[11]Cunningham, *op. cit.,* pp. 27-128.

[12]Edward H. Hempel, *The Economics of Chemical Industries,* John Wiley & Sons, New York, 1939, p. 90.

[13]Felix N. Williams, *The Future of the Chemical Industry,* Monsanto Chemical Company, April 1963, pp. 6-7.

[14]A. D. H. Kaplan, Joel B. Dirlam, and Robert F. Lanzillotti, *Pricing in Big Business,* The Brookings Institution, Washington, D.C., 1958, p. 109.

[15]It has been pointed out that "Advertising outlays for a new product may range from 2 to 10% of the products' sales, and sometimes more, but promotion costs for commodity chemicals such as formaldehyde, sulfuric acid and caustic soda, range from 0 to 0.2% of sales. For this type of product . . . there is little difference between one company's product and another. . . . All sources for the products provide good material, give speedy delivery, have fine technical service groups, and sell for comparable prices." *Chemical and Engineering News,* December 10, 1962, p. 34.

[16]Dow was estimated to produce "more than 1,000 [products] ranging from such basics as chlorine and magnesium to intermediate petrochemicals to finished consumer goods such as . . . Saranicides for Christmas trees, and Handi-Wrap, a plastic film priced low enough for housewives to use it in place of waxed paper." Perrin Stryker, "Chemicals: The Ball Is Over," *Fortune,* October 1961, p. 126. According to one official, Allied Chemical manufactures about 3,500 different products. Lawrence A. Coleman, "Definitions and Characteristics of Today's Chemical Industry" in *The Chemical Industry.* Allied Chemical Corporation, New York, 1959, p. 17. Du Pont has about 12,000 different products and product lines. *Better Living,* E. I. du Pont de Nemours and Company, November-December 1963. Some product lines may include thousands of products. Thus, the fabrics and finishes department of Du Pont manufactures about 18,000 products. *Better Living,* September-October 1963, p. 23.

[17]Monsanto developed a leading detergent — ALL — but later disposed of this business.

[18]This conclusion was based on chemicals and allied products rather than chemicals. Michael Gort, *Diversification and Integration in American Industry,* Princeton University Press, Princeton, New Jersey, 1962, p. 40.

[19]*Better Living,* September-October 1962, p. 20.

[20]It was reported that in 1961 one company had "about 150 different types of homopolymers, copolymers, mixed polymers, or chemically modified polyethylenes. Most are designed for specific uses." Walter S. Fedor, "Thermoplastics: Progress Amid Problems," *Chemical and Engineering News.* May 29, 1961, p. 81. Du Pont was reported to have over 50 types of polyethylene in 1962. Lawrence Lessing, "How Du Pont Keeps Out in Front," *Fortune,* December 1962, p. 207.

[21]Stryker, *op. cit.,* p. 127.

[22]Robert B. Semple, "What Is So Different About the Chemical Industry," *The Commercial and Financial Chronicle,* November 26, 1959, p. 18.

[23]Statement by Roger W. Gunder, President, Stauffer Chemical Co., *The Commercial and Financial Chronicle,* February 6, 1969, p. 57.

[24]Conrad Berenson, *The Chemical Industry: Viewpoints and Perspectives,* Interscience Publishers, New York, 1963, p. 5.

[25]The large investment per worker in the tobacco industry reflects mainly the large inventories that must be kept on hand rather than the use of machinery and equipment.

[26]Under Treasury guidelines chemicals and allied products may be depreciated in 11 years. U.S. Treasury, Internal Revenue Service, "Depreciation, Guidelines and Rules," *Publication No. 456,* Washington, D.C., Revised, August 1964, p. 7.

[27]Annual reports of some companies show such data. For example, in 1968 Union Carbide reported that selling, general, and administrative expenses were 10.8% of total sales. *Annual Report 1968,* p. 22.

[28]1965 was the latest date for which data were available from the three sources used.

[29]In 1967, advertising expenses for Du Pont, Union Carbide and Dow Chemical were estimated between 1% and 2% sales. In contrast, for drug companies the cost averaged

more than 5% and exceeded 20% for some companies (For Johnson and Johnson it was 5.2%, Bristol-Myers 16.5%, American Home Products 9.8%, Warner-Lambert 18.3%, Sterling Drug 20.6%, Miles Laboratories 24.5%). For cosmetics and soaps advertising costs generally exceeded 10%. (For Colgate-Palmolive it was 22.5%, Lever 17.0% and Procter and Gamble 11.1%). *Advertising Age,* August 26, 1968, p. 38.

[30]Labor costs vary in relative importance among chemicals. It has been pointed out that: " . . . While labor costs for a few large tonnage chemicals produced in such high-capital cost installations are relatively low, this does not apply to hundreds of intermediates nor to thousands of more complex end-products made from them. High labor costs are customary in the production of dyes, drugs, medicinal, pharmaceutical, photographic and food chemicals, because these are 'fine' chemicals which require exacting quality control and are customarily produced in small quantities by batch process in vats, autoclaves and other batch vessels. They are tailor-made to rigid specifications, and the quantities produced do not lend themselves to automatic or semi-automatic round-the-clock output." *Formula For Progress, Some Facts About Synthetic Organic Chemicals,* Synthetic Organic Chemical Manufacturers Association of the United States, New York, 1963, pp. 17-18.

Chapter II

Role in the
National Economy

The first use of chemicals dates far back in history. Forty centuries ago the Egyptians made glass, used soda in making soap and dye, and acids in metal making. Early practitioners often were alchemists who sought to transmute baser metals into gold and in the process discovered chemicals such as sulfuric acid and hydrochloric acid.[1]

Chemistry as a science is less than two centuries old. It had its origins late in the 18th century under the leadership of such pioneers as Lavoisier who identified oxygen, hydrogen and other elements and concluded that "a true element was a substance that could not be split up or reduced to any other substance by any chemical means, that a compound was a combination of two or more elements chemically joined. . . ."[2] New discoveries followed quickly with scientists in many countries contributing to the expanding knowledge of chemistry. A particularly important development was the discovery by William H. Perkin, an Englishman, that dyes could be obtained from coal-tar. This discovery in 1856 created the foundation for organic chemicals. Finally, these continuing discoveries culminated in a greater understanding of the nature of atoms and in the formation of a coordinated and systematic science of chemistry.

Developments in the United States

Chemical production was relatively unimportant in this country until the present century; it was mainly a local industry meeting simple needs such as tanning, bleaching, and dyeing. Some chemicals were produced as early as 1635 when the manufacture of saltpeter and alum was started in Boston. Soon after the Revolutionary War, the first sulfuric acid plants were built in this country.

Alexander Hamilton recognized the importance of allied products as early as 1791 when he set up the initial industrial classification system for the Census of Manufactures. He listed some seventeen groups of manufacturing industries which in his words had "grown up and flourished with a rapidity which surprises, affording an encouraging assurance of success in future attempts."[3] At least four of these groups were related to the chemical industry: oils of animals and seeds, soap, spermaceti and tallow candles; starch and hair powder; lampblack and other painters' colors; and gunpowder.[4] However, Hamilton did not include chemical manufacture as such; this was set up as a classification for the first time in the Census of 1879.

Around the turn of the present century, the American chemical industry produced mainly allied products such as patent medicines, paints and varnishes, soap, and fertilizers. These four groups of products accounted for more than half (51.8%) of the value added by manufacture by chemicals and allied products in 1899. Chemicals accounted for only $25.6 million in value added or about one-seventh of the total for the entire chemicals and allied products group. (See Appendix Tables 1 and 3) The more important chemical products were soda ash, sulfuric acid, caustic soda, nitric acid, and glycerin.

World War I provided the major stimulus to the growth of the chemical industry. When the war cut off German supplies[5] the U.S. had to develop its own sources of supply. During that period, the organic chemical industry took firm root domestically although there had been some production earlier. Of particular importance was the production of benzene, toluene, phenol, and naphthalene required either for munitions or by our Allies.[6]

The war underlined the importance of developing and encouraging the U.S. chemical industry. Tariff protection was adopted in 1916 and then extended in 1922. In the 1916 Act, a free list was established for coal-tar crudes and a dutiable list varying from 15% to 30% *ad valorem* plus special levies of 2-1/2 to 5 cents a pound for semi-manufactured and manufactured coal-tar products, dyestuffs, and explosives. The rates were scheduled to be reduced gradually so that after ten years all coal-tars were to be placed on the free list. However, the Tariff Act of 1922 established protection on a permanent basis for the chemical industry. Tariffs of 55% and 60% plus seven cents a pound were imposed on coal-tar products.[7]

During World War I, the Alien Property Custodian had taken over from foreign interests a large number of patents and secret processes, including some for coal-tar processing and dyes. To make these patents and processes available to American producers, the Chemical Foundation was established and underwritten by some thirty chemical companies. By executive order of President Wilson the patents were transferred to the Foundation.[8]

"The Foundation granted "non-exclusive licenses for the use of its patents to any American citizen, copartnership made up of American citizens, or any American company 75 per cent of whose stock was owned by Americans.

"To aid and encourage the companies in the development of the new processes, imports of dyes and dyestuffs were limited and for five years were placed under special regulations. Duties were raised, and all imports of coal-tar products were closely controlled."[9]

During the 1920s and 1930s, the chemical industry expanded dramatically particularly as a result of the development of rayon[10] and compressed gases.[11]

By 1939 chemicals had total shipments of $1.3 billion produced in 1,086 establishments by 158,000 workers, whereas chemicals and allied products had combined sales of $4.3 billion and 371,000 workers in that year. Between World Wars I and II this had become a major sector of the American economy accounting for 7.5% of the volume of all manufacturing.

The development of petrochemicals was a major feature of the post-World War II period. "Petroleum supplanted coal-tar as the major source of benzenoid chemicals, and petrochemical processes almost completely replaced fermentation of carbohydrates to make ethyl alcohol, butyl alcohol, and acetone."[12] This development set the stage for the large scale entry of petroleum companies into the chemical industry with the dramatic impact on competition which is discussed in later chapters.

The past four decades have witnessed dramatic breakthroughs which have contributed a series of chain reactions with the accompanying explosive growth in the chemical industry. Discovery has fed upon discovery and has opened new worlds of opportunities which have been grasped imaginatively by the chemical industry. These developments have included:

1. Greater understanding about giant molecules. The development of polymerization—a method by which materials of high molec-

ular weight are formed through linkage of many simple molecules—added major new dimensions to the chemical industry. Synthetic fibers, plastics, foams, polymeric coatings, and synthetic rubber—which account for such a large proportion of total industrial chemical sales—were the direct results of these developments. It also set the stage for combining organic and inorganic chemicals. One illustration is the substitution of silicone atoms for carbon atoms in organic carbons to obtain materials which are more resistant to high temperatures. Another is the substitution of fluorine for hydrogen in organic compounds (for example, fluorocarbons). Refrigerants and propellants (aerosols) emerged from this research.

2. Expanded knowledge about surface chemistry. Research in this area has been concerned with the physical interactions of substances (for example, water and air, metal and gases). Familiar products resulting from the greater understanding of these interactions include detergents, adhesives, hair sprays, and water repellants.

3. Increasing experimentation with solids. Until very recently little was known about the nature and structure of solids, such as metals, although they have been combined effectively for many centuries (for example, bronze is produced by combining copper and tin). The full potentialities of research in this area remain to be realized. However, the production of diamonds by General Electric and synthetic sapphires by the Linde Division of Union Carbide, provide eye-opening demonstrations of what can be done in the field of gem creation. Equally dramatic was the development by Corning Glass Works of a glass (Pyrocerams) which has many of the characteristics of metal. Lessing has suggested that "This is a seminal discovery, almost on a par with the discovery of the big-molecule structure in organic chemistry, except that crystalline glass has no known counterpart in nature."[13]

To the above development may be added our increasing knowledge of electrons, the intensive efforts to understand photosynthesis (process by which green plants convert water and atmospheric gases into carbohydrates), and the many other frontiers of chemistry.

Of particular interest is the close interrelationship between nuclear energy and chemistry. Dr. Daniel R. Miller, Deputy Director, Division of Research, Atomic Energy Commission, has pointed out:

"On the one hand the uses of nuclear radiation and radioactive techniques have greatly expanded our knowledge in all fields of fundamental chemistry and have extended our capabilities in chemical technology. At the same time and more important for this program . . . the increases in chemical knowledge and understanding have been essential in conserving and improving the efficiency of the many chemical operations required in nuclear energy programs. An inspection of the broad operations carried out in the atomic energy program reveals that it resembles very closely a large chemical industry. This conclusion could be substantiated by a look at the roster of the contractors who operate the large facilities for the Atomic Energy Commission. Mostly they are large chemical companies."[14]

The development of synthetic products during the twentieth century has had drastic impacts upon the economies of many primary product countries. Synthetic rubber undercut a key primary product—natural rubber—of the Malay States and Indonesia. Synthetic nitrogen broke the monopoly of Chilean nitrates which were essential to the production of explosives and fertilizers. Nylon, rayon, and other man-made fibers have had their repercussions on Japanese silk and Australian wool as well as upon American and Egyptian cotton. Plastics are cutting into the traditional markets for construction materials. The dynamic chemical industry has had and continues to have a major impact upon the producers of other natural products as well. Its history is one of inquisitiveness which has led to discovery, to change, and to progress.

Although past discoveries and advances have been fantastic, many scientists are convinced that we have barely scratched the surface. Thus, Dr. John C. Bailar, Jr., of the University of Illinois, has pointed out:

> "In some areas of chemical research, we have made reasonable progress, but in others, our knowledge is still elementary. One might cite, as examples, the structure of the atomic nucleus, the mechanisms of reactions in solids, the nature of heterogeneous catalysis, the origin of the elements, and the passivity of metals. Each of these is in the realm of fundamental research, but it is clear that the solution of the fundamental problems will open the way for important developments in apllied chemistry."[15]

The laboratory, which has been the source of the explosive growth of the chemical industry in the past, continues to provide the ingredients of future growth.

Contributions of Chemicals

The chemical industry makes significant contributions to all phases of our economy. (See Chart II-1) During peace and war it is in the forefront of scientific and technical advancement. Basic chemicals and intermediates generally lose their identification as they are converted into finished goods. As a result, the consumer is rarely aware of the ways in which chemistry makes homes more comfortable, families healthier, and living more enjoyable.[16]

Its products play an ever-growing role in manufacturing industry. In the words of the President's Materials Policy (Paley) Commission "Practically every industry is dependent on the chemical industry to a considerable degree, and this is also true of every household and consumer."[17] Similarly, Walter S. Landis has observed: "Chemistry is the servant of *all* mankind, and of *all* industry. It has probably contributed most to raising the standard of living and improving the various environments of the human race."[18]

The contributions of chemicals to our society are many and diverse:

They replace natural raw materials and help to utilize more efficiently vital resources including labor (for example, synthetic fibers replacing natural fibers).[19]

They play a key role in space technology and in missiles (for example, chemical propellants).[20]

They are widely used as a tool in production (for example, hydrogen peroxide to bleach pulp, dyes for clothing).

They may reduce or eliminate dependence on foreign sources of supply (for example, synthetic rubber).[21]

They create opportunities to develop new industries (for example, the availability of chemical refigerants contributed significantly to the development of the frozen food industry) and new or improved products (for example, use of plastics in phonograph records); the net effect is an important contribution to the number of available job opportunities and to the economic welfare of consumers.

CHART II-1

BROAD SCOPE OF CHEMICALS
AND ALLIED PRODUCTS INDUSTRY

ABUNDANT RAW MATERIALS
from Mine, Forest, Sea, Air, Farm, Oil, Brine and Gas Wells

THE CHEMICALS AND ALLIED PRODUCTS INDUSTRY
in 12,000 plants in the U.S. converts these
raw materials into more than 10,000

CHEMICALS

such as acids and alkalies, salts, organic compounds,
solvents, compressed gases, pigments and dyes
which are used

BY THE CHEMICALS AND
ALLIED PRODUCTS INDUSTRY
To Produce

Cosmetics
Detergents & Soap
Drugs & Medicines
Dyes & Inks
Explosives
Fertilizers
Paints
Pesticides
Plastic Materials
Sanitizing Chemicals
Synthetic Fibers
Synthetic Rubber
And many others

BY OTHER INDUSTRIES
In the Production of

Durable Goods	Nondurable Goods
Aircraft & Equipment	Beverages
Building Materials	Food Products
Electrical Equipment	Leather & Leather Products
Hardware	Packaging
Machinery	Paper & Paper Products
Metal Products	Petroleum & Coal Products
Motor Vehicles & Equipment	Rubber Products
And other products of metal, glass, paper and wood	Textiles

THE ULTIMATE MARKET
(Fundamental human needs)

Health, Food, Clothing, Shelter, Transportation, Communication, Defense and Other Needs

They provide substitute products which reduce costs in many industries.[22]

They contribute to improved levels of living (for example, synthetic fibers which have made possible better clothing with lower cost of upkeep for laundering and drycleaning).

They have contributed to a more adequate food supply for the expanding population throughout the world (for example, better fertilizers).

They contribute to vastly improved health (for example, the miracle drugs and chlorine for water).

They contribute significantly to national defense. According to the Department of Defense ". . . not one single modern weapons system would function without the many valuable products of the chemical industry."[23] It has been estimated, for example, that an atomic submarine requires more than 300 chemical products.

Many of us often fail to realize how much we depend upon industrial chemicals for many everyday items including toothpaste, lipstick, color in our neckties, gasoline, antibiotics, paints, bleach in fabrics, color film, aerosol bombs, water repellents, milk containers, and a host of other products.

"The traffic light? Its brilliant red, green, and amber colors are imparted by such elements as selenium, chromium, and copper. The bridge? Its steel pylons and suspension cables were tempered, treated, hardened or softened with chemicals, long before they were shipped from the mill, and are assured long service life by a variety of protective chemical coatings. . . ."

"But it is polymer chemistry that has given us synthetic fibers, and elastomer chemistry that has contributed synthetic rubber for tires for our cars and trucks and aircraft. Cortisone, vitamin supplements, steroids are products of synthesis chemistry, and fermentation chemistry has given us antibiotics. When you get into petrochemistry, of course, you find its products—and their applications—range from baby oil to rocket fuels, suntan lotion to the Polaris submarine.

"As for our latest supersonic aircraft, the A-11's titanium skin is completely the result of a chemical development; unlike such noble metals as gold, silver and platinum, titanium does not already exist in a metallic state. It must be derived—chemically derived—from its ore."[24]

Clearly, the "ubiquitous American chemical industry" touches every phase of our lives.

The most eloquent testimony to the essential contribution made by chemicals to a modern economy has been given by Russia. In 1958, that country announced a $25 billion, seven year program for its chemical industry. Premier Khrushchev justified this expansion as "the most important factor in further technical progress and in rapid growth of the productivity of communal labor in all branches of the national economy."[25] The proposed program emphasized plastics, synthetic fibers, and synthetic rubber. Again, in the fall of 1963, Russian officials stressed the importance of developing their chemical industry. Premier Khrushchev announced that:

"The latest achievements of science and technology and domestic and foreign practice in recent years have more and more fully revealed the growing potential of the chemical industry, are heightening its role in the development of the productive forces of society."[26]

20

"The chemical industry is moving to the foreground in the national economy because the use of chemical products and synthetic materials offers an opportunity to make radical qualitative transformations in the leading areas of material production. These transformations will permit us to increase the output of products rapidly and to raise their quality with simultaneous savings in capital expenditures and a reduction in production costs....

"Chemistry's successes in the production of synthetic materials have created the conditions for the rapid development of the newest branches of technology; atomic energy, radio-electronics, jet technology and others."[27]

However, in 1969 in connection with a review of a study by the Organisation for Economic Co-operation and Development (OECD) it was reported that " . . . it takes five to seven years on the average to build a new chemical plant [in the U.S.S.R.] as compared with one or two years in the United Kingdom or the U.S."[28]

Finally, it should be noted that our own national economic growth has been influenced in several ways by the chemical industry. The need for new plants in the chemical industry has been one of the major outlets for capital investment. Not only is the plant in place subject to very rapid process obsolescence but the rapid rate of new product development creates rising outlays for plant and equipment. The intensive struggle for product leadership within the industry also contributes to a high rate of investment. The development of new chemical materials has created both investment and employment opportunities outside the chemical industry. For example, the discovery of refrigerants and propellants has contributed to a sharp expansion in the appliance and packaging industries respectively. The use of petroleum and gas as a base for chemicals has meant the creation of vast new industrial complexes, particularly on the Gulf Coast, in the Southwest, and in Puerto Rico, with the stimulating impact upon the economies of those areas.[29]

Relative Importance of the Chemical Industry

During the twentieth century, chemicals and the allied products industries have expanded considerably. Today they are among the largest manufacturing industries. They are leaders in research and development, they provide major outlets for new investments, they are important providers of jobs and payrolls, and they account for a significant proportion of the contribution made by manufacturing activity to our national economic well-being.

This has been true throughout the world as well as in the United States. Sir Peter Allen, chairman of the Board of Imperial Chemical Industries, estimated in 1968 that ". . . something like 3 to 4 percent of world income is produced by chemicals."[30]

Chemicals

The relative importance of chemicals (SIC-281 and 282) may be indicated by a few key relationships in 1967 (See Chart II-2):

Shipments were $21.5 billion or 3.9% of the total for all manufacturing.

Value added by manufacture was $11.6 billion or 4.5% of the total for all manufacturing.

CHART II-2

Chemicals as a Per Cent of all Manufacturing, 1967

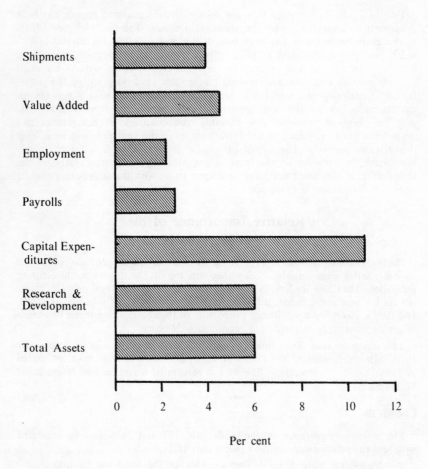

Per cent

Employment was 429,000 or 2.2% of the total for all manufacturing.[31]

Payrolls were $3.4 billion or 2.6% of the total for all manufacturing.

Expenditures for research and development were $1,006 million or 6.1% of the total spent by all industry in 1967.

Capital expenditures were $2,159 million or 10.7% of the total for all manufacturing.

Total assets were $26.1 billion[32] or 6.0% of the total for all manufacturing.

Research and development and capital expenditures play a major role in determining the national rate of economic growth. The chemical industry makes a significant contribution in both areas.

For 1967, the Bureau of the Census reported data for 147 manufacturing industries including SIC 281 and 282.[33]

Basic Chemicals (SIC 281) ranked sixth in shipments, fourth in value added by manufacture, nineteenth in employment, twelfth in payrolls, and second in capital expenditures.

Fibers, Plastics and Rubbers. (SIC 282) ranked seventeenth in shipments, thirteenth in value added by manufacture, thirty-seventh in employment, twenty-ninth in payrolls and fourth in capital expenditures.

If the combined totals for SIC 281 and 282 are compared with the other 145 groups then they ranked third in shipments, third in value added by manufacture, fifth in employment, fifth in payrolls, and first in capital expenditures. However, this comparison, suffers from the infirmity that some of the other 145 categories also could be combined since they cover products manufactured by single companies in the same manner that both organic and inorganic chemicals are produced by a chemical company (for example, electrical machinery).

In 1963, 28.9% of the shipments of chemicals were inorganics and 71.1% were organics. Thermoplastic resins with shipments of $1.3 billion was the most important single group of products accounting for 8.7% of the total. Synthetic rubber (5.7%) and cyclic intermediates (5.1%) were the only other groups, other than the miscellaneous category, with more than 5% of total shipments. These three groups of organic chemicals, therefore, accounted for almost one-fifth of the total shipments of chemicals in 1963 (See Appendix Table 4).

The most important inorganics were the nitrogen group of synthetic ammonia, nitric acid, and ammonium compounds (3.9%), potassium and sodium compounds (3.4%), and aluminum oxide (2.1%).

Historically, a large proportion of the total shipments of chemicals has been assigned to a miscellaneous category by the Bureau of the Census. As products so classified have increased in importance over time, they have been set up in new five digit classifications. In 1963, for example, $3,154 million or one-fifth of the total shipments were classified as miscellaneous acyclic chemicals and chemical products. Included in this group were halogenated hydrocarbons (including carbon tetrachloride, trichloroethylene, and perchloroethylene) which alone had shipments of about $400 million[34] or a larger volume than reported for 19 out of the 20 inorganic products classes and for 16 out of 24 product classes for which separate data were reported. It would be more meaningful for the Bureau of the Census to report products with such a large volume as separate five digit product classes than as part of a miscellaneous category.[35]

Size of Companies

In light of the substantial and expanding volume of business cited above there are many large companies in this industry. One observer has pointed out that:

"Prior to the second World War the chemical industry was pretty much divided into producers of bulk industrial chemicals, producers of intermediates, or end use manufacturers. Now practically every major U.S. company is in chemicals and it sometimes is hard to define the industry precisely."[36]

Of the 500 largest industrial companies in 1968, 28 obtained more than one-quarter of their sales from chemicals. Appendix Table 5 lists these chemical companies, their *total* sales and their total invested capital;[37] the tabulation does *not* include petroleum and other companies which have a large amount of chemical business but whose main activities are in other fields. In many instances, the chemical output of these other companies is greater than that of the smaller companies included in Appendix 5[38] (See Table II-1).

Ten chemical companies were members of the billion dollar club in 1968 (Du Pont, Union Carbide, Monsanto, Dow, Grace, FMC, Allied Chemical, Celanese, American Cyanamid and Olin). However, it was estimated that only the first four had chemical sales of more than one billion dollars.[39]

An additional 126 companies among the 500 largest also produced some chemicals, although that was not their most important activity.[40] The distribution by rank of the 154 companies was as follows:

500 Largest Corporations, 1968

Rank in Sales	Primarily Chemicals	Some Chemicals	Total
1-100	8	48	56
101-200	7	31	38
201-300	6	22	28
301-400	4	15	19
401-500	3	10	13
	28	126	154

It is a significant indication of the opportunities available in this industry and of the relative ease of entry that more than half of the 100 largest industrial corporations and about three companies out of every ten among the 500 largest industrial companies produce some chemicals. Regardless of the basis of comparison, it is evident that the chemical industry ranks high in the hierarchy of American industries.

Chemicals and Allied Products

The relative importance of the chemicals and allied products industries in 1967 may be summarized as follows (See Appendix Table 6):

Shipments were $42.2 billion or 7.6 per cent of the total for all manufacturing. Only five of the twenty-one manufacturing industries

TABLE II-1

Relative Importance of Chemical Sales For 50 Industrial Companies, 1968

Rank	Company	Chemical sales	Total income[a]	Chemical sales as % of total income
		(Millions of dollars)		
1	Du Pont	$3250	$3481	94%
2	Monsanto	1711	1810	94
3	Union Carbide	1675	2686	62
4	Dow Chemical	1450	1723	84
5	W. R. Grace	958	1761	54
6	Standard Oil (N.J.)	933	15873	6
7	Celanese	917	1256	73
8	Allied Chemical	869	1278	68
9	Hercules	639	718	89
10	FMC	625	1387	45
11	Occidental Petroleum	571	1815	31
12	American Cyanamid	522	1040	55
13	Shell Oil	513	4008	18
14	Eastman Kodak	507	2644	19
15	Stauffer Chemical	478	478	100
16	Uniroyal	476	1436	33
17	Phillips Petroleum	447	2130	21
18	Rohm and Haas	423	428	99
19	Mobil Oil	417	7089	6
20	Cities Service	358	1461	25
21	Borden	354	1681	21
22	Standard Oil (Ind.)	342	3994	9
23	Ashland Oil[b]	342	1082	32
24	Continental Oil	333	2443	14
25	IMC	332	502	66
26	Ethyl Corp	331	512	65
27	Gulf Oil	315	5657	6
28	Diamond Shamrock	314	528	59
29	Olin	298	1011	29
30	American Can	278	1633	17
30a	Standard Oil of Calif.	276	4160	7
31	National Lead	275	876	32
32	PPG Industries	261	1058	25
33	Air Reduction	254	440	58
34	U.S. Steel[b]	250	4609	6
35	Tenneco	242	2101	12
36	B. F. Goodrich[b]	240	1144	21
37	American Enka	239	239	100
38	Witco Chemical	221	224	99
39	Pennwalt	208	407	51
40	Pfizer	200	736	27
41	Koppers	199	449	44
42	Air Products	185	205	90
43	Chemetron	179	244	73
44	Swift	170	2832	6
45	Reichhold	161	161	100
46	Goodyear[b]	160	2941	5
47	GAF	150	571	26
48	Wyandotte	147	148	99
49	Sinclair Oil	143	1478	10
50	National Distillers	136	958	14

[a] All financial data for fiscal 1968.   [b] C&EN estimate.

Source: Chemical & Engineering News, June 16, 1969, p. 23 and July 28, 1969, p. 15.

for which data were reported (food and kindred products, transportation equipment, machinery except electrical, electrical equipment and supplies, and primary metals) had larger shipments.

Value added by manufacture was $23.4 billion or 9.0% of the total for all manufacturing.[41] Only four industries had a larger value added (food and kindred products, transportation equipment, machinery except electrical, and electrical equipment and supplies).

Employment was 854,000 or 4.4 per cent of total for all manufacturing. Thus, approximately one job out of every 22 in manufacturing industries was provided by this group of industries which ranked tenth in the volume of employment.[42]

Total payrolls were $6.5 billion or 4.9 per cent of the total for all manufacturing. It ranked eighth in importance on this basis.

Expenditures for research and development were $1,565 million or 9.5% of the total spent by all industries. Only electrical equipment and communications and aircraft and missiles had higher expenditures, largely because of federally financed research.

Capital expenditures were $2,833 million or 14.0% of the total for all manufacturing. Only the primary metals group exceeded this total.

Total assets were $43.1 billion or 9.8% of the total for all manufacturing.[43]

The chemicals and allied products industries also have contributed significantly to foreign trade and to the U.S. export trade surplus as the following data for 1967 demonstrate:[44]

Exports were $2,803 million or 9.2% of the total.

Imports were $963 million or 3.6% of the total.

TABLE II-2

Chemicals As Per Cent of Total Chemicals and Allied Products, Selected Economic Data, 1967

	Industrial Chemicals	Plastic Materials and Synthetics	Total
	(SIC 281)	(SIC 282)	(SIC 281 & 282)
Value added by manufacture	32.8%	16.6%	49.4%
Value of shipments	33.4	17.6	51.0
Capital expenditures	43.0	33.2	76.2
All employees	29.5	20.7	50.2
Payrolls	32.4	20.2	52.6

Sources: U.S. Department of Commerce, Bureau of the Census, *1967 Census of Manufactures,* General Statistics for Industry Groups and Industries Preliminary Report, MC 67(P)-1, Washington, D.C., April 1969, p. 7.

The net export surplus for chemicals and allied products was $1,840 million or 52.9% of the national total of $3,477 million. In 1968 imports and exports of chemicals and allied products were considerably larger.

About half of the size of the chemicals and allied products industries is accounted for by chemicals (SIC 281 and 282). The data for 1967 show that this approximate ratio prevailed for shipments, value added by manufacture, employment and payrolls. However, more than three quarters of the capital expenditures were made by chemicals (See Table II-2).

Summary and Conclusions

The chemical industry makes impressive and vital contributions to all phases of the U.S. economy in peace and in war including: more efficient use of raw materials and manpower, advancement of space and missile technology, creation of new products and processes, stimulus to new industries, reduced dependence on foreign sources of supply, improved levels of living, lower costs to industry, improved health and longer life, increased food supply, national defense, and national economic growth.

The major contributions made by chemicals and allied products are reflected in their high rank in the hierarchy of American industry and in their large share of all manufacturing industries in terms of jobs, shipments, total assets, expenditures for research and development, and capital expenditures. In this connection, it is also significant that more than one half of the 100 largest corporations in the United States produce some chemicals and that almost one-third of the five hundred largest industrial companies in the United States produce chemicals although most of these companies are more heavily engaged in other types of manufacturing activity.

---

[1] A comprehensive history of the chemical industry is contained in the six volume study by Williams Haynes, *American Chemical Industry*, D. Van Nostrand Company, Inc., New York, 1945 to 1954. See also "The Rise of the United States Chemical Industry, 1918-1968," *Chemical Week*, November 16, 1968, pp. 104-49.

[2] Lawrence P. Lessing, *Understanding Chemistry*, Mentor Books, New York, 1959. p. 31. See Chapter 2 for a brief review of the developments which contributed to the modern science of chemistry.

[3] Charles A. Bliss, *The Structure of Manufacturing Production*, National Bureau of Economic Research, New York, 1939, p. 120.

[4] Also included were ardent spirits and malt liquors; and pot and pearl ashes, pitch, tar and turpentine. United States Department of Commerce, Bureau of the Census, *Chemical and Rubber Industry Report*, Washington, D.C., August 1960, p. 3.

[5] Prior to World War I, the major developments in the chemical industry took place in Germany. It has been pointed out that " . . . for many years it was impossible to get an education in organic chemistry without attending a German university." *Formula For Progress*, Synthetic Organic Chemical Manufacturers Association of the United States, New York, 1963, p. 8.

[6] Output of coal-tar dyes increased from 12.2 million pounds in 1914 to 66.2 million pounds in 1919; the value of this output increased from $4.7 million in 1914 to $69.3 million in 1919. U.S. Bureau of the Cenus, *Abstract of the Census of Manufactures: 1919*, Washington, D.C., 1923, p. 171.

[7] Percy W. Birdwell, *What The Tariff Means to American Industries*, Harper and Brothers, New York, 1956, pp. 188-90.

[8]Haynes, *op. cit.*, Vol. 3, p. 261.

[9]Edward H. Hempel, *The Economics of Chemical Industries*, John Wiley & Sons, Inc. New York, 1939, p. 31.

[10]The value of shipments of man-made cellulosic fibers increased from $86.1 million in 1925 to $254.7 million in 1937; value added by manufacture increased from $12.1 million in 1923 to $174.1 million in 1937. U.S. Department of Commerce, Bureau of the Census, *U.S. Census of Manufactures: 1958*, Vol. II, Part I, Industry Statistics, General Summary and Major Groups 20 to 28, Washington, D.C., 1961, p. 28 B-4.

[11]The index of physical output of compressed gases increased from 31.5 (1929 = 100) in 1921 to 143.3 in 1937. Solomon Fabricant, *The Output of Manufacturing Industries, 1899-1937*, National Bureau of Economic Research, Inc., New York, 1940, p. 499.

[15]*Chemical Week*, November 16, 1968, p. 135.

[13]Lessing, "Understanding Chemistry," *op. cit.*, p. 132.

[14]Joint Committee on Atomic Energy, *Hearings on AEC Authorizing Legislation, Fiscal Year 1965*, Part 3, 88th Cong., 2nd Sess., Washington, D.C., 1964, pp. 1346-47.

[15]John C. Bailar, Jr., "The Expanding Universe of Chemistry," *Chemical and Engineering News*, April 20, 1964, p. 114.

[16]*Hercules Annual Report 1968*, p. 13.

[17]President's Materials Policy Commission, *Resources for Freedom*, Washington, D.C., June 1952, Vol. II, p. 103.

[18]Walter S. Landis, *Your Servant the Molecule*, Macmillan Company, New York, 1944, p. 9.

[19]In an interesting study published by the Bureau of the Census, the savings in manpower and resources when one billion pounds of cellulosic man-made fibers replace the amount of cotton were summarized as follows: "The use of 2.3 million acres of cotton land and 150 million man-hours of farm labor is replaced by one million acres of forest land, 15 million man-hours of direct labor for raw materials production, and the use of considerable capital resources . . . in producing these fibers, 42 cents more value was added to in the manufacturing stage, involving an additional 70 million man-hours of direct labor and the use of much more capital." Vivian E. Spencer, "Raw Materials in the United States Economy: 1900-1961," *Working Paper No. 6*, U.S. Department of Commerce, Bureau of the Census, Washington, D.C., 1963, pp. 23, 26.

[20]It has been estimated that 15% of the appropriations for space exploration goes to the chemical industry, "Formula For Progress," *op. cit.*, p. 23.

[21]It has been estimated that during World War II the chemical industry created "a $1-billion synthetic-rubber industry out of almost nothing in two years flat." "The Chemical Century," *Fortune*, March 1950, p. 70.

[22]For illustrations of cost saving substitutions and estimates of the savings involved see Manufacturing Chemists' Association, Inc., *The Chemical Industry Facts Book*, Washington, D.C., 1962, Fifth Edition.

[23]Quoted in *Chemicals*, Merrill Lynch, Pierce, Fenner & Smith, 1958, p. 2. It was pointed out during World War II that "what we think of as an ultra-mechanized war is being fought from a chemical base." Williams Haynes, *The Chemical Front*, Alfred A. Knopf, New York, 1943, pp. v-vi.

[24]"The U.S. Chemical Industry—Keystone of our Economy," *Empire Trust Letter*, Empire Trust Company, New York, June 1964, p. 2.

[25]Cited in *Chemical News*, Manufacturing Chemists' Association, Sept.-Oct. 1958, p. 1.

[26]*The Current Digest of the Soviet Press*, December 25, 1968, p. 6.

[27]*Ibid.*, p. 7.

[28]*Chemical & Engineering News*, March 31, 1969, p. 26.

[29]See Victor R. Fuchs, *Changes in the Location of Manufacturing in the United States Since 1929*, Yale University Press, New Haven, 1962, 218-22.

[30]Sir Peter Allen, "The Chemical Industries of the U.K. and North America: Lessons and Opportunities," *Chemistry and Industry*, August 3, 1968, p. 1037.

[31]The U.S. Bureau of Labor Statistics estimated total employment at 519,700 in 1967. *Employment and Earnings Statistics for the United States for 1909-1968*, Bulletin No. 1312-6, Washington, D.C., 1968, pp. 643, 649.

[32]Federal Trade Commission and Securities and Exchange Commission, *Quarterly Financial Report for Manufacturing Corporations*, First Quarter, 1968, pp. 34, 47.

[33]90 were three digit groups and 57 were four digit for industry groups for which no three digit data were reported.

[34]In 1966 the shipments for this group totaled $509 million.

[35]United States Tariff Commission, *Synthetic Organic Chemicals, United States Production and Sales 1966*, TC Publication 248, Washington, D.C., 1968, pp. 55-58; *Synthetic Organic Chemicals, United States Production and Sales*, TC Publication 143, Washington, D.C., 1964, pp. 56-58.

[36]Charles W. Sexton, The Value of a Conglomerate Acquisition to a Chemical Company," *Chemical Marketing and Economics Meeting Papers*, April 1967, pp. 237-38.

[37]In 1968, W. R. Grace had 54% of its sales in chemicals, Olin had 29% in chemicals and Koppers had 44% in chemicals.

[38]For example, in 1968 out of total sales of $2,644 million reported by Eastman Kodak, 19% was in chemicals, fibers, and plastics; this proportion represented sales of $507 million. *Annual Report* for 1968, pp. 1, 2. Chemical sales were about $500 million or more for Occidental Petroleum, Shell Chemical Co., and Standard Oil Company (New Jersey).

[39]*Chemical & Engineering News*, June 16, 1969, p. 23.

[40]The companies which produce chemicals were determined on the basis of their SIC codes as reported in a survey made by *Fortune*. (*1966 Plant and Product Directory of the 1,000 Largest U.S. Industrial Corporations*, Vol. 1, New York, 1966).

[41]In 1967 chemicals and allied products accounted for 2.2 per cent of the total national income and 2.6 per cent of the private national income (excluding government). Of the other twenty manufacturing industries for which data are reported by the U.S. Department of Commerce, only five made a larger contribution to national income in 1967 than did chemicals and allied products (electrical equipment and supplies, primary meals, non-electrical machinery, food and kindred products and transportation equipment and ordnance). Moreover, chemicals and allied products made a greater contribution to total national income than such vital nonmanufacturing industries as railroads, banking, telephone and telegraph, and electric and gas utilities. *Survey of Current Business*, July 1968, p. 23. These totals for chemicals and allied products do not include many chemical process industries such as paper, rubber, and petroleum.

[42]According to the U.S. Bureau of Labor Statistics, total employment was 1,002,400 in 1967. "Employment and Earnings Statistics for the United States, 1909-68", *op. cit.*, p. 639. The larger total includes the employees in administration and auxiliary establishments who are not included in the Census tabulation.

[43]*Quarterly Financial Report for Manufacturing Corporations*, First Quarter, 1968, *op. cit.*, pp. 34, 47.

[44]U.S. Department of Commerce, Bureau of the Census, *Statistical Abstract of the United States: 1968*, Washington, D.C., 1968, pp. 805, 807.

Chapter III

Growth Trends

The chemical industry has experienced a rate of growth about twice as rapid annually as that for the national economy during most of the twentieth century. This above average rate of growth is reflected in the dollar totals for shipments or sales and value added by manufacture, in the indicators of physical volume such as production and employment, and in the capital invested in the industry.

Limitations of the Data

Measurement of the growth record of the chemical industry is complicated because of the heterogeneous nature of the industry's products, the frequent changes in Bureau of the Census definitions of the industry, the wide variety of new products, the lack of comparability among data compiled by different government agencies, and the fact that many statistical compilations combine data for the chemical industry with those for the allied product industries such as drugs, fertilizers, cosmetics, and soaps.

Census data for chemicals and allied products are available since 1879 but the composition of products included in the industry often has been changed.[1] Hence the reported data require very careful analysis. Usually, the data for earlier years are not available in sufficient detail to make possible all of the adjustments required as a product becomes important or as products have been included or excluded from the Census data.

The Census data for the period 1899 to 1954 have been analyzed and adjusted to obtain data on a basis which is consistent with those made available since 1957 when a comprehensive revision was made in the Standard Industrial Classification.[2] (See Appendix A) For example, various fats and oils[3] were included in chemicals and allied products until the 1958 Census when they were shifted to a different industry group. Since there were 943 establishments[4] producing fats and oils in 1958 as compared with 11,309 establishments remaining in chemicals and allied products it is evident that their inclusion or omission makes a considerable difference.[5]

The most detailed breakdown for major groups of chemical products on a consistent basis is available only for the past quarter of a century in the compilations of the Bureau of the Census; production data are available on a consistent basis only since 1947. The U.S. Department of Commerce, in connection with its estimates of national income has compiled data for chemicals and allied products since 1929; it does not prepare separate data for chemicals. Thus, different series may be analyzed for varying periods of time.

Another limitation of the available data is the lack of comparability in coverage among several series. The Bureau of the Census and Bureau of Labor Statistics data are based on *establishments* which tend to reflect fairly adequately the trends for specific groups of products. The U.S. Department of Commerce and Internal Revenue Service data on the other hand, are based on *company* data which embrace all of a company's activities and hence may not be fully representative of its experience with chemicals. Price indexes are based on specific products and hence provide still a third dimension of definition.

The dollar data reported by various agencies reflect the price inflation which has characterized much of the past three decades. Any attempt to adjust the dollar totals for price changes is affected by the inadequacy of price indexes in terms of coverage, adjustment for quality changes, and the failure to reflect fully all price shading (e.g. actual prices as distinct from list or quoted prices). The further back in years, the less adequate and representative are the price indexes likely to be. However, the price indexes show that chemical prices have risen less than prices generally. As a result, comparisons of growth rates for chemicals and for the entire economy based on dollar volume tend to *understate* by a significant margin the contribution to economic growth made by this industry as will be noted later.

The dramatic changes in the composition of output also influence the significance of long-term comparisons of industry aggregates. Thus, for example, organic chemicals were of minor importance in this country prior to World War I while synthetic fibers (except for rayon), synthetic rubber, and plastics have become significant since 1939.

The changes in the nature of the chemical industry have been mirrored in the operations of many companies. The shift of Du Pont from a company specializing in explosives to a major chemical company after World War I provides a well-known and dramatic illustration. Moreover, the entrance into chemical production by companies with a primary interest in other industries also has been important in the post-World War II years. Illustrations include the large scale production of chemicals by petroleum companies, rubber companies and paper companies and by such large industrial companies as Pittsburgh Plate Glass, National Distillers, Eastman Kodak, Borden, and others.

At the same time, chemical companies have become increasingly interested in integrating forward into the industries producing consumer products which are built on chemical raw materials. Most leading chemical companies have established consumer products departments. Familiar illustrations of end products sold directly to ultimate consumers are Lucite paints (Du Pont), Saran Wrap (Dow), Eveready batteries and Prestone antifreeze (Union Carbide), and Breck shampoos (American Cyanamid). The advertising of various non-cellulosic fibers may also be cited in this connection (for example, Acrilan by Monsanto).

It has been suggested that "An important incentive for the movement into consumer lines is the wider profit margin which results from the considerably higher price for the finished products than for the [chemical] materials."[6] As this trend develops the data measuring a company's entire activity will become increasingly less useful as an indication of trends in the chemical industry. However, it would not affect their usefulness as a measurement of trends for chemicals and allied products.

From the above discussion it is clear that no one series of data is completely adequate to measure the magnitude of growth recorded by chemicals (SIC 281-282) and chemicals and allied products either because it is not available for the entire period, the effects of price inflation, or duplications included in the totals. Thus, for example, shipments and sales data are affected by duplications because they include shipments within the industry; they are also affected by price changes. Data for value added by manufacture and income originating eliminate the duplications but they also are influenced by the price factor. Production data show the changes in physical volume but are not available on a comprehensive and consistent basis for specific groups of products prior to 1947. Data are more complete for the period since 1899 for production workers than for total employment.

When data are cited for the entire chemicals and allied products group, it should be kept in mind that over time, chemicals have accounted for an increasing proportion of the group total. This trend is illustrated by the data for value added by manufacture.[7] In 1899, the proportion of total chemicals and allied products contributed by chemicals was 14.0%, in 1919 it was 30.2%, and in 1939 it was 43.0% (industrial chemicals accounted for 31.0% and fibers, plastics and rubbers for 12.0%). In 1967, the ratios were 33.4% for industrial chemicals (SIC 281) and 17.6% for plastics materials and synthetics (SIC 282). Thus, both components of chemicals shared in the increase to 51.0% in 1967. Clearly, there has been a greater rate of growth for chemicals than for the allied products.

Despite the limitations described above, it is possible to depict through a combination of measurements the general magnitude of growth for chemicals and for the more inclusive chemicals and allied products for varying periods of time.

Shipments or Sales[8]

Chemicals

The explosive growth of the chemical industry has reflected primarily the enormous expansion in the use of chemicals both by industry and individuals as the research laboratories have poured forth their modern miracles.

Initially, the chemical industry found its market primarily in the consumer needs of an agricultural population. During the 20th century it has thrived on the expanded industrial base accompanying the economic growth of the United States. The major market today is in supplying the requirements of industry (including chemical companies) and in furnishing low cost raw materials such as plastics, man-made rubber, synthetic fibers and related items to end-product producers.

The dramatic growth of chemicals (281-282) in the twentieth century is strikingly portrayed by the rise in shipments from $57 million in 1899 to $21,523 million in 1967. These data include intra-industry shipments and hence are not as accurate an indication of growth as the data for value added by manufacture discussed in a later section.

Overwhelmingly, this growth developed in the past quarter of a century. Of the total increase of $21,466 million in shipments since 1899, $20,246 million has taken place since 1939. In other words, some 94% of the growth in dollar shipments of chemicals has developed since 1939. It is fruitful, therefore, to give greatest emphasis to developments during this most recent period (See Appendix Table 9).

In 1967, shipments of chemicals were about sixteen times as large as in 1939 while gross national product was only about eight and a half times as large.[9] Clearly, chemicals have expanded at a far greater rate than the national economy.

The changes in shipments for the major categories of chemicals between 1939 and 1967 are shown in Table III-1.

The exceptional growth reported for chemicals reflects primarily the rapid expansion of newly developed products such as synthetic rubber, plastics materials and non-cellulosic fibers,[10] thus underlining the close relationship between this industry's growth and its large expenditures for research and development.

TABLE III-1
Value of Shipments, Chemicals, 1939 and 1967

	1939	1967	% Increase
	(millions)		
Alkalies and chlorine	$ 102	$ 737	623
Industrial gases	53	567	970
Cyclic intermediates and crudes	173	1,485	757
Inorganic pigments	79	546	591
Organic chemicals, n.e.c.	237	6,582	2,677
Inorganic chemicals, n.e.c.	302	4,179	1,284
Total basic chemicals	$ 946	$14,096	1,390
Plastics materials and resins	83	3,584	4,218
Synthetic rubber	—	927	—
Fibers	247	2,916	1,081
Total plastics materials & synthetics	$ 330	$ 7,427	2,151
Total chemicals	$1,277	$21,523	1,585

n.e.c.—not elsewhere classified.
Sources: See Appendix Tables 7, 8, and 9.

The comparisons are in dollar terms and make no allowance for the price inflation during the period. Actually, prices of chemicals have risen much less than all prices since 1939. The implicit price index used to measure the inflation in gross national product increased by 171%[11] as compared with the rise of 68% for chemicals between 1939 and 1967. After eliminating the effects of price rises, gross national product in real terms increased by 221% and chemical shipments by 903% in this 28 year period.

If chemical prices had risen as much as the implicit price index, purchasers would have had to pay $34.7 billion for the volume acquired in 1967 or $13.2 billion *more* than they actually paid. Of course, with such a price rise fewer units would have been purchased and hence total sales would not have reached that total; the contribution of the chemical industry would have been smaller in real terms.

The increase of almost $20 billion in shipments of chemicals between 1939 and 1967 reflected: (a) the price inflation which developed during that period, (b) the greater breadth of the market resulting from the continuing rise in population, and (c) the phenomenal rise in real per capita expenditures for chemicals as the demands by industry have expanded. The impact of each of these factors during this 28 year period is shown below (See Chart III-1):

Wholesale prices of chemicals advanced by 68% and were responsible for $8,712 million of the increase in the dollar value of shipments between 1939 and 1967.

Population increased from 131,028,000 in 1939 to 199,118,000 in 1967 or by 52%. The increase in population would have resulted in a rise of $664 million in shipments if real shipments per capita had remained unchanged.

The remaining $10,870 million of the $20,246 million increase reflected the more than sixfold rise in real shipments per capita from $9.75 in 1939 to $64.34 in 1967 (in 1939 dollars). The dramatic rise in per capita consumption of the newer products such as plastics and noncellulosic fibers is widely recognized. Significant increases also have developed for older inorganics. Per capita production increased as shown in Table III-2.

CHART III-1

Factors Contributing to the Increase
in Shipments of Chemicals, 1939-1967

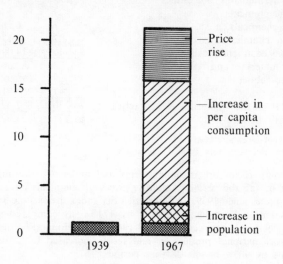

Billions of
Dollars

1939   1967

—Price rise

—Increase in per capita consumption

—Increase in population

TABLE III-2

Per Capita Production of Selected Inorganic Chemicals,
1939 and 1967

	1939	1967
	(pounds)	
Ammonia, synthetic anhydrous	5	119
Chlorine, gas	8	77
Hydrochloric acid	2	16
Nitric acid	3	61
Sodium hydroxide	16	79
Sulfuric acid	73	289

Source: U.S. Department of Commerce, Office of Business Economics, *Business Statistics,* 1967 Biennial Edition, Washington, D.C., September 1967, p. 125 and *Survey of Current Business,* March 1968, p. 24.

The *real* growth rate for chemicals after eliminating the effects of price rises was at the annual rate of 8.9% between 1939 and 1967 as compared with 4.3% for real gross national product. From 1939 to 1965 the real growth rate (based on sales) for chemicals and allied products was 6.3% annually (See Chart III-2).

Chemicals and Allied Products

In 1869, sales of chemicals and allied products totaled about $131 million[12] and by 1899 had increased to $621 million. Largely as a result of the war in-

CHART III-2

Annual Real Growth Rate, 1939-1967

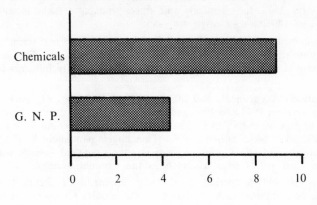

Per Cent

duced stimulus, sales aggregated about $3.5 billion in 1919. During the 1920s there was a consolidation of these gains. Throughout most of this period, sales rose more rapidly than gross national product.

The U.S. Department of Commerce has reported sales for chemicals and allied products (but not for chemicals alone) as part of its national income reports since 1929. Between 1929 and 1939, sales of chemicals and allied products rose moderately as compared with the net decline reported for total corporate sales; as a result they increased in relative importance from 2.9% in 1929 to 3.6% in 1939. During World War II and the early postwar years the ratio increased to 3.9% as sales of chemicals and allied products expanded more rapidly than total corporate sales. However, in 1948, the ratio was 3.6% or the same as before the war; since 1948 the proportion has fluctuated around this level. Thus, when set against the dollar sales performance of all corporations it would appear that the growth of chemicals and allied products has not been particularly marked since the end of World War II.

However, these data do not show the full story. The apparent lackluster performance for all chemicals and allied products between 1947 and 1961 is explained largely by the smaller price rise for those products as compared with the entire economy during that period. Although the wholesale industrial price index increased by 39.0%, the chemicals and allied products index rose by only 6.1% between 1947 and 1966. The effect of these diverse price changes was marked as is shown below:[13]

Corporate Sales, 1947 and 1966

Sales	1947	1966	% Increase
	(billions)		
Total Corporate			
As reported	$347	$1,158	234
in 1957-59 dollars	461	1,106	140
Chemicals and Allied Products			
As reported	13	44	238
in 1957-59 dollars	14	44	214

Between 1947 and 1966, dollar sales increased by about the same proportion for chemicals and allied products (+238%) and all corporations (+234%). However, when adjustment is made for the smaller price increases, the real increase was 214% for chemicals and allied products or substantially greater than that of 140% for all corporate sales.

The contribution of chemicals and allied products in real terms continued to rise more rapidly than that of the balance of the economy. This pattern has been obscured in the dollar totals which were significantly influenced by price changes.

If prices of chemicals and allied products had risen as much as prices generally between 1947 and 1966 and if such higher prices had not resulted in an adverse impact on the volume of sales, then total sales would have been $57.1 billion instead of $43.6 billion in 1966. Thus buyers paid about $13.5 billion *less* for chemicals and allied products than the 1966 physical volume would have cost had their prices risen as much as the national average.[14]

During the 1947-66 period, total dollar shipments of chemicals increased by 409% as compared with the rise of 238% in sales for chemicals and allied products and 234% in the sales of all corporations. Thus, even before adjustment for the smaller rise in prices, shipments of chemicals continued to increase almost twice as rapidly as sales for all corporations. As these data indicate, the lag in dollar sales of all chemicals and allied products was due to the smaller rate of growth of allied products between 1947 and 1966.[15]

Value Added by Manufacture

Value added by manufacture shows how much is contributed to the economy by an industry after deducting from its sales the cost of materials, supplies, fuel, containers, purchased electric energy and contract work. The shipments within the industry are eliminated by this measure and hence it does not suffer that infirmity of the shipments and sales data. The Bureau of the Census considers value added by manufacture: " . . . to be the best value measure available for comparing the relative economic importance of manufacturing among industires. . ."

The growth in the demand for chemicals as inexpensive raw materials for American industry has been a major factor contributing to their growth in relative importance. Value added by manufacture of chemicals increased from an unimpressive $26 million in 1899 to $11.6 billion in 1967; its share of all manufacturing rose from 0.6% at the turn of the century to 4.5% in 1967.

Allied products have experienced less of a dramatic growth. From 3.7% of total value added by manufacture in 1899, the proportion fell to 2.9% in 1919 and then recovered to 3.6% in 1929. In 1939, the proportion was 4.0% and in 1967 it was 4.5%. Clearly, the increase in the relative importance of all chemicals and allied products during the twentieth century has been due overwhelmingly to the vigorous expansion recorded by chemicals.

Largely because of the growth of chemicals, the composite total for chemicals and allied products has steadily moved up the ladder of importance. The 425 manufacturing industries covered in the Census of Manufactures are combined into 21 major manufacturing industries — the two-digit industries. Of these 21 major industries, which comprise the nation's manufacturing base, chemicals and allied products ranked fifth in terms of value added in 1967. It was surpassed in importance only by food, transportation equipment, electrical equipment and supplies, and machinery except electrical.

Trend of Production

The rise in output of chemicals and allied products has far outstripped that for all manufacturing industries regardless of which year is used as the basis for measurement (See Table III-3 and Chart III-3).

Chemicals and allied products output in 1968 was almost fifteen times as large as in 1929 while for manufacturing it was about 4-1/2 times as large.

Chemicals and allied products output in 1968 was more than 10 times the 1939 total while the manufacturing total was about 4-1/2 times as large.

Chemicals and allied products output in 1968 was 5 times the 1947 total while manufacturing output was 2-1/2 times as large.

Chemical output increased significantly more than that for chemicals and allied products and was largely responsible for the growth rate of the broader group.

TABLE III-3

Production Indexes for Chemicals and Allied Products Industry and All Manufacturing, 1899-1968
(1958 = 100)

Year	Chemicals and Allied Products	All Manufacturing Industries
1899	3	11
1909	5	17
1914	7	21
1919	8	24
1929	16	40
1939	21	41
1947	46	71
1954	75	91
1958	100	100
1963	152	133
1968	230	178

Source: For 1899 to 1963: *Census of Manufactures, 1963, Vol IV, Indexes of Production,* Joint Publication of U.S. Bureau of the Census and Board of Governors of the Federal Reserve System, Washington, D.C., 1968, p. 7 (for all manufacturing, and census years 1939-63 for chemicals and allied products). For earlier years for chemicals and allied products: *Census of Manufactures, 1954, Vol. IV, Indexes of Production,* Joint Publication of U.S. Bureau of the Census, Bureau of Labor Statistics and Board of Governors of the Federal Reserve System, Washington, D.C., 1968, p. 3 (adjusted to 1958 base). Data for 1968 from Federal Reserve Board index of industrial production.

The expansion in physical output of chemicals during the post-World War II years can be measured by the comprehensive indexes published by the Board of Governors of the Federal Reserve System for the period since 1947. Between 1947 and 1968 the output of inorganic chemicals increased by 532% and of organic chemicals by 701% (See Appendix Table 15). These increases were several times as large as that in total industrial production and more than twice as large as the increase of 273% in the output of allied products (drugs, cosmetics, soap, paints, fertilizers, etc.) (See Chart III-4).

The annual rate of increase between 1947 and 1968 was 10.0% for chemicals as compared with 6.5% for allied products and 4.5% for total industrial production.[16] Since these data are in physical terms and hence do not reflect price inflation, they demonstrate that chemicals have made a far above-average contribution to the nation's economic growth.

CHART III-3

Production Indexes: Chemicals and Total Industrial Production, 1947-1968

1957-59 = 100

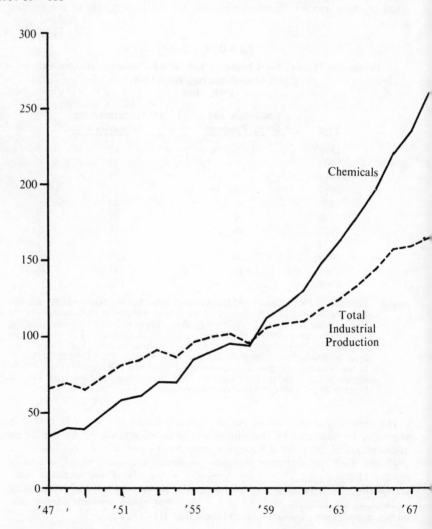

CHART III-4

Per Cent Increases in Production: Chemicals and Allied Products and Total Industrial Production, 1947-1968

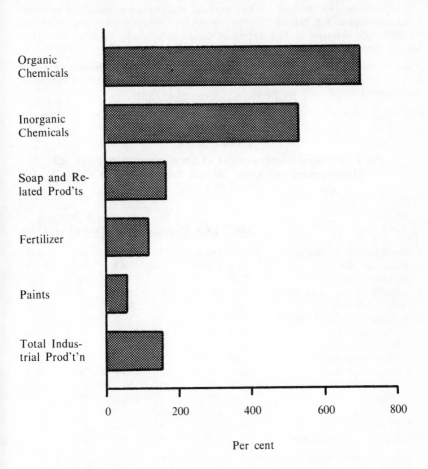

Per cent

The 10% average annual rate of increase in chemical output reflected widely varying annual changes. In three years (1950, 1955 and 1959), the rise exceeded 20 per cent; in three recession years output declined moderately (1949, 1954, and 1958). In 17 out of the 21 years for which data are available, the annual increase exceeded 5%. The size of the annual gains from 1958 to 1963 was greater and more consistent than in the five preceding years (1953 to 1958) when growth was interrupted by two recessions. From 1963 to 1968 increases were about 10% in each year.

Within the chemical industry, there have been widely varying growth rates for different groups of products. Between 1947 and 1968, the largest growth was experienced by plastics materials for which output increased by 2093%; for man-made fibers the increase was 715%. The slowest growth rates were for basic inorganic chemicals (429%) and basic organic chemicals (471%).

For the last five years of this period (1963 to 1968), the pattern was different. The largest growth was recorded by man-made fibers (115%) with plastics materials in second place (78%). The lowest growth was recorded by synthetic rubber (32%) or about in line with the increase in total industrial production (33%) (See Table III-4).

For both the 1947-68 and 1963-68 periods, the growth in the allied products industries lagged far behind that for chemicals. Between 1963 and 1968, for example, the increase of 34% for allied products was only slightly more than half as large as the 60% increase for all chemicals.

An analysis by the U.S. Department of Commerce of the growth in output for 339 products between 1948 and 1965 showed that a number of chemicals were among those with the most rapid rates of increase.[17]

TABLE III-4

Per Cent Changes in Production of Chemicals and Products, All Manufacturing and Total, Selected Periods, 1947 to 1968

(1957-59 = 100)

	1947	1963	% Increase	1968	% Increase 1963-68	% Increase 1947-68
Chemicals and products	41.5	148.5	258	220.4	48	431
Industrial chemicals	34.8	162.5	367	260.4	60	648
Inorganic chemicals	32.0	135.6	324	202.1	49	532
Basic inorganic chemicals	47.0	142.0	202	248.7	75	429
Organic chemicals	36.0	173.9	383	288.3	66	701
Basic organic chemicals	39.7	158.2	299	226.6	43	471
Plastics materials	18.2	224.5	1,134	399.2	78	2,093
Synthetic rubber	NA	135.9	NA	179.6	32	NA
Man-made fibers	44.8	170.1	280	365.0	115	715
Chemical products	48.4	134.2	177	180.4	34	273
Soap and related products	58.9	123.4	110	156.7	27	166
Paints	82.6	107.5	30	129.8	20	57
Fertilizer	62.0	126.0	103	134.1	6	116
All Manufacturing	66.4	124.7	88	166.2	33	150
Total Industrial Production	65.7	124.3	89	164.7	33	151

NA—Not available.
Source: Board of Governors of the Federal Reserve Systems.

Table III-5 lists 24 industrial chemicals which had the highest growth rates in the Commerce study with the changes in output between 1948 and 1965 and for three periods within that span of years. For these 24 products, the growth rate in the 17-year period ranged from 34.8% per year for polyethylene to 7.3% for pentaerythritol. Expansion did not take place at an equal rate throughout the period. Thus, for polyethylene the growth rate in the 1960-1965 period was 17.9% per year as compared with 48.0% annually in the 1948-1953 period and 38.8% from 1953 to 1960. In contrast, output of oxygen expanded 9.3% annually in the earlier period, 12.6% per year between 1953 and 1960 and 25.7% from 1960 to 1965.

Many of the products listed in Table III-5 are relatively new ones which have been developed since World War II. It is these new products with their rapid acceptance and accompanying high growth rates which help to explain the markedly above average growth rate of the chemical industry. However, older chemicals also have experienced growth rates which approximated two or more times the annual growth rate of 4.5% for total industrial production between 1947 and 1965. These include oxygen (15.3%), phosphoric acid (13.7%), benzene (9.2%), hydrogen (9.1%), and nitric acid (8.9%).

TABLE III-5

Per Cent Increase in Output of Rapidly Growing Chemical Products, 1948 - 1965

Product	Unit of measure	Production 1965	Average Annual Rates of Increase			
			1948-65	1948-53	1953-60	1960-65
Polyethylene	mil. lbs.	3,047	34.8	48.0	38.8	17.9
Argon	mil. cu. ft.	1,273	24.7	42.3	22.2	46.8
Non-cellulosic fibers	mil. lbs.	1,777	26.3	30.2	15.5	21.3
Styrene plastics and polyester resins	mil lbs.	2,033	15.9	25.2	11.1	13.9
Oxygen, high purity	bil. cu. ft.	182	15.3	9.3	12.6	25.7
Polyvinyl resins	mil. lbs.	2,312	14.9	18.8	12.9	14.0
Phosphoric acid	thous. short tons	3,845	13.7	17.3	11.7	13.0
Plastics & resin materials	mil. lbs.	11,680	12.9	13.3	12.0	13.7
Plasticizers	mil. lbs.	1,073	12.4	14.6	10.8	12.2
Xylene	mil. gals.	388	11.5	13.1	14.0	6.6
Toluene	mil. gals.	530	11.4	13.2	8.4	14.1
Ammonia, synthetic anhydrous	thous. short tons	8,607	11.4	10.7	11.2	12.3
Perchlorethylene	mil. lbs.	429	11.4	17.6	4.6	15.5
Ethylene glycol	thous. lbs.	1,850	10.0	11.2	11.0	7.4
Formaldehyde	mil. lbs.	3,086	9.9	12.6	7.6	10.5
Benzene	mil. gal.	827	9.2	8.1	7.7	12.6
Hydrogen	bil. cu. ft.	124	9.1	−2.1	14.4	13.7
Nitric acid	thous. short tons	860	8.9	9.3	9.4	7.9
Urea & melamine resins	mil. lbs.	621	8.7	11.5	6.5	9.2
Phenol, natural & synthetic	mil. lbs.	1,229	8.7	5.2	10.6	9.7
Butadiene	mil. gal.	2,708	8.6	11.8	7.3	7.5
Chlorine, gas & liquid	thous. short tons	6,439	8.4	11.3	7.5	6.8
Phthalic anhydride	mil. lbs.	579	7.9	7.4	8.5	7.6
Pentaerythritol	mil. lbs.	69	7.3	21.7	1.9	1.5

Source: Francis L. Hirt, "Patterns of Output Growth," *Survey of Current Business,* November 1966, p. 21.

Trend of Employment

The expansion in demand for chemicals has been reflected in a sharp rise in job opportunities. However, because of the sharp increases in output per man-hour, employment opportunities have increased at a much slower pace than output in the chemical industry.

Production worker employment has been increasing since 1899 with the rise particularly marked during and after World War II. Until 1958, the increase in production worker employment was more rapid than for all manufacturing industries—the increase was somewhat smaller between 1958 and 1967 (16.8% for chemicals and 19.6% for all manufacturing) (Appendix Tables 2 and 16 and Table III-6).

During the post-World War II years, the employment mix or the structure of employment for manufacturing industries has changed significantly. Employment of production workers has not risen so rapidly as total employment. The chemical industry has experienced this shift to a greater extent than all manufacturing. In 1939, 75.3% of the chemical labor force consisted of production workers; the ratio was similar in 1950. However, by 1968 the proportion had declined to 59.6%. For all manufacturing the ratio fell from 82.2% in 1950 to 73.4% in 1968.

This development in the chemical industry has been attributed to "two related trends . . . an intensification of competition and a trend toward integration. These developments have led to greatly expanded sales and marketing staffs, and growing emphasis on laboratory research and development programs."[18] With growth for even the largest company dependent upon innovation and new discoveries, the employment of research and related workers has been expanded markedly in this industry and has accounted for a significant part of the increase in relative importance of non-production workers. These developments reflect the large scale investments in this capital intensive industry (See Chapter VIII).

TABLE III-6

Chemicals, Production Workers, Selected Years, 1899 - 1967

	Number (thousands)	% of All Manufacturing
1899	18	0.4
1914	35	0.5
1919	77	0.9
1929	105	1.3
1939	123	1.6
1947	214	1.8
1958	244	2.1
1963	257	2.1
1966	286	2.1
1967	285	2.0

Source: Derived from Appendix Table 16.

Because of these trends, the changes in the number of production workers no longer provide an accurate guide to the trend of employment opportunities in this industry. Between 1939 and 1968, according to the Bureau of Labor Statistics, *total employment* in the chemicals segment increased from 158,000 to

532,000 or by 237%; the percentage increase for production workers was only 166%. For the allied products industries the increases were 135% and 121% respectively and for all manufacturing industries, 92% and 74% (derived from Appendix Table 17).

Employment in chemicals increased at the annual rate of 4.3% between 1939 and 1968 as compared with 3.0% for allied products and 2.3% for all manufacturing. Between 1947 and 1968, the annual rates of increase were 2.8% for chemicals, 1.7% for allied products, and 1.1% for all manufacturing. Employment opportunities in the chemical industry have risen more sharply than for the allied industries and for all manufacturing.

The increase in employment has been concentrated in plants making the newer products. Thus, since 1947 employment opportunities have increased most in establishments producing plastics materials, non-cellulosic fibers, synthetic rubber, and miscellaneous organics including acyclics. In contrast, there has been little change in the number employed[19] in establishments producing alkalies and chlorine, and industrial gases, while total employment actually has declined for inorganic pigments, intermediate coal-tar crudes, cyclic coal-tar crudes and cellulosic man-made fibers. These trends underline the vital importance of new investments and new products as the source of expanding job opportunities in the dynamic industrial chemical industry.

Chemical Companies Among the 100 Largest Industrials

As the chemical industry has increased in relative importance, companies have grown in size and have accounted for a large number of the 100 largest industrial companies. A.D.H. Kaplan studied the composition of the 100 largest industrial corporations in terms of *total assets* as of six dates between 1909 and 1960.[20] Included in this group in 1909 were only four chemical companies ranked as follows:[21]

Rank	Company
27	E. I. du Pont
29	Virginia Carolina Chemical Company
91	International Salt Co.
96	General Chemical Co. (predecessor of Allied Chemical)

By 1948, eight chemical companies were included in the 100 largest and were ranked as follows:

Rank	Company
8	E. I. du Pont
15	Union Carbide
42	Allied Chemical
52	Dow Chemical
64	Celanese
71	American Viscose
76	American Cyanamid
86	Monsanto

In 1960, there were also eight companies ranked as follows:[22]

Rank	Company
8	E. I. du Pont
16	Union Carbide
(27)	Monsanto
29	Dow
41	Olin Mathieson
51	Allied Chemical
64	American Cyanamid
69	W. R. Grace & Co.

In 1968, the number had increased to 10 as follows:[23]

Rank in Assets	Company
17	E. I. du Pont
18	Union Carbide
29	Dow Chemical
(36)	Monsanto
45	W. R. Grace & Co.
47	Celanese
54	Allied Chemical
86	Olin Mathieson
88	American Cyanamid
89	FMC

Moreover, an additional 46 companies included in the 100 largest industrials produced chemicals although it was not their major business activity. Thus, more than one-half of the 100 largest industrial companies are in the chemical business.[24]

If the list is confined to the 50 largest industrial companies in terms of assets the number increased from two in 1909, to three in 1948, and then to five in 1968. Moreover, in the latter year an additional 23 companies among the 50 largest industrial companies produced chemicals. In some instances (as for example, Standard Oil of New Jersey, Socony Mobil, Shell Oil, and Eastman Kodak), these other companies had chemical sales of $250 million or more annually. The rise in the relative size ranking of chemical companies provides another indication of the dramatic growth achieved by this industry. However, as Kaplan has warned: "Some giants with consecutive membership in the 100 largest throughout the half century bear little resemblance to their earlier namesakes. The product mix of du Pont of 1909 is scarcely that of the present leader in the chemical field."[25]

Changing Composition of Output

The development of new products as well as the improvement of older products has played a primary role in the growth experienced. The chemical industry has been an aggressive innovator. As a result, the composition of its output has changed continuously. Unfortunately, because of changes in classifications and discontinuities in the data available, the changes in composition of output can be painted only in broad strokes. However, the general tendencies are more important than the precise percentages involved.

Prior to World War I, the industry produced mainly inorganic chemicals such as acids and various sodium compounds (especially caustic soda and soda ash). Glycerin was the most important organic chemical in terms of dollar volume.

During World War I, there was a tremendous increase in the production of coal-tar dyes, which were essential to the war effort and which were no longer available from Germany. Similarly, domestic production of compressed gases, especially oxygen, increased markedly.

Between 1919 and 1937, the major development was the phenomenal growth of rayon which became by far the most important product of the industry. Compressed gases extended their World War I gains by a substantial margin while the output of coal-tar products after declining significantly below the wartime totals rose sharply during the 1930s to a new record level. The output of acids and sodium compounds continued to increase but at a slower rate than the total for all groups. Plastics also became increasingly important.

The group totals conceal diverse trends. For example, although the total value of output of acids increased between 1919 and 1937, declines were recorded for hydrochloric and oleic acids while little change occurred for stearic, nitric, and phosphoric acids. On the other hand, sulfuric acid, the most important product in the group, recorded a marked increase in value of output.

Among the compressed gases, carbon dioxide volume declined between 1919 and 1937 in contrast to the large expansion experienced for acetylene, chlorine, and oxygen.

As a result of these trends, the composition of output changed drastically between 1914 and 1937. Rayon, compressed gases, and plastics, which were relatively unimportant before World War I, together accounted for $378 million or 30.8% of the value of output in 1937. In 1937, these three groups of products were the most important—measured in dollar volume—produced by the chemical industry.

Growth has been particularly marked in the more than quarter of a century since 1939. In that year total shipments of chemicals (SIC 281 and 282) were

TABLE III-7

Distribution of Shipments Among the Major Categories of Chemical Products, Selected Years, 1939 - 1967

	1939	1947	1954	1958	1962	1967
			(per cent)			
Alkalies and chlorine	8.0	5.0	4.6	4.3	4.1	3.4
Industrial gases	4.2	2.3	2.3	2.4	2.5	2.6
Cyclic (coal-tar crudes)	2.6	1.5	0.9	1.0	0.8	6.9*
Intermediate coal-tar products	10.9	11.6	8.3	6.9	6.8	
Inorganic pigments	6.2	6.9	4.4	3.5	3.2	2.5
Organic chemicals, n.e.c.	18.6	23.5	25.2	26.3	28.7	30.6
Inorganic chemicals, n.e.c.	23.7	15.1	22.2	23.4	21.3	19.4
Plastics materials and resins	6.5	11.6	14.1	15.7	15.4	16.7
Synthetic rubber	—	5.7	4.1	4.6	4.9	4.3
Cellulosic man-made fibers	19.4	17.0	13.9	6.1	4.7	3.4
Organic fibers, non-cellulosic				5.8	7.7	10.2
TOTAL	100.1	100.0	100.0	100.0	100.0	100.0

n.e.c.—not elsewhere classified.
*Cyclic intermediates and crudes

$1.3 billion. By 1967 the total was $21.5 billion. This tremendous increase reflected the combination of higher prices and greater volume,[26] with volume accounting for the bulk of growth. The increase in volume was influenced to a significant degree by the development of many new products.[27] Howeverm the growth was very uneven among the different groups of chemicals.

The changing composition of chemical industry shipments since 1939 is shown clearly in Table III-7. Actually, each category of products listed recorded an increase in shipments in each of the years shown. The changes in the proportions reflect the different rates of growth rather than declines in the value of shipments for any major group of products. Thus, for example, total shipments of alkalies and chlorine increased by 623% between 1939 and 1967. Nevertheless, its relative share of total shipments of chemical products was more than cut in half because total shipment of chemicals increased by 1,585% in the period covered.

The major contributions to growth in 1939-1967 period were made by organic chemicals particularly the synthetics, which continued to increase in relative importance. Moreover, there was a major shift in the relative importance of end-products from dyes, explosives and intermediates to plastics materials, non-cellulosic organic fibers, and miscellaneous organic chemicals. During this period, petroleum and natural gas replaced coal, cellulose, water, air, and fats and oils as the source of many chemicals.[28]

The more important changes may be summarized as follows:

> Synthetic rubber was produced on an unimportant scale prior to World War II. It became a full-blown industry during that conflict when it became necessary to replace the natural rubber no longer available from the Malay States, Dutch East Indies, and other countries in that area. All of the growth in the relative importance of synthetic rubber had occurred by 1947 since which year shipments have not increased as rapidly as for all chemicals.

> Plastics increased steadily in relative importance from 6.5% of total shipments in 1939 to 16.7% in 1967.

> Organic chemicals, n.e.c. include non-cyclic organic chemicals, solvents, plasticizers, polyhydric alcohols, rubber processing chemicals, etc.[29] In the aggregate, shipments of these products increased from $237 million in 1939 to $6,582 million in 1967; their relative importance increased from 18.6% to 30.6%. The major contribution to this growth has been made by acyclic chemicals and chemical products which account for more than one-half of the total for the group.[30]

Some Census groupings show a decline in relative importance that conceals the dramatic expansion which has taken place for new products classified in those groups. For example, in 1939 synthetic fibers accounted for 19.4% of the shipments of chemicals while in 1967 the proportion was only 13.6%. However, the 1939 total was composed almost entirely of rayon and acetate. Nylon was first introduced on a small scale in that year and polyesters, acrylics, and modified acrylics were not yet available. Shipments of rayon and other cellulosic fibers continued to rise in the postwar years. But the rate of increase was dwarfed by that for the non-cellulosic fibers which in terms of pounds increased from less than one per cent of the combined total to over 50%.[31]

The shift in dollar volume was even more dramatic. Between 1958 and 1963, for example, the shipments of rayon, etc. increased from $723 million to $924 million. Meanwhile, the total for the non-cellulosic group of fibers increased from $688 million to $1,992 million. In 1967, these products accounted for 10.2% of total shipments of chemicals.

The illustrations cited above could be multiplied many times and they are found within companies as well as in the industry.[32] It is evident that the chemical industry is one of the most dynamic in our economy. Change is its theme and keynote. Its enormous investment in research and development has borne fruit in the new products which have assumed key importance in our industrial economy. These new products, in turn, spawn newer products in the intensely competitive environment which characterizes today's chemical industry. Clearly, the overall growth rate of the chemical industry would have been significantly smaller if these new products had not been developed. The record also underlines the necessity of continuing to develop new products if the significantly greater than average growth rates of the past are to be maintained.

Interruptions In Growth: Cyclical Patterns

Growth in our economy usually does not mean a continuous expansion in volume. Historically, both national economic growth and the expansion of specific industries have been interrupted periodically by cyclical influences. During periods of recession, the rate of expansion may be slowed even for strong growth industries (as has been true for electric power) or may be interrupted by brief periods of modest decline in volume (as has been true for the chemical industry).

Tables III-8 and III-9 compare the changes in industrial production and in the output of chemicals between the high and low months of successive business cycles. The dates shown are those which have been designated as turning points for the economy as a whole by the National Bureau of Economic Research.[33] Since a continuous series of data is not available for chemicals, the record over the past 40 years is shown in two separate tables: Table III-8 covering 1923 to 1938 and Table III-9 the 1948-1968 period. (The data for the years 1939 to 1947 are distorted by World War II and hence have been omitted.)

The production series for chemical products[34] from 1923 to 1938 is not comparable with that for chemicals and products during the post-World War II period. Output of chemical products declined less than total industrial production in each of the four recessions between 1923 and 1938; in the Great Depression of 1929 to 1933, the decline in chemical output was less than half as great as total industrial activity (See Table III-8). During periods of expanding activity, on the other hand, output of chemicals and products increased about in the same proportion as industrial production during two of the three periods shown. The combination of smaller declines and about equal increases (with one exception) resulted in a net increase of 67% of output of chemicals and products between July 1924 and June 1938 (two troughs in the business cycle) as compared with the rise of only 8.0% for total industrial production.

TABLE III-8

Industrial Production at Cyclical Turning Points, 1923-1938

	Total Industrial Production	Chemical Products
	(1935-39 = 100, Seasonally Adjusted)	
May 1923	92) down 17	57) down 2
July 1924	75) up 23	55) up 16
October 1926	98) down 6	71) up 2
November 1927	92) up 22	73) up 18
August 1929	114) down 60	91) down 23
March 1933	54) up 77	68) up 47
May 1937	121) down 40	115) down 23
June 1938	81	92

generally follows but less severe

47

Per Cent Changes for Cyclical Periods, 1923-1938

	Total Industrial Production	Chemical Products
May 1923-July 1924	—18.5	—3.5
July 1924-October 1926	+30.7	+29.1
October 1926-November 1927	—6.1	+2.8
November 1927-August 1929	+23.9	+24.7
August 1929-March 1933	—52.6	—25.3
March 1933-May 1937	+124.1	+69.1
May 1937-June 1938	—33.1	—20.0

Source: Board of Governors of the Federal Reserve System, *Federal Reserve Index of Industrial Production,* Washington, D.C., 1943, pp. 45, 95.

TABLE III-9

Industrial Production at Cyclical Turning Points, 1948-1968

	Total Industrial Production	Total Manufacturing	Chemicals and Products	Chemical
	(1957-59 = 100, Seasonally Adjusted)			
November 1948	68.4	68.6	45.3	40.4
October 1949	62.6	63.8	45.8	39.9
July 1953	93.9	95.3	72.4	73.4
August 1954	85.4	85.8	71.2	70.0
July 1957	102.2	102.3	95.4	97.2
April 1958	87.8	87.2	91.2	87.0
May 1960	109.9	110.5	117.6	121.4
February 1961	103.4	102.6	115.0	118.4
December 1968*	168.7	170.1	231.1	273.6

Per Cent Changes for Cyclical Periods

	Total Industrial Production	Total Manufacturing	Chemicals and Products	Chemical
November 1948-October 1949	— 8.5	— 7.0	+ 1.1	— 1.2
October 1949-July 1953	+50.0	+49.4	+ 58.1	+ 84.0
July 1953-August 1954	— 9.1	—10.0	— 1.7	— 4.6
August 1954-July 1957	+19.7	+19.2	+ 34.0	+ 38.9
July 1957-April 1958	—14.1	—14.8	— 4.4	— 10.5
April 1958-May 1960	+25.2	+26.7	+ 28.9	+ 39.5
May 1960-February 1961	— 5.9	— 7.1	— 2.2	— 2.5
February 1961-December 1968	+63.2	+65.8	+101.0	+131.1

*December was not the turning point but rather the latest data available for an expansion that had lasted about eight years.

Source: Board of Governors of the Federal Reserve System, *Industrial Production-1957-59 Base,* Washington, D.C., 1962, pp. S-58, 59, 148, 150; *Survey of Current Business,* March 1969, p. S-4.

Table III-9 shows the indexes and the changes for total industrial production, manufacturing, chemicals and products, and chemicals as compiled by the Federal Reserve Board between 1948 and 1968.[35] The index of chemical production covers the equivalent of SIC 281 and 282.

The above average long term growth for chemicals is indicated by the increase of 577% between November 1948 and December 1968; during the same period the total index of industrial production increased only 147%.

In every post-World War II period of expansion, output of chemicals rose substantially more rapidly than total industrial output or manufacturing output. However, chemical output has not been immune to recessions as declines were recorded in each postwar recession; these declines were usually much more moderate than those recorded for total industrial production or for manufacturing production (See Chart III-5).

The fluctuations in the output of chemicals have been somewhat greater than for chemicals and allied products with declines usually greater and advances more marked. The relatively greater stability for the composite group of chemicals and allied products reflects the fact that it includes drugs, soaps, toilet goods, and cosmetics which are consumer products with more stable demand and a lower growth rate in the aggregate than chemicals.

It is clear from these data that the forces of growth for chemicals have been so strong that they have tended to offset in large part the pressures which operate to reduce demand during periods of general declines in economic activity. Thus, the outstanding growth record of the chemical industry in the post-war period has reflected less than average declines in production during recessions and above average increases during periods of expansion.

Factors Contributing to Growth

The major factors contributing to the above average growth record of chemicals have included the large investment in research and development, the industry's technical know-how, the intense competition among chemical companies, the large-scale military and space demand for chemicals, the broadening of markets through reductions in price, the fact that many customers also are above average growth industries, and the incentives created by a favorable rate of profits.

High Rate of Innovation

Research and development has been the primary driving force behind the sensational growth of the chemical industry. Long before the high pay-off of investment in research was recognized by other industries, the chemical industry was heavily engaged in such activities. The importance of relatively heavy expenditures for R & D is indicated by the steady stream of new products each year. The chemical industry has had a high rate of innovation and of new processes which act to hold down or to reduce costs thus making the use of chemical products more attractive. The discoveries in connection with giant molecules, surface chemistry, and solids are a testimonial to the yield arising from the major investment in research. Dramatic breakthroughs with new products have made significant contributions to the industry's growth as well as to that of the nation.

Thus, for example, Du Pont reported in 1968 that about 45% of its sales were from products added to the company catalogs since 1946.[36]

For Dow, 30% of the 1964 income was derived from products introduced in the preceding ten years while in 1968, 7% of its income was from products introduced in the preceding five years.[37]

A company's growth depends upon the flow of new products and processes. A company must engage in research if it is to participate fully in the growth of

49

the industry and to avoid a decline in its market share. Research is going on simultaneously in a large number of laboratories thus increasing the possibilities of new discoveries. Of the 371,000 scientists and engineers spending full time in industry research and development, as of 1967, 42,000 were employed in chemicals and allied products. Only aircraft and parts and communications and equipment, both engaged in military research, had a larger number of scientists so engaged.[38]

The impact of new discoveries has been reflected in many ways. Chemical products have provided relatively cheap raw materials with qualities that have made them more useful than the products they displace. In this connection, it has been pointed out that the versatility of carbon in terms of number of uses and compounds and its low cost "provided a main driving force behind the chemical industry's expansion in the past 30 years."[39]

The chemical industry is its own greatest competitor. It is constantly obsoleting its own products and generating its own growth by the chemical reactions it builds up from its basic raw materials.

As the limits of knowledge of chemical processes expand, growth is fed by the heightened awareness of the ability to develop profitable opportunities inherent in these new discoveries. It also has made possible the fuller utilization of waste materials of many chemical operations with the accompanying flow of useful products. The opportunities are diverse and often unforseeable. Once a new breakthrough is made, it is rarely possible to determine at the time its full potentialities. The multitude of products created subsequent to the discoveries of giant molecules provide the most dramatic illustration of the unforseen possibilities attending a new development. Technical competence and management "know-how," therefore, are important contributing factors to the growth of the industry.

Initially, the chemical industry seeks to determine the chemical structure of natural products and then to reproduce them in the laboratory. Upon the achievement of this goal, the researchers then seek to improve upon the natural product in terms of both cost and performance as they have done with dyes, rubbers, fibers, leather and many others. Markets are thereby broadened and scarce materials made more plentiful with the resulting stimulus to growth of the chemical industry and of the national economy.

Many industries are based on chemical processes and hence the companies in those industries have chemical know-how which has contributed significantly to growth.[40]

Since almost one-third of the nation's largest corporations already are involved in chemical production in some form, there is a wide base which increases the number of opportunities for the discovery and development of new products. Major contributions to the industry's growth rate have flowed from the research activities of these companies as well as from the efforts of the primary producers of chemicals. The enormous growth in various petrochemicals has undoubtedly been stimulated by the vigorous search for new products and new uses for old products as well as their improvement by petroleum companies.

Favorable Price Relationships

Historically, chemical prices have tended to decline relative to the general price level. Markets have expanded for plastics, for example, as prices have been reduced and new uses have been found for these versatile materials. During the period from 1947 to 1963, wholesale prices of plastic resins and materials fell by 13.0% in contrast to the rise of 33.9% in the general level of wholesale prices; the price index for organic chemicals rose only 2.7% in the same period. Between 1957 and 1968, when the wholesale price index rose 9.8%, the prices of plastic resins and materials fell by 19.9% and organic chemicals declined by 11.8%.

The sensational growth in the demand for polyethylene provides a recent illustration of the important role played by favorable price relationships in the growth of the chemical industry.

The pressure on prices as new companies have entered into production undoubtedly has helped to increase the effective demand for chemicals as they have improved their competitive position vis à vis natural materials. In turn, new and improved chemical products have competed with those already in use and have helped to open up new markets. Moreover, there is considerable pressure for quick acceptance of new products because companies know that within a short period their initial market advantage will be lost because of the intensive competition within the industry.

Above Average Growth of Large Customers

Since the bulk of the industry's demand is derived rather than direct, the fact that some of the industries and products which use chemicals have experienced above average growth also has contributed to the spectacular growth performance of the chemical industry. Included in this category are drugs, rubber and plastics, glass, fluorescent lighting, and detergents. The chemical industry has expanded more rapidly than consuming industries because it has replaced other materials as well as participated in new growth.[41]

Thus, for example, value of shipments increased by 1262% for drugs and 1169% for rubber and plastics between 1939 and 1967; for all manufacturing the rise was 959%. A similar pattern is shown for the 1947-1967 period with increases of 339%, 289% and 249% respectively.[42] It should also be noted that the chemical industry is its own best customer and hence the sharp rise in demand for its products has resulted in a marked expansion in its own use of chemicals.

Growth in Military and Space Demand

The rise in military demand also has contributed to growth largely by laying the groundwork for new products and processes such as those which were developed in World War II and those which have been developed more recently in connection with our missile and space programs. Chemical propellants, for example, have played a key role in "lifting heavy payloads to orbital and escape velocities."[43] Chemical research will continue to be vital in this program.

Spending for research and development on the space program increased substantially over the past decade, but is now expected to decline. The amount is estimated at $3.9 billion in fiscal 1970 as against $4.7 billion two years earlier. In fiscal 1960, the total was about $0.5 billion.[44] It was estimated in 1963 that the chemical industry obtained about 15% of the federal government's appropriations for the development of space and missile systems. As a result, chemical concerns are important Defense Department contractors in aerospace.[45]

Profits and Incentives

Until 1967, the profitability of the chemical industry provided the incentive to undertake new programs and hence contributed to the industry's growth over the years. The industry's rate of return on net worth generally was higher than the average for all manufacturing until 1966. However, according to the First National City Bank, return on net worth for chemical products reached a peak of 21.3% in 1950, fell to 17.7% in 1955, declined further to 12.4% in 1960, and to 11.4% in 1968. During this 18-year period the differential has shifted from 4.2% in favor of chemical products as compared with all manufacturing to 1.7% against chemicals. Thus despite sharply rising demand for chemical products, earnings have not kept pace. Price declines have contributed to this recent unfavorable trend.

In the past, above average rates of return have attracted capital into the chemical industry thereby laying the groundwork for the many new and improved products. These earnings also have been an important source of funds to finance expansion and the development of new products. The large scale capital investment resulted in sharp increases in productivity which in turn contributed to maintaining above average profit rates.

The above average profit rates also have induced companies in other industries to enter the chemical industry. One result has been to broaden the base for research and development and to intensify competitive pressures in this area as well as in the search for new markets. A continuation of the less favorable profits experience of 1967 and in 1968 could modify one of the important inducements to expansion of this industry.

Future Trends

McGraw-Hill Publications' Economics Department has prepared projections for the components of the Federal Reserve Board production index by five year periods from 1967 to 1982. The projections for the several components of chemicals and products are shown in Table III-10. Five factors were considered in making these forecasts:

"1. Past growth trends, as measured by the Federal Reserve Board's indexes of production, which often do not have any direct relationship to tons, pounds, gallons, feet or other units of measurement of production of specific products.

2. The amount and trend of research and development spending.

3. Prospects for development of new products.

4. Prospects for use of new technology and cost-cutting machinery.

5. The implications of projected trends in GNP expenditures by sectors and components for output of specific industries.

The fastest growing industries, such as plastics, man-made fibers, chemicals, appliances and aluminum ranked high in all five of the above factors."[46]

The chemical industry ranks high in at least four of these five areas and hence it is not surprising that the "fastest growing industries" included plastics, man-made fibers, and chemicals. The projected annual growth rate is 10.2% for organic chemicals in the 15-year period or more than twice as much as for all industrial production; for synthetic materials the projected annual growth rate is 11.8% and for plastic materials 13.5%. In contrast to these extraordinary growth rates for chemicals, the projection for allied products (including soaps and related products, paints, and fertilizers) is only 5.5% or moderately higher than the national average (See Table III-10).

TABLE III-10

**Projections For Output of Chemicals and Products and Total
Industrial Production, 1967-1982**

(1957-59 = 100)

	1967	1972	1977	1982	Annual Rate of Increase 1967-1982 (per cent)
Industrial Production	157.9	199.1	253.9	326.6	5.0
Chemicals & Products	203.4	301.4	447.2	664.9	8.2
Industrial Chemicals	234.3	373.3	593.7	941.7	9.7
Inorganic Chemicals	190.5	283.6	418.5	611.4	8.1
Basic Inorganics	236.4	363.8	552.2	826.6	8.7
Other	111.8	146.1	189.2	242.6	5.3
Organic Chemicals	252.9	411.2	667.7	1081.2	10.2
Basic Organic	216.3	314.9	454.1	648.9	7.6
Synthetic Materials	295.6	523.0	915.5	1582.7	11.8
Plastic Materials	343.0	660.3	1244.0	2291.4	13.5
Synthetic Rubber	160.3	214.5	284.4	373.4	5.8
Man-Made Fibers	277.0	446.2	702.3	1080.8	9.5
Chemical Products	171.7	227.6	296.8	380.7	5.5
Soap & Related	150.6	189.5	237.3	295.7	4.6
Paints	128.2	152.3	179.1	208.7	3.3
Fertilizer	140.0	170.4	209.3	259.5	4.2
Other	191.4	262.2	350.8	458.5	6.0

Source   The American Economy, Prospects For Growth Through 1982, McGraw-Hill,
New York, 1969, Statistical Supplement, pp. 12, 22.

Summary and Conclusions

Test tube competition has been the vital stimulating and driving force in the chemical industry. Such competition is so intensive and so widespread that it has become indispensable to competitive success. The industry is constantly obsoleting its own products and processes. It is marked by intensive struggles for product leadership. Extensive research is undertaken not only by chemical companies but by the companies in the various chemical process industries thus broadening the base of research. The pervasiveness of research results in a fuller utilization of waste materials and increases the possibilities of discovery of new products and of the development of greater usefulness for older ones. Technical know-how and an insatiable drive for further knowledge have been among the industry's greatest assets.

The dramatic growth of the chemical industry provides an outstanding demonstration that extensive investment in research and development pays off. (The drug industry provides another illustration.) The recent history is one of inquisitiveness which has led to discovery, to changes, and to progress. An examination of the changing composition of output over time quickly reveals the dynamic contribution of R & D to expanding volume. Rayon and other cellulosic fibers in the 1920s and 1930s, synthetic rubber during World War II and the postwar years, plastics (e.g. polyethylene, polypropylene, styrene, urea, etc.) and non-cellulosic fibers (e.g. polyesters and acrylics) in the 1950s and 1960s all represented major breakthroughs which resulted in the creation of major new markets for the chemical industry.

In addition to the significant contribution to growth made by its research laboratories, the industry has been favored by a large rise in demand because of military and space needs, by the increase in effective demands as markets have broadened when prices for many new products have declined, by the substitution of chemicals for other products, and by many customers who are in industries with above average rates of growth. Finally, the favorable profit record throughout most of the chemical industry's history provided the incentive to make substantial investments in research and to manufacture and market the flow of products developed in its research laboratories; these profits also have helped finance the investment required. The economy has reaped high social dividends from these developments.

Throughout the twentieth century and particularly since World War II chemicals has been one of the great growth industries. The rate of growth has been more than twice as large as that recorded for the entire national economy.

Over the span of the twentieth century, the value added by manufacture by chemicals increased from 0.6% to 4.4% of the total for all manufacturing industries. The expanded contribution made to the economy has been even greater than indicated by these data, which are based on dollar totals, because prices have risen less for chemicals than for the entire economy. Although the relative importance of allied products also has increased during this period (from 3.7% of value added in 1899 to 4.5% in 1967), their record has fallen far short of the growth in the chemicals segment.

The growth of chemicals in dollar terms has developed overwhelmingly since 1939 when total shipments were a little less than $1.3 billion. By 1967, the total had increased to $21.5 billion. While increases were reported for all major product groups, the most outstanding growth rates developed for synthetic rubber, plastics materials, non-cellulosic fibers, and acrylics. These were mainly newly developed products. Since 1939, after eliminating the effects of higher prices, total shipments of chemicals have increased at an annual rate of 8.9% as compared with 4.3% for gross national product. The physical output of chemicals has increased more than twice as rapidly as that for the entire economy.

The exceptional dollar increase since 1939 has reflected in part the price inflation which characterized this period. However, chemical prices rose less (68%) than the implicit price index used to measure the inflation in gross national product (171%). If chemical prices had risen by 171%, purchasers would have to pay $34.7 billion for the volume acquired in 1967 or $13.2 billion *more* than they actually paid. Of course, with such a price rise the actual volume bought would have been less.

The record since 1947 has been similar. As measured by production, the annual rate of increase since 1947 has been 10.0% for chemicals, 4.5% for total industrial production, and 6.5% for allied products. Total employment increased at an annual rate of 2.8% for chemicals, 1.7% for allied products, and only 1.1% for all manufacturing between 1947 and 1968. The chemicals segment has been expanding much more rapidly than the allied products. Clearly, the growth record of the entire chemicals and allied products group of industries has been due in large measure to the tremendous expansion recorded by chemicals.

Despite its great growth rate, the chemical industry has not been immune to recessions. Growth in this industry has been interrupted by cyclical downturns. However, in every recession since 1923, the decline in output of chemicals has been smaller—usually significantly smaller—than that recorded for total industrial production. The industry has been more recession resistant because of the strong underlying growth trend. Prior to World War II, the expansion in chemical output during periods of recovery was only about equal to that for total industrial production but in the post-World War II years, the increases recorded by chemicals usually have been significantly greater than those for all industry. Long-term growth at a faster rate than the economy, therefore, has reflected below average declines and above average expansions.

Finally, it must be emphasized that the dramatic growth rate of the chemical industry has reflected and has been made possible by the large flow of new products it has developed. The volume of older products has increased as the national economy has grown in size. But it has been the sales derived from the new organics, particularly synthetic materials, which have made the difference between an about average growth rate and one which is more than twice as rapid as that recorded by the national economy. There has been no slowing down in the historic high rate of growth. However, a continuation of past trends will depend upon the continued high rate of innovation which has contributed so significantly to the brilliant record achieved by chemicals.

---

[1] For example, at various times the Bureau of the Census had included aluminum, ferro alloys, and lubricating oils among chemicals and allied products. "U.S. Census of Manufactures: 1963," *op. cit.*, p. 28-3.

[2] Further revisions were made in 1958, 1963, and 1967.

[3] Cottonseed oils, linseed oils, soybean oils, vegetable oil, nec., grease and tallow, and animal oil, nec.

[4] The number of establishments producing fats and oils was 998 in 1954, 1,176 in 1947, and 953 in 1939. The Census data for those years as well as earlier years, must be adjusted to make the totals for chemicals and allied products comparable with 1958.

[5] In 1958, fireworks and pyrotechnics, which were shifted to chemicals and allied products, accounted for 67 establishments.

[6] Joseph V. Sherman, "Profitable Formula," *Barron's,* July 20, 1964, pp. 11, 17.

[7] "Value added by manufacture is calculated by subtracting the cost of materials, supplies, containers, fuel, purchased electric energy, and contract work from the total value of shipments." U.S. Department of Commerce, Bureau of the Census, *Census of Manufactures: 1947,* Washington, D.C., 1949.

[8] The Bureau of the Census, U.S. Department of Commerce, usually reports data for shipments while the Office of Business Economics, Department of Commerce, reports data for sales. The former are for establishments while the latter are on a company basis. Both series are net, that is, after discounts and allowances. The Census data also exclude freight charges and excise taxes in most instances while the OBE data include them since they are based on receipts. Both sales and shipments show similar trends and hence changes in the two series may be compared.

[9] An OECD study for the 1956-1966 period found "that an increase of one percent in the gross national product is accompanied by an increase of 2.05 percent in European chemical consumption and 1.81 in chemical consumption in the United States. For plastics materials the elasticity is 3.43 for Europe and 4.45 for the United States." Organisation for Economic Co-operation and Development, *The Chemical Industry, 1967-1968,* Paris, 1969, p. 12.

[10] In 1939, the output of non-cellulosic fibers was nominal. Nevertheless, by 1968 the total output of these fibers was more than twice as large as that for rayon and acetate.

[11] The BLS wholesale price index increased by 151%.

[12] Hempel, *op. cit.*, p. 4.

[13] U.S. Department of Commerce, *National Income and Product Accounts of the United States, 1929-1965,* Washington, D.C., August 1966, p. 143; *Survey of Current Business,* July 1968, p. 46; *Economic Report of the President,* January 1969, p. 282.

[14]Prices of chemicals increased by 19.6% between 1947 and 1966. If the rise had been equal to the national average of 39.0%, purchasers would have had to pay an additional $3.6 billion for the chemicals they bought—$24.9 billion instead of $21.3 billion.

[15]That chemicals were expanding much more rapidly than allied products also is shown by the output data reported by the Federal Reserve Board. Between 1947 and 1966, the increases were 449% for inorganic chemicals and 563% for organic chemicals in contrast to 147% for soaps and related products, 119% for fertilizers, and 54% for paints.

[16]" . . . in developed countries throughout the world the [chemical] industry is expanding at roughly twice the rate of industry as a whole." Allen, op. cit., p. 1037.

[17]Francis L. Hirt, "Patterns of Output Growth," Survey of Current Business, November 1966, p. 21.

[18]National Industrial Conference Board, Chemicals and Allied Products, New York, 1960, p. 17.

[19]But the composition of employment has changed with a declining proportion accounted for by production workers.

[20]A. D. H. Kaplan, Big Enterprise In a Competitive System, The Brookings Institution, Washington, D.C., 1964, pp. 140-51.

[21]Kaplan also included as chemical companies in his 1909 list the following companies which are not classified as chemicals in the present study and hence have been omitted above: American Agricultural Chemical (fertilizers), American Cotton Oil and American Linseed Oil (fats and oils), and Eastman Kodak, Ibid., p. 13.

[22]Kaplan also included Eastman Kodak and Procter and Gamble in his list of chemical companies. Ibid., pp. 131, 150-51.

[23]Fortune, May 15, 1969, pp. 168-70.

[24]Du Pont reported that in 1968 "28 of the top 100 firms are making products that compete directly with Du Pont's firms—and are making inroads on the company's sales." Du Pont, Better Living, September/October 1968, p. 16.

[25]Kaplan, op. cit., p. 138.

[26]When the shipments data are adjusted to eliminate the effects of the price rise of 68%, total volume in physical terms rose more than nine-fold from $1,277 million to $12,051 million in 1939 dollars.

[27]For example, synthetic rubber and non-cellulosic organic fibers, which were inconsequential in 1939, accounted for 4.3% and 10.2% respectively of total shipments in 1967.

[28]In 1965, 93% of the total production of organics in the United States was obtained from natural gas and oil. In Western Europe the proportion was only 73% (the Western Europe figure for 1966 was 77%. Data are not available for U.S.) Organisation for Economic Cooperation and Development, The Chemical Industry, 1966-1967, Paris, 1968, pp. 93-94.

[29]"Census of Manufactures: 1963," op. cit., p. 28A-5.

[30]In 1963 shipments of acyclic chemicals and chemical products accounted for $2,600 million out of the total of $4,840 million for the entire organic chemicals, nec group.

[31]"Census of Manufactures: 1963," op. cit., pp. 28B-14-15.

[32]For example, in the five year period 1958 to 1963, Monsanto reported that fibers had increased in relative importance from 23.1% to 26.7% of sales and that plastics, synthetic resins and surface coatings had increased from 20.1% to 24.8%. On the other hand, the relative share of heavy chemicals declined from 3.1% to 2.0% and of rubber and oil chemicals from 8.6% to 7.2%. 1963 Annual Report, p. 16. From 1963 to 1968 the relative importance of fibers had risen to 29.2%, plastics, resins and coatings fell to 23.0%, heavy chemicals were unchanged at 2.0% and rubber and oil chemicals declined to 6.3%. 1968 Annual Report, p. 4.

[33] U.S. Department of Commerce, Bureau of the Census, *Business Cycle Developments,* January 1964, p. 61.

[34] For the 1923-1938 period the chemical products index included paints, soaps, rayon, industrial chemicals, explosives and ammunition, and other chemical products. The chemical products index was given a weight of 6.27% in the industrial production index. Of this total, industrial chemicals accounted for 1.71% paints for .78%, soaps for .45%, and rayon for .60%. For reasons of national security, no weights were indicated for explosives and ammunition and other chemical products, *Federal Reserve Bulletin,* October 1943, p. 6.

[35] Chemicals and products have a total weight of 7.58% in the industrial production index or somewhat larger than in the earlier series. Chemicals have a weight of 3.84% (inorganics, 1.14% and organics and synthetic materials 2.70%) and chemical products a weight of 3.74%. Chemical products include drugs, soaps, toiletries, paints, and fertilizer. Board of Governors of the Federal Reserve System, *Industrial Production—1957-59 Base,* Washington, D.C., 1962, pp. S-14-15.

[36] *Better Living,* January/February 1968, p. 24.

[37] Dow Chemical Company, *1964 Annual Report,* p. 3 and *1968 Annual Report,* p. 3.

[38] "Statistical Abstract of the United States: 1968," *op. cit.,* p. 529.

[39] Soule, *op. cit.,* p. 102.

[40] It has been suggested that the "chemicalization of industrial processes and products" may be increasing. Harold G. Vatter, *The U.S. Economy in the 1950s: An Economic History,* W. W. Norton & Company, Inc., New York, 1963, p. 170.

[41] It has been reported that " . . . chemical sales to the automotive industry are growing at a rate more than double the growth rate of the automotive industry itself." Thomas F. Willers, "The Outlook For Chemicals." An address before the National Industrial Conference Board 1969 Sales Management Conference, Los Angeles, California, May 8, 1969, p. 2.

[42] Between 1947 and 1968, total physical output of rubber and plastics products increased 290% as compared with the rise of 151% in the Federal Reserve Board index of industrial production.

[43] "The Chemical Industry Facts Book," *op. cit.,* p. 127.

[44] *The Budget of the United States Government, Fiscal Year 1970,* Washington, D.C., 1969, pp. 90-91.

[45] "The Chemical Industry Facts Book," *op. cit.,* p. 136.

[46] *The American Economy, Prospects For Growth Through 1982.* McGraw-Hill, New York, 1969, p. 22.

Chapter IV

Structure of the Chemical Industry

Economists judge the competitive position of an industry in two ways: (a) its structure and (b) its performance. The structure of an industry is concerned with the size of companies, the extent to which activity is concentrated in the largest companies, and the ease with which new competitors may enter the industry's product markets. Performance usually is measured in terms of relative prices and price changes, rate of economic growth, profit rates, productivity, labor costs and other economic measures.

This chapter deals with various aspects of the structure of the chemical industry. In one respect the structure is similar to that found in many other mass production industries; namely, several large companies and a number of smaller ones. In such industries the largest companies usually account for a significant proportion of the total volume. A small number of large firms need not connote limited competition. In many industries the most vigorous and intensive competition takes place between industrial giants as the experience with cigarettes and automobiles has so well demonstrated.

For many products, the percentage accounted for by the largest firm and/or firms usually is significantly larger than their share of the entire industry. This is especially true in the chemical industry which is highly specialized for most of its products. As a result, the largest firms have a relatively larger share of the market for many specific products than is indicated by the aggregate data.

A measure frequently employed to measure bigness in the chemical and other industries is the concentration ratio. Such ratios measure the proportion of an industry's economic activity or of a product's volume accounted for by a designated number of large companies, usually the four largest (Big Four) or the eight largest (Big Eight). Concentration usually is measured in terms of one or more of the following economic variables: sales or shipments, employment, value added or income originating, and assets (gross or net).[1] The higher the proportion accounted for by the largest companies, the greater is alleged to be the control over the market.

Limitations of Concentration Ratios

It is very difficult to obtain meaningful concentration data for many products. The underlying data, for example, are very unsatisfactory in many instances. Problems of definition are important. What is an industry? How effectively do the available data delineate the industry in terms of products, firms, or geographic location? In this connection Jesse J. Friedman has warned that the Census

". . .classifications were not designed to establish categories necessarily denoting coherent or relevant markets in the true competitive sense, or to provide a basis for measuring market power. . .products classified in one 4-digit or 5-digit category may compete for the same market with products classified in other categories. Frequently, products grouped together in a single 4-digit classification, while related in the sense that they may be manufactured in the same plants, or from the same types of raw materials, or by similar production processes, are nevertheless destined for basically noncompetitive uses and markets."[2]

Moreover, the available data usually do not include imports so that the relative share of a market reported for a Big Four may be overstated for products with a significant volume of imports. This factor may affect comparisons over time when imports account for a growing share of the American market.

The existence of some degree of concentration is not equivalent to the absence of competition. Some industries with high concentration are among the most competititve in our economy.[3]

Betty Bock has pointed out:

"Whatever the universe and whatever the relative sizes of companies, a concentration ratio serves simply to identify the share of a given number of large companies as distinct from the share of all other companies operating in the same markets; but 'concentration' as a measure refers to the industry and product classifications for which the Bureau of the Census collects data—and these may not be equivalent in all cases to 'markets' in the competitive sense."[4]

The percentage of a market accounted for by a small number of companies is not the important point. How companies respond to various market stimuli is the real test of the extent of competition and the significance of concentration ratios. Big Fours in highly concentrated industries may compete among themselves with a vigor and intensity that is as great, if not greater, than the competition found in industries much less concentrated.

Finally, the combination of companies comprising the Big Four or Big Eight may vary for the different products in an industry and for the same product at different times. This has been the situation in the chemical industry as is shown below. Clearly, the interpretation of concentration ratios must be handled with great care. Even when the basic data are homogeneous and statistically accurate, their significance is subject to considerable dispute. This problem is compounded when the underlying data do not provide an accurate portrayal of the market facts.

Extent of Concentration in Chemicals

The largest companies account for a smaller share of the chemical industry's volume than do the largest companies in other large industries including steel, aluminum, automobile, rubber, office equipment, and tobacco. In 1967, Du Pont had sales of $3.1 billion or 14.4% of total chemical (SIC 281-282) shipments of $21.5 billion. The four largest chemical companies (Du Pont, Union Carbide, Monsanto, and Dow) had total sales of $8.6 billion in 1967 or 40.0% of the industry's total.[5] Both of these ratios actually overstate the relative importance of these companies since their total sales include allied products.[6] Thus, on an overall basis, the chemical industry is one of the less concentrated among major industries.

For individual product markets, a different picture emerges. On this narrower basis, concentration ratios for chemicals are among the highest for any manufacturing industry. Only tobacco manufactures and rubber products report higher concentration ratios. Table IV-1 lists 36 chemical product classes (five digit) for which data were compiled by the Bureau of the Census for 1963. This tabulation shows the percentage of total shipments accounted for by the four largest companies. These 36 concentration ratios fell into the groups on page 61.

The product classes with the highest concentration ratios tend to have the smallest average volume of shipments. Thus, in 1963 the eight product classes with concentration ratios in excess of 75% had average shipments of $261.8

TABLE IV-1

Percent of Value of Shipments Accounted For by Four
Largest Companies, Chemicals and
Allied Products, 1963

SIC		Percent Accounted for By Big Four	Value of Shipments
			(millions)
28231	Acetate yarn	100	$ 250.3
28140	Cyclic (coal-tar) crudes	95	79.3
28212	Regenerated cellulosic products, except rayon	94	327.6
28132	Acetylene	87	93.5
28242	Other noncellulosic synthetic organic fibers	86	472.7
28195, 28196	Aluminum oxide and other aluminum compounds	85	422.4
28232	Rayon yarn (viscose and cuprammonium process)	85	398.6
28133	Carbon dioxide	78	49.9
28134	Elemental gases and compressed and liquefied gases, n.e.c	73	244.6
28124	Other alkalies	70	27.6
28192	Inorganic industrials household bleaching compounds	70	200.0
28162	Other white opaque pigments	64	50.4
28215	Synthetic resin adhesives	60	29.3
28193	Sulfuric acid	60	193.9
28184	Pesticides and other organic agricultural chemicals	54	223.4
28151	Cyclic intermediates	53	758.6
28216	Synthetic resins for protective coatings	53	272.2
28219	Plastics and resin materials, n.e.c.	52	60.4
28220	Synthetic rubber	52	862.3
28153	Synthetic organic pigments, lakes and toners	51	111.7
28123	Sodium hydroxide (caustic soda)	51	209.7
28182	Miscellaneous acyclic chemicals and chemical products	51	3,153.9
28121	Chlorine compressed or liquefied	51	164.0
28198	Chemical catalytic preparations	50	75.2
28152	Synthetic organic dyes	48	243.1
28194	Inorganic acids, except nitric and sulfuric	47	166.3
28163	Chrome colors and other inorganic pigments	45	151.8
28213	Thermoplastic resins and plastics materials	43	1,302.0
28197	Potassium and sodium compounds	43	513.3
28214	Thermosetting resins and plastics materials	41	420.0
28191	Synthetic ammonia, nitric acid and ammonium compounds	38	587.8
28183	Synthetic organic chemicals, n.e.c.	34	418.9
28217	Custom compounding of purchased resins	32	184.6
28185	Ethyl alcohol and other industrial organic chemicals, n.e.c.	32	192.3
28181	Miscellaneous acyclic chemical products	29	200.5
28199	Reagent and high purity grades of inorganic chemicals, and other inorganic chemicals, n.e.c.	29	825.8

Source: U.S. Department of Commerce, Bureau of the Census, *Concentration Ratios in Manufacturing Industry, 1963,* Part 1, A Report for the U.S. Senate Committee on the Judiciary, Subcommittee on Antitrust and Monopoly, 89th Cong., 2nd sess., Washington, D.C., 1966, pp. 177-180.

Concentration Ratio Big Four - Percent	Product Classes No.	Percent	Shipments in 1 Millions	Perc of Tot.	
75-100	8	22.2	$ 2,094	15.3	
50-74	16	44.5	6,403	46.7	
25-49	12	33.3	5,205	38.0	..8
	36	100.0	$13,702	100.0	$380.6

million but accounted for only 15.3% of the total shipments covered. On the one hand, twelve product classes with concentration ratios of less than 50% accounted for 38.0% of the total shipments and had average shipments about one and two thirds as large per product class as the group with the highest concentration ratios. Thus, when the relative importance of each product class is considered, the level of concentration is not as high as when attention is focused on the number of product classes alone.

Trend of Concentration Ratios

The combination of new entrants and lower growth rates for the largest companies appears to have resulted in some reduction in the extent of concentration in the chemical industry. Concentration data are available for seven four digit groups for 1954 and 1966. For six groups, including the relatively important plastics materials, the degree of concentration was reduced while for one group the ratio rose (See Table IV-2). The decreases in concentration were substantially greater than the increase.

For the period 1954 to 1963 data were available for 16 five digit groups; the concentration ratio declined for ten, was unchanged for two, and increased for four (See Table IV-3).

TABLE IV-2

Percent of Total Shipments By Four Largest Companies By Chemical Groups, 1947, 1954, 1958, 1963, and 1966

SIC	1947	1954	1958	1963	1966	Shipments, 1966
						(millions)
2812 Alkalies and chlorine	70	69	64	62	63	$ 783
2813 Industrial gases	83	84	79	72	72	550
2815 Intermediate coal-tar prods.	NA	58	54	54	52	1,483
2816 Inorganic pigments	NA	67	69	68	64	582
2818 Organic chemicals, n.e.c.	NA	59	55	51	46	6,541
2819 Inorganic chemicals, n.e.c.	-	-	34	31	29	3,845
2821 Plastics materials & resins	44	47	40	35	32	3,533
2822 Synthetic rubber	NA	53	60	57	56	955

Source: U.S. Department of Commerce, Bureau of the Census, *Annaul Survey of Manufactures:* 1966, Value-of-Shipment Concentration Ratios by Industry, M66 (AS)-8, Washington, D.C. 1968, pp 13-14.

TABLE IV-3

Per Cent of Total Shipments By Four Largest Companies By Chemical Product Classes, 1954, 1958 and 1963

SIC	Product Class	1954	1958	1963	1963 Shipments
		----(per cent)----			(in millions)
28121	Chlorine compressed or liquefied	54	52	51	$ 164.0
28123	Sodium hydroxide (caustic soda)	57	55	51	209.7
28124	Other alkalies	86	77	70	27.6
28133	Carbon dioxide	80	80	78	49.9
28134	Elemental gases and compressed and liquefied gases, n.e.c.	-	73	73	244.6
28140	Cyclic (coal tar) crudes	89	89	95	79.3
28151	Cyclic intermediates	55	52	53	758.6
28152	Synthetic organic dyes	64	56	48	243.1
28153	Synthetic organic pigments, lakes & toners	53	50	51	111.7
28162	Other white opaque pigments	-	64	64	50.4
28163	Chrome colors & other inorganic pigments	-	47	45	152.8
28181	Miscellaneous acyclic chemical products	44	39	29	200.5
28182	Miscellaneous acylic chemicals & chemical products	64	59	51	3,153.9
28183	Synthetic organic chemicals, n.e.c.	-	34	34	418.9
28184	Pesticides and other organic agricultural chemicals	43	52	54	223.4
28185	Ethyl alcohol & other industrial organic chemicals, n.e.c.	-	42	32	192.3
28192	Inorganic industrial household bleaching compounds	61	60	70	200.0
28193	Sulfuric acid		58	60	193.9
28195〉 28196〉	Aluminum oxide and other aluminum compounds	89	88	85	422.4
28198	Chemical catalytic preparations	-	61	50	75.2
28212	Regenerated cellulosic products, except rayon	-	95	94	327.6
28220	Synthetic rubber	52	54	52	862.3
28231	Acetate yarn	100	100	100	250.3
28232	Rayon yarn (viscose & cuprammonium process)	79	78	85	398.6

Source: U.S. Department of Commerce, Bureau of the Census, *Concentration Ratios in Manufacturing Industry, 1963*, Part I, A Report for the U.S. Senate Committee on the Judiciary, Subcommittee on Antitrust and Monopoly, 89th Cong., 2nd Sess., Washington, D.C., 1966, p. 177.

Similar data also are available for 24 five digit product classes for 1958 and 1963 (See Table IV-3). For 13 product classes, the ratio declined and for four it remained unchanged; it rose for seven product classes. The relative importance of the product classes is shown below:[7]

Change in Concentration Ratio 1958-1963	Shipments (millions)	Percent of Total
13 decreases	$6,080	67.5
4 unchanged	964	10.7
7 increases	1,966	21.8
	$9,010	100.0

Product classes accounting for about two-thirds of the total shipments in 1958 recorded a decline in concentration between 1958 and 1963.

The Bureau of the Census also has compared concentration ratios based on production for sale data in 1937 compiled for the Temporary National Economic Committee (TNEC) with those based on dollar shipments in 1958 for twelve "substantially comparable" seven digit chemical products. The data are reproduced in Table IV-4.

TABLE IV-4

Proportion of Shipments in 1958 and of Production in
1937 Accounted For By Four Largest Producers

Product Ratio Increased	1958 Shipments (in millions)	Percent Accounted for by Four Largest Companies	
		1937	1958
Carbon dioxide, solid (dry ice)	$ 26.3	65	77
Nitrous oxide	4.7	91	94
Iron blues (prussian blue, milori blue) . .	4.0	68	72
Sodium phosphate, tribasic	8.4	77	82
Aluminum sulfate, com'l. and iron free	32.1	82	95
Total	75.5		
Ratio Unchanged			
Sodium bichromate and chromate	19.0	100	100
Ratio Reduced			
Sodium hydroxide (caustic soda)	154.1	59	52
Nitric acid	14.2	81	70
Ammonia, anhydrous	132.7	90	41
Ammonium sulfate	33.1	76	71
Hydrochloric acid made from salt	4.5	86	80
Hydrochloric acid made from chlorine, byproduct and other	20.7	86	57
Total	359.3		

Source: *Concentration Ratios in Manufacturing Industries, 1958, Part II.* Report prepared by the Bureau of the Census for the Subcommittee on Antitrust and Monopoly of the Committee on the Judiciary, United States Senate, Washington, D.C., 1962, p. 487.

Although the 12 products compared represent a relatively unimportant proportion of the chemical industry they do suggest a tendency for concentration to have declined somewhat. Declines were reported for six products with total shipments more than four times as large as for the five products for which concentration increased. One was unchanged.

Scattered data suggest that the extent of concentration has declined during the past few years. Estimates of plant capacity published by the trade press illustrate these tendencies. These data may yield somewhat different results than actual production or shipments because of differing rates of plant utilization which in turn may reflect in part the age of plants. Nevertheless, they probably do indicate the general trends. Table IV-5 shows the *percent of capacity* accounted for by the four largest producers in each of the years indicated for 16 products.

TABLE IV-5

Changes in Percent of Total Capacity Accounted For By Four Largest Producers, Selected Years, 1959 to 1968

Product	Year	Percent	Year	Percent	Change in Percentage Points
Benzene-petroleum base	1960	49	1968	32	—17
Butadiene	1960	50	1968	46	— 4
Chlorine	1959	58	1967	57	— 1
Cumene	1962	64	1966	61	— 3
Ethylene	1959	69	1968	48	—21
Methanol	1960	74	1968	68	— 6
Orthoxylene	1961	95	1968	62	—33
Phthalic anhydride	1960	77	1968	53	—24
Polypropylene	1962	86	1967	69	—17
Polyvinyl chloride	1960	49	1967	43	— 6
Styrene	1959	82	1968	63	—19
Sulfuric acid	1961	40	1968	33	— 7
Synthetic phenol	1960	68	1966	67	— 1
Toluene	1960	45	1966	35	—10
Vinylacetate monomer	1960	84	1967	73	—11
Vinyl chloride monomer	1962	58	1967	58	— 0

Sources: Derived from various issues of Chemical Week, *Chemical and Engineering News,* and *Oil, Paint and Drug Reporter,* 1959 to 1969.

It is apparent that the large expansion in capacity for most of the products listed in Table IV-5 has resulted in some instances in marked reductions in the share of total capacity accounted for by the four largest producers. For 15 of the

16 products the proportion of capacity accounted for by the four largest producers declined between 1959-1961 and 1966-1968; for one product it remained unchanged.

Changing Composition of Big Fours

Comparisons such as those made above do not show the full picture because the four largest companies in an industry or in a specific market are not a static group. Over time, the composition of the group of largest companies often changes.

In terms of total sales, the four largest chemical companies in 1954 were (1) Du Pont, (2) Union Carbide, (3) Allied Chemical, and (4) Olin Mathieson. In 1968, Monsanto was in third place and Dow was the fourth largest chemical company.[8] W. R. Grace had a larger sales volume than Dow but this was due to its large non-chemical operations.

Similarly, the Bureau of the Census has reported that for each of the five four digit industry groups for which data were available for 1947 and 1958, the composition of the four largest companies changed between those two years so that at least one of the four largest in 1947 no longer was in that group in 1958.[9] Where such a situation develops, the relative share accounted for by a constant group of four companies over time would be less in the terminal year than shown by "Big Four data" based on the four largest companies in each year. The raw concentration data conceal changes in relative position within a particular market and hence obscure the full effect of competitive forces where dynamic changes may be taking place.

Additional light is thrown on the changing composition of the largest companies in a specific market by the data for capacity discussed earlier. For the 16 products in Table IV-5 there was a change in the composition of the Big Four in fourteen instances and changes in position among the Big Four for the other two products as shown below:

Benzene (petroleum based): Monsanto, a new entrant, replaced Hess Oil in the Big Four. The four largest companies in 1960 accounted for 32.6% of the capacity in 1965 or 4.4 percentage points less than reported by the new Big Four.

Butadiene: In 1968, Sinclair replaced Enjay Chemical as the fourth largest producer. The 1960 Big Four accounted for 41.7% of the 1968 volume as compared with 50% in 1968.

Chlorine: Between 1959 and 1967, Hooker replaced Allied as the fourth largest producer. The four largest producers in 1959 accounted for 55% of the capacity in 1967 or 2 percentage points lower than for the 1967 Big Four.

Cumene: Clark replaced Allied. The Big Four in 1962 accounted for 50.5% of the 1966 capacity or 10.3 percentage points lower than the Big Four in that year.

Ethylene: Shell replaced Gulf Oil. The four largest companies in 1959 accounted for 47.2% of the 1968 capacity or 0.7 percentage points lower than reported for the new Big Four in that year.

Methanol: Borden, Celanese and Tenneco replaced Union Carbide, Commercial Solvents and Monsanto-Hayden. The Big Four in 1960 accounted for 45.3% of the 1968 capacity or 22.5 percentage points lower than reported for the new Big Four on that date.

Orthoxylene: Sinclair, Cities Service and Commonwealth Oil replaced Enjay, Suntide and Delhi-Taylor. The Big Four in 1960 accounted for 34.7% of 1968 capacity or 27.5 percentage points lower than reported for the new Big Four on that date.

Phthalic anhydride: Between 1960 and 1968, Monsanto replaced Allied as the largest company and Hooker and Koppers replaced American Cyanamid and Reichhold in third and fourth place. American Cyanamid, one of the Big Four in 1960, withdrew from the industry. The remaining three members of the 1960 group accounted for only 45% of the 1968 capacity or 8 percentage points less than the new Big Four.

Polypropylene: Shell replaced Dow. The Big Four in 1962 accounted for 54.7% of the 1967 capacity or 14.1 percentage points lower than the Big Four on that date.

Polyvinyl Chloride: Thompson Apex and Tenneco replaced Monsanto and Borden. The Big Four in 1960 accounted for 38.7% of the 1967 capacity or 3.9 percentage points lower than the Big Four on that date.

Styrene: Cos-Mar replaced Shell. The Big Four in 1959 accounted for 56.4% of the 1968 capacity or 6.6 percentage points lower than the Big Four on that date.

Sulfuric acid: The Big Four remained the same in 1961 and 1968 but Tennessee Corp. replaced Du Pont in third place.

Synthetic phenol: Between 1960 and 1966, Monsanto replaced Dow as the largest producer. Hooker replaced Allied in the Big Four.

Toluene: Ashland replaced Sun. The Big Four in 1960 accounted for 32.7% of the 1966 capacity or 1.8 percentage points lower than the Big Four on that date.

Vinyl Acetate: Celanese replaced Shawinigan. The Big Four in 1961 accounted for 47.5% of the 1967 capacity or 23.4 percentage points lower than the Big Four on that date.

Vinyl Chloride Monomer: No change in the Big Four between 1962 and 1967. However, Union Carbide fell from second place to fourth and Ethyl rose to second place. In 1962 the Big Four accounted for 58.1% of capacity and in 1967 for 57.6%.

The foregoing data illustrate that changes do take place among the four largest producers, as measured by capacity, in relatively short periods of time. These illustrations underline one of the limitations of concentration ratios as a measure of competition. Certainly, it is evidence of dynamic competition when companies lose their relative position to other firms who expand more rapidly to meet new needs or to companies which enter an industry. Unfortunately, ratios for unidentified Big Fours do not reflect these changes. Such measures definitely tend to understate the competitive forces at work in a dynamic industry such as chemicals.

Significance of Concentration in the Chemical Industry

The high concentration ratios found for chemicals reflect the underlying economic characteristics of the industry, particularly the heavy investment required in plant and equipment, and to some extent the mergers that have taken place. Professor Simon Whitney has noted the importance of "(1) ability to install the complicated automatic equipment which makes possible the most efficient processing of chemicals and recovery of by-products; and (2) ability to finance and utilize extensive research, to launch new products which may bring no return for years, and to reduce risks by diversifying output."[10]

The manufacturers of chemicals are mass producers. They turn out their products by the thousands of tons. The mechanisms employed are huge and costly, embracing all forms of tanks, retorts, stills, pipes, tubes etc.[11] Bigness in the chemical industry is required, therefore, because of its complex manufacturing processes. Many by-products can be most profitably employed on site or in continuous processing.

This is the economic background which requires large corporations. The *Fortune* listing of the 100 largest industrial corporations in 1968 included eight industrial chemical producers, excluding the oil companies. There were also 48 other companies producing chemicals in the top 100.

The total capital invested in chemicals and allied products was $24 billion in 1963.[12] The investment *per production worker* in that year averaged $45,800 for the chemical industry or more than twice as large as for all manufacturing.[13] No other manufacturing industry except petroleum and tobacco (where a huge investment in inventories is required) requires such a large provision of capital per worker.

The significance of concentration ratios in the chemical industry is affected by: (1) the relative ease of entry and (2) the extensive interproduct and interindustry competition. The number of producers has been increasing in many markets. Moreover, the new entrants usually are either other large chemical companies or industrial giants whose main activity is in other industries. In the latter connection the movement into chemicals by many large petroleum companies has been particularly significant. While the extent of interproduct and interindustry competition varies, it plays a role for most chemical products.

The intensity of competition is not determined solely or primarily by the number of competitors. Accordingly, concentration ratios, which are also subject to many infirmities because of the inadequacies of the data on which they are based, cannot be used to determine the effectiveness of competition.

Finally, fewness of sellers has inhibited neither price competition nor nonprice competition for many chemical products. Nor has it prevented the development of excess capacity for many organic chemicals. Clearly, concentration ratios must be examined qualitatively as well as quantitatively to determine their impact upon competition.

The Number of Competitors

The relative ease with which new competitors may enter a product market with the accompanying increase in the alternatives available to buyers is an important element in the competitive structure of an industry. The potential competitor, who often becomes an actual competitor, exercises a powerful restraint on those already in the market.

The number of companies producing a product in the chemical industry can be increased either (a) by the organization of a new company, (b) by the entry of established companies whose main area of operations is in other industries or overseas, and/or (c) by an extension of product lines by companies already in the industry. All three methods of entry have been important in the chemical industry.

Many of the newly organized companies have been joint ventures, often with one of the established chemical companies as a partner, as is noted later. Competition from new entries from other industries has been particularly significant in recent years with the major thrust from petroleum companies. Foreign companies also have been establishing plants in this country to an increasing extent. Moreover, because of the nature of the production process and the interrelationship of products and stages of production, the introduction of new product lines by existing companies also has been an important method of entry.

Number of Companies and Establishments

As a result of changes in classification, the data for all chemical industries as reported by the Bureau of the Census are not comparable over the years. For example, as noted earlier, vegetable and animal oils (soybean oil, linseed oil, vegetable oil, cottonseed oil, grease and tallow, etc.) were included in the Census definition of chemicals prior to the 1958 Census. In 1958, the companies in this industry had 963 plants which were no longer included in the total for Chemicals and Allied Products.[14]

The number of establishments producing basic chemicals increased from 1,015 in 1939 to 1,905 in 1963, a rise of 87.7%. The number producing fibers, plastics, and rubber increased from 71 in 1937 to 577 in 1963, a dramatic expansion of 713% (See Table IV-6 and Chart IV-1). New producers may enter a market by creating a new establishment or by producing new product lines in existing establishments. Accordingly, the changes in the number of establishments do not give a complete picture of the dynamic pattern which has characterized the competitive picture for many chemical products.

The pattern of increases in the number of establishments has varied widely among products. For older products, such as alkalies and chlorine, the number of establishments recorded only a small increase between 1939 and 1963. For synthetic rubber, a small rise is shown between 1947 and 1963. For industrial gases and synthetic fibers, moderate increases took place. The most dramatic increases in the number of establishments took place for plastics materials, a relatively new and rapidly growing group of products, and for organic chemicals, n.e.c., which includes such products as acids, solvents, and plasticizers (see Table IV-7).

The changes in the *number of companies* in the chemical industry appear to have paralleled those shown for establishments although the Census data available on a company basis are less complete. The Bureau of the Census reported an increase in the number of companies from 18 in 1947 to 19 in 1963 for alkalies and chlorines and a decrease from 13 to 8 in the same period for cyclic (coal tar) crudes. The number of companies producing industrial gases increased from 69 to 104, those producing synthetic rubber from 5 to 16 and those manufacturing plastics materials from 94 to 391 in the same period. These are substantial increases in the total number of competitors. However, it must be kept in mind that these industries include a number of product categories so that all of the companies were not directly in competition with each other for each product.

This is the background against which Dow Chemical has plaintively observed:

"The Chemical industry, historically competitive, has become a most strenuous testing ground. New competitors - diversifying from other fields, or starting from scratch with package plants, or coming from overseas - almost outnumber our long-time competitors. Whenever we look up, it seems, one more brand-new competitor comes charging at us. In this testing we have seen markets shifted, prices beaten down, profit margins pressured. And it still goes on."[15]

CHART IV-1

Number of Establishments, Selected Years, 1939-1963

Number

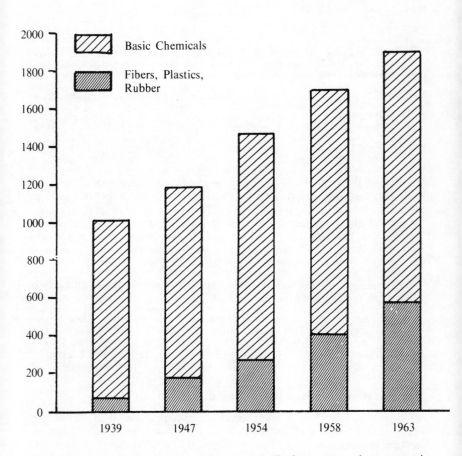

And Du Pont has observed that "The sweet smell of success . . . has attracted a swarm of competitors."[16]

Since 1947, the number of establishments producing basic chemicals and synthetic materials has increased at a relatively faster rate than for all manufacturing industries. During the same period, output of basic chemicals and synthetic materials also increased much more rapidly than for all manufacturing (See Table IV-8).

TABLE IV-6

Number of Establishments, Census Years, 1939 - 1963 .

	Chemicals and Allied Products*	Basic Chemicals (281)	Fibers, Plastics, Rubbers (282)
1939	7,945	1,015	71
1947	8,916	1,180	181
1954	10,154	1,474	273
1958	11,309	1,698	407
1963	11,996	1,905	577

*Excludes all vegetable and animal oils, except fatty acids, which were formerly included in Chemicals and Allied Products and includes fireworks and pyrotechnics which were formerly included in miscellaneous manufactures.

Sources: U.S. Department of Commerce, Bureau of the Census, *1963 Census of Manufactures;* Vol. II, Industry Statistics, Part I, Major Groups 20 to 28, Washington, D.C., 1966, p. 54; *Census of Manufactures: 1958,* Vol. II, Industry Statistics, Part I, Major Groups 20 to 28, Washington, D.C., 1961, pp. 20H-4, 28-2, 28A-6, 7, 288-4; *U.S. Census of Manufactures: 1954,* Vol. II, Industry Statistics, Parts 1 and 2, Major Groups 20 to 28 and 29 to 39, Washington, D.C., 1957, p. 28G-5 and p. 39D-5.

Many of the new establishments in the chemical industry have been relatively small in size as measured by the number of employees. However, employment alone does not give a good picture of size in terms of dollar volume because of the large capital investment required in the chemical industry. Nevertheless, the data are of interest because they show the relatively larger increase in the number of smaller establishments both for basic chemicals and synthetic products as measured on this basis (See Table IV-9).

Small companies play an important competitive role in the chemical industry. American Cyanamid has emphasized:

> "Some of our keenest competition. . .comes from the host of smaller firms that make resins. . . Many small firms don't have technical laboratories. They wait until we've helped a customer solve his problems and then they move in. Lacking this kind of overhead, they offer their resins at a lower price."[17]

The Petroleum Industry and Chemicals

Competitive patterns in the chemical industry have been dramatically changed by the large scale entry of companies whose primary activity has been in other industries.

> "As diversification has become the popular route for corporate expansion, organic chemicals have displayed considerable appeal to entrepreneurs in other industries seeking investment opportunities for surplus cash. Among these have been several oil companies who found themselves supplying more and more feedstocks to neighboring chemical plants whose technology was becoming increasingly similar to their own. *The flame of interest was further fanned by engineering and construction firms, many of whom have*

gone to great lengths to place themselves in position to offer their clients complete process designs and highly automated plants on a guaranteed turnkey basis.... "[18] (italics added).

Because they have ample raw materials which are basic to chemicals and they have the processing know-how, petroleum companies have participated in the chemical industry since the 1920s.[19] This participation was given a substantial stimulus by the increasing use of petroleum and natural gas as raw materials in the 1950s. At the end of 1967 the gross capital investment in chemical plants by oil companies was $6.4 billion here and abroad.

TABLE IV-7

Number of Establishments for Important Categories of Chemicals, Selected Years, 1937 to 1963

Industrial Inorganic and Organic Chemicals (SIC 281)

	Alkalies and Chlorine	Industrial Gases	Cyclic (Coal-Tar) Crudes	Intermediate Coal-Tar Products	Inorganic Pigments	Organic Chemicals n.e.c.	Inorganic Chemicals n.e.c.
1939	33	379	45	73	59	119	307
1947	32	371	46	93	95	167	376
1954	29	428	43	107	104	275	488
1958	34	491	45	115	99	334	580
1963	38	456	36	141	96	464	674

Fibers, Plastics, Rubbers (SIC 282)

	Plastic Materials & Resins	Synthetic Rubber	Cellulosic Manmade Fibers, plus Organic Fibers, Non-cellulosic
1937	34	NA	33
1939	41	NA	30
1947	123	20	38
1954	206	21	46
1958	349	18	40
1963	509	24	44

NA - Not available.

n.e.c. - not elsewhere classified.

Sources: U.S. Department of Commerce, Bureau of the Census, *1963 Census of Manufactures,* Vol. II, Industry Statistics, Part I, Major Groups, 20 to 28, Washington, D.C., 1966, pp. 28A-8-9, 28B-5; U.S. Department of Commerce, Bureau of the Census, *U.S. Census of Manufactures: 1958,* Vol. II, Industry Statistics, Part I, Major Groups 20 to 28, U.S. Government Printing Office, Washington, D.C., 1961, pp. 28S-6-7, 28B-4.

TABLE IV-8

Changes in Number of Establishments and Production, All Manufacturing Industries and Chemicals, 1947 to 1963 and 1954 to 1963

	Percent Increase, 1958-63		Percent Increase, 1954-63	
	Establishments	*Production*	*Establishments*	*Production*
All manufacturing	29.5	88.1	8.8	44.7
Basic chemicals (SIC 281)	61.4	367.5	29.2	135.1
Fibers, plastics, rubber (SIC 282)	303.5	504.7	154.2	219.4
Total (SIC 281 and 282)	87.6	398.5	45.9	153.7

Sources: U.S. Department of Commerce, Bureau of the Census, *1963 Census of Manufactures,* Vol. II, Indsutry Statistics, Part I, Major Groups 20 to 28, Washington, D.C., 1966, pp. 86, 28A-8-9, 28B-5; Board of Governors of the Federal Reserve System, *Industrial Production—1957-59 Base,* Washington, D.C., 1962, pp. S-59, S-103, S-151; *Industrial Production Indexes, 1961-1965,* Washington, D.C., November 1966, pp. 19, 34.

TABLE IV-9

Number of Establishments By Size of Employment, 1947, 1954, 1958, 1963

	1947	1954	1958	1963	Percent Increase 1958-63	Percent Increase 1954-63	Percent Increase 1947-63
Basic Chemicals (SIC 28)							
1-19 employees	NA	685	836	1010	20.8	47.4	NA
20 or more employees	NA	789	862	897	4.1	13.7	NA
Fibers, Plastics, Rubbers (SIC 282)							
1-19 employees	47	81	154	234	64.9	213.6	440.4
20 or more employees	134	192	253	323	27.7	68.2	141.0
Total							
1-19 employees	NA	766	990	1264	27.7	65.0	NA
20 or more employees	NA	981	1115	1220	9.4	24.4	NA

NA — Not available.

Source: U.S. Department of Commerce, Bureau of the Census, *1963 Census of Manufactures,* Vol. II, Industry Statistics, Part I, Major Groups 20 to 28, Washington, D.C., 1966, pp. 28A-8-9, 28B-5.

Petroleum companies have expanded their annual capital investment in the chemical industry very sharply as is shown below for the United States:

Annual Capital Expenditures in
Chemical Plants By Petroleum Companies

	(millions)
1957	$125
1959	175
1961	325
1963	275
1965	525
1967	825

In 1967, investment in chemical plants was $825 million or three times the 1963 total. Throughout the free world, petroleum companies invested $1,565 million in chemical plants of which $740 million was outside the United States. At the end of 1967, the gross investment in chemical plants by American petroleum companies was $5,040 million and the net investment was $3,050 million.[20] Chemical sales of petroleum companies exceeded $5 billion in 1968.[21]

The extent to which petroleum companies have entered the chemical industry is shown by a study prepared by the National Petroleum Council. It found that of approximately 465 plants making petrochemicals, about 165 were "owned or operated" by oil and gas companies in 1962. For 11 products, the proportion in the hands of petroleum companies exceeded 50% (for example, benzene, butadiene, toluene and cumene); for five products the proportion was between 25% and 50% (e.g., acetone, ethylene, and naphthalene).[22]

It was estimated in 1967 that "Petrochemicals account for over 30% of the tonnage and over 60% of the value of all organic chemicals produced in the United States, so that the importance of the oil and gas companies' position is obvious."[23]

One of the largest domestic chemical producers among the petroleum companies is Standard Oil Company (New Jersey) whose worldwide chemical operations reached $932 million in 1968 for such products as butyl rubber, polypropylene, hydrocarbons, ammonia, plastics, resins, and basic chemical raw materials.[24] This volume was greater than the total sales of companies such as Rohm and Haas, Stauffer Chemical, and Hooker Chemical.

The estimated volume of chemical sales in 1968 for a number of petroleum companies is shown in Table IV-10.

The oil companies have played a role for a number of products including: butadiene (Phillips, Shell, Sinclair, Enjay Chemical, Chevron Chemical); synthetic rubber (Shell, Phillips, Enjay Chemical); polypropylene (Shell, Enjay Chemical); acetone (Shell, Standard Oil of Cal., Skelly, Enjay Chemical); orthoxylene (Cities Service, Enjay Chemical, Chevron Chemical, Sinclair); epoxies (Shell); ethylene (Gulf Oil, Enjay Chemical, Phillips, Mobil Chemical, Atlantic-Richfield, Continental Oil, Shell); styrene (Amoco, Shell, Sinclair); toluene (Amoco, Chevron, Enjay, Gulf, Hess, Shell, Sinclair, Texaco); polyethylene (Gulf, Phillips, Shell); paraxylene (Sunray DX, Chevron Chemical, Shell, Enjay); phenol (Chevron Chemical, Shell, and Skelly); and petroleum-naphthalene (Ashland Oil, Tidewater, Sun, Cities Service, Texaco). Additionally, there are some oil companies that produce these and other products in joint ventures with chemical, rubber, and companies in other industries.

Crawford H. Greenewalt, former president of Du Pont, summarized the competition from petroleum companies as follows:

" . . .We in the chemical industry have come to recognize the oil industry as a formidable competitor whose inroads into our traditional markets have become very substantial.

" . . .We have felt the sting of competition from petroleum producers in various ways. We find ourselves with comparable materials in the same market place, with competing processes seeking the establishment of new markets, and with similarly persuasive lures in the search for scientific and managerial talent."[25]

In the period since 1959, the degree of competition from petroleum has been further intensified and so these observations remain pertinent.

TABLE IV-10

Chemical Sales of Petroleum Companies, 1968

	(millions)
Standard Oil Company (New Jersey)	$932
Occidental Petroleum	571
Shell Chemical Co.	513
Phillips Petroleum	447
Mobil Oil	417
Cities Service	358
Standard Oil Co. (Ind.)	352
Ashland Chemical Co.	342
Gulf Oil	342
Standard Oil of California	276
Tenneco Inc.	242
Continental Oil	195
Sinclair Oil	143
Union Oil Co. (California)	121
Coastal States Gas	110
Standard Oil Co. (Ohio)	104

Source: Chemical Week, April 19, 1969, p. 26, and *Chemical & Engineering News,* June 16, 1969, p. 23.

Competition From Other Non-Chemical Companies

In addition to petroleum companies, Eastman Kodak (photographic supplies), Borden (dairy products), National Distillers (distilling), Firestone (rubber), and many others have become important factors in the chemical industry. W. R. Grace, originally largely in shipping, now derives about two-thirds of its revenues from chemicals.

In the immediate post-World War II years the shortages of certain chemicals prompted former buyers such as Eastman Kodak and Pittsburgh Plate Glass[26] to start producing their own materials. These concerns have significantly expanded their line of chemicals over the years. The major rubber companies also have become an important factor in the industry with the production of synthetic rubber, vinyl resins, and ethylene.

A rough indication of the extent to which other industries already had entered the chemical industry by 1954 was shown in a study prepared by Michael Gort who examined the product lines of 111 large manufacturing companies. The 111 companies included 14 chemical companies which in 1954 were estimated to hold 45.6% of the assets of all companies in the industry.[27]

Gort found that 97 manufacturing companies excluding chemical companies, produced 213 chemical products in 1954 as compared with 161 products produced by 14 companies classified as Chemicals and Allied Products. He concluded that "Frequency of activity in chemical industries was especially striking for companies in the paper; petroleum; rubber products; stone, clay, and glass; and food products industry groups."[28]

The reason for the attractiveness of chemical products to other industries is indicated by Gort's finding that:

> "A rapidly growing industry tends to attract resources from existing firms based primarily in other sectors of the economy as well as from new firms or from those within the industry. . . The most decisive influence in the choice of an industry as a diversification outlet, however, was not its growth rate but its rate of technological change."[29]

The chemical industry clearly is one in which high growth rates and rapid technological change have been characteristic.

New Entry: Product Markets

The barriers to entry to individual product markets do not appear to be significant in the chemical industry. The ability to buy "turn key" plants undoubtedly has facilitated entry. Moreover, many chemical products and processes are interrelated and thus the technical know-how is available or readily obtainable to add to product lines.

The trade press contains numerous announcements of companies which have joined the ranks of existing producers:[30]

Acetic acid: FMC entered in 1968 and Monsanto was scheduled for 1970. Their entry increased the number of producers from 6 to 8.[31]

Acrylics fiber: Between 1962 and 1968 the number of producers increased from 4 to 6 with Dow-Badische, Union Carbide, and Tennessee Eastman as new entrants and Dow withdrawing (Table VI-10).

Benzene: Between 1960 and 1965, eleven companies entered the industry and one dropped out (See Chapter VI).

Cumene: Coastal States and Marathon Oil entered in 1967. They added capacity estimated at 100 and 120 million pounds respectively.[32]

Methanol: Georgia-Pacific Corp. and Mercury Chemicals & Petroleum Inc. were reported to be new entrants with large plants.[33]

Nylon: Between 1962 and 1968, the new entrants included: Fiber Industries, Rohm and Haas, Courtaulds North America (See Table VI-9, Chapter VI).

Ortho-xylene: In 1968 and 1969, Phillips, Southern Petrochemicals, and Southwestern Oil Refining were scheduled to start producing this product.[34]

Phthalic anhydride: The new producers include Union Carbide, and Grace between 1960 and 1962; Stepan Chemical by 1964; and Hooker and U.S. Steel Chemicals by 1968 (See Chapter VI, Table VI-3).

Polyester fibers: Between 1962 and 1966, new entrants included: Monsanto, FMC, American Enka, Phillips Fiber. Between 1966 and 1968: Hystron Fibers, Dow-Badische, Allied Chemical (Table VI-11, Chapter VI).

Polyethylene: There were seven entrants between 1953 and 1956, four more between 1956 and 1959, and three between 1959 and 1962. Gulf and Columbia Carbon entered this market after 1964 (See Chapter VI).

Polypropylene: Since 1962 Alamo, Rexall and Shell have entered. The latter has one of the largest capacities in the industry. The three new firms accounted for 30.5% of total capacity.[35]

Polyvinyl chloride: Allied Chemical became a producer in 1967, Stauffer and Ethyl entered somewhat earlier.[36]

Styrene: Since 1959 capacity has more than doubled. Such new producers as Amoco, Cos-Mar, El Paso, Marbon, Shell and Sunray-DX have entered. In 1968 they accounted for more than one-third of total capacity.[37]

Toluene diisocyanate (TDI): Wyandotte Chemicals began producing in 1967.[38]

Vinyl acetate: Since 1961 Monsanto, Borden and National Starch and Chemical have entered. In 1967 they accounted for 27.5% of total capacity.[39]

There has been a considerable number of new entrants into the production of a wide variety of chemicals. Generally, the new entrants have been large companies (chemical and non-chemical) which have extended their product lines. In many instances, the new producers soon have become important competitors in terms of volume. The accompanying expansion in capacity has contributed to the pressure on the prices of a number of chemicals.

Chemical companies as well as companies in other industries constantly are seeking opportunities for investment in chemical products. This search is implemented by their large expenditures for research and development. The net result has been persistent pressures upon existing producers, both large and small, to improve their products and to expand their own capacity in order to meet these competitive threats. One evidence of these tendencies is the overcapacity which has developed for many chemical products, mainly organics, in recent years. New entry is a potent force which makes competition workable in the chemical industry.

Summary and Conclusions

Although chemical markets may be oligopolistic, they have been characterized by intensive competitive pressures. Of particular importance in this connection has been the ease of entry into many chemical markets—particularly the organics.

The number of companies producing specific chemicals has increased significantly as a result of the organization of new companies (often joint ventures), the entry of established companies from other industries, and/or the extension of product lines by chemical companies. Competitive pressures affecting many chemical products have been dramatically intensified by the large-scale entry of companies whose primary activity has been in other industries. The major invasion into the chemical markets has been from the petroleum industry. In many instances, the new producers soon have become important competitors in terms of volume. The result has been persistent pressures upon existing producers, both large and small, to improve their products and services and to expand their own capacity in order to meet these competitive threats. In addition, as is discussed in Chapters XI to XIII, imports have been playing an increasing competitive role for many products.

Most chemical markets are characterized by several large companies and a number of smaller ones. This is similar to the structure in other mass production industries. However, the biggest companies in the chemical industry account for a smaller share of the industry's total sales than is typically found in large manufacturing industires. On the other hand, the proportions of volume of specific products accounted for by the four largest companies are among the highest for any manufacturing industry. Concentration ratios in the chemical industry tend to be smaller for the higher volume products than for those with smaller volume.

The combination of new entrants and different growth rates for companies in the industry has resulted in a reduction of concentration in the chemical industry; for some products the reductions in concentration have been marked. This tendency has been more significant than indicated by the raw data because the composition of the four largest companies in the chemical industry and for specific products has changed over time. Leading companies in the chemical industry have lost their relative position to other companies which have expanded more rapidly to meet new needs or to companies which have entered the industry. Thus, the relative share of total shipments accounted for by a constant group of large companies has declined more than indicated by the data for unidentified successor Big Fours. The published data obscure the full effects of competitive forces which have resulted in significant changes in the position of individual competitors. This is evidence of dynamic competition.

The high concentration ratios found for chemicals reflect the underlying economic characteristics of the industry, particularly the heavy investment required and the accompanying economies inherent in large scale production. Such ratios are subject to many infirmities because of the inadequacies of the data on which they are based. Accordingly, they cannot be used to determine the effectiveness of competition. The significance of these concentration ratios also is affected by relative ease of entry.

Fewness of sellers has not inhibited intensive competition for many chemical products. Nor has it prevented the development of excess capacity for many organic chemicals with the accompanying pressures on prices.

---

[1] Each of these bases of measurement is not available for every industry. Thus, shipments may be an unsatisfactory basis for measurement because of the large scale duplication which occurs when there are heavy shipments between plants in the same classification. See Jesse J. Friedman, *Concentration in American Industry,* Report of the Subcommittee on Antitrust and Monopoly to the Committee on the Judiciary, United States Senate, pursuant to S. Res. 57, Washington, D.C., 1957, p. 193.

[2] *Ibid.,* p. 5.

[3] John Perry Miller, "Measures of Monopoly Power and Concentration: Their Economic Significance," in *Business Concentration and Price Policy,* Princeton University Press, Princeton, N.J., 1955, pp. 130-131.

[4] Betty Bock, "New Patterns of Concentration in Manufacturing," *Business Management Record,* National Industrial Conference Board, July 1963, p. 43.

[5] In 1963, the Big Four in primary aluminum accounted for 100% of total output, in automobiles 99%, tires and inner tubes 70%, cigarettes 80%, and typewriters 76%. Senate Subcommittee on Antitrust and Monopoly, *Concentration Ratios in Manufacturing Industry, 1963,* Part 1, Washington, D.C., 1966, pp. 9, 21, 25, 231.

[6] In 1968, it was estimated that these four companies had a total income of $9,700 million of which $8,086 million or 83.36% were chemical sales. *Chemical & Engineering News,* June 16, 1969, p. 23. If chemical sales accounted for the same share of total income in 1967, the Big Four would have accounted for 33.3% of the industry's sales.

[7] Between 1954 and 1958, 13 five digit groups accounting for 83.5% of the shipments had declines in concentration ratios, four with 6.7% of the shipments recorded no change, and 7 with 9.8% of the shipments had increases.

[8]"The News Front Directory, 7,500 Leading U.S. Manufacturers," *News Front*, 1961, p. 74 and "The Fortune Directory," *Fortune*, June 15, 1968, p. 188.

[9] *Concentration Ratios in Manufacturing Industry, 1958.* Report prepared by the Bureau of the Census for the Subcommittee on Antitrust and Monopoly of the Committee on the Judiciary, United States Senate, 87th Cong., 2nd Sess., U.S. Government Printing Office, Washington, D.C., 1962, Part 1, p. 434. The Bureau of the Census has pointed out: "Based upon the 1957 revision of the Standard Industrial Classification Manual, the content of Major Group 28, Chemicals and Allied Products, has been significantly changed in 1958 from the prior information published on the previous classification system." U.S. Department of Commerce, Bureau of the Census, U.S. *Census of Manufactures: 1958,* Vol. II, Industry Statistics, Part II, Major Groups 20 to 28. Washington, D.C., 1961, p. 28-1.

[10]Simon N. Whitney, *Antitrust Policies,* The Twentieth Century Fund, New York, 1958, Vol. 1, pp. 227-28.

[11]For a discussion of the influence of these factors in the rayon industry, see Jesse W. Markham, *Competition in the Rayon Industry,* Harvard University Press, Cambridge, Mass., 1952, ch. 3.

[12]*Economic Almanac, 1967-1968,* National Industrial Conference Board, The Macmillan Company, New York, 1967, p. 275.

[13]*Ibid.,* p. 276.

[14]"Concentration Ratios in Manufacturing Industry, 1958," Part I, *op. cit.,* pp. 470,472.

[15]*Dow Chemical Company Report for June 1, to December 31, 1962,* p. 6.

[16]*Management Newsletter,* January 1967, p. 1.

[17]*Cyanamid Magazine,* Winter 1961, p. 5.

[18]J. P. Cunningham, "The Challenges in Marketing for Organic Chemicals," in *Chemical Marketing: The Challenges of the Seventies,* American Chemical Society, Washington, D.C., 1968, p. 27.

[19]Shell and Standard Oil of New Jersey were in the chemical business in the 1920's— "but most started taking chemical production seriously in the late '40's or '50's." *Chemical Week,* November 16, 1968, p. 136.

[20]Richard C. Sparling and Norma J. Anderson, *Capital Investments of the World Petroleum Industry, 1967,* The Chase Manhattan Bank, New York, December 1968, pp. 18-25.

[21]*Chemical & Engineering News,* February 17, 1969, p. 16.

[22]*Chemical Manufacturing Facilities of the Petroleum and Natural Gas Industries,* The National Petroleum Council, Washington, D.C., 1963, p. 8. The total number of petrochemical plants increased from 465 in 1962 to 510 in 1963. *The Oil and Gas Journal,* September 2, 1963, p. 112.

[23]Frank Sciancalepore, "Basic Characteristics of the Chemical Industry," in *Chemical Marketing Research,* edited by N. H. Giragosian, Reinhold Publishing Corp., New York, 1967, p. 12.

[24]*Chemical Week,* April 19, 1969, p. 26.

[25]*The New Competition in Our Changing Economy,* an address before the American Petroleum Institute, Chicago, Illinois, November 11, 1959, pp. 3-4.

[26]25% of the PPG volume was accounted for by chemicals in 1968. *Chemical Week,* February 15, 1969, p. 21.

[27] One of the limitations of the Gort material for the present study is that he defined the chemical industry more broadly to include some allied products industries. Included in this group of companies were Procter & Gamble Co., Colgate-Palmolive Co., Sherwin-Williams Co., and Merck & Co., Inc., Michael Gort, *Diversification and Integration in American Industry,* Princeton University Press, Princeton, N.J., 1962, pp. 162-63.

[28] Gort, *op. cit.,* pp. 38-40.

[29] *Ibid.,* p. 6.

[30] For illustrations of new entrants into 23 product markets in the early 1960s see Jules Backman, *Competition in the Chemical Industry,* The Manufacturing Chemists' Association, Inc., Washington, D.C., 1964, pp. 14-17.

[31] *Chemical Week,* January 18, 1969, p. 47.

[32] *Ibid.,* February 4, 1967, p. 33.

[33] *Oil, Paint & Drug Reporter,* November 4, 1968, p. 3.

[34] *Chemical Week,* January 13, 1968, p. 29.

[35] *Oil, Paint & Drug Reporter,* July 23, 1962 and *Chemical Week,* March 4, 1967, p. 38.

[36] *Oil, Paint & Drug Reporter,* November 19, 1962, p. 46 a d *Chemical Week,* January 7, 1967, p. 32.

[37] *Oil, Paint & Drug Reporter,* February 9, 1959, p. 44 and September 30, 1968, p. 33.

[38] *Annual Report 1968,* pp. 5-6.

[39] *Oil, Paint and Drug Reporter,* May 15, 1961, p. 42 and *Chemical Week,* August 12, 1967, p. 74.

Chapter V

Competition in the Chemical Industry

Competition means rivalry. The significance of any type of rivalry and its effectiveness cannot be determined by any simple yardsticks. Conclusions concerning the effectiveness of competition, therefore, necessarily involve judgment factors. The abstract ideal of pure or perfect competition, often used as a theoretical standard, exists mainly in textbooks but usually cannot be attained in the real world.[1]

The prerequisites for pure or perfect competition are: a significant number of buyers and sellers so that no one can influence the price, homogeneous or standardized products, ease of entry and exit, operation at full capacity, and a static economy, that is no changes in tastes, incomes, habits, etc. All of these conditions obviously are not present in the chemical industry. Nor are they found in other industries.

Effective competition has been defined as a pattern of behavior in which ". . . no one seller, and no group of sellers acting in concert, has the power to choose its level of profits by giving less and charging more."[2]

The ability to control price and quality and thus profits may be significantly influenced by several factors: the number of competitors, the availability of substitute products, the ease of entry into an industry, the extent to which its products are standardized, the extent to which producers act independently, the presence of predatory actions, the stage of growth of the industry, and the extent of excess capacity. The number of competitors and growth were discussed in the two preceding chapters.

This chapter deals with key aspects of competition including: the availability of substitute products (interproduct and interindustry competition); the nature of price competition, the extent of non-price competition, including competition in service. The relationship of joint ventures, reciprocity, and patents to competition in the chemical industry also are reviewed. Competition from imports is discussed in Chapters XI and XII.

Competitive Products

There are one or more substitutes available for almost every chemical product. These may be either other chemicals or materials produced by other industries. The availability of substitute products among chemicals may be called *interproduct competition* while the ability to substitute the products of other industries may be described as *interindustry competition*. The buyer of chemicals, therefore, usually has a choice among varying numbers of alternatives to meet his needs.

The availability of substitute products affects competition for various chemicals to a significant degree. Of particular importance is the fact that the industry deals with industrial buyers, who usually are familiar with substitute products and their relative prices. Interproduct and interindustry competition therefore may affect prices in many instances. The ability to develop substitute products also induces the so-called "test tube" rivalry which is so vital in the chemical industry. The availability of substitute products influences the magnitude and definition of the market and hence the significance of concentration ratios which are based on single products. Clearly, substitute products add a significant dimension to competition in the chemical industry. Moreover, new products are developed for so many existing items that "product obsolescence" becomes one result of competitive pressures.[3]

Interproduct Competition

Interproduct competition has played an increasingly important role in the chemical industry. Chemical products generally have multiple end uses. A score of industries easily may have requirements for a single basic chemical. That chemical may meet competition in one or more of these uses from a variety of other chemicals. Among synthetic products there often is vigorous competition for markets. One interesting aspect of competition in the chemical industry is similar to the drug industry. Not only are other companies seeking to develop new products which will compete successfully with existing products but within a company a similar search usually is underway. For instance, Du Pont has developed synthetic products, such as Dacron polyester fiber, which compete with natural fibers as well as with other synthetic fibers it produces itself.

Illustrations of interproduct competition among inorganic chemicals include:

Caustic Soda (sodium hydroxide) can be substituted for soda ash in some uses.

Chlorine "competes with numerous other oxidizing agents, bleaches (hydrogen peroxide, sulfur dioxide), and bactericides."[4]

Sulfuric acid competes with hydrofluoric acid in oil refining alkylation processes; with phosphoric in coke oven ammonia recovery; with electrolytic processes in phosphoric manufacture; with other explosives in the manufacture of TNT, etc.; with by-product hydrochloric acid in the manufacture of hydrochloric by the salt and sulfuric processes. Manufactured sulfuric competes with by-product material and spent acid. Sulfuric must compete with mechanical means in descaling metals and competes with other drying agents, other sulfonating agents, and other light oil recovery processes.

Among synthetic products there also is considerable interproduct competition:

Nylon successfully competed with rayon in tire cord; fiber glass and polyester fibers are now competing with nylon.[5]

Acetate, polyester film, and unplasticized vinyl chloride film compete for use in computer and sound tape.[6]

"Four major resins are competitive for bottle markets on a price-performance basis. At 20¢ per lb., polyethylene and polystyrene are the cheapest; but polypropylene is close behind at 22¢ per lb. while polyvinyl chloride molding compounds sell at 28-32¢ per lb. - Acrylics . . . at 35-37¢ per lb. are out of the running for most markets."[7]

". . . polypropylene competes directly with conventional polyethylene in film form as a packaging wrap; its strength and clarity will make it a formidable competitor if prices can be made equal. In molded plastic products, polypropylene competes with linear polyethylene and its greater strength should give it a competitive advantage as the price premium narrows. In fibers it competes primarily with nylon, and its resistance to abrasion and stretching should permit it to gain a share of the synthetic fabric market."[8] In closures for cosmetics, toothpaste, etc., it competes with urea molding materials.[9]

Epoxies "virtually replaced" phenolic and also resinous materials as inner lining for beer cans. In turn, hydrocarbon resins replaced epoxies at a lower cost.[10]

Glycerine, pentaerythritol, and sorbitol compete in a number of end uses.

In some instances chemical products compete not only with other chemical products but with products of other industries as well. Illustrations include:

Dacron polyester fiber with cotton and wool and with rayon and nylon.

Polyethylene with paper and with cellophane.

Nylon with hog bristles in brushes and with cellulose acetate.

Titanium dioxide with white lead and with lithopone.

Many chemicals are used to make other chemicals. But the processes used are not static. On the contrary, the production process is dynamic and subject to change as the research laboratories have developed more economical and more efficient processes. The result has been an accelerated rate of *interprocess competition* throughout the chemical industry.

Heavy chemicals have been affected significantly by changing technology:

". . . late in the '50s, Du Pont pioneered the chloride process to replace the sulfate method of making titanium dioxide. . . . In sulfuric acid manufacture, the contact process continued to supplant the chamber technique; and in chlor-alkali production, the mercury cell accounted for 5% in '45, almost 20% in '60."[11]

The changes in process used to make acrylonitrile have been described as follows:

"Initially (1940) . . . ethylene and chlorine were reacted to form the chlorohydrin which in turn was reacted to form acrylonitrile.

"In 1952 . . . reacting methane and ammonia to produce hydrogen cyanide, which in turn is reacted with acetylene to form acrylonitrile. . . .

"In 1960, . . . propylene was reacted with ammonia directly to produce acrylonitrile. . . .

"The net effect of this changing technology was to decrease the demand for ethylene oxide, chlorine, and hydrogen cyanide."[12]

Similarly, it has been noted that "acetic acid has at various times been made from three different raw materials by ten different processes."[13]

The illustrations could be multiplied many times as any review of the trade press will quickly show. As cost-price pressures develop, the search for new processes becomes intensified in order to shave costs wherever possible.

Keen interproduct competition from other chemicals may not be present for every chemical product. However, where it is found the competitive picture is affected, the competitive situation for each product must be examined separately. The only generalization that applies to the chemical industry is that no single competitive pattern is applicable. Moreover, as research and development has increased in importance, there has undoubtedly been a reduction in the number of products insulated from the competition of other chemical products.

Interindustry Competition

A significant aspect of competition in the chemical industry is the extent to which its products compete directly with those produced by other industries. This is particularly true for plastic materials and synthetics (SIC 282) which accounted for total shipments of $7,427 million in 1967. Many of these products had to carve a share out of existing markets held by other materials.[14]

It should be emphasized that the concept of interindustry competition deals with what is produced, not with who produces it. Thus, polyethylene may be produced by a chemical company or a petroleum company. This is not considered to be interindustry competition. Only competition between the products of other industries and products of the chemical industry are embraced by this definition. The role in the chemical industry of companies whose main activity has been or is in other industries was discussed earlier.

There are many familiar illustrations of interindustry competition including synthetic rubber with natural rubber, the miracle fibers—nylon, Dacron, Orlon, Acrilan, etc.—with cotton and wool, and cellophane with various packaging materials including aluminum foil and paper products. That producers in these other industries have not stood by idly in the face of this competition is indicated by the efforts of cotton textile producers to improve their product through styling and other measures.

Illustrations of substitutions of chemicals for products of other industries have included:

- Corfam for leather in shoes.
- Nitrocellulose, then alkyds, then vinyl and styrene—butadiene latices for linseed oil in finishes.
- Acetal resins for die cast zinc and aluminum in many automotive and machinery components—for brass in bushings and valves, for steel in oil field piping.[15]
- Polyethylene for kraft paper in multiwall bags and for tinplate and glass.
- Formaldehyde resins for metal.
- Nylon for steel in automobile speed gears and acrylic resins for glass in tail lights.

Synthetics and plastics have become increasingly important to American industry. For example, three-fourths of our rubber requirements are now furnished by synthetic rubber. Plastics are occupying a greater role in the important building products market.

The increase in interindustry competition for plastics has been described by the U.S. Department of Commerce as follows:

"Plastics materials have found application in every segment of the economy, and their penetration in new uses and as replacements for older materials will continue to increase. Plastics materials are molded, fabricated, or processed by many methods into countless items or components.

"The extremely wide range of properties available in the plastics materials, such as light weight, ease of fabrication, physical toughness, chemical resistance, and color selection, has contributed to ever-widening acceptance for civilian and military uses. In various applications these materials can be found to be competing with, or replacing, metal, wood, paper, and glass."[16]

The problem of market definition under these conditions was highlighted in the *Cellophane Case.*[17] The Supreme Court found that ". . . Du Pont produced almost 75% of the cellophane sold in the United States, and cellophane constituted less than 20% of all 'flexible packaging material' sales." The Court refused to confine the market to cellophane and defined it more broadly as flexible packaging materials, including aluminum foil, glassine, waxing papers, sulfite bag and wrapping papers, pliofilm, polyethylene, Saran, and Cry-O-Rap. The Court held "That market is composed of products that have *reasonable interchangeability* for the purposes for which they are produced—price, use and qualities considered " (italics added). Cellophane was sold in competition with other chemicals (e.g. polyethylene) as well as products of other industries.

Because of the difficulties encountered in measuring markets and the lack of meaningful data, the significance of concentration ratios also is affected by interindustry competition as was noted earlier.

The availability of substitute products is a vital economic fact of life in the chemical industry. It influences the competitive environment within which decisions must be made concerning pricing, sales strategy, research and development, and technical services and other forms of non-price competition.

Price Competition

The chemical industry formerly was regarded as one in which price stability characterized the pattern of behavior for its products. During the 1930s, chemical prices were fairly stable while during the inflation of the 1940s and 1950s, prices rose significantly less than the general price level. As a result observations such as the following by Robert F. Lanzillotti were not unusual: "The relative infrequency with which chemical price quotations are altered over the course of the business cycle is particularly evident from an analysis of business cycle movements since the general recovery of the 1930s. It is to be noted that this relative insensitivity of chemical prices to fluctuations in market demand operates on the upswing as well as the downturn."[18]

The relative stability of prices combined with price leadership and identical bidding on government contracts generally were cited to "prove" that price competition was not present for most chemical products. The fact that price leadership and identical bidding may be consistent with price competition has been ignored because prices remained relatively stable. This image of the chemical industry was shattered in the 1960s. Overcapacity and price cutting became the rule rather than the exception for many chemical products and attempts by price leaders to raise prices have frequently failed. Price shading and sales below list price became a way of life for many organic chemicals including the plastics.

Many illustrations may be cited to show the widespread price cutting that developed in the early 1960s.[19] The following headlines in five quarterly summaries of prices by *Chemical and Engineering News* in 1962 and in the first half of 1963 tell the story for that period:[20]

> *July 1962:* "Chemical Prices Continue to Decline: Price cuts during the second quarter centered on aromatics, and their derivatives, antibiotics, and polyols."

> *October 1962:* "Price Pattern Still Marked by Declines: Competitive pressures are highlighted by price increases that failed to stick."

January 1963: "Chemical Prices Continue Downward Trends: Last quarter of 1962 did little to change trend that prevailed all year; pressure is already building for more cuts this year."

April 1963: "Most Chemical Price Changes Are Downward: Price weakness haunts organics, although prices of many inorganics, such as cadmium, ferric, and sodium salts, climb."

July 1963: "Chemical Prices Still Face Downward Pressure: Phthalic anhydride is worst hit item among organics; most inorganic prices are holding steady or increasing."

Among the products for which price declines in 1962-63 were attributed to overcapacity were acetone, benzene, caustic soda, carbon black, acrylonitrile, phthalic anhydride, toluene, phenol, naphthalene, glycerin, hydrochloric acid, and nitrogen. Other chemicals for which price reductions were reported in this period include: polystyrene, polypropylene, polyvinyl alcohol, acrylic fibers, ethylene-diamine, sodium benzoate, vinyl acetate, xylene, propionates, and phthalate and adipate plasticizers.[21] This list includes a number of large volume products.

The development of excess capacity reflected the entry of new competitors, particularly petroleum companies, as well as the substantial new investment by companies already producing the affected products. The pressure to obtain volume under these conditions was intensified. The desire to broaden markets, which has been the policy of some companies, also has encouraged price cutting against a background of large increases in capacity.

Price cutting continued for many products despite the general price inflation after 1965. Thus, it was reported in 1968 that "The soaring capacity and eroding price are symptoms of the transition to big plants that is also shaking industrial chemical markets for ammonia, methanol, and ethylene."[22] A year later, it was reported that for ammonia "list prices have not meant much."[23] Other illustrations of price shading include the following:

Benzene: Prices were cut sharply in 1967-68 as consumption and exports declined creating considerable overcapacity (See Chapter VI).

Phenol: In 1967-68, the market was described as chaotic and actual prices were four cents or more below the list price of 11-1/4 cents a pound (See Chapter VI).

Trichlorethylene: Prices were reduced in 1968 "to bring list into line with the current market."[24]

Polyester Fiber: List prices reduced in 1967 to end "prevalent off-list pricing."[25]

Ethylene oxide: Prices have "eroded." One EO buyer reports that negotiated tags are about 9¢/lb., delivered, vs. a nominal list price of 15.5¢/lb., tanks, delivered."[26]

Ditertiary butyl peroxide: List prices were cut in 1968 "to bring them in line with market conditions."[27]

Polystyrene: "Widespread discounting by all producers" in 1968.[28]

ABS resin: "Depressed by overcapacity recently."[29]

Detergent range alcohols: Market prices were "as low as 13.5 cents a pound" compared with a list price of 20 cents."[30]

Although many price increases were reported in the 1967-1969 period, it is evident that competitive pressures resulted in lower prices for many important chemicals. Moreover, as is shown in Chapter VII, in a number of instances where prices were increased, they did not hold as other companies refused "to follow the leader."

To the chemical executive, price stability for many organic chemicals was a myth which he devoutly wished was reality.

The net effect of the price cutting in the 1960s was a steady erosion in the Bureau of Labor Statistics wholesale price indexes for organic chemicals and plastics during a period when wholesale industrial prices first remained steady and then advanced. As compared with the 1957-1959 period, the BLS index of organic prices had declined 12.4% and plastic resins and materials by 19.5% by December 1968; during the same period the BLS index of wholesale prices increased 9.8%. However, prices of inorganic chemicals rose by 14%.

It must be kept in mind that some chemical prices have recorded only nominal changes or advanced during this period so that the composite indexes include a number of products with declines much larger than the average. Table V-1 shows the percentage changes for organic chemicals as of December 1968 from the average prices in the 1957-59 period.

Declines were recorded for half of the 52 organic chemicals for which BLS publishes prices on a 1957-59 base; no change in price was reported for two

TABLE V-1

Percent Change in Organic Chemical Prices, December 1968 Compared with 1957-59 Average

Percent Change	No. of Prices
+50.1 to 60.0	1*
+40.1 to +50.0	1
+30.1 to +40.0	0
+20.1 to +30.0	1
+10.1 to +20.0	6
+0.1 to +10.0	15
0	2
−0.1 to −10.0	9
−10.1 to −20.0	3
−20.1 to −30.0	6
−30.1 to −40.0	3
−40.1 to −50.0	3
−50.1 to −60.0	1
−60.1 to −70.0	1
TOTAL	52

*November 1968

Note: There have been excluded from this tabulation four products available since December 1966 and one available since December 1967.

Source: Derived from data published by the U.S. Department of Labor, Bureau of Labor Statistics.

products. The declines exceeded 10% for 17 products. The actual decline in chemical prices probably has been greater than shown because the BLS indexes do not include some products which have fallen sharply in prices (e.g. polypropylene, polyethylene, and sorbitol), nor does it reflect all price shading.

Clearly, this is a picture which differs significantly from the stereotype of an industry whose prices are maintained unchanged over long periods of time without regard to changing economic conditions.

Identical Bids

Do identical bids reflect competitive pressures or collusion? There is no general or single answer to this question. Each case must be examined within the framework of the economic forces affecting the product or products involved. Identical bids in government contracts sometimes are considered to reflect an absence of price competition.

Professor Robert Lanzillotti concluded that identical bids in the chemical industry "constitute fairly conclusive evidence of the presence of some form of collusion which flows from the concentrated structure of the markets in question."[31] His conclusion was based upon an examination of bids in 73 transactions reported by the Joint Economic Committee.[32] However, the Joint Economic Committee warned that the selection of its materials does "not suggest that these abstracts are representative, either of the volume of the kinds of identical bids actually received by the Federal agencies during the years in question."[33]

This point is well illustrated by the material for chemicals and allied products for which there were only 12 abstracts. One abstract covered 42 cases of zinc oxide for which the bids were identical. The remaining 12 abstracts covered scattered cases involving only 12 products. The bids generally involved dollar amounts of less than $10,000. The data also contained a surprisingly large number of instances where there was *not* identical bidding for the few unrepresentative chemical products covered. This is certainly a very unsatisfactory and inadequate sample on which to base sweeping generalizations.

Any discussion of identical bids must start from the premise that: ". . . *collusive bids* are unlawful whether they be identical or not; *independent bids* are lawful whether they are identical or not."[34] Where collusion does prevail, it may be reflected in an absence of identity in bids. In this connection, Professor Paul W. Cook, Jr. has observed: ". . . I would certainly bet that most conspiracies involving public tenders are conspiracies to rotate the low bid—and the business."[35] The electrical price conspiracy which did so much to revive interest in and concern about identical bidding did *not* involve identical bids. Rather, the essence of the conspiracy was the filing of *different bids* for some products in order to influence the flow of orders.[36] There is a substantial difference between identical bids and collusive rigging of bids which may or may not be identical.

How do identical bids come about without collusion? They are most likely to be found where products are standardized, there are relatively few sellers, small amounts are involved for specific bids, price lists or catalogues are available, and buyers are well informed. These conditions prevail generally for chemicals. Under such circumstances it would be anticipated that both prices *and* terms of sale would be identical in the overwhelming majority of instances.

Of critical importance in this group of factors is the standardized nature of chemical products. Competitive forces press toward an identity of prices for standardized products. If a producer tries to charge informed business purchasers (who make up the bulk of buyers of chemicals), a higher price he will lose volume. If he charges a lower price than his competitor, the latter will lose volume unless he meets the cut. For such products, bids on government contracts cannot vary much from prices to other purchasers. Temporary deviations may take place but prices are quickly adjusted. The expectation concerning identity of prices in competitive bidding and their significance is markedly different when the bid is made on complex products which must be manufactured to order.

Most chemicals are produced by a relatively small number of producers. In such an environment, each seller is promptly aware of the actions taken by his competitors. It is especially easy to determine competitors' past bids on government contracts since the bids are made public. In contrast, if deviations take place in prices offered to private purchasers they are much more difficult to ascertain.

The relative volume involved in such bidding can be an especially important factor. To cut prices in an effort to secure an unimportant volume of government business does not make much sense to the businessman, particularly if one possible result is to undermine his entire price structure.[37] Hence, on small orders the tendency would be to quote list prices.

Identity in price bidding also is facilitated when the companies circulate price catalogues and price lists. Such identical prices can be arrived at independently although the prices charged by competitors may be a major factor in the price established. When identical prices are quoted to private customers, they are neither illegal nor uneconomic. To the extent that deviations from list prices take place in private transactions they may be secret—in contrast to the advertised nature of bids on public contracts. On the other hand, it has been noted that reductions in prices under sealed bids become known immediately to other buyers who then refuse to pay prices higher than those quoted on such bids.[38]

It is sometimes stated that identity of bids must involve collusive action because bids are to be opened in the future and bidders could not independently arrive at an identical price in light of the uncertainty involved in evaluations of future conditions.[39] Except in periods of marked economic change (such as a major price inflation or deflation) many prices do not change frequently nor by significant amounts. Minor changes in economic conditions generally are not reflected in most industrial prices. Against this background, the most logical basis on which to bid is to assume that the prevailing prices will continue in effect.

From the foregoing analysis, it seems evident that identical bids generally are to be expected for chemical products and that this development is not *per se* evidence of a lack of price competition. On the contrary, it is the competitive forces and the economic characteristics of the products involved that result in identical bids.

Nonprice Competition

Nonprice competition is of major importance throughout American industry. It embraces all actions which are designed to attract business through means other than price reduction.[40] The emphasis is upon such factors as quality, service, product performance, development of brand names, advertising, and credit terms. By emphasizing nonprice factors, a company attempts to maintain or increase its sales at a given price or within a given range of prices. Under price competition a firm attempts to increase its volume or to maintain its share of the market by lowering its price.

The opportunity to give considerable emphasis to nonprice factors is more limited for sellers of standardized industrial products such as chemicals than for consumer goods or for differentiated industrial products. Nevertheless, since it is unavoidable that prices will be identical for standardized products sold to knowledgeable industrial buyers, ways are sought to emphasize nonprice factors.

Smaller companies often find it easier to compete in nonprice terms than through price. The following description as to how a small chemical manufacturer competes is illuminating:

> "To meet the lower prices of large production runs, he offers rapid service, products tailored to the customer's exact specifications. Where the large company promotes sales through heavy advertising, the small firm stresses personal contact and service. When his accounts turn into captive customers through competitive mergers, he relies on his flexibility, switches to a new product or a new customer."[41]

Nonprice competition in the chemical industry takes the form of technical service, emphasis upon quality, improvement of products through research and development, and to a limited extent, the development of brand names. Product differentiation is not important.[42] The extent to which each type of nonprice competition is emphasized varies among products.

Technical Services

A significant aspect of nonprice competition in the chemical industry is making available technical services to customers. As one Union Carbide official has observed:

> ". . . the salesman must offer more than a good product. He must offer also the technology required to help his customers toward profitable application of the product. Because customers have come to expect a liberal share of technical know-how along with purchased materials, companies in the chemical and plastics industry have established specialized research and development facilities, manned by able, professional experimentalists, to assist customers in the proper and profitable use of standard products and in the development of new applications for existing products and of commercially-acceptable, new products for specific applications. Such assistance to customers defines the mission of technical service and application research."[43]

Since many chemicals—particularly inorganic—are identical in their physical composition, the quality of technical service becomes the differentiating factor which may become "the major justification for customer loyalty."[44]

A survey by *Chemical Week* in 1962 reported that the average cost of technical services was 1% to 2% of sales and that it varied for different products.[45]

The important role of technical services in the chemical industry has been succinctly summarized by David H. Dawson of Du Pont:

> ". . . Nowadays, with more complex products and heightened product competition, the need for technical aid has grown greatly. The customer will give his business to the producer who helps him solve his problems and enhance his earnings. That this is proceeding to great lengths is evident from the magnitude and rapid growth of our new Chestnut Run end-use research and technical service establishment near Wilmington.

> "Much of the work in these laboratories is directed towards the cultivation of markets once or twice removed from our own. In the case

of synthetic yarns, we have found it productive, and frequently necessary, to study not only their weaving or knitting into fabrics, not only the dyeing and finishing of these fabrics, but their conversion into garments—cutting and sewing techniques, yes, and consumer care of the garments. In plastics, especially the newer types, it is often necessary to work out the design of a plastic component for use in an automobile or a washing machine and only then go to work with our immediate customer, the supplier of molded or extruded parts, on methods of producing the parts.

"Customers in today's chemical industry markets are wooed also in indirect ways such as assistance on financial controls, credit, and business methods. We have, for instance, issued a detailed manual on how to set up and run a paint store, and another on credit policies. Other types of aid include such things as product publicity, directed to the ultimate consumer, and increasingly heavy appropriations for advertising at each stage of distribution down to the end-product user. This is often aimed at establishing and enhancing the value of the chemical producer's trademarks."[46]

Technical services embrace a wide variety of activities including problem solving, development of process knowledge, product development, design of equipment, and market research. Dow reported in 1967 that it had inaugurated a new "instant solvent analysis" that reduced the time required to analyze chemical samples for its customers.[47] Technical services are especially important in connection with new products. For example, it has been reported that Dow Corning "had to work directly with molders to teach them how to use its silicone molding resin."[48]

Celanese has reported that "In many cases, [its] personnel may relate not only to the purchasing department of the customer, but also to its manufacturing, research, finance, merchandising, styling, advertising and publicity as well as to the customer's top management. . . . We share with mill customers the job of developing new fabrics in new textures, patterns, and colors."[49]

Allied Chemical reports that ". . . the company has developed an extensive technical service capability. Specialists experienced in all aspects of the industry and having available production-sized fabricating equipment work with customers to design and demonstrate new plastics applications, to improve productivity in customers' plants, and to tailor products and facilities to meet specific customer requirements."[50]. Allied also has established a Fibers Technical Center to provide "customers with the strong sound technical support they require."[51]

Professor Phillips has pointed out that there

". . . has been a sharpening of service competition among rubber producers, both for new customers and for new markets. Included are technical services performed for buyers. . . .

"In most cases the smaller rubber fabricators, in particular, do not have the chemical background, research laboratories, or technical facilities to solve the problems arising in usage of various synthetic rubber grades. Accordingly the technical service staffs of the rubber producers provide an important aid in the fabrication of synthetic rubber products."[52]

The profits squeeze in the 1960's has placed many chemical companies on the horns of a dilemma. Cuts in technical service costs may appear to be logical to maintain profit margins. But against the background of intensive price competition, such services became even more important if volume were to be retained.

Some companies resolved the problem by making the services available on a more selective basis determined by the size of the customer and his growth potential.[53] Sometimes price has been raised with the cost of services cited as the reason.[54]

Brand Names

Relatively few brand names for chemicals have much significance to the ultimate consumer. A major exception is synthetic fibers. Creslan, nylon, Orlon, Dynel, Acrilan, Zefran and other fibers have become increasingly familiar names to buyers. The producers of these fibers have given great attention to the ultimate consumer through advertising in order to stimulate demand for their specific product.

Chemical Week reports that "Most polyester producers emphasize stringent brand name marketing programs to make sure the fiber's reputation is not sullied by misuse." Louis Laun of Celanese Fibers Marketing Co. stated that "Licensed fiber-brand name programs assure the shopper that the shirt does contain the necessary amount of polyester to provide good performance."[55]

Brand names are more significant for the allied products industries such as drugs and paints. However, chemical companies do sell some consumer products under brand names. Illustrations include Union Carbide's Everready batteries and Prestone antifreeze, Du Pont's Lucite paints, Dow's Saran Wrap, and Mobil Chemical's Hefty household bags.

Competition and Intercompany Relationships

Several types of relationships which may affect the intensity of competition have developed among chemical companies. Joint ventures, reciprocal buying, and patent licensing have been described by some writers as evidence that the industry is characterized by "peaceful and collaborative coexistence." According to Alfred Kahn, the underlying philosophy of the industry has been " . . . where interests might otherwise conflict, collaborate."[56] On the other hand, Dr. Simon Whitney has concluded that these activities ". . . constitute, in major part, attempts to : (1) spread the risk; (2) avoid setting up top-heavy systems of distribution; (3) share technology—and, it is true, sometimes divide international markets at the same time; and (4) buy products where they are cheapest. These policies are not peculiar to the chemical industry."[57]

Joint Ventures and Competition

The modern joint venture usually is designed to establish a new company on a permanent basis with a continuing relationship between the partners. These permanent relationships are in contrast to the joint venture which in yesteryear was designed as a temporary arrangement to handle a specific project. However, sometimes one of the partners may finally take over the entire operation. Thus, for example, Chemstrand, which originally was organized by Monsanto and American Viscose, was later taken over 100% by Monsanto. Joint ventures have been used widely in the chemical industry.[58]

Joint ventures are formed for a variety of reasons. The joint venturers are not seeking partners merely to share profits. Rather, they are formed because each of the partners has a contribution to make either in terms of technical know-how, marketing know-how, or financial or other resources. Joint ventures have been undertaken in the chemical industry to:

(1) Combine diverse technical abilities of companies in different industries.[59]

(2) Obtain technical resources beyond the capacity of single companies.

(3) Combine availability of raw materials with knowledge as to how to convert them into complex finished products.[60]

(4) Spread the risk and thus facilitate raising capital.

(5) Create new products.[61]

(6) Combine the sales techniques of one company with the production know-how of another.[62]

Some writers[63] and public officials[64] have recognized the advantages of the joint venture to the companies involved, but have charged that such arrangements: (1) tend to limit the present and potential competition in the product market affected, (2) tend to result in domination of the product market because of the economic power of the parent companies, and (3) tend to lessen competition in other product lines in which the two companies already are competing. Many of the benefits outlined are real while the criticisms are speculative.

The basic factor affecting decisions to enter a market is the outlook for demand for a product. Where a market is static, the joint venture can only gain a share of the market at the expense of existing companies. However, in an expanding market, the joint venture and its competitors can grow in absolute terms although one or more of the latter will have a *decreasing relative share* of the market.

The chemical industry generally ranks high in terms of its competitive ferment. Competition is dynamic, not static. It takes many forms and appears from diverse quarters. The competitive pattern for organic chemicals has been particularly vigorous as was noted earlier.

For polyethylene the number of competitors increased from 2 in 1954 to 15 in 1967; 2 of these competitors are joint ventures, with a total capacity of 300 million out of an industry total of 4.5 billion pounds.

In 1959, two of the producers of ethylene were joint ventures (Petroleum Chemicals and Jefferson Chemicals) with a combined estimated capacity of 450 million pounds or 8.0% of the total. The largest of these joint ventures (Jefferson Chemicals) ranked sixth in capacity. In the following nine years, six new joint ventures entered of which two replaced individual producers. One of the earlier joint ventures (Petroleum Chemicals) was taken over by one of the partners and hence lost that status. Thus, in 1968 seven of the 23 producers were joint ventures and accounted for 3,250 million pounds or 19.6% of the total capacity of 16,605 million pounds. The largest joint venture (Union Texas Wyandotte-Marbon) was the seventh largest company in the industry.

Of the nine companies producing nylon, one which started as a joint venture (Chemstrand) has lost that status. The two remaining joint ventures (Fiber Industries and Beaunit-El Paso Natural Gas) accounted for 170 million pounds out of a total capacity of 1,356 million pounds in 1968.

Goodrich-Gulf and Texas-U.S. Chemical have remained the second and third largest producers of butadiene since 1955. However, the former was taken over by Goodrich in 1969.

In petroleum based benzene, the largest joint venture (Union Atlantic) ranked seventeenth in capacity in 1965.

These data, which reflect only one aspect of the competitive picture, do not support any theory of dominance or ability to exclude new entries by joint ventures. Clearly, there is nothing about a joint venture which necessarily will place it in a dominant position in a market or which will assure its continuous growth in relative importance in the chemical industry.

Paul Rand Dixon, then Chairman of the Federal Trade Commission, has suggested: "There is justifiable doubt that business strategists can treat one another as belligerents in one market when they are allies in another."[65] Although such a development is possible, it should not be overlooked that in a large chemical company each product division often is more concerned with its own profitability than with the activities of other divisions.

The vigorous price competition which has dominated many chemical markets in recent years indicates that partners in one venture do not use a kid gloves approach in other markets in which the parents meet. Each company is under pressure, regardless of its corporate relationships in special areas, to compete vigorously in all markets in order to justify the investment required for the manufacture of each of its product lines.

Nor is there any reason to believe that the product market will necessarily be dominated by the joint venture as a result of the greater economic power of the two parent companies. First, the areas marked by the prevalence of joint ventures have been markets in which the existing firms are large ones. In petrochemicals, for example, joint ventures involve some of the largest corporations in the country. Secondly, the parents are not acquiring an existing firm but almost invariably are creating a new competitor. Thirdly, despite their large resources, the parents commit limited amounts to the joint venture and both parents usually must be in agreement if these amounts are increased. Moreover, because of their size both parents usually have competing demands from other activities upon their limited (rather than unlimited) resources. Finally, joint ventures often provide for research and development as a key element in their plans, thus indicating that economic growth in terms of new and better product lines, rather than market foreclosure, is the primary motive in their formation.

In summary, the positive contributions of joint ventures to more effective competition in the chemical industry have been minimized by critics while their anti-competitive effects appear to have been considerably exaggerated. Joint ventures usually increase competition by permitting the entry of new competitors into markets. Clearly, joint ventures do not result *per se* in a lessening of competition. On the contrary, competition generally appears to have been intensified by joint ventures in the chemical industry.

The Penn-Olin Case

Penn-Olin[66] was the first joint venture case to be decided by the Supreme Court under the Celler-Kefauver Act.[67] Penn-Olin was formed in 1960 by Olin Mathieson and Pennsalt to produce sodium chlorate in the southeastern part of the United States. Pennsalt had produced this chemical at a plant in Portland, Oregon and sold a small amount (8.9 per cent of the sales in 1960) in the Southeast. Olin Mathieson had never produced sodium chlorate commercially. However, it had acted as Pennsalt's sales agent for sodium chlorate in the southeastern territory for several years before Penn-Olin was formed. In addition, Pennsalt and Olin produced and competed in the sale of nonchlorate chemicals.

Prior to the organization of Penn-Olin, "over 90%" of the southeastern market was held by Hooker Chemical Corporation and American Potash & Chemical Corporation, both of whom had entered the industry in 1955 and 1956 by the merger route. Pittsburgh Plate Glass entered the industry after Penn-Olin. In 1959, the total capacity was 41,150 tons. By 1962, the total had more than doubled and was divided as follows:

	Tons
Hooker	32,000
American Potash	22,500
Penn-Olin	26,500
Pittsburgh Plate Glass	15,000
Total	96,000

Prior to the organization of the joint venture both Pennsalt and Olin had been considering whether to build their own plants. The district court found that it was "impossible to conclude that as a matter of reasonable probability both Pennsalt and Olin would have built plants in the Southeast if Penn-Olin had not been created." Accordingly, there was "no basis for concluding that Penn-Olin had the effect of substantially lessening competition." It also found that "no reason exists to suppose that Penn-Olin will be a less effective competitor than Pennsalt or Olin would have been. The contrary conclusion is the more reasonable."[68]

However, the Supreme Court found that the lower court "erred" in failing to consider "the probability that one would have built 'while the other continued to ponder.'"[69] The Court observed that "the existence of an aggressive, well equipped and well financed corporation engaged in the same or related lines of commerce waiting anxiously to enter an oligopolistic market would be a substantial incentive to competition which cannot be underestimated."[70] The case was remanded to the lower court because, the Supreme Court concluded, "a finding should have been made as to the reasonable probability that either one of the corporations would have entered the market by building a plant, while the other would have remained a significant potential competitor."[71]

On October 12, 1965 the District Court held that "the Government has failed to sustain its burden of establishing by a preponderance of the evidence that, but for the joint venture, Pennsalt as a matter of reasonable probability would have individually entered the Southeastern chlorate market."[72] The Government appealed this decision to the Supreme Court. By an equally divided court (Justice Marshall not participating) the lower court's position was affirmed without opinion. Thus, the Penn-Olin joint venture finally was held not to be in violation of the Clayton Act.[73]

Potential Competition: The main thrust of the Supreme Court's decision in Penn-Olin dealt with the role of potential competition and the failure of the lower court to evaluate the competitive effects if the joint venture had eliminated a potential competitor.

The Court failed to distinguish between potential competition and a potential competitor. The effects of potential competition are not diluted because one potential competitor is eliminated unless it is the only company which may enter the market. These two companies were not the only potential competitors. According to the Department of Justice:

Rumor around the industry suggested that a number of chemical companies had that very idea [entry]: The Solvay Division of Allied Chemical Corporation, Wyandotte Chemicals, the Columbia-Southern Division of Pittsburgh Plate Glass, Virginia Smelting Company.[74]

Nor does this list exhaust the number of potential competitors. Producers of chlorine and caustic soda also could enter this market if the profits were attractive enough.[75] In 1959, there were at least thirty-six producers of chlorine in the United States.[76] Most of these companies had plants in the southeastern part of the United States.

Potential competitors usually cannot be identified in advance. The willingness and ability of a company to enter a market will be determined by its past experience, the products now handled, technical know-how, cost-price-profit relationships, funds available for investment, competing opportunities to use capital funds, and the philosophy of management (is it expansionist-minded or not). Moreover, the number of and identity of potential competitors change as economic conditions change. An improvement in cost-price-profit relationships, for example, will increase the number of potential competitors, while a narrowing of profit margins will have the reverse effect.

The inability to identify specific potential competitors is one reason why economists have been more concerned with the conditions of entry than with the identity of the entrants. Who was willing to predict some fifteen years ago that most of the petroleum companies would enter the chemical industry or that companies such as Eastman Kodak, W. R. Grace, and many others would, in a short period of time, obtain one-quarter or more of their sales volume from the production and sale of chemicals? The enormous expenditures for research and development have changed the conditions of entry significantly in many industries and have increased the magnitude of potential competition both from identical products and closely substitutable products.

Greater attention also must be given to the differing impact on the market of actual and potential competition. The competitive effects differ significantly in intensiveness and in effectiveness. The main impacts of potential competition are negative to the extent that they create a barrier to the ability of existing competitors to take advantage of their position by raising prices, by limiting output, or by refusing to innovate. In contrast, actual competition makes a positive contribution because it stimulates affirmative competitive responses to counter possible gains by the new competitor.

The sodium chlorate market provides a good illustration of this point. Although the presence of potential competitors undoubtedly was known to Hooker, its competitive reactions did not take place until after Penn-Olin was formed:

"After Penn-Olin's plan to build a plant at Calvert City became known, Hooker employed a new salesman who was a specialist in pulp and paper sales, and installed a pulp and paper research laboratory for its customers. It offered its customers five-year contracts guaranteeing them a firm price during the contract period. It also proposed to increase its selling efforts generally."[77]

These are the competitive responses to actual competition. Hooker didn't undertake these developments while both Olin and Pennsalt were "pondering." They were undertaken only after those two companies had acted by organizing Penn-Olin.

Where the joint venture adds an actual competitor to the market the positive contribution made to competition is far greater than that made by potential competitors "waiting on the edge of the market." The significance of one actual plus one potential as posed by the Court depends primarily upon whether the parent which remains potential is the only company in that position. If it is merely one of a group of potential competitors its impact upon competition, as it stands poised over the market, is minimal. Its elimination as a potential competitor does not dilute the restraining effects of potential competition.

Reciprocal Buying and Competition

The essence of reciprocal buying may be summed up as "we'll buy from you if you buy from us."[78] During the 1960's, reciprocal dealing came under increasing attack as an anticompetitive practice, particularly in connection with efforts by the government to prevent conglomerate mergers or to reverse them after they had taken place. Thus, the government sought to make LTV divest itself of Jones and Laughlin Steel Corp. on several grounds including the charge that the merger may substantially lessen competition because "The power . . . to benefit from reciprocity and reciprocity effects in the sales of their products will be substantially enhanced."[79]

Reciprocity has been described as "another non-price means of influencing the purchase decision."[80] It was estimated in 1965 that "About 60 percent of the companies on *Fortune's* 500 list . . . conduct reciprocal affairs."[81]

Chemical companies sell a large proportion of their output to and buy a large part of their raw materials from other chemical companies. Thus, there often is a considerable volume of buying and selling between pairs of companies who simultaneously are purchasers and suppliers.[82]

A National Industrial Conference Board study concluded that "Reciprocity appears most likely to be a way of life when the parties deal in homogeneous products with a high proportion of fixed costs; where price competition is relatively orderly; and potential buyers and sellers use each other's products in large amounts. Such transactions are more likely to occur in industrial than in consumer markets. . . ."[83]

A 1961 poll by *Purchasing* concluded that: ". . . reciprocity is a major factor in buyer-seller relations" in the basic raw material industries.[84] It is not unique to chemicals. According to some writers, reciprocal buying generally has been associated with the larger and more diversified firms which have a greater opportunity to act in the dual capacity of buyer and supplier with respect to another company.[85]

The anticompetitive effects alleged to attend reciprocal buying include: preemption of part of the market to the favored seller, increase in market power for large diversified firms, discouraging potential entrants into the industry, concealing secret rebates, and reduction in competition and efficiency.[86] In effect, it is claimed that bigness breeds bigness with reciprocal buying contributing to the result. The Supreme Court has held that "reciprocity made possible by [mergers] is one of the congeries of anticompetitive practices at which the antitrust laws are aimed."[87] Consolidated Foods had acquired Gentry, which manufactured dehydrated onions and garlic. The Court found that "Consolidated did undertake to assist Gentry in selling. . . . Reciprocity was tried over and over again and it sometimes worked."

It was reported in 1961 that the larger firms have a greater opportunity as well as a greater propensity to engage in reciprocity buying.[88] However, more recent studies are not available. It is probable in light of the Supreme Court decisions and the actions taken by the Department of Justice and the Federal

Trade Commission since 1961 that a significantly different picture prevails currently. In any event, as Professor George J. Stigler has pointed out: ". . . systematic quantitative study of the extent of reciprocity has never been made."[89]

A special study prepared for President Richard Nixon concluded: "The economic threat to competition from reciprocity (reciprocal buying arrangements) is either small or nonexistent: monopoly power in one commodity is not effectively exploited by manipulating the price of an unrelated commodity."[90]

Professor Ferguson also has emphasized reciprocity is not dependent upon the existence of market power.

> "The fact that reciprocity is often practiced by firms without market power is strong evidence that there are legitimate reasons for the practice. . . . The inevitable conclusion is that reciprocity is not a phenomenon that depends on market power, and the removal of market concentration would not eliminate the factors that give rise to reciprocity."[91]

Joel Dean has observed that reciprocal buying may in itself be a form of competition in oligopolistic markets.

> "In most cases, reciprocal trading is just one of the many forms that competition takes in oligopolistic industries. In some other cases, reciprocity is a symptom of market power but nothing more than a symptom. Reciprocity doesn't add anything to the market power. It is just a way to exercise it."[92]

The allegation that efficiency and competition tend to be lessened because a company is willing to sacrifice the quality of its purchases in order to promote better sales relations with its customers,[93] does not seem applicable to chemicals which are standardized and which in most instances sell at identical prices.[94] The chemical processes require materials of a designated quality. However, despite the identity of products there may be differences in delivery, services rendered, credit terms, and other nonprice factors. It has been reported that one chemical company, Dixon Chemical and Research, was able to maintain its sales "by offering better and faster delivery service to counter the reciprocal pressure of its big competitors."[95]

When the element of coercion is present reciprocal buying is held by the antitrust enforcement agencies to be analagous to tying arrangements. And since tie-ins generally are condemned as suppressing competition, the Federal Trade Commission concluded that coercive reciprocal buying should be similarly condemned. The real problem, however, arises not when coercion is present, but when it is only implied by the market setting.

Several companies have been charged by the government with engaging in illegal reciprocity. Two illustrations are General Dynamics—Liquid Carbonic and GAF Corp. In 1957 General Dynamics merged with Liquid Carbonic, the largest firm in the carbon dioxide industry. In 1962, the government brought a civil antitrust suit charging a violation of the Clayton Act and the Sherman Act because of the defendant's special sales program involving reciprocity.

The District Court Judge held in 1966 that this acquisition violated Section 7 of the Clayton Act since it created "leverage reciprocity," the ability to obtain sales through the systematic application of buying power. General Dynamics had substantial power, but gained no competitive advantage from it until the merger, since it sold the overwhelming proportion of its items to the government. Thus, the merger was held to permit this purchasing power to be used against suppliers who could now use a product manufactured by a division of General Dynamics.

The reciprocity arrangement also was held to have violated Section 1 of the Sherman Act, since at the time of the merger both General Dynamics and Liquid Carbonic had the intent to use the anticompetitive practice of reciprocity to increase sales of the acquired firm. The Court held that reciprocity based on either coercion or on mutual patronage is anticompetitive when it affected an amount of commerce that was considered to be substantial. In late 1966, under a consent decree General Dynamics agreed to divest itself of Liquid Carbonic. They were forbidden to use reciprocity power to obtain sales of carbon dioxide or other industrial gases.[96]

In March 1969, GAF Corp. gave the FTC an affidavit in which the company "agreed to pursue a policy with its suppliers and customers by which all GAF sales will be made solely on the basis of price, quality and services, and all GAF purchases will be made at the lowest price and most favorable terms."[97] Other companies which agreed to discontinue reciprocity as a result of Federal Trade Commission charges included: American Standard Inc. (January 24, 1968), Union-Camp (February 2, 1969) and U.S. Steel (June 13, 1969).

Firms engaging in reciprocal buying must be scrupulously careful in their dealings. If they keep formal records of the volume of purchases and then seek to induce the seller to make reciprocal purchases they will be vulnerable to antitrust actions. Occasional purchases in relatively small volume do not create a problem. It is the systematic arrangement which has been subject to challenge as an antitrust violation.

There may be good business reasons for reciprocal buying. As Corwin Edwards has noted " . . . concerns become one another's customers because each is the best and cheapest source of supply for what the other wants."[98]

Obviously, it doesn't make sense to say that a company should not buy from a supplier who also is a good customer. If quality, service, and price are equal among competing sellers, it is illogical to hold that if you deal with your friends you are guilty of an anticompetitive act. In response to the following question: "when those features may all be equal . . . would you say that the company would be free to deal with its friends or should they toss up a coin. . . .?", Rufus E. Wilson, chief of the FTC Division of General Restraints answered: "I don't see anything wrong with going along and helping out your Yale brothers or your fellow Shriners or your friends."[99]

It is good business policy to study the market carefully to make sure that a preferred seller is charging the lowest prices and offering the best terms of sale available. The rugged competition experienced for many chemicals suggests that few companies in this industry will continue a policy of reciprocal buying if a better product, better service, or a lower price can be obtained elsewhere. There appears to be little hesitancy by chemical companies to turn to other suppliers or to produce the product themselves. It is difficult to obtain the economic leverage required for the coercive application of reciprocal buying in such competitive markets. And in the absence of elements of coercion, the practice of reciprocal buying does not appear to be inherently anticompetitive although it may give an advantage to the seller involved.

Patents and Competition

Patents have played an important role in the development and growth of the American chemical industry. In light of the large R&D expenditures made by the chemical industry, it is not surprising that over the past half century the number of chemical patents granted annually has increased by a far larger amount than for industry generally. It has been estimated that "more than 20 percent of all U.S. patents issued are chemical patents."[100] In some instances, as is illustrated by polypropylene, several companies develop the product and claim the patent rights.[101] Often bitter battles have developed between chemical companies claiming patent rights for the same or substantially the same products.[102]

There has been considerable criticism that patents have had an anticompetitive effect in many industries, including chemicals. Agreements with chemical companies in other countries have been subject to particular criticism. It must be recognized that in many instances, European patent owners have insisted upon restrictive clauses as a condition for licensing American companies to produce the product. As Simon Whitney has pointed out:

> "Many of the quantity limitations on new products and refusals to license them have been conditions imposed by their European originators in licensing them to the American producers. There are progressive chemical industries in both hemispheres, and the terms on which patented knowledge could be exchanged have had to be mutually acceptable."[103]

A leading case involved various patents and processes of Du Pont and Imperial Chemical Industries which had reached an arrangement in 1920. In 1951, a district court held that the "agreements irrespective of their *per se* legality, were instruments designed and intended to accomplish the worldwide allocation of markets; their object was to achieve an unlawful purpose—an illegal restraint of trade prohibited by section one of the Sherman Act."[104] The resulting decree provided for "compulsory licensing of patents at reasonable royalty"[105] and affected such products as nylon and sodium.[106] Imperial Chemical Industries subsequently combined with Celanese to organize Fiber Industries which produces Fortrel in competition with Du Pont's Dacron which was "originally developed by ICI and later licensed to Du Pont."[107]

The patent system is designed to give the inventor an exclusive right for 17 years. Sometimes the patent may be used to keep out competitors. This appears to have been the effect of the polyethylene patent rights Du Pont obtained from Imperial Chemical. A number of companies entered this industry after 1952 when the court decree made this possible. It should be noted, however, that in the chemical industry when a product or process patent is issued other researchers often soon develop competing products or processes in what the industry calls an "end run."

Similarly, successful antitrust suits against National Lead and Du Pont resulted in a decree under which they had to grant non-exclusive licenses at reasonable royalties for titanium compounds.[108] Francis G. Masson subsequently concluded that this ". . . change in patent licensing policy . . . has been a significant influence in easing the barriers to entry."[109]

On the other hand, patents do not always play a primary role in determining ease of entry. Thus, after reviewing the role of patents in the rayon industry, Jesse W. Markham concluded:

> "The extent to which patents have limited the number of rayon producers in the United States is not clear but most of the available evidence indicates that considerations other than patent rights have been the determining factors since 1918. . . . The period since 1930, by which time nearly all basic patents had become public property, has been marked by a complete absence of new entrants to the industry. Obviously, therefore, more significant factors than the legal monopolization of specific processes restrict entry to the rayon industry."[110]

In this connection, too, it is interesting to note that since World War II, Du Pont has listed the majority of its patents as available for licensing, and has aided several firms to enter chemical lines in which it was the leading producer. Simon Whitney has noted that:

"The most spectacular reaction of Du Pont to the post war antitrust attacks has been its policy of helping to get competitors into operation on the basis of its own patents and technical information. The chief examples have been in metallic sodium (licensed to National Distillers Products Corporation), nylon and cellophane. The question has been asked whether Du Pont will want to compete vigorously against firms it has deliberately helped to set up, and whether the government's policy of inducing or harrying it to create competitors really promotes 'the competition the antitrust laws were designed to nourish.' Observers of the chemical industry have as yet found no signs of a slackening in competitive efforts."[111]

A key facet of competition in the chemical industry is the availability of substitute products. Although other companies may not be able to produce the patented product they can and do produce substitutes which will meet similar or identical needs.

The ability to obtain patent protection provides the incentive to spend enormous sums for research and development. Unless some advantage is obtained by a company why should it spend large sums for these purposes? And when a new product or process is discovered why should the company make large investments for its production if the results of its research were to be made generally available without restriction immediately?

In some instances, competitors are encouraged to enter the field with competitive products because they also can obtain patent protection. There are many illustrations of patented products subject to intense competition as is noted throughout this study. The man-made fibers are illustrative. For many uses, Acrilan, Orlon, nylon and other products are substitutable. A number of different companies entered the field, therefore, despite the patent protection for nylon held by Du Pont.

Similarly, when Du Pont patented Delrin, Celanese responded by seeking a patent for Celcon. Both products are strong and durable plastics which can be used as replacements for metals.[112]

Cellophane is another illustration of a product whose patent does not insulate it from competition by a variety of substitute products such as Glassine, aluminum foil, Pliofilm, polyethylene, Saran, and other flexible packaging materials.

Patents relating to the production of SBR, neoprene, butyl, and nitrile synthetic rubbers did not prevent the development of the others such as polyisoprene and polybutadiene.

In connection with Monsanto's patent of All, Wroe Alderson points out:

". . . all the patentee received was limited market entry protection. He was only one of the suppliers competing for a place in the family wash even though he only could offer the presumed advantages of washing clothes with a low sudsing detergent. It is characteristic of monopolistic competition that a number of competitors offer to perform the same function, each claiming that his product is different and therefore best."[113]

Similarly, in connection with a patent for Krillium, a product which would "change the structure of soil almost instantly," Alderson reported "A rash of soil conditioners came into existence a year or two after Krillium was announced, but all soon fizzled out—Krillium was a failure, too. . . . For nearly a year Monsanto was the only producer of a soil conditioner, thus enjoying a very unprofitable monopoly."[114]

The frequency with which companies develop new products which compete with those they already are producing is well known in the chemical industry.

Patents do not necessarily inhibit price competition as has been amply demonstrated by organic chemicals in recent years. Despite patents for many of these products, price cutting has been most extensive. Moreover, many of these products must compete with others produced either by the chemical industry or with those produced by other industries. Thus, competitive pressures often are inherent in the creation of new products which are "protected by patents."

It is possible of course to utilize patents as an anticompetitive device. Such practices can be and must be dealt with under the antitrust laws. But instances of abuses are not the basis for a condemnation of all patents nor do they suggest that all patents will be accompanied by anticompetitive practices. Patents have a constructive role to perform, particularly in the chemical industry, in which "test tube" competition has been such a vital force over the years.

Summary and Conclusions

There are no precise yardsticks to determine the effectiveness of competition in any industry. One approach is to seek out and to focus upon evidence of variations from the norms of perfect competition as outlined in theory. On the basis of that standard, every industry would fall short of the theoretical ideal. Alternatively, the long term record of performance of an industry, as reflected in its growth, prices, profits, research and development, and related areas might be examined. The performance generally has been superior for the chemical industry in terms of the usual standards: prices have declined more or risen less than the general price level while growth, profits, and research and development expenditures have been above the average, often by considerable margins. Unfortunately, there is no way to determine whether the record would have been even better within a different competitive framework or to measure the extent of any improvement that might have taken place under such circumstances.

The availability of substitutes adds a significant dimension to competition in the chemical industry. Chemicals face competition from other chemicals (interproduct competition), from other processes (interprocess competition), and from products of other industries (interindustry competition). The availability of these alternatives influences the environment within which decisions must be made concerning pricing, sales strategy, research and development, and various forms of nonprice competition.

In recent years, price cutting, often quite sharp, had replaced price stability as a major characteristic of many chemicals, particularly the organics. Price reductions were associated with excess capacity, the entry of new producers, the expansion of foreign production, and the desire to broaden markets. Identical bids in goverment contracts are to be anticipated for chemicals because they are identical or closely identified products, small amounts usually are involved in individual transactions, price lists are published, there are relatively few sellers, and information on past bids in publicly available. The competitive pressures and the economic characteristics of the products involved result in identical bids.

Nonprice competition in the chemical industry emphasizes technical services, quality, and product improvement through research and development. The availability of technical services is the most important form of nonprice competition; brand names have been significant mainly for synthetic fibers.

Joint ventures have resulted in an increase in the number of competitors in some chemical markets. Often, when one chemical company participates in a joint venture, others also have organized such companies thus increasing the number of competitors. The vigorous competition which has dominated many chemical markets in recent years indicates that partners in one joint venture do not use a kid gloves approach when they meet, as they often do, in other markets.

Chemical companies sell a considerable volume of products to other chemical companies. However, as a result of keen competition, there appears to be little hesitancy by chemical companies to shift to new suppliers or, in some instances, to produce a product themselves.

Patents have been of considerable importance in the chemical industry. In some instances they have facilitated a limitation over the number of producers. However, judicial actions have modified some of these restrictions. The presence of a patent also tends to intensify research efforts to find substitute products or alternate processes, sometimes leading into entirely new areas of technology. Thus, because of the many substitute products available and the intensive research activities of most chemical companies, competition often develops despite the protection of patents. That patents do not inhibit price competition has been amply demonstrated by organic chemicals in recent years.

[1] Professor George Stigler has noted the categories of pure theory "are designed to simplify analyses, not to characterize specific industries." George J. Stigler, *Five Lectures on Economic Problems*, Macmillan Co., New York, 1949, p. 47.

[2] *Report of The Attorney General's National Commitee to Study the Antitrust Laws*, Washington, D.C., March 31, 1955, p. 320.

[3] ". . . the rapid introduction of new herbicides, each designed for a specific job rather than for a broad spectrum of applications [is] challenging the dominance of the older, multi-purpose products." J. F. Bourland, "The Challenge in Marketing for Agricultural Chemicals" in *Chemical Marketing:. The Challenges of the Seventies*, American Chemical Society, Washington, D.C., September 1968, p. 9.

[4] Malcolm J. Harkins and Charles E. Wallace, "The Chemical Industry" in *The Development of American Industries*, edited by John G. Glover and Rudolph L. Lagai, Simmons-Boardman Publishing Corp., New York, 1959, p. 307.

[5] *Chemical Week*, March 29, 1969, p. 37 projected that by 1973, polyester fibers will have the largest share of the tire market.

[6] *Modern Plastics*, January 1963, p. 93.

[7] *Chemical Week*, April 5, 1969, p. 48.

[8] *Chemicals - Basic Analysis*, Standard & Poor's, Industry Surveys, October 25, 1962, p. C-39.

[9] *Modern Plastics*, January 1963, p. 112.

[10] *Chemical Week*, September 15, 1962, p. 122.

[11] *Chemical Week*, November 16, 1968, p. 136.

[12] Giragosian, *op. cit.*, p. 46.

[13] Sciancalepore, *op. cit.*, pp. 21-22.

[14]For an interesting evaluation of savings in manpower and in use of resources when cellulosic man-made fibers are substituted for cotton, see Vivian E. Spencer, "Raw Materials in the United States Economy: 1960-1961," *Working Paper No. 6,* Bureau of the Census, U.S. Department of Commerce, Washington, D.C., 1963, pp. 23, 26.

[15]David H. Dawson, "Opportunities Ahead for the Chemical Industry," before the National Federation of Financial Analysis Societies, Richmond, Va., May 2, 1961, pp. 6-7.

[16]U.S. Department of Commerce, Business and Defense Services Administration, *U. S. Industrial Outlook 1968,* Washington, D.C., December 1967, p. 132.

[17]*U.S. v. E.I. du Pont de Nemours & Co.,* 351 U.S. 377, 379, 404, 405 (1956).

[18]Robert F. Lanzillotti, "Pricing of Chemical Products," *Chemical and Engineering News,* April 30, 1962, p. 100. See also George W. Stocking and Myron W. Watkins, *Cartels in Action,* The Twentieth Century Fund, New York, 1964, p. 395; *Fortune,* December 1937, p. 157.

[19]For a number of illustrations in other industries see Testimony of Jules Backman, *Hearings on Economic Concentration,* before the Subcommittee on Antitrust and Monopoly of the Committee on the Judiciary, United States Senate, 89th Cong., 1st Sess., Washington, D.C., Part 2 (1965), pp. 896-98.

[20]See issues of July 30, 1962, pp. 65-68; October 29, 1962, pp. 56-58; January 21, 1963, pp. 52, 54; April 29, 1963, pp. 62-64 and July 29, 1963, pp. 52-54.

[21]*Chemical and Engineering News,* October 29, 1962, p. 56; January 21, 1963, p. 53; April 29, 1963, pp. 63-64; July 29, 1963, p. 53.

[22]*Chemical Week,* February 3, 1968, p. 36.

[23]*Ibid.,* January 11, 1969, p. 57.

[24]*Chemical Week,* March 2, 1968, p. 39.

[25]*Ibid.,* August 5, 1967, p. 67.

[26]*Ibid.,* February 3, 1968, p. 36.

[27]*Ibid.,* March 23, 1968, p. 54.

[28]*The Wall Street Journal,* December 3, 1968.

[29]*Ibid.,* January 7, 1969.

[30]*Ibid.,* May 20, 1968.

[31]Robert F. Lanzillotti, "Pricing of Chemical Products," *Chemical and Engineering News,* April 30, 1962, p. 102.

[32]Joint Economic Committee, *93 Lots of Bids Involving Identical Bids Reported to the Department of Justice by the Federal Procurement Agencies in the Years 1955-60,* U.S Government Printing Office, Washington, D.C., August 1961, pp. 18-39. At the request of the Joint Economic Committee, the U.S. Department of Justice made available every fifth abstract in its files dealing with identical bidding for the years 1955 to 1960. These data had been filed with the Justice Department under the Armed Services Procurement Act of 1947 and the Federal Property and Administrative Services Act of 1949. In 1952, government officials reached agreements ". . . to eliminate reporting of identical bids except in those instances where the procurement agencies are able to supply additional, substantiating evidence that the antitrust laws have been violated." (p. vii.)

[33]*Ibid.,* p. viii.

[34]C. Brien Dillon, "But the Other Referee Said!" *The Texas Law Review,* June 1961, p. 784.

[35]Paul W. Cook, Jr., "Fact and Fancy on Identical Bids," *Harvard Business Review*, January-February 1963, p. 68. See also Cyrus V. Anderson, "Legal and Economic Aspects of Price Uniformity," *Chemical and Engineering News*, April 30, 1962, p. 104.

[36]See Jules Backman, *The Economics of the Electrical Machinery Industry*, New York University Press, New York, 1962, pp. 135-37.

[37]Professor Vernon A. Mund, a severe critic of identical bids, has recognized that small volume orders may provide no inducement to depart from prevailing list price. Vernon A. Mund, "Identical Bid Prices," *The Journal of Political Economy*, April 1960, p. 161.

[38]See, for example, testimony of Ralph J. Cordiner, *Hearings on Administered Prices*, before the Subcommittee on Antitrust and Monopoly, Senate Committee on the Judiciary, 87th Con., 1st Sess., 1961, part 28, p. 17,673.

[39]*Identical Bidding in Public Procurement*, Report of the Attorney General Under Executive Order 10963, July 1962, pp. 7-8.

[40]See Jules Backman, *Price Practices and Price Policies*, The Ronald Press Co., New York, 1953, ch. 4.

[41]*Chemical Week*, June 18, 1955, p. 42.

[42]Joe S. Bain, *Industrial Organization*, John Wiley & Sons, New York, 1959, p. 220.

[43]Arthur B. Steel, "Technical Service and Application Research-Industrial Chemicals and Plastics," in "Chemical Marketing: the Challenge of the Seventies," *op. cit.*, p. 104.

[44]John M. Rathmell, "The Service Components in Chemical Product Marketing" in *Papers of Chemical Marketing and Economics*, September 1966, p. 29. See also R. W. McCullough, "Organization of the Technical Service Effort," *Ibid.*, pp. 91-94.

[45]*Chemical Week*, June 2, 1962, p. 29.

[46]*Opportunities Ahead for the Chemical Industry*, An address before the National Federation of Financial Analysts Societies, Richmond, Va., May 2, 1961, pp. 13-14.

[47]*The Dow Chemical Company, 1967 Annual Report*, p. 5.

[48]*Chemical Week*, June 2, 1962, p. 30.

[49]*Celanese Annual Report 1968*, pp. 6, 7.

[50]*Allied Chemical 1966 Annual Report*, p. 12.

[51]*Allied Chemical Corporation Annual Report 1967*, p. 12.

[52]Charles F. Phillips, Jr., *Competition in The Synthetic Rubber Industry*, The University of North Carolina Press, Chapel Hill, N.C., 1963, pp. 209-10.

[53]*Chemical Week*, November 3, 1962, p. 33.

[54]Dry cleaning and other solvents, *The Wall Street Journal*, December 11, 1968; polymethylene polyphenylisocyanate, *Ibid.*, March 17, 1966.

[55]*Chemical Week*, August 5, 1967, p. 68.

[56]Alfred E. Kahn, "The Chemical Industry" in *The Structure of American Industry*, edited by Walter Adams, The Macmillan Co., New York, 1963, 3rd edition, p. 249. See also Stocking and Watkins, *op. cit.*, p. 392.

[57]Simon Whitney, *Antitrust Policies*, Twentieth Century Fund, New York, 1958, Vol. 1, p. 236.

[58]A Federal Trade Commission study reported that 46 joint ventures were formed in chemicals and allied products in 1966, 32 in 1967, and 27 in 1968. For all industry, the totals were 157, 111, and 105. *Chemical Week*, June 7, 1969, p. 16.

[59]For example, Goodrich-Gulf combined the technical knowledge of petroleum and of synthetic rubber possessed by the two parents. In 1969, Goodrich acquired sole ownership of this joint venture.

[60]Petrochemicals provide an outstanding illustration with petroleum and chemical companies establishing the joint ventures.

[61]For example, Dow Corning Company combined Dow Chemical's know-how in chemistry and Corning's know-how with glass to produce silicones.

[62]Penn-Olin provides an illustration.

[63]Corwin D. Edwards, "Conglomerate Bigness As A Source of Power," *Business Concentration and Public Policy,* National Bureau of Economic Research, Princeton University Press, Princeton, New Jersey, 1955, p. 343.

[64]Paul Rand Dixon, *Joint Ventures: What Is Their Impact on Competition,* an address before the Economic Club of Detroit, Michigan, March 12, 1962, 7 Antitrust Bulletin 397 (1962), and Richard W. McLaren, *Current Antitrust Division Policy on Mergers, Acquisitions and Joint Ventures,* An Address before the Town Hall of California, May 27, 1969, pp. 14-17 (mimeo).

[65]Dixon, *op. cit.,* p. 12. See also Stocking and Watkins, *op. cit.,* p. 389.

[66]*United States v. Penn-Olin Chem. Co.,* 378 U.S. 158, 164 (1964).

[67]The Celler-Kefauver Act, 64 Stat. 1125 (1950), 15 U.S.C. Sec. 18 (1964), amended the original Sec. 7 of the Clayton Act, 38 Stat. 731 (1914), to prohibit the acquisition of the whole or any part of the assets of another corporation " . . . where in any line of commerce in any section of the country the effect of such acquisition may be substantially to lessen competition or to tend to create a monopoly."

[68]217 F. Supp. 128-31.

[69]378 U.S. 173.

[70]*Ibid.,* p. 174.

[71]*Ibid.,* pp. 175-76.

[72]*U.S. v. Penn-Olin Chemical Co.,* D.C. Del., 246 F. Supp. 917, in Commerce Clearing House, *1965 Trade Cases,* Chicago, Illinois, 1966, pp. 81-90.

[73]*U.S. v. Penn-Olin Chemical Co.,* 389 U.S. 308 (1967), in Commerce Clearing House, *1967 Trade Cases,* Chicago, Illinois, 1968, p. 84, 752. See also Robert Pitofsky, "Joint Ventures Under the Antitrust Laws: Some Reflections on the Significance of Penn-Olin," *Harvard Law Review,* March 1969, pp. 1007-63.

[74]Post-Trial Brief of the United States, p. 10, *United States v. Penn-Olin Chem. Co.,* 217 F. Supp. 110 (D. Del. 1963).

[75]Sodium chlorate "is produced commercially by the electrolysis of an acidified solution of salt (sodium chloride). The process is closely akin to that used in the commercial production of chlorine and caustic soda." *United States v. Penn-Olin Chem. Co.,* 271 F. Supp. 110, 115 (D. Del. 1963).

[76]*Chemical Week,* March 7, 1959, pp. 114, 117.

[77]*United States v. Penn-Olin Chem. Co.,* 217 F. Supp. 110, 126 (D. Del. 1963), rev'd, 378 U.S. 158 (1964).

[78]"Reciprocity Smirks Behind the Sales Smile," *Chemical Week,* November 22, 1958; p. 39. See also *The Wall Street Journal,* June 26, 1963 and December 4, 1963.

[79]*Complaint in Civil Action No. 69-438,* U.S. District Court, Western District of Pennsylvania, April 14, 1969.

[80]Leonard S. Simon, "Economic and Legal Determinants of Reciprocal Buying," *Chemical Marketing and Economics Papers,* September 1966, p. 37.

[81] Edward McCreary, Jr. and Walter Guzzardi, Jr., "A Customer Is A Company's Best Friend," *Fortune,* June 1965, p. 180.

[82] In Germany, 22% of the output is used in the chemical industry, in France 20%, and in The Netherlands 25%. Organisation for Economic Co-operation and Development, *The Chemical Industry, 1967-1968,* Paris, 1969, p. 25.

[83] Betty Bock, *Mergers and Markets,* Fifth Edition, Studies in Business Economics, Number Ninety-Three, National Industrial Conference Board, New York, 1966, p. 194.

[84] Leonard Sloane, "Reciprocity: Where Does the P.A. Stand?," *Purchasing,* November 20, 1961, p. 71.

[85] G. W. Stocking and W. F. Mueller, "Business Reciprocity and the Size of Firms," *The Journal of Business,* April 1957, p. 76. See also Melvin Mandell, "Reciprocity-Industry's Secret Sales Weapon," *Dun's Review and Modern Industry,* September 1960, p. 32.

[86] Stocking and Watkins, *op. cit.,* p. 404. See also Robert M. Hausman, "Reciprocal Dealing and the Antitrust Laws," *Harvard Law Review,* March 1964, pp. 879-80 and Rufus E. Wilson, "A Look At Reciprocity-Today," an Address before the Trade Relations Association, Inc., Colorado Springs, Colorado, September 26, 1968, pp. 3-4.

[87] *FTC v. Consolidated Foods Corp.,* 380 U.S. 592, 594 (1965).

[88] In the *Purchasing* poll, 78% of the purchasing agents of companies with a volume over $50 million annually said that reciprocity was a factor in their sales or purchases but it was a factor for less than half the firms with sales volume below $10 million. Sloane, *op. cit.,* p. 72.

[89] George J. Stigler, "Reciprocity", *Working Paper for The Task Force On Productivity and Competition,* 1969, p. 1.

[90] *The Task Force On Productivity and Competition* (George J. Stigler, chairman), 1969, p. 20.

[91] James M. Ferguson, "Tying Arrangements and Reciprocity: An Economic Analysis," *Law and Contemporary Problems,* Summer, 1965, p. 579.

[92] Joel Dean, "What The Courts Are Deciding: An Economist's View," in *The Climate of Antitrust,* National Industrial Conference Board, Inc., New York, 1963, p. 33.

[93] Milton Handler, "Emerging Antitrust Issues: Reciprocity, Diversification, and Joint Ventures," in "The Climate of Antitrust," *op. cit.,* p. 9.

[94] D. S. Ammer, "Realistic Reciprocity," *Harvard Business Review,* January-February, 1962, pp. 116-17.

[95] Mandell, *op. cit.,* p. 34.

[96] *U. S. v. General Dynamics Corp.,* 258 F Supp 36, in Commerce Clearing House, 1966 Trade Cases, Chicago, Illinois, 1967, pp. 83, 038-62 and 83, 370-77.

[97] *The Wall Street Journal,* March 19, 1969.

[98] Corwin D. Edwards, *Maintaining Competition,* McGraw Hill Book Company, New York, 1949, p. 179.

[99] Wilson, *op. cit.,* p. 4.

[100] *Oil, Paint and Drug Reporter,* March 28, 1968.

[101] In June 1963, Du Pont and Montecatini, a leading Italian producer agreed to grant non-exclusive licenses to each other whichever company obtains the patent rights. *The New York Times,* June 14, 1963.

[102] Polyethylene provides an illustration. This dispute was finally settled by an agreement between Du Pont and Phillips Petroleum to exchange patent rights. *Chemical and Engineering News,* September 4, 1961, p. 25.

[103]Whitney, *op. cit.,* p. 247.

[104]*United States vs. Imperial Chemical Industries, Ltd.,* 100 F. Supp. 504, 592 (S.D.N.Y. 1951).

[105]Corwin D. Edwards, *Big Business and the Policy of Competition,* The Press of Western Reserve University, Cleveland, Ohio, 1956, p. 143.

[106]Whitney, *op. cit.,* p. 213. Before the Court's decision had been handed down, Du Pont licensed Chemstrand to produce nylon, *Ibid.,* pp. 216-17.

[107]*Chemical Processing,* February 1961, p. 26.

[108]*U.S. vs National Lead Co.,* 63 F. Supp., 513 (S.D. N.Y. 1945); 332 U.S. 319 (1947).

[109]Francis G. Masson, "Structure and Performance in the Titanium Industry," *Journal of Industrial Economics,* July, 1955, p. 227.

[110]Markham, *op. cit.,* pp. 23-24.

[111]Whitney, *op. cit.,* p. 225.

[112]*Christian Science Monitor,* April 2, 1963.

[113]Wroe Alderson, "A Marketing View of the Patent System in *Patents and Progress,* edited by Wroe Alderson, Vern Terpstra, and Stanley J. Shapiro, Richard D. Irwin, Inc., Homewood, Illinois, 1965, p. 231.

[114]*Ibid.,* p. 232.

Chapter VI

Patterns of Competition

In the two preceding chapters, various aspects of competition in the chemical industry were discussed in broad terms with illustrations drawn from a wide spectrum of products. However, the competitive pressures and structure described prevail in myriad combinations within the industry because of its many thousands of products.

To illustrate varying competitive patterns, nine important products have been selected for a brief survey: two inorganic chemicals (chlorine and sulfuric acid), one primary organic chemical (benzene), three organic intermediates (phenol phthalic anhydride, and butadiene), and three organic chemical end products, (synthetic fibers, polyethylene, and synthetic rubber). With one exception (phthalic anhydride) these are fairly large volume products.

For each product, the major competitive factors have been identified and briefly summarized. It must be emphasized that an in depth examination of competition could result in a good sized volume for each product. Nevertheless, even these brief reviews show clearly the significantly different combinations of competitive factors which are found in the chemical industry.

Benzene

Benzene is an important petrochemical. About four-fifths of the output is used to manufacture styrene, phenol, and other polymer intermediates. Thus, it is a basic raw material for an important part of the organic chemical industry. Benzene originally was derived from coal tar. However, since the mid-fifties there has been a dramatic shift to petroleum so that more than 80% of the output is now derived from that source — and the proportion will continue to grow. In 1966, 955 million gallons of benzene were produced.[1] Since the average sales price was 24 cents a gallon, output had a value of $230 million.[2] Production totaled 969 million gallons in 1967.[3] Output has risen sharply in the postwar period from 168 million gallons in 1947.

In 1960, there were 54 producers of benzene with a total capacity of 572 million gallons. In 1968, there were 51 companies that produced benzene with a capacity of 1,268 million gallons. This included 35 petroleum based companies that had a capacity of 1,141 million gallons and 16 coal-derived benzene producing companies with a capacity of 127 million gallons.[4]

Most of the expansion has been concentrated in petroleum benzene capacity which more than doubled from an estimated 359 million gallons for 18 producers in 1960 to 809 million for 32 producers in 1965. By 1968 capacity had been increased further to 1,141 million gallons and the number of producers to 35. Thus, 14 companies entered this industry between 1960 and 1965 while an additional three companies had entered by 1968. One of the latter group, Commonwealth Petrochemicals, had the second largest capacity in 1968 (See Table VI-1).

There is much less concentration of benzene capacity than for most other chemicals. For example, Enjay and Commonwealth, the two largest producers, each account for less than 10% of the total industry capacity. Five of the ten largest producers in 1965 had not produced benzene five years earlier. The four largest producers in 1960 accounted for 50.4% of the capacity while in 1965, the Big Four accounted for 37.0% and included one company which was a new entrant. By 1968 the Big Four accounted for only 30.7% and included one new producer.[5]

Benzene provides a natural means of diversification for petroleum companies in view of their raw material position, familiarity with technology, and the availability of plant designs and processes. The development of dealkylation processes facilitated the conversion of toluene into benzene and "the thought of upgrading 19 cents a gallon toluene into 34 cents a gallon benzene appealed to many [petroleum] companies."[6] However, it has been reported that "When the price difference between benzene and toluene reaches 6-7 cents per gallon, hydroalkylation units . . . are usually the first to be shut down because they are the least economical."[7]

TABLE VI-1

Petroleum Based Benzene Capacity, 1960, 1965 and 1968

	1960	1965	1968
	(millions of gallons)		
Enjay	54	79	108
Commonwealth	—	—	100
Shell	60	96	82
Monsanto	—	65	70
Gulf Oil	32	59	70
Dow	—	50	57
Mobil Chemical	—	30	50
Union Carbide	—	10	50
Sunray DX Oil	15*	48*	48
Atlantic Richfield	18	36	42
Texaco	—	30	40
Union Oil	—	22	39
Hess Oil	35	30	35
Coastal States	—	—	33
Sinclair	—	—	32
Ashland Oil	8	30	30
Cosden	—	9	29
Chevron Chemical	31	35	25
Phillips	—	22	22
Signal Oil	7	22	20
Crown Central	—	38	20
Tenneco	—	15	15
Sun Oil	20	15	15
Standard Oil (Indiana)	30**	15	10
All others (7 cos.)	49	—	—
All others (8 cos.)	—	53	—
All others (11 cos.)	—	—	99
Total	359	809	1,141

*Includes 6 million gallons from Suntide in 1960 and 25 million gallons in 1965 later merged into Sunray DX Oil.

**Includes 15 million gallons from Amoco Chemicals; by 1965 Whiting plant closed down.

Sources: Chemical and Engineering News, March 20, 1961, p. 118; *Hydrocarbon Processing,* September 1965, p. 2111. Stanford Research Institute, *Chemical Economics Handbook,* Menlo Park, California, 1968, pp. 618, 5020H-L.

In 1962, nine companies were reported to have plants with a capacity of 144 million gallons a year to produce benzene from toluene.[8] When benzene prices were cut to 25 cents a gallon in 1962, production through this process became less attractive and output was cut back. Early in 1964, it was reported that several units had been closed while others were operated only occasionally because of the narrow spread between the prices of toluene and benzene.[9] Nevertheless, by 1965 total capacity based on the toluene process had increased to more than 200 million gallons[10] and by 1970 was expected to exceed 400 million gallons.[11]

To some extent, capacity can be shifted to other products. Thus, for example, in 1962 Signal Oil & Gas Company shifted to the production of cyclohexane at its 15 million gallon plant "although by a relatively simple catalyst switch the company can return to benzene production on short notice."[12]

One alternative for plants using the dealkylation process has been to "hydrogenate kerosene for jet fuel."[13] Ashland Oil and Refining shifted its plant to the production of naphthalene.[14]

The relative magnitude of exports of benzene has played an important competitive role. Such exports have averaged about 10% of output. As exports decline, the available supplies increase domestically and create pressure on prices as was evident in the 1967-68 period. Benzene capacity overseas is increasing much more rapidly than in the United States with an adverse impact on our exports and an accompanying intensification of competitive pressures in this country.

The tremendous increase in capacity periodically results in an excess supply with accompanying pressures on price. Thus, the price of benzene was reduced by 3 cents a gallon three times in 1961 and 1962 — from 34 cents to 25 cents as a result of overcapacity. Again in 1967-68, decreasing exports and declines in domestic consumption led to an "oversupply" of benzene and prices fell by 4 cents a gallon.[15]

Benzene provides an interesting illustration of a product for which tight supply and satisfactory profit opportunities attract new companies into production. However, the same opportunity is grasped simultaneously by a number of existing producers with the resulting development of excessive capacity. Sharp price cuts then take place and reduce the profitability of producing benzene whereupon some producers seek to shift those facilities to more profitable products.

Chlorine

Chlorine, a bulk chemical derived largely from common salt,[16] has been produced in the United States since 1896. It has "thousands of end uses"[17] in a large number of chemical processes particularly as a bleaching agent in the pulp and paper industry and as a bactericide. In 1965, the value of shipments was $179.8 million. The increases in the value of shipments since 1958 have been as follows:[18]

Years	Millions
1958	$117.4
1963	164.9
1964	173.5
1965	179.8

The value of shipments does not include chlorine consumed captively at the same plant site — a significant portion of total chlorine consumption.

In the electrolysis process, which accounts for "practically all" the chlorine produced.,[19] caustic soda (sodium hydroxide) is produced as a by-product. The yield of caustic soda is about 10% more by weight than that of chlorine and this ratio cannot be significantly varied. Consumption of chlorine has tended to grow more rapidly than that of caustic soda. The result has been the problem of periodically disposing of an excess supply of caustic soda.[20] Competition from soda ash (sodium carbonate) also is a factor in these markets.

In 1969, it was reported that the oversupply of caustic soda "has lowered prices to the point where new markets are coming into range. The loser: soda ash . . . . Caustic makes headway when its price approaches parity with soda ash on an equivalent sodium oxide content — i.e., a caustic price about 30% higher that that of soda ash."[21] As with so many other chemicals, relative prices play an important role in determining the market for caustic soda.

The production of chlorine increased at an average annual rate of 9% between 1947 and 1968. Output figures for selected years between 1947 and 1968 are shown below:[22]

Years	Million Short Tons
1947	1.4
1951	2.5
1958	3.6
1963	5.5
1967	7.6
1968	8.5

The capacity of leading producers in 1959, 1963, and 1967 is shown in Table VI-2.

TABLE VI-2
Chlorine Capacity, 1959, 1963, and 1967

Company	(Tons per Day)		
	1959	1963	1967
Dow Chemical	4085	4315	7000
Pittsburgh Plate Glass	1750	2010	2100
Diamond Alkali	1215	1280	1800
Hooker Chemical	820	890	1500
Olin Mathieson	590	970	1400
Allied Chemical	860	900	1100
Wyandotte Chemical	550	880	1000
Pennsalt	605	680	830
Stauffer Chemical	360	570	700
FMC	460	600	600
Ethyl Corporation	377	470	520
Monsanto Company	183	275	310
Du Pont	257	255	280
General Aniline and Film	50	230	230
Other producers	1400	1380	2495
Total	13,562	15,705	21,865

Source: *Chemical Week,* March 7, 1959, p. 114 and *Oil, Paint and Drug Reporter,* April 22, 1963, p. 30, September 9, 1963, p. 9, and May 1, 1967, p. 9. Somewhat different capacity estimates for some companies in 1959 are shown in *Chemical and Engineering News,* December 14, 1959, p. 38.

Before World War I there were only five companies in the business.[23] During World War I, two new companies entered the merchant market and several pulp and paper mills installed facilities to produce chlorine for their own use. Three producers entered production in the 1920s when chlorine was "widely adopted as a direct bleach for paper and to a lesser extent for water sterilization and sewage disinfection."[24]

Since World War II, most increases in production have been by firms already producing chlorine or by new small installations for captive use. In 1966, 34 companies were producing chlorine at 68 plant locations.

The shift towards greater use of chlorine in chemical production[25] was accompanied by a greater volume of production for captive use. In addition, several producers of chlorine integrated forward. As a result, although only about 35% of chlorine was produced for captive use in 1937 the proportion was an estimated 50% in 1965.[26]

Capital investment per ton is high because of "the exceedingly corrosive nature of the products and the automatic controls used in plants . . . and the electro-chemical process requirements." In 1965, the estimated cost for a 100 ton per day plant was about $50,000 per ton-day of chlorine capacity. In addition, "the larger producers also have extensive investments in product distribution facilities, such as specially constructed corrosion-resistant tank trucks, railroad cars, and barges, and also thousands of steel cylinders for chlorine."[27]

Nevertheless, it apparently has been economical to operate relatively small plants. Some pulp and paper concerns operate plants with capacities of less than 10 tons per day as compared with installations with capacity of 100 to 150 tons a day by other producers.[28] In 1966, it was reported that a discount of $6 per ton was in effect for pulp and paper producers "to discourage do it yourself chlorine plants."[29] However, "Some pulp and paper companies and a number of chemical companies (Shell, Goodrich) have recently elected to make their own."[30]

New entries have not been attracted for merchant sales in recent years. Among the explanations advanced for this situation are: chronic surpluses of the joint product, caustic soda; the presence of more attractive investment opportunities in some of the newer, faster growing chemicals; the difficulty of entering a market where a large percentage of production is consumed captively; moderately high capital costs; and industry opinion that profits generally are low for this product.[31] However, existing producers have expanded capacity as is shown in Table VI-2.

In 1959 the four largest producers accounted for 58% of capacity and the top eight firms, 77%.[32] In 1967, the ratios were about the same.

The competitive significance of these concentration ratios is limited because of the availability of substitute products for some uses. Thus, chlorine "competes with other oxidizing agents and bleaches, such as hydrogen peroxide, and bactericides such as ammonia compounds."[33]

Because of identical bids for government chlorine purchases several investigations have been conducted to determine whether there is price fixing of chlorine.[34] These investigations resulted in no convictions. However, "In New York State, nine chlorine companies consented to refrain from price fixing in selling liquid chlorine to state and municipal agencies."[35] These municipal purchases were generally in small amounts and accounted for only a minor percentage of the chlorine volume.

In 1964, the U.S. Department of Justice accused 9 companies of manipulating the prices of chlor-alkali products (chlorine, caustic soda, and soda ash). Under a consent decree early in 1967, seven of the nine companies agreed to review their prices and to issue new price lists. The new price lists varied among companies as additional selling zones were established by one company, a special discount was eliminated by another, and other changes were announced by other companies.[36] A number of treble damage suits were instituted by municipalities as a result of alleged price fixing for chlorine.

Chlorine is an homogeneous product, nearly all of which is produced by a single process, and the price charged by each company is common information to all. Hence, there is little reason to expect different prices. List prices often remain unchanged for several years. However, periodically sales at discounts are reported.[37]

Phthalic Anhydride

Phthalic anhydride, a synthetic organic chemical originally based on the by-product coke industry, was produced in small quantities up to 1939 and became a bulk commodity chemical after World War II. In 1947 production was 137.5 million pounds and the value of shipments was $17 million. Output in 1966 was 675.2 million pounds and sales were 365.4 million pounds; the value of sales was $34.6 million.[38] In 1967, output was 727 million pounds.[39] Estimated capacity for selected dates since 1955 is shown in Table VI-3.

TABLE VI-3

Phthalic Anhydride Capacity, Selected Dates, 1955 to 1968

(millions of pounds)

Company	1955	Dec. 1960	Dec. 1962	Jan. 1964	Oct. 1968
Monsanto	55	110	150	113	185
Allied Chemical	135	157	203	130	157
Hooker	—	—	—	—	100
W. R. Grace	—	—	50	44	75
Koppers	17	23	25	50	75a
Union Carbide	—	—	50	50	75
Chevron Chemical	10	18	45	30	68
Witco Chemical	—	20	50	50	50b
Stepan Chemical	—	—	—	40	50
USS Chemicals	—	—	—	—	43
Reichhold Chemical	13	60	60	29	30
Sherwin-Williams	3	6	10	20	20
Pittsburgh Coke & Chemical	14	36	60	40	—
Heyden-Newport	—	—	10	12	—
Thompson Chemical	—	—	10	10	—
American Cyanamid	65	65	65	—	—
Amoco Chemical	—	15	15	—	—
Total	312	510	803	618	928

Source: *Petro/Chem. Engineer*, February 1963, p. 56; *Chemical Week*, December 10, 1960, p. 87 and January 18, 1964, p. 62 and *Oil, Paint and Drug Reporter*, October 21, 1968, p. 42.

a Construction of a new 130 million pound capacity per year plant to be started in mid-1969. Koppers, *1968 Annual Report*, p. 1.

b In 1969, Witco announced it was closing its plants and withdrawing from the industry. *Chemical Week*, April 12, 1969, p. 73.

Phthalic anhydride production formerly fluctuated with steel production since coal tar naphthalene — a major raw material — is manufactured as a by-product with coke and coke gases used in the manufacture of steel. The shortages of naphthalene in the 1959 to 1961 period and the resulting high price encouraged the production of naphthalene as a petroleum derivative.[40] In addition, ortho-xylene has been increasingly used as a feedstock for phthalic anhydride.

The largest current use (about 50%) of phthalic anhydride is in the manufacture of phthalate plasticizers which are added to vinyl resins to impart flexibility. The exact ratio between vinyl resins and plasticizers is reported to be somewhat sensitive to phthalic anhydride prices. However, for the large producers of phthalate plasticizers, who are basic in phthalic anhydride, the interdependence of plasticizers and phthalic anhydride prices is not too important.

The second major outlet for phthalic anhydride is in the production of alkyd resins (25-30%) which are used in surface coatings. Increased competition from acrylate based paints and various other water emulsions have, to a large extent, slowed down the growth rate of the alkyd based paints. A growing use for phthalic anhydride has been in the manufacture of polyester resins which accounted for one-sixth the use in 1967.[41]

In 1917, the selling price of phthalic anhydride was $4.23 a pound. The following year, the discovery of a new process caused the price to fall to $2.85. By 1920, it had declined to 46 cents a pound; in 1930 it was 13 cents a pound. Production increased rapidly as new markets were developed. Output increased from 138,800 pounds in 1917 to 45.2 million pounds in 1937. In the latter year there were six producers.[42]

During much of the first decade after World War II the low price of 14-1/2¢ per pound of phthalic anhydride encouraged a large growth in its use.[43]

Between 1955 and 1962 six additional firms entered the industry and capacity increased at a rapid rate (see Table VI-3). The entries were encouraged by a higher price—between 16-1/2¢ and 20-1/2¢ per pound—and the absence of technical obstacles. In addition, profits before taxes during the period were generally regarded as being attractive.[44]

The combination of new entries and expansion by the firms already in the industry reduced the extent of concentration markedly. In 1955, the largest producer accounted for 43.3% of total capacity; in October 1968, the largest company (Monsanto) accounted for only 19.9% and it had moved up from second place replacing Allied. The share held by the four largest producers declined from 87.2% to 55.7%.

Most of the new phthalic anhydride capacity was captive. The U.S. Tariff Commission estimated that about one quarter of all phthalic made in 1959 was used captively; by 1968 the proportion appeared to be more than 50%.[45]

The increase in new capacity ran far ahead of production. At the end of 1960, phthalic anhydride capacity was rated at 510 million pounds per year as against demand for about 390 million pounds. By December 1962 capacity was estimated at 803 million pounds. As a result of a decline in prices, capacity was reduced as two companies withdrew from the market and others closed down one or more plants. Reported closedowns and the volume involved in the years 1961 to 1963 were as follows:[46] (See Page 116).

A new expansion in capacity took place which increased the total to 910 million pounds by 1968. As capacity is increased, some marginal facilities usually are closed down. In 1969 it was reported that: "Shutdown of high-cost phthalic anhydride plant capacity may offset capacity additions and incremental expansions in 1969 to extent of the supply pinch . . . . There will not be as much improvement in phthalic anhydride availability as had been anticipated."[47]

Company	Location	Capacity (million lbs.)	Year Closed
Allied Chemical	Buffalo, New York	12	1961
	Calumet, Ill.	36	1962
American Cyanamid	Bridgeville, Pa.	25	1962
Amoco	Joliet, Ill.	15	1961
Koppers-Pittsburgh Plate Glass	Kabuta, Pa.	26	1962
Monsanto	St. Louis, Mo.	45	1962, 1963
Oronite	Richmond, Calif.	20	1963
Reichhold	Detroit, Mich.	20	1963
Total		199	

Monsanto was scheduled to close down a 40 million pound facility in mid-1969. USS Chemicals shut down a 43 million pound plant (however, it started-up a 125 million pound plant at the same location). Witco was reported to have withdrawn from phthalic anhydride production in 1969.[48]

Many of the new captive producers "not only installed adequate capacity for their own needs but, in the interest of economy, constructed larger plants and became sellers on the open market."[49] Finally, there has been an increase in European capacity.[50]

Excess capacity led to a precipitous decline in prices starting in 1961. By July 1963 the price had dropped to 8-1/2 cents a pound for molten and 9 cents for flake — less than half its 1959 high of 20-1/2 cents. Between January and July 1963 the price fell from 14 cents to 9 cents — a drop of over 30%. In the following 2-1/2 years, prices fluctuated between 8-1/2 cents and 11-1/2 cents a pound. A new rise starting in 1966 brought the price back to 14 cents.[51] This rise in prices reflected a tight supply-demand situation as lower prices stimulated growth because they gave customers "unexpected cost advantages."[52] One result was the sharp increase in capacity reflected in Table VI-3 and a renewed concern about overcapacity. For this product, the level of prices and of capacity appear to act and interact upon each other fairly promptly.

Polyethylene

Polyethylene, a thermoplastic resin, has become the most important plastic material. Its growth since World War II has been extraordinary. It had the largest rate of annual growth among 381 products. Output increased at an average annual rate of about 35% from 1948 to 1965. However, in recent years the growth rate has slowed down. From 1948 to 1953 it was 48%, almost 39% from 1953-1960, and about 18% from 1960-1965.[53] In 1967 total sales of polyethylene aggregated $529 million.[54]

The growth in demand has been so rapid that periodically shortages have developed. In 1965 when such a shortage developed, exports were reduced and some producers adjusted by "withdrawing several of their low-priced resins from the market . . . . Dow Chemical discontinued production of six broad specification resins . . . Union Carbide stopped production of its wide specification, low density PE resins. . . ."[55].

Low density or conventional polyethylene (0.940 and below) which is lower in price accounted for 73.4% of total sales of 3,459 million[56] pounds in 1967 and high density polyethylene (sometimes called linear or low pressure) accounted for 26.6%.[57] The main uses for the high density product are in blow molding and injection molding which provided the outlet for more than three-fifths of the sales in 1967. The major use for the conventional product is packaging film and sheet. Important uses in 1967 are shown in Table VI-4.

TABLE VI-4
Uses of Polyethylene, 1967

	High Density	Low Density
Blow molding	41%	*10%
Injection molding	22	13
Film and sheet	4	43
Wire and Cable	4	11
Pipe and conduit	4	—
Other extrusion	3	—
Extrusion coating	—	13
Exports	9	10
Miscellaneous	13	—
	100	100

*Includes miscellaneous.
Sources: Oil, Paint and Drug Reporter, October 9, 1967, p. 9 and October 23, 1967, p. 9.

The estimated capacities of producers of polyethylene for selected years are shown in Table VI-5. Capacity figures may be overstated "since productivity of a high pressure polyethylene plant decreases rapidly as resin density increases."[58]

TABLE VI-5
Polyethylene Capacity, 1964 and 1967
(millions of pounds)

	High Density		Low Density	
	July 1964	Oct. 1967	July 1964	Oct. 1967
Allied	50	150	—	25
Celanese	120	140	—	—
Columbian Carbon	—	—	—	100
Dow	25	100	150	300
Du Pont	60	75	360	625
Texas Eastman	—	—	120	175
Goodrich-Gulf	15	—	—	—
Gulf (Spencer)	—	—	135	400
Grace	80	—	—	—
Hercules	80	80	—	—
Monsanto	50	50	130	130
National Distillers (A-B Corp)	—	—	275	450
National Petrochemicals	60	125	—	—
Phillips	116	160	—	—
Rexall	—	—	130	250
Sinclair-Koppers	25	50	70	125
Union Carbide	60	125	650	870
	741	1,055	2,020	3,450

Source: Oil, Paint and Drug Reporter, July 20, 1964, p. 9, July 27, 1964, p. 9, October 9, 1967, p. 9, October 23, 1967, p. 9.

Prior to 1952 Du Pont and Union Carbide were the only producers of poly-ethylene, with the former having the patent license. On July 30, 1952, Judge Sylvester J. Ryan rendered a final decree in the Imperial Chemical Industries and Du Pont case. He ordered them to license all applicants at a reasonable royalty for all processes and patents that they had shared.[59] As *Fortune* said later, "The race for polyethylene capacity started the next day."[60]

The 1953-56 period saw an explosive growth with the entry of seven additional producers. Between 1956 and 1959, there were four more entries and by 1962 three additional producers had entered the industry.[61]

Table VI-5 shows capacity separately for high density and low density poly-ethylene in July 1964 and October 1967. The combined capacity on the latter date was 4.5 billion pounds or an increase of more than 2 billion pounds in 5 years. Further increases took place after 1967. In 1967, the four largest producers of the high density product accounted for 54.5% of capacity and the Big Four for low density accounted for 68.0%.

As the table shows, Columbia Carbon entered this market after 1964. Only Union Carbide was among the four largest producers both for high density for which it was the fourth largest producer and low density for which it had the largest capacity. Two of the four larger producers of low density polyethylene (Gulf and National Distillers) did not produce high density polyethylene. Dow, which was among the four largest producers of the low density product in 1964, has been replaced by Gulf in 1967. For the high density product, Grace and Hercules were in the Big Four in 1964 but had lost those positions to Allied Chemical and Union Carbide in 1967.

In 1968, it was reported that "Five of the 10 high-density polyethylene producers have expansions under way; two new newcomers are preparing to enter the market, and several oil companies are reportedly considering this polymer."[62]

Since 1955 polyethylene producers have been integrating vertically (both forward and backward) and horizontally. The extent to which producers have integrated backwards toward their basic raw material has been summarized as follows:

"Du Pont is among the four top U.S. producers of synthetic resins and about the only 'major' still largely dependent on outside raw-material sources. Monsanto moved into the company of Union Carbide and Dow as bigtime fully integrated polyethylene producers when its Chocolate Bayou unit began operating last year. Other PE makers in the same situation include Rexall Chemical (via its association with El Paso Natural Gas at Odessa, Tex.); Spencer Chemical (recently acquired by ethylene supplier Gulf); Phillips at Pasadena, Tex.; Texas Eastman (Longview, Tex.); Goodrich-Gulf (Port Neches, Tex.); USI, another major PE producer, supplies its own ethylene at Tuscola, Ill."[63]

Prices of polyethylene have declined steadily. The decline has reflected periodic excess capacity and the entry of numerous new producers. Other significant factors which contributed to lower prices for polyethylene have been the interproduct competition among different plastics and the attempts by polyethylene producers to enter markets formerly held by more conventional materials. Low density polyethylene declined from 41 cents a pound in the mid-1950s to 14-1/2 cents a pound in 1967 and the high density product fell from 47 cents in 1957 to 20 cents by 1967. During periods when the increase in demand slows down, the pressures on price intensify as was true in 1967 when prices were cut about 4 cents a pound.[64] However, in 1968 prices firmed as demand again expanded rapidly.

Intense interproduct competition has been a major characteristic for plastic resins. And polyethylene as one of the fastest growing products in those markets has experienced significant competition for its various uses.

In molding applications, polyethylene competes with more conventional materials such as glass, wood, tin, steel and aluminum. Conventional polyethylene also competes with cellophane in the packaging film market. "Other film contenders include polyvinylidene chloride, cellulose acetate, butyrate, vinyls, Pliofilm, oriented polystyrene, Mylar, polycarbonate, and nylon."[65] Polyethylene also has been used as a coating for paper cartons, thus competing with glass and wax manufacturers. High density polyethylene is used increasingly in the intensely competitive packaging industry particularly for containers for bleach, detergents and other household items.

There is also price competition with polypropylene in bottles and other blow molded products and in toys, housewares, and other injection molded goods. It was reported in 1963 that:

> ". . . About 55% went into toys and housewares. Since price is an important factor in both these applications, considerable competition exists, not only among polyethylene producers but also from other thermo-plastics."[66]

Many dairy companies have been using plastic bottles. It has been reported that "Consumers prefer nonbreakable, leakproof plastic containers to paper or glass — when the prices paid are equal. However, penny-conscious housewives don't buy if plastic runs up the cost."[67]

Sulfuric Acid

Sulfuric acid, first produced in 1793,[68] has been called the "workhorse chemical." By tonnage it is the largest inorganic chemical product, it is inexpensive and it has hundreds of uses in many different industries.

Output is derived primarily from sulfur. "It takes 33.3 lbs. of sulfur to make 100 lbs. of acid; thus a rise of $1 in the cost of sulfur should be roughly reflected by a 33¢ increase in the price of acid."[69] As the price of sulfur rose in the mid-1960s, with accompanying increases in the cost of sulfuric acid, considerable research developed in connection with the use of other raw materials including stack gas at new coal-fired electric power plants and gypsum.[70] The usefulness of these competitive sources of raw materials depends upon the availability of and the price of sulfur.

In 1967 total sulfuric acid production was 28.8 million tons of which commercial shipments were 12.5 million with a value of $252 million. Captive production was 57% of the total.[71] About 4% of the output in 1967 was produced as a by-product at copper, zinc and lead plants.[72] Fluctuations in sulfuric acid production have tended to follow the business cycle because of its wide use in industry.

Between 1950 and 1962 sulfuric acid capacity more than doubled. Capacity recorded only minor changes for the next three years but then was expanded by more than 10 million tons between January 1, 1965 and January 1, 1968 (See Table VI-6). New plants are considerably larger in size than the older ones. Modern contact plants can produce 1,000 to 1,500 or more tons per day as compared with 500 ton plants a decade earlier.[73]

Total capacity of 91 producers in 1968 was 36.6 million tons. The largest producers are listed in Table VI-7.

TABLE VI-6

Sulfuric Acid Capacity, 1950-1968

January 1	Million Short Tons 100% Concentration
1950	12.1
1955	17.4
1960	22.6
1962	25.2
1965	25.1
1967	34.7
1968	36.6

Sources: U.S. Department of Commerce, Business and Defense Services Administration, *Sulfuric Acid Industry*, Washington, D.C., January 10, 1962, pp. 3, 4; *Chemicals*, September 1967, p. 10; and Stanford Research Institute, *Directory of Chemical Products*, January 1968.

TABLE VI-7

Sulfuric Acid Capacity, January 1, 1968

(1000 tons)

Allied Chemical	3443
Stauffer Chemical	3300
Tennessee Corporation	2710
Du Pont	2631
Olin Mathieson	1714
W. R. Grace	1343
Chemicals, Inc.	1225
National Lead	1100
Texas Gulf Sulphur	1068
Continental Oil	1028
Armour Agricultural Chemical	1018
Occidental Chemical Company	1000
79 other companies	15039
Total	36619

The four largest companies had a capacity of 12,084,000 tons or 33.0% of the total on January 1, 1968 as compared with 39.7% for the same Big Four in 1961, as smaller companies increased their capacity more than did the Big Four. Tennessee Corporation moved up to third place in 1968 from fourth in 1961.

There seems to be little incentive for new companies to enter this industry except for captive use because plants must be big and costly and large volume must be produced for sale at relatively low unit prices. It has been pointed out that "Large users, such as fertilizer and explosives manufacturers, usually own and operate their own acid plants because they find it cheaper to make acid than to buy it."[74] Much of the new plant capacity is for captive, onsite use and hence is located in the phosphate-rock producing areas rather than in the market areas.[75]

Since sulfuric acid is corrosive as well as bulky, transportation costs tend to be high. As a result, markets are regional rather than national and hence all of the producers are not directly in competition.

Sulfuric acid competes with several other chemicals. The U.S. Department of Commerce reports that "Sulfuric acid is facing greater competition from hydrochloric acid for iron and steel pickling, and from the chlorine process for making titanium oxide. Other improved plastic products have been displacing cellophane and cellulose."[76]

The list price of sulfuric acid remains unchanged for long periods of time in spite of the fact that output fluctuates both seasonally and with the business cycle. Thus, the list price was unchanged from June 1953 to December 1964. However, it has been reported that "Although the published prices of sulfuric acid have remained constant for some time, they generally are ignored and the acid is sold at prices well under list."[77]

Synthetic Fibers

One of the leading growth industries in recent years has been synthetic fibers. The synthetics are chemically produced fibers that include nylon, the polyesters (Du Pont-Dacron, Beaunit Mills-Vycron, Tennessee Eastman-Kodel, Fiber Industries-Fortrel), the acrylics (Monsanto-Acrilan, Du Pont-Orlon, American Cyanamid-Creslan, Dow-Zefran), the modified acrylics (Union Carbide-Dynel and Tennessee Eastman-Verel), and glass fibers. Another entrant in this competitive race was polypropylene fiber in 1961.

From 1948 to 1965 production of synthetic fibers increased more than twenty-five fold. The average annual rate of increase was 21.3%, the eleventh largest advance among 381 products.[78] Total shipments of non-cellulosic synthetic organic fibers were $2,181 million in 1967.[79]

TABLE VI-8

Per Cent Relationship of United States Synthetic Fiber Production to Total Man-Made Fiber Production, Selected Years, 1940-1968

(millions of pounds)

Years	Total Man-Made Fibers	Synthetic Fibers	Rayon & Acetate	Synthetics As Percent of Total
1940	475.8	4.6	471.2	1.0
1945	842.2	50.1	792.1	5.9
1950	1,405.3	145.9	1,259.4	10.4
1955	1,715.8	455.1	1,260.7	26.5
1960	1,882.7	854.2	1,028.5	45.4
1965	3,586.2	2,059.2	1,527.0	57.4
1966	3,920.1	2,401.1	1,519.0	61.3
1967	4,030.6	2,642.5	1,388.1	65.6
1968	5,181.4	3,587.1	1,594.3	69.2

.Source: Textile Organon, February 1969, p. 28.

Table VI-8 shows the great increase in production of synthetic fibers since 1940 and the slower rate of growth of rayon and acetate, the cellulosics. In 1940, the output of synthetic fibers was equal to only 1% of the total production of man-made fibers. By 1950 the proportion had risen to 10.4% and by 1968 to 69.2%. Thus, these synthetics now account for more than two-thirds of the total man-made fiber production.

The tremendous growth of the new synthetic fibers has developed because:

"Both the chemical and textile industries have been motivated by the necessity of novelty and variety in fibers and fabrics for the maintenance of old markets and the development of new. Interfiber price competition has also been instrumental in the search for new fibers, for the high prices of silk in the pre-World War II period and of wool in the postwar period have been a lure to the developers of nylon and other new synthetics."[80]

This rapid growth has reflected the many uses for synthetic fibers including carpets, hosiery, men's and women's clothes, tire cord, and other products. Permanent press apparel is one of the latest outlets for polyesters. Intensive research has resulted in improved color, luster, and texture and has improved the competitive position as compared with natural fibers.

The first "miracle" fiber was nylon 66 which was made available in 1939. Until 1954 Du Pont was the sole producer. After the government threatened an antitrust action against Du Pont in 1951, the company licensed Chemstrand (now Monsanto) and a few years later licensed some smaller producers. Another process (nylon 6) for manufacturing nylon was introduced in Germany and was adopted by American Enka and Allied Chemical among others.[81]

The estimated capacity to produce nylon by six companies in 1962 was 657 to 687 million pounds. By 1968, six additional companies had entered the industry and capacity was estimated at 1,356 million pounds (See Table VI-9).

Between 1954 and 1962, the nylon market changed markedly from one in which Du Pont was the sole producer to one in which there were six producers and Du Pont accounted for only about half of the total output. By 1968 there were 9 important producers and three small ones and Du Pont accounted for 42.8% of total capacity. A 10th important producer (Dow-Badische) was about to enter the market.

TABLE VI-9

Annual Capacity, Nylon, 1962 and 1968

	1962	1968 Total	Nylon 6	Nylon 66
		(millions of pounds)		
E. I. du Pont de Nemours & Co.	325-350	580		580
Monsanto Co.	175-180	240		240
Allied Chemical Corp.	80	173	173	
Fiber Industries, Inc.		120		120
American Enka Corp.	45	90	90	
Beaunit Corp.	4	50	10	40
Firestone Syn. Fibers Co.	28	45	45	
Rohm and Haas Co.		30	30	
Courtaulds North America Inc.		20	20	
Three small companies		8		
Total	657-687	1356	368*	980*

*Two small companies with combined capacity of 6 million pounds have capacity for both products and one with 2 million pounds capacity produced nylon 6.
Sources: Chemical Week, June 23, 1962, p. 81; Stanford Research Institute, *Chemical Economics Handbook*.

At the same time, other synthetic fibers were becoming competitively important. In 1948, Du Pont introduced Orlon, the first of the acrylics. By 1962, Chemstrand (now Monsanto), American Cyanamid, and Dow Chemical had entered this market. Union Carbide and Dow-Badische Company entered the market after 1962. The sharp increase in capacity for acrylics between 1962 and 1968 is shown in Table VI-10.

TABLE VI-10

Acrylics Capacity, 1962 and 1968
(millions of lbs.)

Company	Product	1962	1968
Du Pont	Orlon	120	230
Monsanto	Acrilan	50	200
American Cynamid	Creslan	27	55
Dow-Badische	Zefkrome	—	45
Union Carbide	Dynel	—	30
Tennessee Eastman	Verel	—	25
Dow	Zefran	12	—
Total		209	585

Source: *Chemical and Engineering News,* October 8, 1962, p. 21; *Chemical Week,* December 15, 1962, p. 37; Stanford Research Institute, *Chemical Economics Handbook,* 1968.

Du Pont's share declined from 57.4% in 1962 to 39.3% in 1968.

Capacity for polypropylene which is used to make plastics and fiber has expanded rapidly. Capacity reached 635 million pounds in 1967 and plans were made for an increase to 1 billion pounds. By 1968 about 140 million pounds were used by fiber producers. The largest producer is Hercules.[82] Dow withdrew from production of polypropylene in 1967 "because we felt that other plastics offered better profit potential for us."[83]

In this country Du Pont developed Dacron polyester fibers in 1953. By 1962 Tennessee-Eastman, Beaunit Mills and Fiber Industries also were producing polyesters and the total capacity reached 210 million pounds.

In the following six years, eight new producers entered the industry and capacity was increased to 1,375 million pounds (See Table VI-11). Du Pont which accounted for 76.2% of the capacity in 1962 had 43.6% in 1968. Moreover, three additional producers were scheduled to enter the field: Hystron Fibers, Allied Chemical, and Dow Badische. Clearly, the huge expansion in capacity was accompanied by significant changes in the structure of the industry. The dramatic expansion in consumption of polyesters reflected a 45% decline in prices, an increase in the number of end uses and the "popularity of permanent-press fabrics."[84]

In addition, other fibers with more limited uses have been introduced. From 1948 to 1965 production of textile glass fibers increased more than thirty times. The average annual rate of increase was 22.5%.[85] In the late 1960s there were ten producers [86] Output of glass fibers in 1968 was about 400 million pounds.[87] Glass fiber has been used in combination with other synthetics. In 1968 Goodrich introduced a tire made with polyester cord plies and a fiberglass belt.[88]

TABLE VI-11

Capacity, U.S. Polyester Fiber Plants, 1962, 1966, 1968

Company	1962	1966	1968
	(million pounds)		
Du Pont	160	400	600
Fiber Industries (Celanese-ICI)	30	200	300
Tennessee Eastman	10	100	150
Beaunit	10	45	70
Hystron Fibers (Hercules-Farbwerke Hoechst)	—	—	60
Monsanto	—	15	45
FMC	—	25	40
Dow Badische	—	—	30
American Enka	—	10*	30
Allied Chemical	—	—	15
Phillips Fibers (Phillips Petroleum, Rhone-Poulenc)	—	10	25
Midland-Ross	—	5	10
	210	810	1375

*Filament only.
Source: Chemical Week, August 5, 1967, p. 63.

Nylon, the various polyesters, acrylics, polypropylene fibers, and modified acrylics compete for many uses among themselves; they also are engaged in vigorous competition with rayon and the natural fibers. For example, both the acrylics and polyesters compete with wool in the apparel field. However, the polyester staple is seldom used in 100% form. Usually it is blended with cotton and/or wool. In this competition with natural fibers, relative prices often are significant.[89] However, of great importance is the fact that the entire market has expanded and thus there have been many opportunities for new as well as older fibers.

Tire cord provides an excellent illustration of the keen competition between fibers. In 1958, for example, nylon accounted for 27.3% of the total production of tire cord; by 1963 its share was 50.5% and in 1967 it was 69.9%. Rayon's share of the market during the period declined from 70.8% in 1958 to 28.0% in 1967.[90] However, some companies such as American Enka produce both nylon and rayon tire cord. Competition with other fibers also has developed in such diverse fields as upholstery, belting, felts and filtration materials.

The extent to which cotton and wool have lost ground to the man-made fibers is shown by the per capita consumption data (Table VI-12).

TABLE VI-12

U.S. Per Capita Consumption of Textiles, Selected Years, 1950-1968

	1950	1954	1958	1963	1968
	(pounds)				
Man-made fibers	9.5	8.7	9.6	14.4	26.6
Cotton	29.3	23.8	21.3	21.8	22.0
Wool	4.5	2.7	2.4	3.0	2.3
Total	43.3	35.2	33.3	39.2	50.9

Source: Textile Organon, March 1969, p. 54.

A BLS study concluded that "Each decrease in price and each new fiber has increased the manmade fiber group's competitive strength with respect to the natural fibers (cotton, wool, silk), and allowed the new industry to capture a larger share of the fiber market."[91]

Since 1950, per capita consumption has declined sharply for cotton and wool while it has increased markedly for man-made fibers. In 1968 for the first time, the per capita consumption of synthetic products was greater than that of the natural fibers. This shift has reflected the improved price relationship as the prices of man-made fibers have declined relative to the natural fibers, the greater ability to control quality, intensive marketing efforts, greater expenditures for R and D, and greater product innovation.

The competitive situation for all textiles has been affected by the quotas limiting imports of cotton textiles into the United States. Japan agreed to quotas for a few items in 1956; quotas were adopted for all cotton textiles from 1957 to 1961.[92]

In 1962 a Long-Term Arrangement (LTA) for cotton textiles was entered into by various exporting countries. The LTA provides that when a country finds its cotton textile market has been disrupted by shipments from another country, it may request the latter to restrict those shipments to a level no lower than those in the first of 12 of the 15 months immediately preceding. Should the exporting country not honor this request, the importing country can restrict imports to that level. We have entered into bilateral arrangements under the LTA with 22 countries covering all types of cotton textiles.[93] As a result of the Kennedy Round negotiations there was a 3 year extension of the Long-Term Arrangement. The countries importing textiles agreed to tariff cuts of from 15% to 20% and some adjustments in import quota levels.[94]

Foreign competition has been increasingly important for products of man-made fibers. In 1966, imports were nearly 800 million square yards as compared with only 151 million in 1961.[95] Because of the large inflow of these products, the industry sought to have import quotas established for man-made fibers. In 1969 the Nixon Administration sought to open negotiations with Far Eastern and European countries on an international textile agreement, covering wool and man-made fibers as well as cotton. The President noted that textile imports are "a special problem which has caused very great distress in certain parts of this country."[96]

One of the distinguishing characteristics of the man-made fibers is the important role played by non-price competition. Ultimate consumers know little about the properties and uses of most chemicals primarily because they never see them. But in connection with the fibers, large sums are spent on advertising by each producer to convince the retail consumer and the textile manufacturer of the superiority of his own products.[97] Moreover, the chemical companies work with the textile manufacturers to indicate how their fibers can best be used and to show them the qualitative advantages associated with each one.

Relatively few chemical brand names have much significance to the ultimate consumer. A major exception is found in synthetic fibers for which many of the brands cited earlier have become increasingly familiar. The producers of these fibers have given considerable attention to the ultimate consumer in order to stimulate demand for their specific product. Some illustrations include:

> Monsanto's "Wear Dated" program for Acrilan garments guarantees that garments made of Acrilan will give a consumer a year's normal wear or it will be replaced or the money "refunded." It has also advertised the Big Red A for carpets and other products.

American Cyanamid emphasizes in its advertising of Creslan that it has a staff fashion designer to help manufacturers style clothes made out of that product.

Du Pont assists knitwear manufacturers in their use of Orlon and also advertises institutionally.

Dow's Zefran is promoted "at the fashion level through trade and magazine media."

The synthetic fiber manufacturers also emphasize high quality standards. *Chemical Week* reported that: "Before any fiber producer allows its fiber tradename to be placed on a garment, the fabric must meet a set of specifications and standards of quality."[98] Clearly, non-price factors are more significant in the synthetic fiber market than in that for most inorganic or organic chemicals.

The emphasis given to non-price competition has not insulated synthetic fibers from waves of price cutting such as those experienced from 1966 to 1968. These price reductions had a significant impact on sales and earnings of the companies involved. Celanese reported in 1966 that its increases in dollar sales were limited by lower prices for acetate filament, polyester, and nylon[99] and that in 1967 its financial results were affected by the fact that "the polyester market was quite soft through most of the first three quarters. . ." and "Nylon . . . was plagued with over-capacity and low prices throughout the year."[100]

Business Week summarized the competitive and price picture succinctly: "As new 'miracle' fibers have caught fire, so has the competition; old and new producers have rushed to build new plant to cash in on the trend. Inevitably this has meant overcapacity and price-cutting."[101] These developments have been worldwide.[102]

Prices of nylon and other synthetics fibers were cut in 1966 and 1967 as over-capacity developed throughout the world. In 1968 they increased and were slightly above the 1966 level. From 1960 to 1968, the BLS price index of man-made fiber textile products declined by 6.9% despite the rise in the general price level in the latter part of the period; during this period the prices of cellulosic fibers recorded only small changes with a decline in 1961 offset by a rise in the following seven years.

Synthetic Phenol

Phenol is a key product in the organic branch of the chemical industry. It was one of the products developed by the industry to meet the needs of World War I. Up to 1914 our production was about one million pounds annually and consisted solely of natural phenol derived from coal-tar distillates. During World War I, in response to rapidly rising demand, various synthetic processes were developed based on the large available supply of benzol. By 1918, output had reached 107 million pounds. In the early post-World War I years, a decline in price from 45 cents to 6 cents per pound resulted in a shutdown of the synthetic plants. However, expanding demand in 1923 led to production of the synthetic product by four firms. Since then, synthetic phenol has accounted for the bulk of the output.[103] In 1967, 1,356 million pounds of synthetic and natural phenol were produced[104] with a value of about $48.8 million.

For trend of production for selected years since 1954 see next page.[105]

In 1967 and 1968, a number of new projects was announced and as a result it was projected that capacity "could easily hit 2.5 billion pounds"[106] by 1970. However, it is expected that when these new plants comes on stream, "producers will phase out their smaller operations to avoid overcapacity."[107]

Year	Production (millions of pounds)
1954	418
1959	692
1963	896
1966	1,347
1967	1,356
1968	1,374

In recent years, capacity to produce synthetic phenol has expanded markedly from about 500 million pounds on an annual basis in 1955 to 1,401 million pounds in 1966. Estimated capacities are shown in Table VI-13. In addition, natural phenol capacity is about 60 million pounds. The main producers are Koppers, Allied and U.S. Steel.[108]

In early 1969 capacity was estimated at 1,550 million pounds. The expansion then in process was expected to add around 825 million pounds by 1971 and an additional 300 million pounds in 1972. If these increases are attained, capacity will be about 2,700 million pounds in the early 1970's.[109]

TABLE VI-13
Synthetic Phenol Capacity, 1960, 1963, and 1966
(millions of pounds)

Company	1960	1963	1966
Monsanto	145	205	285
Dow Chemical	220	256	271
Union Carbide Plastics	110	110	250
Hooker Chemical	65	125	130
Allied Chemical	90	110	125
Reichhold	70	90	90
Shell	50	55	50
Chevron Chemical	50	50	50
Skelly Oil	—	50	50
Hercules Powder	30	45	50
Clark Oil	—	30	50
Schenectady Chemicals	—	20	—
Total	830	1,146	1,401

Source: Chemical and Engineering News, March 20, 1961, p. 124 and May 13, 1963, p. 97; Oil, Paint and Drug Reporter, April 11, 1966, p. 9.

Two new producers—Skelly Oil & Refining and Clark Oil & Refining—entered synthetic phenol production late in 1963.[110]

The use of synthetic phenol has grown enormously while that of natural phenol shows little change. Synthetic production rose from 509 million pounds in 1956 to 1,323 million in 1968; the output of natural phenol only increased from 40 million to 51 million pounds.[111]

The four largest producers accounted for 68.1% of synthetic capacity in 1960 and 66.8% in 1966. Hooker became one of the four largest producers (See

Table VI-13). In 1969, U.S.S. Chemicals, a new entrant, was scheduled to open a large plant with a capacity of 200 million pounds.[112]

Competitive pressures have intensified as new facilities have been developed for captive use, which accounts for a growing proportion of total output. The supply available for open market purchase often is increased when new captive facilities are opened and in some instances the producer for captive purposes finds he has a surplus available which also is sold in the market. In 1947, sales were equal to 88.7% of total output of synthetic and natural phenol; in 1959 the ratio was 58.4% and in 1966 it was 42.4%.[113]

The large growth in foreign production of phenol affected the domestic market by reducing the amount sold abroad by our producers in 1962. Between 1955 and 1961, phenol exports ranged between 36.7 million and 48.4 million pounds annually except in 1957.[114] In 1962, exports declined to 11.8 million pounds.[115] They reached a low of 8.1 million pounds in 1966 and then rose to 13.0 million pounds in 1967 and 28.2 million pounds in 1968.[116]

The major markets for phenol are phenolic resins (about 50% of the market), phenolic molding compounds, epoxy resins, and caprolactam nylon.

Phenol competes with other chemicals for some markets. In the production of caprolactam (used in the manufacture of nylon), phenol competes with cyclohexane and toluene. Although only one company—Allied Chemical—manufactures caprolactam by using phenol, it is the second largest outlet for this product. The most important use of phenol is in the production of phenolic resins which meet "strong competition" from other plastic materials such as polystyrene and rigid vinyl resins.[117] Phenolic molding compounds compete with polycarbonates and epoxies. However, phenol is not adversely affected by this competition because these substitute products also utilize phenol.[118]

The development of capacity in excess of demand, the loss of export markets, and the addition of new captive production periodically have been accompanied by sharp pressures on price. Between July 1961 and January 1963, for example, the price of synthetic phenol was reduced five times from 17 cents to 11-1/4 cents a pound.[119]

In 1967-1968, the list price was maintained at a 11-1/4 cents a pound but a "chaotic" market made the "going price" 7 to 8 cents. In the spring of 1968, a new list price of 8 cents a pound was announced to bring it into line with the market.[120]

Synthetic Rubber

The synthetic rubber industry had its start just prior to World War II. However, as a result of the requirements for rubber during the war, a major industry was literally created by the government overnight.[121] Thus, output in this country increased from only 8,000 long tons in 1941 to 1,000,000 long tons in 1944.[122] In 1955 and 1956, government operations were terminated when the government-owned plants were sold to private industry.[123] In 1955, output of synthetic rubber was close to 900,000 long tons. In 1967, output exceeded 1.8 million long tons and sales had a value of $918 million.[124] Captive sales were 62% of the total in 1964.[125]

There are various methods of producing general purpose synthetic rubber: regular S-type, cold S-type, cold oil masterbatch, cold oil black masterbatch, and cold and regular black masterbatch. It was reported by the Attorney General that:

" . . . in the first years of private ownership some companies had near monopolies on certain types of rubber . . . this pattern of plant specialization was gradually broken down, as most companies expanded to offer a rounded variety of products. At present [1960] there is a well-developed competitive potential in most categories of production."[126]

By 1962, it was reported that: " . . . the competitive potential in the various categories of production [ranged] from 9 to 11 producers. The only exception is in the minor black masterbatch category, now reduced to five competitors . . . ."[127].

Because almost two-thirds of the rubber is used to make automobile tires, the larger producers have been subsidiaries of tire companies (e.g. Goodyear, Goodrich-Gulf Chemicals, Firestone); other companies are affiliated with the petroleum industry (e.g. Enjay Chemical, Phillips, Shell Chemical).

Table VI-14 shows the increase in the capacity to produce synthetic rubber between 1955 and 1965. Capacity and output doubled in that decade. This large increase reflected mainly expansion by established producers. One observer has pointed out that: "Expansion . . . was undertaken in order that existing firms might have capacity to produce a complex line of synthetic rubbers."[128] However, three of the smaller producers making S-Type rubber (Dewey and Almy, General Tire and Rubber Co. and International Latex) entered the industry after 1955.

TABLE VI-14
Synthetic Rubber Capacity, May 1, 1955, December 31, 1961 and December 31, 1965
(1,000 long tons)

Styrene (S) Type

Company	May 1, 1955	Dec. 31, 1961	Dec. 31, 1965*
Goodyear Tire	146.5	277.3	306.5
Firestone Tire	129.6	271.5	271.5
Goodrich-Gulf	95.0	280.5	266.0
Copolymer Rubber	49.0	133.0	166.7
Texas — U.S. Chemical	88.0	143.0	156.0
Phillips Chemical	69.4	127.0	110.0
Shell Chemical	94.0	104.0	104.0
American Synthetic Rubber	44.0	75.0	100.0
United Carbon	62.0	69.8	77.2
General Tire	—	71.0	71.0
U.S. Rubber	22.2	32.0	32.0
All others including Dewey and Almy Division of W. R. Grace and International Latex	—	20.5	30.0
Total styrene-butadiene	799.7	1,604.6	1,690.9
Butyl-Humble Oil & Refining now Enjay Chemical Division	90.0	155.0	172.5
Neoprene and nitrile	188.0	199.0	230.0
Total	1,077.7	1,958.6	2,093.4

* Anticipated capacity.

Source: Second Report, (1957), p. 22, *Seventh Report,* (1961), pp. 7, 21, 22 and *Tenth Report,* (1964), pp. 19, 27.

There has been some change in the relative ranking of different producers since 1955. However, the aggregate data do not show the full picture. It was noted in the 1961 Report that:

" . . . as compared with the time of disposal, each leading producer must now oppose a substantially greater number of competing companies. This had resulted from new entrants to the industry and the gradual process of plant diversification in most of all categories of production."[129]

A considerable volume of synthetic rubber is produced captively for the tire companies. This limits the ability of competitors to substitute new types of synthetic rubber. For example, in connection with butyl rubber one trade publication reported: "Big hurdle facing Esso: trying to convince tire producers to buy butyl rubber even though they own their own synthetic rubber plants."[130] However, the non-affiliated companies do plan an important competitive role. In describing the price cutting in the industry, *The Journal of Commerce* reported "In some instances, the cuts were started by companies with no direct affiliation with companies making rubber products."[131]

In 1939, practically no synthetic rubber was used. By 1947, the consumption of natural rubber and synthetic rubber were about equal (562,656 and 559,700 long tons). In 1967, synthetic rubber consumed was 1,628,258 long tons as compared with only 488,848 for natural rubber.[132] In most instances, some natural rubber is used in combination with the synthetic product.

In 1967 output of butyl rubber in the U.S. was 114,000 long tons.[133] Columbian Carbon, a subsidiary of Cities Service, became the second producer of butyl rubber in 1963 when it commenced operation at a 17,500 ton per year plant at Lake Charles, Louisiana.[134]

Nitrile rubber was produced by 5 companies in 1964 while neoprene was made available by only one company.[135] However, during 1967 Petro-Tex "began marketing neoprene synthetic rubber from a Common Market supplier in anticipation of production from its own neoprene plant, which is expected to begin operation in 1969."[136]

A considerable amount of competition also prevails among synthetic rubbers, new forms of which have been developed as a result of intensive research. Thus, styrene-butadiene (SBR) which accounted for 742,000 long tons or 82.9% of the total output of synthetic rubber in 1955 accounted for only 65.1% of the total in 1967. On the other hand, polybutadiene and polyisoprene (so-called "synthetic natural rubber") which was introduced commercially in 1960 accounted for 10.6% of the output in 1967.[137]

The Attorney General reported that 7 producers of polybutadiene would have a capacity of almost 200,000 long tons in 1966 while 2 producers (Goodyear and Shell) of polyisoprene would have a capacity of 100,000 long tons in 1966.[138] Goodrich-Gulf entered the latter market so that in 1968 there were three producers with capacity of 127,000 long tons; additional capacity was scheduled to bring the total to 170,000 long tons in 1969.[139]

In his review of the synthetic rubber industry, the Attorney General reported that for these new products there is " . . . an apparent ease of entry and the prospect of vigorous competition with existing rubbers."[140]

The research laboratory has added a significant dimension to competition in this area. Although patents have been important, the Attorney General has reported " . . . patents have constituted no barrier to . . . entry into synthetic rubber production."[141]

An interesting illustration of the relationship between research and competition developed for butyl rubber. The Attorney General reported:

> "Even as Jersey Standard affiliates were acquiring the sole domestic butyl-producing facilities, technological developments were destroying the basis of dangers inherent in the monopoly position. The advent of tubeless tires in 1954 spelled the decline in importance of inner tubes, butyl's unique market."[142]

While each synthetic has special properties, they do compete for many uses among themselves and with natural rubber. Price may play a role in such substitution. For example, the relatively slow rate at which polyisoprene was replacing natural rubber for which it was the "synthetic twin" has been attributed to its higher price.[143] It has been estimated that "In nearly 40 per cent of rubber uses, synthetics are competitive price-wise with natural rubber when selling from three to four cents per pound under the latter rubber."[144]

Paul J. Lovewell and William S. Penn of USR Research Company have indicated that in the 1980s synthetic rubber producers will face 3 major problems: (1) technology advancing more rapidly than ability to apply it because the cost of manufacturing technology is high in relation to financial resources, (2) growing difficulty in meeting world-wide capital requirements, (3) demand for automobile tires may be adversely affected by growth of non-automobile mass transit facilities as a result of greater traffic congestion.[145]

In 1966, the four largest synthetic rubber producers accounted for 56% of total shipments and the eight largest producers 78% (in 1954, the ratios were 53% and 81% respectively).[146] These concentration ratios do not reflect the natural rubber and reclaimed rubber consumed in 1966. If allowance is made for the consumption of natural rubber in 1966 (554,128 long tons), the Big Four in the synthetic field probably accounted for about 42% of the combined total; if allowance also were made for the reclaimed rubber used (264,506 long tons), the ratio would be 37.6%.[147]

The nature of price and nonprice competition for synthetic rubber has been summarized by the Attorney General as follows:

> " . . . Instead of price competition producers have emphasized competition on the basis of improved quality, product differentiation through development of rubber grades more exactly suited to specific fabricating applications, and extensive provision of helpful technical services to customers.

> "This is not to say that there has been a complete absence of price competition among SBR producers through the years. *In the export market, for example, it is an open secret that there has long been widespread cutting of the published prices by most producers.* And in the domestic market, after the first few years our surveys began to notice increasing evidence of *scattered private discounting of published prices.* Some of this, it is true, involved sale of 'off-specification' rubber, unsuitable for its intended range of application but still of some use to manufacturers whose products required less rigid standards. However, much of this discounting was explained merely as the need 'to meet competition' in certain markets. This discounting became so widespread late in 1962 that a 10 percent discount from published prices was generally made official in an effort to work off accumulated stocks. Although in 1963 published prices were again raised and are still basically maintained at their former levels, our more recent surveys continue to note *evidence of scattered discounting*"[148] (italics added).

In 1968, polyisoprene rubber prices were reduced as a result of the decline in natural rubber prices (with which it competes directly) and because of overcapacity.[149] Prices were reduced by 1/2 cent a pound in October 1967 and 1 cent a pound in January 1968 to a range of 18.5-23 cents a pound, depending on grade.[150] Apparently competitive pressures have been reflected in periodic sales of synthetic rubber below list price.

Butadiene

Butadiene is one of the basic raw materials used in producing synthetic rubber. Most of the facilities to produce butadiene originally were built by the U.S. Government and then later sold to private industry. Table VI-15 shows capacity for selected dates from May 1, 1955 to 1968.

Several points may be noted in connection with these changes in capacity.

1. Total capacity in 1968 was more than 4-1/2 times as large as in 1955.

2. Seven companies with 45.5% of the capacity, also produced synthetic rubber.

3. Since the transfer of government plants to private industry, one company (Publicker in Sept. 1956) has withdrawn from the industry but seven new producers have entered the industry.

4. There has been considerable change in the relative importance of the producers in the industry since 1955. Petro-Tex, the third largest producer in 1955, had the largest capacity in 1968. Union Carbide advanced to sixth from

TABLE VI-15

Butadiene Capacity, 1955, 1960, 1963, and 1968

(1,000 short tons)

	May 1 1955	Dec. 31 1960	1963	1968
Petro-Tex Chemical Corp.	90	200	200	550
Goodrich-Gulf Chemicals, Inc.	95	148	148	350
Texas-U.S. Chemical Co.	95	148	148	350
Sinclair (formerly Texas Butadiene & Chemical Corp.)	---	100	121	260
Phillips Chemical Co.	74	112	112	221
Union Carbide Corp.	30	45	45	204
Firestone Tire & Rubber Co.	---	60	60	180
Petroleum Chemicals Inc.—Cities Service	64	80	80	160
Odessa Butadiene Co.—El Paso	---	50	50	159
Shell Chemical Co.	50	70	70	144
Enjay Chemical	87	120	120	130
Copolymer Rubber & Chemical Corp.	23	40	55	130
Monsanto	---	---	20	106
Dow Chemical Company	8	32	32	70
Mobil Chemical	---	---	45	40
Chevron Chemical	14	16	16	32
Publicker	84	---	---	---
Other	---	---	---	222
Total	714	1,221	1,322	3,308

Source: Sixth Report, (1960), p. 21; *Oil, Paint and Drug Reporter,* April 15, 1963, p. 9; *Chemical Week,* September 14, 1968, p. 54.

ninth largest. Texas Butadiene (acquired by Sinclair), which was not in the 1955 list, was the fourth largest company in 1968, advancing from sixth place in 1960.

The proportions of sales made captively to adjacent unaffiliated copolymer plants, and in the open market, were as follows in 1955 and 1964.[151]

| | Percent of Sales | |
| | May-December | |
	1955	1964
Captive sales	44	43
To unaffiliated adjacent plants	28	22
Open market	28	35
Total	100	100

Open market sales of butadiene are "sold under long term contracts. Occasionally full requirement clauses are used."[152]

The trend in this market in the first decade after plants were sold by the government to private industry in 1955, has been summarized by the Attorney General as follows:

"In butadiene, this true open market has been growing perceptibly in recent years as new producers have entered the field and markets outside synthetic rubber have developed. As an accompaniment, the traditional market leaders have been losing ground and the potential for effective competitive rivalry has broadened."[153]

In 1955, when the plants were sold to private industry, butadiene was priced at 15 cents a pound. By 1968, the price had declined to 9-1/2 cents a pound.

Summary and Conclusions

There are many patterns of competitive pressures in the chemical industry. Price competition, non-price competition, foreign competition, ease of entry, technological development, interproduct competition and interindustry competition appear in varying combinations. The distinguishing characteristics of the competitive factors for these nine products may be highlighted as follows:

Benzene: Against a pattern of rapid growth there has been a considerable number of new entrants in recent years, particularly from the petroleum industry. Petroleum companies account for a large and growing proportion of the output. Concentration ratios are much lower than for most other chemicals with the largest company accounting for less than 10% of total capacity. Excess capacity has been accompanied by sharp declines in price and some shift of capacity to other uses.

Chlorine: A major bulk inorganic chemical with a key by-product, caustic soda, whose market has expanded more slowly than that for chlorine. There have been relatively few new entrants since World War II despite unimportant technical barriers to entry. However, capital investment per ton is high because of the corrosive nature of the product. Chronic surpluses of caustic soda have resulted in great pressure on those prices and acted to discourage new entrants. Most of the new entrants produce for captive use; about half of the output is used captively. The Big Four account for 58% of total capacity. Interproduct competition plays a role. There has been some identical bidding in government contracts.

Although list prices remain unchanged for long periods of time, periodically there are sales at a discount from list.

Phthalic Anhydride: This product became a bulk organic after World War II and the number of producers increased from six at that time to 13 in 1964 in response to good profit margins. Between 1955 and 1968 the proportion of capacity accounted for by the Big Four declined sharply from 87.2% to 55.7%. About half of the capacity is captive with some companies producing in excess of their needs and hence adding to the free market supply. Excess capacity here and a large expansion in foreign capacity have been accompanied by sharp declines in price. There have been several withdrawals from the industry because of these price reductions. The level of prices and of capacity appear to interact upon each other fairly promptly.

Polyethylene: This has been a tremendous growth product in the past two decades. There were two producers in 1953, nine in 1956, and 17 in 1967. Companies from other industries, largely petroleum, have been among the new entrants. One result has been replacement of some of the Big Four by other companies over time. Polyethylene is subject to intensive interproduct and interindustry competition. Prices have been declining with an accompanying sharp expansion in its use.

Sulfuric Acid: This is one of the largest inorganic products. It is inexpensive and has widespread use. More than half the output is used captively. There has been a large increase in capacity but only a few new entrants. The Big Four accounted for 33% of capacity in 1968. Although there are some 50 sulfuric acid producers, much of the product must be marketed locally or regionally because it is bulky and corrosive and is subject to high transportation costs. Interproduct competition is becoming increasingly important. List prices may remain unchanged for many years although actual prices often are below these list prices.

Synthetic Fibers: This is a leading growth industry with intensive interproduct and interindustry competition. There is a small but growing number of producers for each of several products. For example, the number of nylon producers increased from 6 in 1962 to 9 in 1968; in the same period the number of producers of acrylics increased from 3 to 6 and polyester producers from 4 to 12. These products vigorously compete with each other and with the natural fibers. Nonprice competition is more important for synthetic fibers than for other chemicals. Brand names are significant. Large expansions in capacity have been accompanied by large price declines in recent years. The intensification of foreign competition has led to the demand for import quotas similar to those in effect for cotton textiles.

Synthetic Phenol: This major organic chemical has virtually taken over the market from natural phenol which is largely produced by steel and coal companies. The captive market expanded from a little more than 10% in 1947 to more than 50% in 1966. Excess capacity has developed. A large growth in foreign capacity periodically results in a decline in exports which back-up on the American market. Phenol is subject to interproduct competition and has experienced severe price reductions in recent years.

Synthetic Rubber: Synthetic rubber is produced largely by rubber tire manufacturers and some petroleum companies. There has been little change in the number of producers since 1955 when the industry was turned over to private ownership by the U.S. Government. However, capacity has more than doubled since then. Large scale captive production limits the opportunities for new producers. New types of synthetic rubber are growing in importance. Price plays a role in determining the extent of substitution for natural rubber. Ratios based on synthetic rubber output alone overstate the extent and significance of concentration by a considerable margin because of the continuing importance of natural rubber and reclaimed rubber. Price cutting develops periodically. Nonprice competition is important in terms of quality and technical services.

Butadiene: This is a basic raw material to produce synthetic rubber. A little less than half of the capacity is owned by companies which also produce synthetic rubber. Total capacity has expanded sharply but new entry has not taken place. Only about one-third of the output is sold in the open market; the balance represents captive sales or sales to unaffiliated adjacent plants. Prices have been reduced over the years.

------

[1] United States Tariff Commission, *Synthetic Organic Chemicals, United States Production and Sales, 1947,* Washington, D.C., 1949, p. 7 and *Synthetic Organic Chemicals, United States Production and Sales of Tar and Tar Crudes, 1966,* TC Publication 248, Washington, D.C., 1968, pp. 2-3.

[2] The value of total sales would vary from this figure depending upon the proportion sold overseas.

[3] United States Tariff Commission, *Synthetic Organic Chemicals, United States Production and Sales of Tar and Tar Crudes, 1967,* Preliminary, Washington, D.C., February 1969, p. 3.

[4] Stanford Research Institute, *Chemical Economics Handbook,* Menlo Park, California, 1968, pp. 618, 5020 H-L.

[5] If the capacity of the Big Four is related to total capacity including coal derived benzene, their share was only 28.4%.

[6] *Chemical & Engineering News,* March 20, 1961, p. 119.

[7] *Chemical Week,* March 2, 1968, p. 17.

[8] *Ibid.,* November 3, 1962, p. 76.

[9] *Chemical Week,* February 8, 1964, p. 63.

[10] *Oil, Paint and Drug Reporter,* June 14, 1965, p. 36.

[11] *Ibid.,* January 29, 1968, p. 3.

[12] *Ibid.,* November 5, 1962, p. 49.

[13] *Chemical and Engineering News,* July 9, 1962, p. 25.

[14] *Chemical Week,* November 3, 1962, p. 75.

[15] *Ibid.,* March 2, 1968, p. 17.

[16] "Approximately 3,700 pounds of salt is required to produce 1 ton of chlorine and 1.12 tons of co-produced caustic." U.S. Department of Commerce, *Chemicals,* March 1965, p. 1.

[17] *The Chemical Industry Facts Book,* The Manufacturing Chemists' Association, Inc., 5th edition, 1962, p. 3. See also W. L. Faith, Donald B. Keyes, and Ronald L. Clark, *Industrial Chemicals,* 2nd Edition, John Wiley & Sons, New York, 1957, p. 262.

[18] U.S. Department of Commerce, Bureau of the Census, *Inorganic Chemicals and Gases, 1962,* Washington, D.C., December 5, 1963, p. 3; April 28, 1967, p. 3.

[19] U.S. Department of Commerce, Business and Defense Services Administration, *Alkalis and Chlorine Industry, Review of 1963 — Outlook for 1964,* Washington, D.C., January 22, 1964, p. 1 and *Chemicals,* June 1967, p. 4.

[20] "There have been years when caustic soda was in such surplus of supply that it was dumped into the sea. . . " Walter K. Gutman, "Chemicals," in *Investing in American Industries,* ed. by Lester V. Plum, Harper & Brothers, New York, 1960, p. 124.

[21] *Chemical Week,* April 19, 1969, p. 55.

[22]*Survey of Current Business,* September 1961, p. 14. U.S. Department of Commerce, Bureau of the Census, *Inorganic Chemicals and Gases,* Washington, D.C., April 28, 1967, p. 3; *Summary for 1967,* May 9, 1968, p. 2.

[23]Mathieson Alkali, Dow Process, Pennsylvania Salt, Hooker Electro Chemical, and Niagara Alkali. William H. Martin, "Potential Competition and the United States Chlorine-Alkali Industry," *The Journal of Industrial Economics,* July 1961, p. 235.

[24]In 1964, water and sewage treatment accounted for 1.2% and pulp and paper 14.9% of the chlorine used. *Chemicals,* June 1964, p. 4.

[25]Chemical uses accounted for approximately 49% of all chlorine produced in 1935 and 74% in 1967. Theodore Sheets, Jr., "Trends in Chlor-Alkali Industry," *Chemical Engineering Progress,* October, 1957, p. 482 and *Oil, Paint and Drug Reporter,* May 1, 1967, p. 9.

[26]Martin, *op. cit.,* p. 241 and *Chemicals,* March 1965, p. 11.

[27]*Chemicals,* March 1965, pp. 12-13.

[28]Ecusta Paper Co., six tons per day; Eastern Mfg. Co., six tons and S. D. Warren Co., five tons. See *Chemical Week,* March 7, 1959, pp. 114, 117.

[29]*Chemical Week,* December 10, 1966, p. 25.

[30]*Ibid.,* p. 26.

[31]Martin, *op. cit.,* p. 245 and *Chemical Week,* August 5, 1961, p. 46.

[32]See also *Concentration Ratios in Manufacturing Industries, 1958,* Report prepared by the Bureau of the Census for the Subcommittee on Antitrust and Monopoly of the Committee on the Judiciary, United States Senate, 87th Cong., 2nd Sess., U.S. Government Printing Office, Washington, D.C., 1962, p. 130.

[33]"The Chemical Industry Facts Book," *op. cit.,* p. 8.

[34]The U.S. Department of Justice conducted a federal grand jury investigation in Philadelphia in 1961. John Wiley Jones Co's. Western Division (distributor for Stauffer Chemical) and Tops Chemical (distributor for Dow) were indicted by the State of California in March 1961. *Chemical Week,* April 1, 1961, p. 18. In December 1938 nine principal liquid chlorine producers accepted a cease and desist order issued by the Federal Trade Commission in connection with price agreements and monopolistic practices. Simon Whitney, *Antitrust Policies,* Twentieth Century Fund, New York, 1958, Vol. I, pp. 197, 249.

[35]*Chemical Week,* January 7, 1961, p. 17.

[36]*The Wall Street Journal,* April 14, 1967.

[37]*Chemical Week,* February 17, 1968, p. 29.

[38]"TC Publication 248," *op. cit.,* p. 14.

[39]United States Tariff Commission, *Synthetic Organic Chemicals, United States Production and Sales of Cyclic Intermediates, 1967,* Preliminary, Washington, D.C., April 1969, p. 6.

[40]*Ibid.,* June 2, 1962, pp. 60-61.

[41]Peter H. Spitz, "Phthalic Anhydride Revisited," *Hydrocarbon Processing,* November 1968, p. 163.

[42]United States Tariff Commission, *Synthetic Resins and Their Raw Materials, Report No. 131,* Second Series, Washington, D.C., 1938, p. 100.

[43]"The 14-1/2 cent basis for phthalic anhydride in the early years of its development did more than anything else to stimulate the growth of the synthetic coatings industry in this country." *Chemical and Engineering News,* November 12, 1956, pp. 55, 68.

[44]*Petro/Chem. Engineer,* February 1963, p. 56.

[45]*Oil, Paint and Drug Reporter*, October 21, 1968, p. 42; United States Tariff Commission, *Synthetic Organic Chemicals, United States Production and Sales, 1962, TC Publication 114*, Washington, D.C., 1963, p. 14.

[46]*Chemical Week*, January 18, 1964, p. 59.

[47]*Oil, Paint and Drug Reporter*, April 14, 1969, p. 35.

[48]*Chemical Week*, August 2, 1969, p. 27.

[49]*Petro/Chem. Engineer*, February 1963, p. 56.

[50]See *Chemical Week*, July 1, 1961, pp. 16-17, August 20, 1966, pp. 78, 80 and August 17, 1968, p. 76.

[51]*Oil, Paint and Drug Reporter*, December 18, 1967, p. 32.

[52]*Chemical Week*, August 20, 1966, p. 80.

[53]Francis L. Hirt, "Patterns of Output Growth," *Survey of Current Business*, November 1966, p. 21.

[54]United States Tariff Commission, *Synthetic Organic Chemicals, United States Production and Sales of Plastics and Resin Materials, 1967*, Preliminary, Washington, D.C., 1969, p. 4.

[55]*Chemical Week*, May 22, 1965, p. 64.

[56]A production of 13 billion pounds of polyethylene is projected for 1980 by G. A. Fowles and M. W. Osborne of B. F. Goodrich Chemical Co., "Plastics Marketing: The Challenge of the Seventies," in *Chemical Marketing: The Challenge of the Seventies*, American Chemical Society, Washington, D.C., September 1968, p. 38.

[57]"United States Production and Sales of Plastics and Resin Materials, 1967," *op. cit.*, p. 4.

[58]*Chemical Week*, May 19, 1962, p. 137.

[59]*U.S. vs. Imperial Chemical Industries Ltd.*, 100 F. Supp. 215 (S.D.N.Y., 1951)

[60]*Fortune*, February 1954, pp. 136, 166.

[61]Goodrich-Gulf withdrew from the high density market in 1965, *Oil, Paint and Drug Reporter*, February 8, 1965, p. 3.

[62]*Chemical Week*, April 6, 1968, p. 40.

[63]*Ibid.*, February 15, 1964, p. 31.

[64]*Chemical Week*, October 14, 1967, p. 117.

[65]For example, "Now, say polyethylene makers, the larger bakers are showing a real interest in PE film because of its lower cost." *Chemical Week*, May 9, 1959, pp. 41-42.

[66]*Chemical & Engineering News*, March 4, 1963, p. 27.

[67]*Chemical Week*, April 6, 1968, p. 41.

[68]Theodore J. Kreps, *The Economics of the Sulfuric Acid Industry*, Stanford University Press, Stanford, California, 1938, p. 16.

[69]*Chemical Engineering*, April 25, 1966, p. 106.

[70]*Chemical Week*, October 12, 1968, p. 83 and May 11, 1968, p. 55, *Journal of Commerce*, May 23, 1968, p. 8.

[71]U.S. Dept. of Commerce, Bureau of the Census, Current Industrial Reports, Series M 28A (67)-13 Supplement 1, *Sulfuric Acid 1967*, Washington, D.C., November 7, 1968, p. 2.

[72]By-product production 1,114,881 long tons. U.S. Department of Interior, Bureau of Mines, *1967 Minerals Yearbook,* Vol. I-II, Washington, D.C., 1968, p. 1088.

[73]*Chemicals,* September 1967, p. 10.

[74]Faith, Keyes, and Clark, *op. cit.,* p. 750.

[75]"The greatest expansion occurred during 1965 and 1966 when capacity increased about 9.6 million tons. Most of this new capacity was centered in the south (especially Florida) near large phosphate rock mines." *Chemicals, op. cit.,* p. 10.

[76]*Chemicals, ibid,* September 1967, p. 10. See also *Chemical and Engineering News,* August 1, 1966, p. 15.

[77]*The Wall Street Journal,* February 24, 1964. That there has been wide recognition of these sales below list price over time is indicated by the following reports. In 1958, for example, decreased demand caused by a fall in steel production was accompanied by a shading of list prices. See *Chemical and Engineering News,* April 7, 1958, p. 7. It was reported in 1961 that "Price weakness and lower discounts were more evident than in 1960." "Sulfuric Acid Industry," *op. cit.,* p. 3. See also *Journal of Commerce,* January 6, 1961 which referred to sales "several dollars a ton below scheduled prices."

[78]Hirt, *op. cit.,* p. 21.

[79]U.S. Department of Commerce, Bureau of the Census, *1967 Census of Manufactures.* General Statistics for Industry Groups and Industries, Summary Series, Washington, D.C., April 1969, p. 7.

[80]Joseph Airov, *The Location of the Synthetic-Fiber Industry,* The Technology Press of the Massachusetts Institute of Technology, Cambridge, Massachusetts and John Wiley & Sons, New York, 1959, p. 19.

[81]Jack Blicksilver, *Man-Made Fibers: A Growth Industry for the Diversifying South,* Research Paper No. 20, Georgia State College of Business Administration, Atlanta, Georgia, June 1961, pp. 9-10.

[82]*Chemical Week,* December 9, 1967, p. 56.

[83]The Dow Chemical Company, *1967 Annual Report,* p. 9.

[84]*Chemical Week,* August 5, 1967, p. 61.

[85]*Survey of Current Business,* November 1966, p. 21.

[86]*Textile Organon,* September 1968, p. 160 and February 1969, p. 28.

[87]*Ibid.,* February 1969, p. 28.

[88]The B. F. Goodrich Company, *Annual Report 1968,* p. 8.

[89]*Chemical Week,* April 15, 1961, p. 76.

[90]*Textile Organon,* March 1961, p. 35, March 1964, p. 35, November 1968, p. 195.

[91]William J. Marshall, "Manmade Fibers: Industry Growth and Price Trends," *Monthly Labor Review,* October 1968, p. 32. See also U.S. Department of Commerce, *Growth Pace Setters In American Industry,* 1958-1968, Washington, D.C., October 1968, pp. 68-69.

[92]U.S. House of Representatives, Ways and Means Committee, *Foreign Trade and Tariff Proposals,* Part 6, 90th Cong., 2nd Sess., Washington, D.C., 1968, p. 2522.

[93]*Ibid.,* p. 2389.

[94] *Textile World*, September 1967, pp. 46, 48.

[95] *Chemical Week*, December 9, 1967, p. 52. However, imports of noncellulosic fibers were equal to only 2.1% of domestic supply in 1966. "Growth Pace Setters In American Industry, 1958-1968," *op. cit.*, p. 70.

[96] *The Wall Street Journal*, February 7, 1969, p. 5.

[97] For example, Celanese has reported that in 1968, its marketing organization was " . . . supported by $23 million worth of sales promotion and advertising, using all media from direct mail to prime-time commercial television . . . " *Celanese Annual Report 1968*, p. 6.

[98] *Chemical Week*, February 24, 1962, p. 45.

[99] *Celanese Annual Report* for the year ended December 31, 1966, p. 25.

[100] *Celanese Annual Report, 1967*, p. 3.

[101] *Business Week*, October 12, 1968, p. 141.

[102] *The Economist* (London), September 3, 1966, pp. 934-35.

[103] "Synthetic Resins and Their Raw Materials," *op. cit.*, p. 111.

[104] "United States Production and Sales of Cyclic Intermediates, 1967," *op. cit.*, p. 6.

[105] *Oil, Paint and Drug Reporter*, February 3, 1964, p. 37 and February 10, 1964, p. 33; U.S. Department of Commerce Business and Defense Services Administration, *Chemicals,* Quarterly Industry Report, March 1969, p. 26.

[106] *Oil, Paint and Drug Reporter*, April 17, 1968, p. 5.

[107] *Chemical Week*, November 4, 1967, p. 29.

[108] *Oil, Paint and Drug Reporter*, April 11, 1966, p. 9.

[109] *Ibid.*, March 3, 1969, p. 29.

[110] *Oil, Paint and Drug Reporter*, February 3, 1964, p. 9.

[111] U.S. Department of Commerce, Business and Defense Services Administration, *Chemicals,* Quarterly Industry Report, March 1969, p. 26.

[112] *Ibid.*, March 3, 1969, p. 29.

[113] *Chemical and Engineering News*, September 2, 1963, part 2, p. 100 and "TC Publication 248," *op. cit.*, p. 14.

[114] *Oil, Paint and Drug Reporter*, February 26, 1962, p. 47.

[115] U.S. Department of Commerce, Bureau of the Census, *United States Export Statistics*, Report FT 410, Part II, 1962 Annual, Washington, D.C., May 1963, p. 225.

[116] U.S. Department of Commerce, Business and Defense Services Administration, "Chemicals," *op. cit.*, p. 27.

[117] *Chemical Week*, September 22, 1962, and August 19, 1961, p. 93.

[118] *Chemical Week*, August 19, 1961, p. 93.

[119] *Oil, Paint and Drug Reporter*, February 26, 1962, p. 68 and *Chemical and Engineering News*, February 4, 1963, p. 23.

[120] *Oil, Paint and Drug Reporter*, June 10, 1968, p. 5.

[121] For a description of the historical development of the industry, see Charles F. Phillips, Jr., *Competition in the Synthetic Rubber Industry*, University of North Carolina Press, Chapel Hill, 1963, pp. 17-67.

[122] *First Report of the Attorney General on Competition in the Synthetic Rubber Industry*, Washington, D.C., May 1, 1956, p. 1. This was the first of ten annual reports prepared at the request of the Congress. The subsequent reports are cited below as Second Report, Third Report, etc.

[123] *Public Law 205*, August 7, 1953.

[124] "TC Publication 248," *op. cit.*, p. vii. In 1968, the value of shipments exceeded $1 billion. "Growth Pace Setters In American Industry, 1958-1968," *op. cit.*, p. 147.

[125] *Tenth Report*, (1964), p. 21.

[126] *Sixth Report*, (1960), p. 9.

[127] *Eighth Report*, (1962), p. 11.

[128] Charles F. Phillips, Jr., "Market Performance in The Synthetic Rubber Industry." *The Journal of Industrial Economics*, April 1961, p. 141.

[129] *Seventh Report*, (1961), p. 29.

[130] *Chemical Week*, May 28, 1960, p. 66.

[131] *The Journal of Commerce*, January 21, 1962, p. 25A.

[132] U.S. Department of Commerce, Bureau of the Census and Business and Defense Services Administration, *Current Industrial Reports: Rubber, Supply and Distribution for the U.S., Summary for 1967*, April 10, 1968, p. 6.

[133] Rubber Manufacturers Association, *Rubber Industry Facts, 1968 Edition*, September 1968, p. 16.

[134] *Seventh Report*, (1961), p. 5 and *Tenth Report*, (1964), pp. 26-27.

[135] *Tenth Report* (1964), p. 27.

[136] *1967 Annual Report: Tenneco Inc.*, p. 26.

[137] "Rubber, Supply and Distribution for the U.S.", *op. cit.*, p. 2.

[138] *Eighth Report*, (1962), pp. 4-5 and *Tenth Report*, (1964), p. 16.

[139] *Chemical Week*, March 23, 1968, p. 58.

[140] *Sixth Report*, (1960), p. 40.

[141] *Tenth Report*, (1964), p. 11.

[142] *Fifth Report*, (1959), p. 34.

[143] *Chemical Week*, June 15, 1963, pp. 103-104, 108.

[144] Phillips, *op. cit.*, p. 136 and *Chemical Week*, March 23, 1968, p. 56.

[145] *Oil, Paint and Drug Reporter*, May 26, 1969, p. 5.

[146] U.S. Department of Commerce, Bureau of the Census, *Annual Survey of Manufactures: 1966*, Value-of-Shipment Concentration Ratios by Industry, M66(AS)-8, Washington, D.C., 1968, p. 14.

[147] U.S. Department of Commerce, Office of Business Economics, *Business Statistics*, 1967 Biennial Edition, Washington, D.C., September 1967, p. 180.

[148] *Tenth Report*, (1964), pp. 14-15.

[149] It has been estimated that users "save from 2 cents to 5 cents per pound in processing and handling cost" for polyisoprene as compared with natural rubber. Edwin H. Sonneckin, "World Outlook For The Rubber Industry," *Chemical Marketing and Economics Papers*, September 1966, p. 49.

[150]*Chemical Week,* March 23, 1968, pp. 57-58.

[151]Derived from *Sixth Report* (1960), p. 23 and *Tenth Report,* (1964), p. 24.

[152]*Seventh Report,* (1961), p. 19.

[153]*Tenth Report,* (1964), p. 36.

Chapter VII

Prices And Price Policies

Proper pricing is an important ingredient of satisfactory profits. However, pricing procedures are difficult to pin down. A considerable amount of pricing appears to be based on inadequate information or a "feel of the market" or just plain hunch. While pricing cannot be reduced to mathematical formulas, an understanding of the forces which influence them is of vital concern to a company.[1]

Factors Considered In Pricing

Chemical prices are set by corporate officials rather than in an auction market such as a commodity exchange. There are many factors which a price official must consider and evaluate when he administers prices. These include the economic characteristics of product, competition, demand, costs, distribution system used, legal factors, political factors, and public relations.[2] The combination of these factors which may be significant varies for different products produced by a company and for the same product over a period of time. The freedom of action by the price administrator is limited by the operation of these forces. There is no way in which these factors can be fed into a computer to determine the "right" price. It is the informed judgment of the price maker which fuses these several factors into a final decision concerning price. Pricing is an art, not a science.

Price Policies

A price policy represents a broad program which a company establishes to guide the pricing decisions by its officials. Such a policy generally will cover the goals of pricing (e.g. to attain target returns on investment, to meet competition, to seek to retain or to increase market shares), the assignment of pricing responsibilities, and the various practices or procedures used in setting prices (e.g. quantity, cash, and/or functional discounts, geographic pricing practices,[3] internal methods for handling price changes, etc.). In some companies, pricing policies are formally spelled out; in most companies they are not. Policies may be dynamic (as when a company assumes the initiative in changing prices) or passive (as when a company follows the lead of others). A company often has varying pricing practices for different products.

Price policy in the chemical industry is difficult to summarize because of the wide variety of products sold. It is probably safe to say that most pricing practices used by other industries are followed for one or more chemical products.

In a competitive situation, such as that which characterizes many chemical products, it is particularly important to establish a pricing policy and then to operate within that framework. Otherwise, countermoves to competitor's actions may be made without full consideration of their implications and effects. In this connection, Monsanto's pricing policy has been summarized as follows:

". . . while we intend to remain competitive—aggressively competitive—we will not be stampeded either into selective or general market price reductions on the basis of rumors or isolated lower prices. There's just not enough margin left in the prices of most common chemicals to continue lowering them."[4]

There are many ingredients of a price policy as was noted earlier. Du Pont's pricing policy has been summarized as follows:

"Our price is based upon the obvious elements of conducting a business. The probable factory cost of manufacture is calculated. Expected sales and distribution charges are added. We then consider what return on investment is desirable, appropriate and consistent with our own long-term risk and tax exposure, and, finally, we make an appraisal of the use value of the product to the consumer, as well as of its worth in relation to competitive counterpart or alternate materials. The end result is usually a compromise of these various factors. . . .

"Ideally, an established product for which the price must fall below the level of a reasonable target return, stability considered, will be dropped and give way to expansion in more promising directions. . . .[5]

"The corporation's Executive Committee, while having a corporate target return in mind, does not expect the same rate of return from all departments. It recognizes differences in earnings potential by product groups; but it expects each to approximate an optimum rate in the light of such facts as the age and degree of stabilization of the product line, the elasticity of the demand, whether the product is mainly for use by other departments in Du Pont, or whether it is a by-product of another Du Pont product.

". . . a target return is something that is achieved only on an over-all basis, by mixing the high-return with the low-return products."[6]

Target returns are not easy to realize for individual products in the intensely competitive environment in which many chemicals are sold. This is particularly true for the new products, including plastics and other organics, which have been subject to considerable price cutting. It also has been difficult to achieve targets for inorganics. Thus, an official of Wyandotte Chemicals testified that for alkalies:

"My company's price schedules at the outset were f.o.b. mill prices. They were based on cost of production when operating at 80% of capacity, plus a reasonable profit. However, . . . we soon discovered that we could not sell 80% of our production in the area in which we have the lowest freight rate. Therefore, we found it necessary to reach out and take business nearer our competitors' plants where the customer enjoyed a lower freight rate from our competition than he did from us. Naturally, in order to obtain this business, it was necessary for us to meet the competitors' price . . . delivered to the customers' plant."[7]

Although pricing goals and policies may not always be achieved they do provide a plan of action for an orderly and consistent approach to pricing. In the intensely competitive chemical industry, it has become increasingly difficult to achieve predetermined target rates of return.

Economic Characteristics of the Product

The emphasis given to different pricing factors varies among products depending upon their characteristics. As was noted in Chapter I these include: importance of substitute materials, is it a by-product or a main product, changes in products and in processes, the extent of standardization of the product, the

142

need for specialized equipment by customers, the importance of derived demand, the high rate of innovation, the relative ease of entry by new producers, and the difficulty of determining costs for many of these products.

Whether a product is one which is produced and sold in large quantities— so-called commodity chemicals[8]—or a specialty or new product is particularly important. For the former, producers have little ability to control or influence the price. As *Chemical Week* has pointed out: "Products like ethylene, ammonia, heavy acids, chlorine, caustic, oxygen and nitrogen are commodities. They do not differ from one another, prices must be competitive, and so the highest-profit producer is the one with the lowest cost."[9]

According to the Brookings Institution study:

". . . Du Pont sells a number of standardized products having little prospect of being dressed up, either through innovation or improvement of service facilities, and others somewhat more differentiated (but not originated by Du Pont), the prices of which apparently are beyond its control. Because of this the company regards its price policy on these standard products as simply that of 'meeting competition,' in contrast to new products which are expected to meet a rigorous return and pay-out test."[10]

Du Pont has observed that "Any newcomer who wishes to sell [sulfuric] acid must be prepared to meet the price quoted elsewhere. If he cannot pull his costs down far enough to make a profit at that figure, he must abandon his plans to enter the market."[11]

In contrast, for a new product with unique characteristics, the producer has greater freedom in setting the price, particularly in the early stages of its sale. However, "If he quotes too high a figure, he will drive away potential customers and restrict the product's future growth."[12] Thus, this "freedom" is tempered by market forces and a concern about being priced out of the market.

Specialty products often have more stable prices than bulk commodities. W. R. Grace & Co. has reported that "specialized items developed to meet parituclar market requirements" are characterized by "long-term customer relationships and price stability. . . ."[13]

By producing an item with special characteristics it is possible to be insulated at least in part against price pressures. Because of "the downward trend of commodity chemical prices", Pennsalt has been "upgrading basic chemicals to specialties and intermediates." The company has reported that "the upgrading approach . . . pays off." To achieve this objective the company increased its captive use of hydrofluoric acid from 10% of its output in 1957 to close to 50% in 1967 and produced "specialties in both the laundry and dry cleaning field, and in metal processing."[14]

For polyvinyl chloride it has been reported that:

". . . producers are concentrating more and more on compounds produced to serve the particular needs of each customer so that he may improve or broaden his product. Compounds bring 3 to sometimes 20¢ more per pound than general purpose resin. This is now going on to such an extent that it broadens the average price of resin sold by a considerable percent. The polyethylene producers, too, are concentrating more and more on satisfying their various customers with formulations tailored to their needs, although several have said they intend to concentrate on no more than two or three types, such as film and coating grades. The first would concentrate on upgraded prices for specific formulations—the other would cut production costs by concentrating on his own specialty."[15]

143

W. F. Christopher of Hooker Chemical has effectively summarized the difference in pricing commodity-type and specialty chemicals as follows:

> "Different rules apply to different types of products. Undifferentiated, commodity-type chemicals move at 'competitive' market prices leaving little room for discretionary price action. Unique, specialty-type chemicals permit a range of price action depending on the price and availability of substitutes that can serve the same function . . . .

> "The growth cycle of the product affects the degree of pricing freedom. When a new product is introduced there is usually considerable latitude for discretion in pricing. As volume and profitability increase, competition is attracted in the form of identical or substitute offerings, and the room for freedom in pricing is reduced. As the product moves on to large volume and competitive selling, it becomes more and more a commodity-type product with little or no room for discretionary pricing. . . .

> "In undifferentiated, commodity-type products, price competition is seldom the route to profitability. The market will allow no producer a price advantage, and the inelasticity of demand will allow no increased total volume. So sales still are made on such nonprice considerations as service, quality, technical assistance, salesmanship, promotion, and packaging."[16]

The period during which a company tends to have a large amount of freedom in pricing has been decreased appreciably as research laboratories pour forth their stream of substitute and competing products. Two Du Pont products illustrate the point. That company made large investments in nylon and Delrin acetal resin. For nylon, it had many years in which to recoup the investment while for Delrin, an equivalent product (Celcon) was sold competitively within a year by Celanese and hence Du Pont's freedom of pricing action was curtailed.

In effect, there is a broad spectrum which ranges from a high degree of discretion in pricing decisions (within the framework of market pressures) for new specialties at one extreme to little or no freedom of action for commodity chemicals at the other.[17] Between these two extremes there are varying degrees of discretion in pricing as a product moves through its life cycle from a specialty to commodity status.

The more successful a new product, the more certain that competitors will seek to produce an equivalent product. Competitors are always waiting in the wings ready to move into any area that appears to be very profitable. Companies, therefore, are circumscribed in their freedom of action even during the early stages of the marketing of a new product. If they price at levels that make the product too attractive to potential competitors, the process of erosion of their areas of "freedom of action" starts earlier and moves faster.

Role of Competition

Because of the intensely competitive environment in which most chemical products are sold, this factor plays a major role in pricing. Competition from other producers of the same product, from newly developed products and processes in the chemical industry (interproduct competition), from products of other industries (interindustry competition), and from imports (foreign competition) affect chemical pricing decisions to varying degrees. One important aspect of this competitive situation is reflected in price leadership—and sometimes lack of followership as is noted later.

Competition from Other Producers: There has been an intensification of competition as new producers have entered the chemical industry, as former customers have produced or threatened to produce their own materials, as foreign markets have shrunk for some products with the "displaced exports" backing up on our domestic market, and as over-optimism combined with the foregoing developments has created problems of excess capacity for many products. As the economics of the industry and advances in technology have resulted in steadily larger plants "Newcomers to the field often build substantially higher volume than can be sold in the early years of production."[18] The result has been excess capacity and pressure on many prices.

The significance of competitive actions in chemical pricing has been well summarized by John L. Gillis of Monsanto: ". . . each Monsanto salesman has standing instructions to notify St. Louis whenever any customer tells him of a price offer lower than our existing prices. He is told also to get adequate evidence of the offer. . . .

"At one level or another we spend a great deal of time on pricing decisions. We try to keep a current audit on the pricing of all major products so we can *anticipate* possible market price changes rather than be caught by surprise when a competitor acts"[19] (italics added).

In light of the Robinson-Patman Act, it is important to obtain evidence of competitive offers whenever a price is cut to a particular customer to meet competition. In addition to compiling supporting documentation, Union Carbide requires the following procedures to be followed in such situations:

> "The Regional Managers should confirm by letter to the customer when we are agreeable to meeting a competitive price. . . . Letters to both contract and spot customers must contain the following statements:
>
> '. . . we elect to meet the competitive price for *(material)* outlined (in your letter of (*date*) or in your (*date*) conversation with Mr. _____). Therefore, effective (*date*), the following price will apply:
> (Quote competitive price)
> This price will be in effect until further notice from us or until expiration of the competitive offer, whichever first shall occur.' "

The Union Carbide procedure also provides that the salesmen should "reinvestigate the competitive situation" periodically. If their "competitor withdraws his offer," the recipient of the "competitive price" is promptly notified that it no longer applies and "that all subsequent orders are to be billed at schedule."

In other words, it is important to know who are the competing companies and how their officials have reacted to changing situations in the past. What is their philosophy of pricing? Are they aggressive or defensive in the pricing area? This knowledge must also extend to other products which compete for the same end uses. Only by having such knowledge can pricing officials plan their strategy and determine what price moves and counte moves will be most profitable.[20]

Interproduct Competition: Interproduct competition is a vital factor in chemical product pricing since the prices of alternative products available must be given heavy weight. And this means recognition that a product which is not competitive at the prevailing price may be very competitive if its price is reduced. Thus, the price official must be concerned with all the products which can be substituted for the one he is pricing. The following are illustrative:

> Natural glycerine usually is priced about 1% below synthetic glycerine.[21]

Natural phenol "historically has always been priced a few cents lower" than the synthetic product.[22]

Maleic anhydride prices were reduced as a "reaction to lower benzene prices."[23]

Synthetic fiber pricing is affected by the growing number of such products.

"Extreme weakness" in leather prices was cited by Du Pont as a factor creating "marketing problems" for Corfam in 1967; prices were reduced for Corfam in that year."[24]

Price of natural alcohol was reduced because of competition from synthetic alcohol.[25]

Prices were reduced by American Cyanamid for XT acrylic-based polymer "to win a larger share of the food packaging market now held by glass, paper, and other plastics."[26]

Foreign Competition: As foreign countries have recovered from the destructive effects of World War II, their capacity to produce has been significantly expanded for many products, including chemicals. Increasingly, competition from imports has played a role in our domestic pricing decisions, particularly those to reduce prices. For example, a cut in the price of hydrogen peroxide by Allied Chemical was designed in part to "more effectively meet foreign competition." Other products for which prices have been reduced at least in part because of foreign competition include: vinyl resins, dyestuffs, acrylic fiber, citric acid, sulfamic acid, urea, trichloroethylene, sodium bichromate and ethyl vanillan. By offering to sell at lower prices importers affect prices even if they make no sales.

With the expansion of world markets and the development and growth of foreign competitors, American companies must consider the entire world situation in their pricing decisions for many products. Import prices, tariffs, and prospective changes in tariffs all must be analyzed. In this connection it is becoming increasingly difficult to treat excess domestic supplies as salable at low prices abroad as often has been done in the past. Newly created and growing chemical industries in foreign countries insist upon protection against this practice and where that protection is not forthcoming they take retaliatory action. Moreover, there is no reason why American companies, selling in foreign markets characterized by shortages, should sell below the locally established prices. In other words, domestic chemical prices are now more closely tied in with world prices than has been true at any time since before World War I.

Role of Demand

The level of demand and the desire to expand are given considerable weight in chemical pricing. Demand cannot be considered independently of the available supply or of the capacity to produce. Scattered price increases for chemicals in the early part of 1964 were headlined as follows: "Prices of Key Products Firm as Heavy Buying Cuts Excess Capacity."[27] Earlier the prices of many of the affected products had been cut under the pressure of excess supplies.

Meeting the customer's needs is an important aspect of price policy. One unidentified chemical executive has stated that his company's pricing philosophy involved two considerations:

"The first is that the price should be such that the profit on the product will reflect satisfactory return on our investment. The second is that the price should be such that it reflects *a satisfactory value in features given to a customer.* Unless these two criteria are reasonably met, there is reason to question our having the product in our line"[28] (italics added).

Use value is particularly important in connection with new products which are designed to compete with existing products. Then it is important to determine what price will encourage the customer to make the substitution when consideration is given to technical factors as well as to price. Where a specific use can be met by a number of products with differing prices, depending on the quality sought in the final product, a decision must be made concerning the specific quality market in which penetration is sought in order to determine the potential sales at any given price.

While in other industries, price increases in the post-World War II period almost invariably have been explained in terms of costs, chemical companies also have frankly stated that prices have been raised for other reasons, including: strong demand,[29] better market conditions,[30] higher prices for end products,[31] and to adjust depressed prices.[32] These four reasons are clearly related to improved demand. Under conditions of strong demand it has been possible to make upward price adjustments to correct previous sharp price declines and to improve a company's profit position.

However, prices have sometimes declined despite "strong demand."[33] For new products, as is noted below, prices often are reduced in order to "broaden markets" and thus to increase effective demand. The lower prices by attracting greater volume contribute to lower unit costs which in turn make sales at those prices profitable.

Price reductions have been made effective for many products in order to broaden the market. Even when such reductions are due to other forces, they may have a very favorable impact on effective demand. Thus Du Pont has reported that the "substantial rate of growth in the market for synthetic fibers [was] stimulated by a long-term downward price trend which broadens market penetration."[34]

For some products price and volume are inextricably tied together. Because of the large investment required to produce many products, it is very important to determine the elasticity of demand—even though the calculation necessarily will be very rough. It has been reported that "Statistical studies have indicated that individual plastics frequently have a price elasticity factor of 2 to 3—i.e., a 1% price decline resulted in a 2 to 3% volume increase. The effect upon profits, however, was often the reverse as the expanding volume was not sufficient to compensate for the drastically reduced profit margin."[35]

Although chemical prices do not move up and down like a yo-yo in response to every change in demand, the experience in the 1960s indicated that they are not immune to downward pressures when supply exceeds demand by a wide margin.

Role of Costs

Costs are only one factor considered in pricing as some companies specifically recognize in their pricing policy statements. Actually, it is extremely difficult for a company to determine costs for many chemical products for a variety of reasons. Joint products or by-products may be developed from a single process or by the use of a single plant so that cost allocation often tends to be extremely difficult and hence must be arbitrary. Research laboratories are working on numerous projects simultaneously and in addition must make allowance for failures as well as successes. As a result it is almost impossible to assign all research costs to specific products.[36] Of considerable significance is the fact that chemical production usually involves greater overhead than most other industries. Large investment in facilities, high rate of obsolescence, and large expenditures for research and development combine to make overhead costs relatively high. Incremental costs (costs incurred for added output) are very low for chemicals—it doesn't cost much more to operate at full capacity than at 50% of capacity. However, incremental prices set the floor below which prices cannot be cut without increasing out of pocket losses. The floor "depends on the out-of-pocket cost of the lowest cost producer(s)."[37]

Because of the relatively large overhead costs, increases in volume act to cut total unit costs—often by significant proportions. Where demand is elastic, the lower prices will act to stimulate demand substantially as has been evident for plastics in recent years. The result is a decline in unit costs which makes it profitable to sell at the lower prices. In this type of situation, lower prices lead to lower costs.

Under these conditions, price determines cost, rather than the reverse. Thus price declines may create pressures to cut costs in order to maintain profitability. Charles H. Sommer, chairman of Monsanto Company, has pointed out that the pressure of lower prices "has speeded up plant modernization and improvements, and has put pressure on production costs with rather remarkable results." This development characterized many chemicals during the 1960s when price declines were widespread for organics.

When price increases are announced, chemical companies often follow the practice of companies in other industries of attributing such increases to higher costs.[38] Both increases and decreases in prices have been related to changes in raw material costs.

Price increases

Phthalic anhydride—when prices rose for naphthalene[39]

Anhydrous sodium bisulfite—because of higher prices for caustic soda[40]

Copper cyanide—because of higher copper prices[41]

Sulfuric acid—when prices rise for sulfur[42]

Surfactant prices—when ethylene and propylene oxide prices rose[43]

Price decreases

Phthalic ester plasticizers—followed lower prices for phthalic anhydride[44]

Phenol—because of lower prices for benzene[45]

Phthalic plasticizers—because of lower prices for alcohols[46]

Closely related to costs as a reason for raising prices is the claim that higher prices are required to induce construction of new capacity. Thus it was stated that the price of phenol was increased to induce "construction of new capacity to keep up with growing demand."[47] Similarly, a higher price for vinyl chloride monomer was justified in part because "construction of additional capacity has been restricted" as price declines had made it "difficult to obtain a return on investment that is high enough to justify the outlay."[48]

Chemical companies also have emphasized that lower costs, due to improved manufacturing efficiency or because of greater volume, have made possible reductions in the prices of many new products.[49]

W. F. Christopher of Hooker Chemical has warned:

"In directing pricing policy toward profit goals, the simplest technique, and one too often used is the 'cost plus' method of establishing prices. In the cost-plus-margin version this method makes price calculations easy. The only fault is that the answers are usually wrong. . . .

"Cost-plus approaches can easily result in prices (a) higher than the market will permit, or (b) lower than the market is willing to accept in relation to the value offered. Fortunately, market considerations usually take over at this point and appropriate adjustments are made in the calculated price so that the product can be sold. . . .

"A question is in order here. If market considerations take over to adjust the calculated price based on cost, why not begin with these considerations in the first place? And why not study in detail the market influences on price with the care and attention now commonly given to the cost considerations? If the market sets, or limits the price, why not try to find out as exactly as possible just what these determinants are? Then cost, so far as it can be known, will be seen in a more constructive light—not as a determiner of price, but as a determiner of the profitability of any given price action."[50]

This is the meat of the cocoanut. Costs determine profitability. As is evident from the preceding sections, competition, the use value of the product, and the efforts to broaden demand usually are of primary importance in price determination. When these factors result in prices which do not yield satisfactory profits at the prevailing level of costs a company must either reduce its costs or withdraw from producing the affected product.[51] It cannot merely add to its costs, however determined, some desired profit margin and expect that consumers will pay that price.

Excess Capacity

In the 1960s, a potent factor affecting prices has been the development of excess capacity for many important chemicals. Supply and demand have gotten out of balance generally because of factors inducing an expansion in total capacity rather than because of declines in demand although the latter development may sometimes be important. Large increases in excess capacity have developed for several reasons:

1. New competitors have entered many markets with the accompanying increases in capacity at a faster rate than demand has been expanding. High profits induce new entries, whose additions to total supply create pressures on price and act to reduce the profit margins since the expanded output cannot be sold at the existing price level. The overcapacity which developed for synthetic fibers in 1966 and 1967 resulted in part because a large number of new producers entered the industry here and abroad while the established producers were adding to their capacity (See Chapter VI). The result was intensive pressure for lower prices and in turn lower profits. Similarly, benzene capacity is periodically overexpanded as existing producers and new entries have responded to tight market conditions and favorable price relationships by increasing capacity.

2. Misjudgment of immediate increases in demand has resulted in a mad scramble to increase capacity. Chemical producers looking at the developing

countries saw a tremendous market for fertilizers. Many companies rushed to expand capacity in the mid-1960s and to enter the industry. When the potential demand did not become effective, large scale overcapacity developed and chaos in prices became the order of the day.

3. Great strides in technology often have been accompanied by enormous increases in the size of plant that will be most economic to operate. One result has been to make obsolete many smaller plants and another has been to create excessive capacity. For example, for ammonia, new plants with a capacity of 1,000 tons or more per day had much lower costs per unit than older 400 tons per day plants. The development of larger plants results in a new dimension to competition which puts pressure on all producers to install the more efficient larger plants and to retire the excess capacity represented by the smaller less efficient plants. But it takes time to close down these less efficient plants because they can continue to operate so long as they make some contribution to overhead costs. During that period, excess capacity is present and as the larger more efficient plants seek to operate at effective capacity, prices are lowered. Jonnard has pointed out that "Price cuts are often caused by the newer producers with new and simpler plants. . . ."[52] In time, the less efficient plants are retired and a new supply-demand balance is achieved.

4. Excess capacity may develop for one or more by-products or co-products because capacity is increased to supply the main product. An outstanding illustration is provided by chlorine and caustic soda. The two products are produced in a fixed relationship with 1.1 pounds of caustic soda for every pound of chlorine. The demand for chlorine has been expanding more rapidly than that for its co-product. The result has been periodic gluts on the market for caustic soda with the resulting slashes in prices.

5. When capacity is built for captive use, the most economic size of plant may dictate a larger capacity so that merchant sales must be made if it is to be operated at most efficient levels. Thus, not only is the company's former demand removed from the market place but it also adds to net market supplies and thus contributes to depressing price. Phthalic anhydride and synthetic phenol provide illustrations (See Chapter VI).

6. Foreign trade has affected the domestic supply—demand situation for some products and resulted in excess capacity for domestic producers. In the late 1960s, for example, competition from imports contributed to the excess capacity of man-made fibers. Similarly, the loss of foreign markets may temporarily result in overcapacity as exports are reduced. Phenol in the early 1960s is an illustration.

7. Supplies may be increased because a new source is developed. As new and bigger chemical complexes are built and as technology becomes more sophisticated, supplies are sometimes supplemented by a flow of by-products. Jonnard has reported, for example, that in 1954 "industry production of almost 500 million pounds of acetone was augmented by about 50 million pounds of by-product acetone from the new cumene-phenol plants. With these new producers in the market, the price dropped from 8-1/2¢ per lb. in April to 7¢ per lb. in less than a year, with unofficial prices lower than that."[53]

Prompt response of prices to conditions of oversupply resulting from the above developments characterized the chemical industry during the 1960s.

Price Leadership

Price leadership and followership is found throughout American industry. Many companies, large and small, exercise little or no initiative in the determination of many prices. They compete by following the leadership of other companies which assume the initiative in making changes in prices.

Price leadership is particularly important for standardized products such as chemicals. The initiative for price changes usually is taken by one of the larger companies in the industry. The leader is not always the same company. The price leader determines the timing and magnitude of the price change. Some company must raise or lower price in response to changing conditions and it is usually one of the larger companies that does so. Such firms often have more adequate staffs to evaluate economic developments.

Consistent matching of the prices of the leader by other sellers over long periods may develop without any agreement and without any coercion by one firm over the others. Each company acting independently in its own interest may compete by following the leadership of another firm and all the firms acting in this manner produce the phenomenon known as price leadership. Competitive conditions and sometimes changes in costs clearly provide the motivation for price "followership" for most of the companies involved. Nevertheless, some economists have labeled such price leadership as "tacit collusion."[54] Tacit collusion is a possibility under these conditions and indeed price leadership has been practiced in collusive agreements. But price leadership is not necessarily collusive action nor is it usually contrary to the public interest.

There generally will be a reluctance to raise or lower prices in the absence of a major change in the economic conditions affecting the product. The initiating factor may be a significant rise in labor costs, changes in raw material costs, large increases or decreases in demand, changes in the prices of substitute products, a general condition of inflation, surplus capacity, or some other factor. Usually all or most companies in an industry are affected similarly by such developments. This is why price leaders (who act as barometers) usually have been followed when they raise prices as well as when they reduce prices.

Price leaders were closely followed by other companies throughout most of the inflationary period after the end of World War II. However, it should be emphasized that the general tendency for many companies to follow practically all price increases in the earlier postwar years did not reflect "tacit collusion" as has been suggested. Rather, it reflected to a large extent the inflationary environment in which those patterns emerged. Under conditions of inflation, strong pressures push up prices, wages, and profits. Often the blame for the price rise is directed at one group. This is reflected in the claims by industry that higher prices were the result of higher labor costs and the claims by labor that higher prices resulted from the desire for higher profits. Such claims ignore the fact that the fundamental pressures for higher prices, higher wages, and profits are generated by fiscal or monetary inflation. At such time, the reason for prompt price followership by practically all firms is found in these inflationary pressures.

That a large company made the first move was less important than the fact that their competitors were anxious to raise prices, too, and felt that they had to wait until the largest companies had done so. The departure from the early postwar practices in the early 1960s took place for a number of products for which price increases were not followed and had to be cancelled. Clearly new competitive influences were developing.[55]

In the 1960s, there was considerable price cutting in the chemical industry as was noted earlier. Generally such price cuts were followed by other companies.[56]

The typical pattern has been first a shading of list prices by one company, then other companies compete by shading their prices, and finally an announcement is made of a new and lower list price. It must be recognized that the formal change in list price is only a recognition of the price decline which already has taken place. In such circumstances, the apparent leader in reducing the price is really a price follower. For example, when Du Pont reduced the price of methanol by 2 cents a gallon in 1967, the *Oil, Paint and Drug Reporter* stated: "It can be assumed that Du Pont's move merely reflected an earlier decline in actual market prices, which always run substantially below list prices."[57]

While a number of price increases were announced and apparently held during this same period, chemical companies in some instances had to rescind price increases which other companies failed to follow.

The 38 instances listed in Table VII-1 cover only a small proportion of the many chemical products which are sold. Undoubtedly, there are other illustrations which could be added to the list. Nevertheless, the experience demonstrates that chemical producers can not arbitrarily raise prices without considering economic pressures. Most of the leading chemical companies as well as several smaller ones had this experience. Chemical producers are not free to raise prices merely because only a few companies produce the particular item. Competitive pressures resulting from excess capacity and the threat of loss of markets are potent forces which restrict the freedom to set prices—even of oligopolists. Clearly, these developments reflect the price competition which was very much in evidence in the 1960s.

Contractual Arrangements

Many chemicals are bought under contracts which cover a purchaser's needs for a year or longer. Illustrations include: caustic soda, sulfuric acid, phthalic anhydride, aluminum sulfate, alum, and maleic anhydride. The contract includes a price but this may be changed periodically by the seller. The buyer usually must be given advance notice if the price is to be increased for products covered by the contract. A typical provision is the following:

> "Seller may increase any price hereunder on the first day of any calendar quarter-yearly period by delivering or mailing written notice to Buyer at least fifteen (15) days prior to such day. Buyer, however, shall have the right to cancel the undelivered portion of the material to which such increase in price applies by delivering or mailing written notice to Seller prior to the date when such increase is to become effective."

A decision to change prices may be made at any time and the timing need not coincide with the contract notice period. Thus, it is fairly typical when prices are increased for products covered by such contracts, that the price change becomes effective immediately for spot sales and a month or two later for contract sales. For example, in February 1964, the price of phthalic anhydride was increased at once on spot sales while on contract sales the effective date was April 1, 1964.[58]

The spot price of hydrofluoric acid was increased December 1, 1967 while on contract shipments the price change became effective January 1, 1968.[59] When

Table VII-1
Price Leaders Who Were Not Followed, 1961-69

Product	Company Announcing Price Changes	Date	Refused to Change Prices
Polyethylene	Du Pont	January 1961	Union Carbide and U.S. Industrial Chemicals
Urea	W. R. Grace & Spencer	June 1961	Other producers
Polystyrene compounds	Union Carbide Plastics	October 1961	Monsanto
Polystyrene, general purpose	Rexall Chemical & Dow	do	do
Nitrogen products	Allied Chemical	December 1961	Other producers
Polyvinyl chloride films and resins	Pantasote Co.	February 1962	
Polyethylene	Allied Chemical	August 1962	Union Carbide
Hydrofluoric acid	Dixon Chemical	do	Leading producers
Aluminum sulfate (Michigan Territory)	Allied Chemical	do	Other producers
Perchloroethylene	Dow	September 1962	Du Pont
Acrylonitrile	Union Carbide	March 1963	American Cyanamid
Polyvinyl chloride copolymer resins	Monsanto	do	Other producers
Chloride acetate copolymer	Diamond Alkali	do	Other producers raised price by ½ cent instead of 1 cent and Diamond cut back increase
Hydrofluoric acid	Allied Chemical	February 1964	Stauffer Chemical
Polyethylene	Dow	do	Union Carbide
Tetramethyl and tetraethyl lead	Nalco	September 1964	Du Pont and Ethyl
Alcohols for plasticizers	Union Carbide	December 1964	Enjay Chemical
DDT	Allied Chemical	Winter 1964	Other producers
Sulfuric acid	Allied Chemical raised price by $1.50 a ton	August 1965	American Cyanamid increased price by $1.10 a ton which Allied met
Methanol	Commercial Solvents	March 1966	Other producers
Polyethylene film	Du Pont raised price by two cents	April 1966	Union Carbide and others increased price by ½ cent and then Du Pont matched the more modest hike
Pentaerythritol	Hercules, Reichhold, Tenneco	April 1966	Celanese Corp.
Sodium phosphate compounds		April 1966	Olin Mathieson Chemical cut a price increase in half
Hydrofluoric acid	Pennsalt	May 1966	Some other producers
Acetal resin	Du Pont	October 1966	Celanese Plastics Co.
Chlorine	Allied Chemical raised prices $4 a ton (east of Rockies)	December 1966	Other companies increased price by $2 a ton; Allied matched that price
Sulfur Dioxide	Essex Chemicals	February 1967	Other producers
X-Ray Film (Cronex medical)	Du Pont	February 1967	Eastman Kodak and others
Sodium tri-polyphosphate	Hooker	June 1967	Other producers
Anhydrous lithium chloride	Foote Mineral	December 1967	Lithium Corp. raised prices 2½¢ or half the Foote increase
Propylene (glycol and oxide)	Wyandotte raised price by one cent	March 1968	Union Carbide and Olin followed but Dow increased price by only one-half cent and postponed effective date for three months; others lowered prices to meet this price
Calcium chloride	Dow	March 1968	Allied raised prices by 50 cents a ton instead of $1
Polyethylene (low density film grade resins)	Dow	April 1968	Other producers
Styrene	Dow	April 1968	Other producers
Polystyrene	Monsanto	May 1968	Other producers
Caustic Potash solution	Dow	June 1968	Other producers
Chlorinated solvents (Trichlorethylene and perchlorethylene)	Dow	September 1968	PPG Industries
Phenol (price in Western territory)	Union Carbide	December 1968	Other producers

vinyl chloride monomer prices were increased by B. F. Goodrich Chemical it was announced that "Contract prices will be lifted according to contract stipulations."[60] Trimethylene chlorobromide spot prices were increased early in October 1968 with "Contract tags . . . raised January 1, 1969."[61] For plastics the role of contract prices has been described as follows:

> "On the bottom level of the price structure are contract prices. These go to purchasers that agree to buy large amounts within a certain time, generally three months. For this they get a 1 or 2¢ discount under the *going* price. If the price goes up during the contract period the supplier generally protects the purchaser; if it drops he lowers the contract price also. The purchaser is thus well-protected. There are enough contracts in force so that when the industry makes a general price change there is always an excuse for confusion since contract prices are a confidential matter between seller and buyer; sellers become cautious about disturbing their price relations with contract buyers."[62]

On the other hand, price reductions usually are effective at the same time for spot and contract sales. Moreover, the buyer is free to buy elsewhere. A typical contract contains a provision like the following:

> "If Buyer furnishes proof to Seller that Buyer can purchase from a manufacturer in any contract year any of the aforesaid materials produced within the United States, of the same quality as the then undelivered quantity hereunder during such contract year, and at a lower price than is then in effect under this Agreement, then if Seller shall not reduce the price hereunder to such lower price for the aforesaid quantity, Buyer may purchase such quantity from the other manufacturer, whereupon Buyer's commitment under this Agreement shall be reduced by the quantity so purchased."

Long term contracts are attractive to the seller because cost economies can be effected by a more even and better planned flow of deliveries, and because his selling costs are reduced. To the buyer, there are the advantages of an assured source of supplies, the avoidance of short-term price fluctuations, a reduction in purchasing department costs, and sometimes the ability to negotiate a more favorable price or terms of sale. Aimison Jonnard of Esso Chemical Co. reports that "Risks of a new capital investment are occasionally reduced by offering customers a long-term contract (e.g. five years) at a price lower than list, one-year contract or spot prices. . . . Such prices are not usually published, but are sometimes generally known because the prospective producer presumably contacts a good many prospects before signing some as customers."[63]

Pricing New Products

The pricing of new products is important to chemical companies because a large proportion of the sales volume is derived from such products. For example, in 1969 Roger W. Gunder, president, Stauffer Chemical Co., reported that "one-third of our sales come from products that were in the research lab five to ten years ago."[64]

New products fall into two categories: (1) those which are minor modifications of, identical with, or equivalent to existing chemical products as, for example, various polyester and acrylic fibers and (2) those which are entirely new products to the chemical industry as, for example, polyethylene and Corfam poromeric material. In pricing new products, a company has much less freedom of action for products in the first group than for those in the second group.

The fact that an equivalent product is available to meet the specific need means that the new product must be slotted into the existing price structure with due allowance for differences in quality, processing problems, and savings made possible by its use. In other words, the product may be a new addition to the producing company's line but not to the market. The primary factor considered in pricing such a "new" product is the price of competing or substitute products. Costs can play a role in the decision as to whether the company should manufacture the product because, in relationship to the prevailing price structure, they indicate whether the venture can or will be profitable; however, costs neither determine nor influence the price.

For products which are genuinely new to the chemical industry several factors must be considered: (1) the prices of equivalent products already on the market; (2) the magnitude of research and development costs and the philosophy concerning how this investment should be recovered; (3) estimates of demand for existing products and their elasticity; (4) alternative estimates of production and selling costs; (5) estimates of the customer's use cost; and (6) "what the probable future price of the new product and competitive products will be."[65]

Du Pont's philosophy for pricing new products has been summarized as follows:

". . . the manufacturer cannot be arbitrary in setting a price. If he quotes too high a figure, he will drive away potential customers, and restrict the product's future growth. If he quotes too low a figure, he will have no chance to recover his costs and in years to come make a profit. . . .

". . . Thus, the market and the costs set the introductory price. When and if the market expands, and manufacturing can be made more efficient by virtue of increased volume and improved process equipment, the introductory price can be adjusted downward."[66]

Du Pont has summarized its profits objectives for new products as follows:

"If our contribution of an improved or new product is an exceptional achievement because of long and expensive research and development and a high permanent investment hazard, and if it affords profitable opportunities to consumers or converters, we feel we are entitled to an exceptionally good return and we ask a corresponding price for it. If our contribution has been only a moderate one, then we determine upon a price that will give us a profit consistent with our work, effort, and risk."[67]

The evolution of pricing for new products has been succinctly summarized as follows:

"Traditionally, new chemical products are introduced at prices that reflect low initial demand and correspondingly high unit production costs.

"Then as markets grow, economies of larger scale production justify lower prices, which in turn permit penetration into new markets. Also, process improvements or new processes utilizing lower-cost raw materials often trim production costs.

"But eventually these once special products achieve—or more properly, are relegated to—commodity status. At this point capacity is sufficient to satisfy known markets, new markets are difficult to find, and further growth approaches the rate of general industrial growth. No longer does a price cut expand the market; and if one producer cuts the price to garner a larger share of the existing market, his advantage is short-lived since other producers must either match his price or lose their business to him."[68]

In connection with new products, demand usually is an unknown. Costs are so closely related to volume and to decisions concerning the allocation of research costs and starting-up expenses that almost any cost figure desired can be obtained. For new products, the philosophy of pricing may be the primary determinant of the initial offering price. Should a price be set high initially and then reduced as experience with consumer acceptability, production techniques, and costs is accumulated? Or should a much lower price be set initially to tap a mass market from the outset? One large company has indicated it will not use the initial low price in the hope of developing markets because the expected volume often does not materialize. Market research data sometimes are helpful in determining which approach to adopt. A higher price may help to create a better image for a product and thus add to the willingness of consumers to buy it over long periods of time. This is particularly true when the higher price is associated with quality.

The phrases "to broaden the market" or "to increase sales" are found frequently in statements explaining price reductions.[69] Dow reported a major price cut for ethyleneimine as part of a "planned program to make this new chemical building block commercially attractive for its many potential applications."[70] Emphasis also is given to improving technology with the accompanying lower costs as a factor making possible lower prices.[71]

It is not always possible to sell large quantities of a new product when it is first introduced. Industrial buyers want to make sure that no production problems will arise in its use and that it can live up to its advertised capabilities and performance. Small volume initially also reflects the inability or unwillingness of producers to build the facilities to manufacture large quantities until the extent of market acceptance is tested and determined. Sometimes, the introduction of a new product on a small scale permits its use in higher priced products and may add to the consumer awareness of the product on a prestige basis. For example, Corfam, was initially used only in high priced shoes. After a product is introduced and any "bugs" are eliminated, intensive efforts are made to educate potential buyers as to the advantages inherent in its use. With expanding ability to manufacture the product, the prices are then reduced to broaden the market.

Summary

Pricing policies provide a plan of action for an orderly and consistent approach to pricing. It is desirable to formulate such policies even though the goals set forth are not always attained. For example, in the competitive chemical industry it has become increasingly difficult to attain target returns.

Chemical prices are determined by a number of factors which vary in relative importance, depending upon the product to be priced. Of greatest importance are:

1. Competition—from other producers of the same product, from equivalent or substitute products, and from imports.

2. The level of demand and the desire to expand demand.

3. The relationship of capacity to demand—particularly excess capacity.

4. The use value to the buyer.

5. Changes in cost, particularly for raw materials, However, costs generally do not play a major role in pricing. Rather they are important primarily in determining the profitability of the product at a given level of prices.

The discretion in pricing available to chemical companies ranges over a wide spectrum, from substantial latitude for highly specialized products at one extreme to little or no discretion for bulk or commodity chemicals at the other. As a product moves from specialty to commodity status, the degree of latitude in pricing available to a company is steadily reduced. For new products, the extent of freedom in pricing depends on whether it is an entirely new product to the chemical industry or whether it is merely an addition to a company's product line of an already available product. In the latter case, the price must be slotted into the existing market and hence a company has little latitude in its pricing unless it can differentiate its product in some way. However, for an entirely new product considerable discretion is available and a company must decide at what price the product should be introduced. Where a natural product already is available, its equivalent cost is an important factor in the decision. Usually, the initial price is reduced if such an action will broaden demand.

Trends Of Prices

Prior to 1800, chemicals generally were relatively scarce and high in price. Edward H. Hempel has summarized the history of prices for earlier centuries as follows:

> "From the days of the Pharaohs until long after the Middle Ages, chemicals were definitely expensive. . . . Roman dyers could pay very high prices for Egyptian alum and natural saltpeter, Spanish copper salts, Sicilian sulphur, and Adriatic purple, because it was only to the very rich that they sold the goods which they dyed with these materials. . . .

> "Even 1,500 years later, when French, Spanish, Dutch and English traders ventured forth into new lands and after two or four years' absence brought home new spices, precious stones, new dyestuffs, perfumes, and chemical raw materials in larger quantities, prices did not come down appreciably. The silk and velvet dyers of Lyons, the linen industries of Flanders and Brussels . . ., the soap makers of Marseilles, London, and Amsterdam, the painters, glass makers, hatters, tanners, and armorers of France and Western Europe—all used more chemicals than had been used in the days of Rome, but they did not pay much less for them in their respective currencies. . . .

> "Only after the French revolution, when the French government again encouraged the chemical sciences and manufactures and the new machine industries began to create new markets, did the supply of chemicals gradually increase in every land and chemicals begin to lose their rarity values. The discovery of new processes for making cheaper substitutes (Leblanc soda for potash, etc.) not only filled the increasing demand, but finally sent prices of chemical products on their downward trend."[72]

Between 1800 and 1890, chemical prices declined sharply in the United States. During that period the Warren-Pearson index of all wholesale prices declined by 36.4% while their index of five chemicals and drugs fell by 78.9%.[73] Hempel reports that by 1880, chemicals already had become a "penny business". The industry "sold at least 60 per cent of its entire output at an average price of 2.6 cents per pound."[74]

1890-1913: In the first few years of this period, prices continued the decline that had been taking place since the Civil War. By 1896 the long decline reached its low point and prices began a rise which brought the general wholesale price level in 1913 to a level 24% higher than in 1890. Prices of chemicals and allied products (no chemicals price index available for this period) followed a similar trend. However, the rise after 1896 reached its high point in 1902 and then these prices moved irregularly lower. In 1913, prices of chemicals and allied products were 9.6% higher than in 1890. Thus, these prices rose less than half as much as all wholesale prices in the pre-World War I period.

1913-1939: This period witnessed very wide gyrations in wholesale prices, largely during and immediately after World War I. The chemicals price index reached its peak during the war while the general level of wholesale prices continued to rise until 1920. The following tabulations show the comparisons for several key dates:[75]

	Wholesale Price Index	Chemicals and Allied Products	Chemicals
	------ (1926 = 100) ------		
1913	69.8	80.2	89.9
1918	131.3	182.3	187.3
1920	154.4	164.7	166.5
1939	77.1	76.0	84.7

Per Cent Changes—Selected Periods

1913-20	121	105	85
1920-39	—50	—54	—49
1913-39	10	—5	—6

The chemical industry began its fabulous development in this country during World War I. When German supplies were cut off, chemical prices rose sharply. Between 1913 and 1918 the chemical price indexes doubled. However, as American production expanded, the price index trended downward; the low point was reached in 1932-33. During the balance of the 1930s, prices rose moderately. In 1939, the average level of chemical prices was 6% *lower* than in 1913, although the total wholesale price index was 10% *higher*.

1939-1951: During World War II, chemical prices increased 14% as compared with the 37% rise in the total wholesale price index.

Prices continued to rise through 1948 as the deferred price inflation of World War II developed. Prices declined moderately in 1949 and then surged upward again under the impact of the price inflation attending the Korean War. Chemicals, plastics materials, and the general level of wholesale prices reached a new postwar peak in 1951. Between 1945 and 1951 chemical prices increased 49% as compared with the rise of 67% for the WPI (See Chart VII-1).

During this entire period, the general price level more than doubled, largely under the impact of World War II and the Korean War. Between 1939 and 1951 wholesale prices increased as follows:

	Per Cent
Chemicals............................	69
Chemicals and allied products............	97
All wholesale........................	129

CHART VII-1

Wholesale Price Indexes: All Commodities and Chemicals, 1926-1968

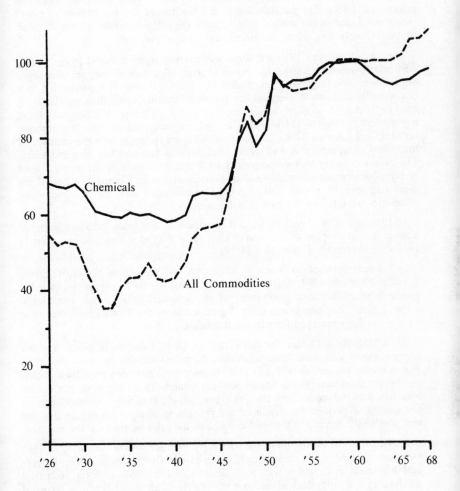

1957-59 = 100

Chemicals

All Commodities

The rise for chemicals was only a little more than half as large as that for all wholesale prices during this period.

1951-1964: Between 1951 and 1964, chemical prices declined by 3.5%, prices of plastics materials were reduced by about 25%, and chemicals and allied products declined about 4%. Prices of organics and inorganics recorded diverse changes. The prices of inorganics rose by 20.6% while prices of the more important organics[76] declined by 15.3%. The wholesale price level for all commodities increased 3.9%.

Between 1951 and 1958, chemical prices fluctuated within a narrow range while prices of plastics materials declined fairly steadily for a net drop of 15.4%.

Between the 1958 and 1964 period, the general wholesale price level moved within a very narrow range. The trend for chemical prices was markedly different, with the index declining 5.7% (organic chemical prices declined 11.1% and prices of plastics materials declined 11.9%,[77] while inorganic chemical prices rose 2.8%). The published data did not record the full decline in prices which developed in the early 1960s, because the official indexes do not show all of the price shading which developed during that period.[78]

The period between 1960 and 1964 was marked by widespread price cutting, particularly among the organics; prices of inorganics showed only small changes on balance. The large scale expansion of facilities during that period led to a considerable amount of overcapacity for many products including acrylonitrile, acetone, benzene, carbon black, caustic soda, glycerine, maleic anhydride, naphthalene, nitrogen, phenol, plastics, polyethylene, sodium tripolyphosphate, sorbital, and toluene. This situation resulted from the entry into the industry of many new competitors as well as the expansion of facilities by older producers. The excess capacity was accompanied by a steady erosion in the average level of prices of organic chemicals and of plastics materials. During this period the increasing size of plants and improved technology, with the accompanying economies, resulted in declines in unit costs.

In 1964, prices of chemicals were at their lowest level since 1950 and prices of plastics materials were at the lowest level since the index was first compiled in 1947 (See Appendix Tables 18 and 19).

Few prices declined as much as chemicals and plastics in the early 1960s. Between 1958 and 1964, only 11 groups of prices out of 73 subgroups included in the nonfarm-nonfood component of the wholesale price index recorded a larger decline than chemicals. Only 3 groups out of the 73 declined more than 11.0%, the drop recorded for plastics materials.

These data do not show the full extent of the real decline in prices. Quality improvements also have been equivalent to price declines in some instances. For example, cellophane which is sold by the pound has been improved so that the buyer can obtain more square feet per pound. Thus, the price per square foot has declined more than the price per pound. Similarly, improvements in the quality of plastics have reduced the processing costs of buyers so that the real cost to the buyer has declined more than the price he paid for the material.

1964-1968: The escalation of the Viet Nam War starting in the spring of 1965 was accompanied by an accelerating rise in prices. By December 1968, the general wholesale price index was 9.3% above the 1964 level and the industrial wholesale price index had advanced 8.9%. Prices of chemical products recorded mixed trends during this period of price inflation, as follows:

160

	1964	**December 1968**	**% Change**
		(1957-59 = 100)	
Inorganic chemicals	103.0	114.9	+11.6
Organic chemicals	88.7	87.6	−1.2
Chemicals	94.2	97.9	+3.9
Plastic resins and materials	89.0	80.5	−9.6

The increase of 3.9% in the composite price index for chemicals resulted from the rise of 11.6% for inorganic chemicals since prices of organic chemicals declined moderately. Prices of plastic resins and materials fell by 9.6% with all of the decline taking place in 1968; the index had remained about unchanged from 1964 to 1967.

Despite the general price inflation, many chemical prices were reduced in this period. For example, *Chemical Week* reported that in 1967 it had listed 182 increases and 90 decreases for chemical and drug prices.[79] There were many sales below list price for chemical products during this period so that on balance it seems evident that chemical prices contributed little to the prevailing general price inflation in the 1965-68 period.

Price declines have not been confined to the United States. For many products it has been noted that "Real price erosion in the world chemical industry has been widespread and since 1959 falls of 2 or 3 percent and even of 4 per cent in the year have been met by many companies, particularly those committed to plastics, synthetic fibers, and organic chemicals, and this against a background of inflation running at an average of 3 per cent per annum."[80]

Declines For Selected Products

Many chemical prices have declined while the prices of products in which they are used have advanced or shown little change. Du Pont reports the following diverse changes in prices between 1957 and 1967:

Dacron polyester fiber for dresses declined 60% but prices of dresses rose 19%.

Orlon fiber for sweaters dropped 16% but sweater prices rose 7%.

Nylon for hosiery fell about 50% but hosiery prices declined by only 1%.

The index of Du Pont's sales prices fell amost 15% in contrast to the rise of 13% in the consumer price index.

Among the other price reductions reported during that ten year period were the following:

Urea fertilizer from $120 to $130 a ton to $90 a ton.

Lucite acrylic resin from 59 cents a pound to 45.5 cents.

Corfam from $1.24 a square foot in 1963 to 98 cents.

Polyethylene film for packaging food from 53 cents a pound in 1959 to 37 cents in 1967.[81]

The illustrations cited above cover many newly developed products.

Such price declines have also developed for key organic chemicals as they "have approached and entered the billion-pound category." The following are illustrative:[82]

	1958	**1968**	**% Decline**
	(cents per lb.)		
Ethylene	5	3	40.0%
Ethylene oxide	15	10	33.3
Vinyl chloride	12	6	50.0
Acrylonitrile	27	15	44.5
Benzene	5	3	40.0
Phenol	18	9	50.0
Styrene	12	8	33.3

Prices of New Products

The price history of most new chemicals products has been one of sharp price reductions as each product evolved from a specialty with limited markets to one with much broader uses. As was noted earlier, the leading companies have followed policies of reducing prices for these products. However, in some instances the quality has been significantly improved while prices have held fairly steady.

Simon Whitney concluded that "over the long run the prices of chemicals which have come into mass production and gained wide markets generally came down very sharply."[83] Some illustrations of reductions in the prices of new products are summarized below:[84]

Nylon: This product involved a research cost of $6 million and an investment of $21 million in manufacturing facilities to Du Pont before it was produced commercially. Because of the uniqueness of the product, it has been held that Du Pont's "pricing policy could be much more autonomous" than for its other products. Prices recorded only minor changes between 1945 and 1955. However, quality improvements were effected which Du Pont concluded had "economic consequences for our customers analagous to price reductions because this improvement [has] permitted lower processing costs and higher yields of first-grade cloth." That Du Pont held the price below "what the traffic could bear" is indicated by the "gray market" which developed "at premiums usually $1 per pound or more." Moreover, the relative stability of price took place against the large increase in labor costs and the general price inflation that characterized the post-World War II decade. This is the background for the "view of the company that the price history of nylon has been one of continuous decline in *real price*"[85] (italics added).

Teflon TFE Fluorocarbon Resin: Price was reduced twelve times, from $18 a pound in 1944 to $3.25 in 1964.

Polyethylene Resins: Reductions in prices usually have been accompanied by and often have stimulated large increases in the use of a product. For polyethylene resins, for example, Chart VII-2 shows the changes in the *unit value*[86] per pound and in output. From 1955 to 1962, the unit value of polyethylene sales dropped from 39 cents a pound to 23 cents a pound, a decline of more than 40%. During this same period the average level of wholesale prices increased by 8.3%. Thus, the *real* decline in polyethylene prices was greater than shown by unit values alone. Sales of polyethylene resins increased from 350 million pounds in 1954 to 2,016 million pounds in 1962. Because of this tremendous increase in volume, total dollar sales expanded from $138 million to $463 million despite the sharp decline in prices. Between 1962 and 1967, the unit value declined further to 16 cents a pound, a decline of 30%. Output in 1967 was 3,799 million, an increase of 88.4% in four years. The total value of the output increased to $646 million. Clearly, the decline in average unit value continued to be accompanied by much more than proportionate increases in volume.

Acrylonitrile: This product is used largely in the production of acrylic fibers. During the decade, 1953 to 1962, unit values per pound fell about 60% (all wholesale prices advanced 8.5%). Output increased steadily (except in 1960) and in 1962 reached 360 million pounds, as compared with 57 million pounds in 1953. Because of the sharp decline in unit prices, the value of this production increased from $22 million to only $54 million. Between 1962 and 1967, the unit value per pound declined an additional 20% and production almost doubled (671 million pounds in 1967). The value of total output increased sharply to $81 million.

CHART VII-2

**Polyethylene Resins: Production and Unit Value,
By Years, 1955-67**

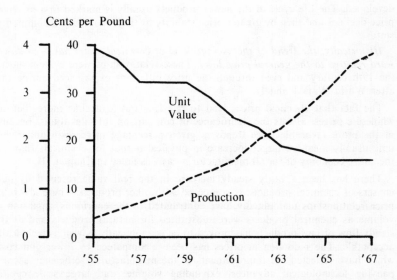

Billions of Pounds

Cents per Pound

The significant contribution made by new technology to these patterns of declining prices for new products was summarized by Du Pont in 1960 as follows:

"Had there been no improvement in technology, the price of many products would have to be far above present levels . . . five Du Pont products, all made for 20 years or more, prove this dramatically. Cellophane costs about 62 cents a pound now [1960]; made the way it was at the time of its commercial debut, it would cost $6.00. Had there been no progress, Du Pont would have to charge $4.00 a pound for neoprene synthetic rubber, instead of 40 cents. Nylon, made with pre-World War II techniques, would be three times its present price; 'Freon' refrigerants would cost $1.75 per pound instead of 25 cents; and 'Duco' finishes would have to be priced far above today's figures. Duco black automotive lacquer, for example, would be $10.00 a gallon, rather than $2.90. Adding to the value today is the fact that the products have improved in quality over the years."[87]

Summary and Conclusions

During the half century since the modern chemical industry developed in World War I, the broad trend of chemical prices has been downward except during the four wars that occurred during this period. These tendencies have been particularly marked for organic chemicals and plastics materials which have more than cancelled out the price raising effects of the Korean War. The development of new products and the accompanying competitive pressures have resulted in significant declines in the prices of these chemicals. For the older and more mature inorganic chemicals—which had previously undergone similar price reductions—the tendency was for prices to rise moderately until the Viet Nam War was accelerating and then to rise more rapidly.

In the 1960s, there was a significant intensification of competitive pressures with an accompanying downward trend in organic chemical prices even during the Viet Nam War. The trend toward lower prices has been most clearly reflected for new products for which the initial or introductory prices have been reduced sharply as the ability to expand output and to broaden markets has developed. The life cycle of the newer products usually is marked first by sharp price declines and then by greater price stability as they, too, reach a commodity status.

Historically, the trend of the average level of chemical prices has been downward relative to the general price level. These relationships were evident during the 19th century and even through the price inflations experienced during and after World Wars I and II.

The fact that chemical prices tend to rise less and to decline more than all wholesale prices, affects the significance of comparisons of sales totals. Because of the more favorable price trends, a given percentage increase in dollar volume usually means a larger increase in physical output for chemicals than for the entire economy or for all manufacturing as was noted in Chapter III.

There has been a fairly steady increase in the real value received by purchasers of chemical products as compared with other products. These favorable price relationships undoubtedly have contributed to the enormous expansion in volume as chemical products were substituted for natural products and as the steady flow of new products has proved to be economically as well as technically acceptable. The reduction in prices has been accompanied by lower unit costs which have reflected the improvements in the manufacturing efficiency accompanying technological advances, expanding volume, and large scale capital investments.

[1]Comprehensive reviews of the pricing policies and practices of Du Pont and Union Carbide are contained in A. D. H. Kaplan, Joel B. Dirlam, and Robert F. Lanzillotti, *Pricing in Big Business,* The Brookings Institution, Washington, D.C., 1958.

[2]Jules Backman, *Pricing: Policies and Practices,* National Industrial Conference Board, New York, 1961, *passim.*

[3]Broadly speaking, prices may be quoted either f.o.b. at the plant or delivered (e.g. freight equalization, freight allowed, zone, postage stamp). An examination of 1,766 chemical and drug prices listed in *Chemical and Engineering News,* April 29, 1963, pp. 65-76, showed that 393 or 22.3% were quoted f.o.b. plant; the balance were some type of delivered price.

[4]John J. Gillis, "The Legal Aspects of Pricing," the Chemical Buyers Group, National Association of Purchasing Agents, The Hilton Hotel, Chicago, Illinois, May 8, 1962, p. 7.

[5]Cited in Kaplan, et al., *op. cit.* pp. 150-51.

[6]*Ibid.,* pp. 151-52, 155.

[7]Testimony of Bert Cremers, vice president of Michigan Alkali Division, Wyandotte Chemicals Corporation, *Study of Pricing Methods,* hearings before Senate Subcommittee on Interstate and Foreign Commerce pursuant to S. Res. 241, Washington, D.C., 1948, pp. 1082-83.

[8]A distinction should be made between chemicals which are homogeneous for all producers of a particular grade (e.g. sulfuric acid) and those for which there may be differences among producers (e.g. plastics). In the latter case, emphasis may be placed upon differences in quality.

[9]*Chemical week,* November 16, 1968, p. 141.

[10]Kaplan et al, *op. cit.,* p. 154.

[11]*The Story of Competition in the American Market,* E. I. du Pont de Nemours and Company, 1959, pp. 28-29.

[12]*Ibid.*

[13]W. R. Grace & Co., *1967 Annual Report,* p. 8.

[14]Pennsalt Chemicals Corporation, *Annual Report 1967,* pp. 7-8.

[15]"Let's Stop Kidding About (ugh) Prices," *Modern Plastics,* April 1969, p. 94.

[16]W. F. Christopher, "New Approach On Pricing Urged," *Journal of Commerce,* March 28, 1962.

[17]A similar spectrum may be found for some products. For example, polyethylene has a high value in use for wire cable for which quality standards are very high and very rigid in contrast to its value for molding some products such as waste baskets, for which the quality of the polyethylene is not as important. In addition, the cost of the polyethylene is a much smaller part of the total cost in the first category than in the second. Finally, all producers are not able to produce polyethylene of the high quality required for wire cable, although many seek to upgrade to this higher value market. In effect, the lower end is priced as commodity while the upper end is a specialty.

[18]Wilbert F. Newton, "Inorganic and Heavy Chemicals" in *Chemical Marketing: The Challenge of the Seventies,* American Chemical Society, Washington, D.C., 1968, p. 17.

[19]Gillis, *op. cit.,* pp. 7-8.

[20]International Minerals and Chemicals is reported to have "completely simulated most of its major competitors' major operations on a computer, including demands, prices, hypothetical competitive responses," *Chemical Week,* April 5, 1964, p. 92.

[21]*The Wall Street Journal,* November 11, 1963.

[22] *Ibid.*, January 28, 1963.

[23] *Oil, Paint and Drug Reporter*, July 16, 1962, p. 427.

[24] *Annual Report 1967*, p. 14.

[25] *The Wall Street Journal*, January 9, 1968.

[26] *Chemical Week*, February 3, 1968, p. 33

[27] *The Wall Street Journal*, March 16, 1964.

[28] G. Clark Thompson and Morgan B. MacDonald, Jr., "Survey of Business Opinion and Experience: Pricing New Products," *The Conference Board Record*, January 1964, p. 7.

[29] "Acetate yarn prices are moving up to list under pressure of heavy demand," *Chemical Week*, March 2, 1968, p. 40. See also *Celanese Annual Report 1967*, p. 6.

[30] Sodium benzoate price increase by Monsanto, *The Wall Street Journal*, June 8, 1967.

[31] Allied Chemical in raising the price of phthalic anhydride noted the rise of prices of some plasticizers made from that product. *Ibid*, September 4, 1963.

[32] Dow when it raised prices of synthetic glycerine. *Ibid.*, March 4, 1964.

[33] "Prices for chlorine, and particularly its co-product, caustic soda, . . . were off significantly despite strong demand." Wyandotte Chemicals Corp., *Annual Report 1968*, p. 4.

[34] *Annual Report 1967*, p. 15.

[35] G. A. Fowles and M. W. Osborne, "Plastics Marketing: The Challenge of the Seventies" in *"Chemical Marketing: The Challenge of the Seventies,"* op. cit., p. 33.

[36] ". . . many chemicals, . . . such as ethylene and its derivatives, come from integrated complexes producing a large number of intermediate products, co-products, and by-products, where it is a matter of choice how costs are divided, and prices determined." Aimison Jonnard, "Chemical Economics and Price Forecasting," in *Chemical Marketing Research*, Reinhold Publishing Corp., New York, 1967, p. 196.

[37] *Ibid.*, p. 198.

[38] American Cyanamid attributed an increase in aluminum sulfate prices to "rising labor and maintenance costs."(*The Wall Street Journal*, December 2, 1963.) Rexall Chemical indicated it raised the price of polystyrene resins to sustain research. (*Ibid.*, March 16, 1964.) Air Reduction attributed higher prices for welding gases in part to higher costs of capital equipment. (*Ibid.*, January 9, 1963.) An increase in prices of perchlorethylene by Du Pont was attributed to "increased costs for labor, raw materials, and transportation." (*Press Release*, September 8, 1967.) Prices were raised for sulfonated naphthalene formaldehyde condensate tags by Diamond Shamrock because of the "continual sharp rise in raw-material costs." (*Chemical Week*, February 3, 1968, p. 33.)

[39] *The Wall Street Journal*, June 16, 1959.

[40] *Ibid.*, March 24, 1964.

[41] *Press Release*, E. I. du Pont, November 16, 1967.

[42] *The Wall Street Journal*, January 22, 1969.

[43] *Chemical Week*, March 22, 1969, p. 87.

[44] *The Wall Street Journal*, July 24, 1962.

[45] *Ibid.*, March 27, 1962.

[46] *Chemical Week*, April 5, 1969, p. 27.

[47]The Wall Street Journal, December 13, 1968.

[48]*Ibid.*, January 22, 1969.

[49]Acrylamide-American Cyanamid (*Ibid.*, July 6, 1963), silicone molding compound—Dow Corning (*Chemical Week*, May 20, 1967.) Elvax and terpolymer resins—Du Pont (*Press Release*, February 6, 1969).

[50]Christopher, *op. cit.*

[51]The Industrial and Biochemicals Department of Du Pont has reported that out of 24 typical products manufactured in 1930, 10 had been dropped (e.g. acetic acid, lead acetate, calcium arsenate) by 1950 and 4 others before 1960 (e.g. sodium phosphate, chromic acid). *Better Living*, September-October 1962, p. 20.

[52]Jonnard, *op. cit.*, p. 197.

[53]*Ibid.*, p. 206.

[54]George J. Stigler, *The Theory of Price*, The Macmillan Co., New York, 1952, p. 234.

[55]Among the non-chemical products for which price increases had to be reversed were: aluminum ingots, grocery bags and wrapping paper, bleached sulphite, bleached Kraft pulp, light heating oils, multiwall shipping sacks, aluminum siding and sheet, plywood, steel plates, corrugated containers, copper water tube and pipe, zinc, oil circuit breakers, water heaters, aluminum cans, welding steel tubing, glass fiber roving, flannel, tool steel, and steel strapping.

[56]One exception was styrene butadiene polymer. *Chemical Week*, November 3, 1962, p. 72; November 17, 1962, p. 157; November 24, 1962, p. 76; December 1, 1962, p. 72; and December 15, 1962, p. 127.

[57]*Oil, Paint and Drug Reporter*, December 4, 1967, p. 32.

[58]*The Wall Street Journal*, February 21, 1964.

[59]*Chemical Week*, December 2, 1967, p. 47.

[60]*Ibid.*, February 1, 1969, p. 31.

[61]*Ibid.*, October 12, 1968, p. 60.

[62]"Let's Stop Kidding About (ugh) Prices", *Modern Plastics*, April 1969, p. 92.

[63]Jonnard, *op. cit.*, p. 220.

[64]*The Commercial and Financial Chronicle*, February 6, 1969, p. 57.

[65]Giragosian, *op. cit.*, p. 290.

[66]"The Story of Competition in the American Market," *op. cit.*, pp. 28-29.

[67]Kaplan, et al., *op. cit.*, p. 153.

[68]*Chemical Week*, April 27, 1968, p. 5.

[69]See Jules Backman, *Pricing: Policies and Practices*, National Industrial Conference Board, New York, 1961. For statements by Du Pont in connection with methanol, polyethylene resins, silicon, and Dacron polyester staple (see p. 77), Imperial Chemical for titanium (see p. 118), Monsanto for fumaric acid (see p. 118), Rohm and Haas for acrylic acid (see p. 119).

[70]The Dow Chemical, *1966 Annual Report*, p. 4.

[71]Teflon, Mylar polyester film, fibrous potassium titanate, and urethane elastomers by Du Pont (*"Pricing: Policies and Practices," op. cit.*, p. 78), polypropylene film by National Distillers. *The Wall Street Journal*, May 22, 1962.

[72]Edward H. Hempel, *The Economics of Chemical Industries,* John Wiley and Sons, Inc., New York, 1939, pp. 157-58.

[73]U.S. Department of Commerce, Bureau of the Census, *Historical Statistics of the United States, Colonial Times to 1957,* Washington, D.C., 1960, pp. 115-16.

[74]Hempel, *op. cit.,* p. 159.

[75]In connection with long term comparisons, it most be kept in mind that the components of the chemical price index have been changed over time. For a detailed tracing of these changes from 1800 to 1963 see Jules Backman, *Chemical Prices, Productivity, Wages, and Profits,* The Manufacturing Chemists' Association, Washington, D.C., November 1964, Appendix A.

[76]In 1958, organics accounted for 69.2% of total shipments.

[77]These price trends were similar to those in Europe. Thus, the OECD reported in 1964 that "Prices of basic inorganics and fertilizers have been stable in most countries over the last year or two, whereas, in other branches of the chemical industry, for example, plastics materials, and above all, basic organics prices have sometimes declined appreciably. This downward movement can be attributed partly to the reduction in world raw material prices and to technical progress, but a further cause appears to have been fierce competition in the sectors of the industry where capacity may have outstripped temporarily the expansion in demand." Organisation for Economic Cooperation and Development. *The Chemical Industry, 1962-1963,* Paris, February 1964, pp. 20-21. See also pp. 77, 94-95.

[78]"List prices, of course, are not infrequently as much as 50% higher than actual prices." Jonnard, *op. cit.,* p. 203.

[79]*Chemical Week* January 6, 1968, p. 29.

[80]Sir Peter Allen, "The Chemical Industries of the U.K. and North America: Lessons and Opportunities," *Chemistry and Industry,* August 3, 1968, p. 1040. See also Organisation for Economic Co-operation and Development, *The Chemical Industry, 1967-1968,* Paris, 1969, pp. 30-31.

[81]*Better Living,* September/October 1967, pp. 5-7.

[82]J. P. Cunningham, "The Challenges In Marketing For Organic Chemicals," in *Chemical Marketing: The Challenge of the Seventies,* American Chemical Society, Washington, D.C., 1968, p. 26.

[83]Simon N. Whitney, *Antitrust Policies,* Vol. I, The Twentieth Century Fund, New York, 1958, p. 252.

[84]A. D. H. Kaplan has described similar patterns of price decline for ammonia, synthetic methanol, ethylene glycol, and triethanolamine. *Big Enterprise In A Competitive System,* The Brookings Institution, Washington, D.C., 1964, pp. 160-62.

[85]*Ibid.,* pp. 103-8.

[86]Unit value reflects the average sales price and is derived by dividing dollar sales by the number of pounds sold. The changes in this average will not be identical with the changes in price because it also is affected by changes in the relative proportion of lower price and higher price units sold.

[87]E. I. du Pont de Nemours & Co., *The Story of Prices, 1960,* p. 22.

Chapter VIII

Productivity Trends

Rising productivity has been the key to economic growth in the United States. Putting more people and more capital to work as population and wealth have grown has also contributed toward the greater output of goods and services shared by each new generation. But by far the larger part of this nation's growth has resulted from the more effective use of its people, its capital and its natural resources, that is, increased productivity.

As early as the 18th Century, this link between productivity and economic growth had already been perceived by Adam Smith. He pointed out:

> "The annual product of the land and labour of any nation can be increased in its value by no other means, but by increasing either the number of its productive labourers, or the productive powers of those labourers who had before been employed. . .in consequence either of some addition and improvement to those machines and instruments which facilitate and abridge labour; or of a more proper division and distribution of employment."[1]

The chemical industry has made an extraordinary contribution to national economic growth. The United States Department of Commerce has observed that "In the case of the chemical industry, the ever-increasing ability to use capital and natural resources more efficiently has spurred output to heights not even dimly imagined only a decade ago. . . This increased efficiency has brought important benefits to customers, stockholders and employees."[2]

An increasing number of workers, supervisory officials and scientists have been employed by the industry and their productivity has been heightened. Direct employment has been multiplied many times. At the same time employment in other industries has benefited indirectly by the cheaper materials and improved technology made possible by the research findings of the chemical industry.

In the following sections, the trend of productivity for chemicals and allied products and for chemicals is briefly reviewed. This is followed by an examination of the outstanding program of research and development and the large capital investments which have contributed so markedly to the industry's superior performance. Comparative trends abroad are then reviewed.

Measurement

Over the years efforts have been made periodically to measure changes in productivity for chemicals and for allied products. These studies have estimated changes in productivity on one or more of the following bases:

    1. Factor productivity—output related to the combined input of capital and labor.

    2. Output per employee—output related to the total number of employees.

    3. Output per manhour—output related to the total number of manhours either for all employees or for production workers alone.

169

4. Sales or value added per employee—mainly used to make international comparisons.

Because of the lack of data showing trends in capital and other inputs, productivity generally has been measured in terms of output per employee or output per manhour. However, John W. Kendrick has prepared data which measure productivity relative to the combined input of labor and capital or what is technically designated as "total factor productivity." According to Kendrick:

> "The term 'productivity' is generally used rather broadly to denote the ratio of output to any or all associated inputs, in real terms. Ratios of output of particular inputs may be termed 'partial productivity' measures, the most common of which is output per manhour. Partial productivity ratios, while useful for measuring the saving in particular inputs achieved over time, do not measure over-all changes in productive efficiency, since they are affected by changes in the composition of input, i.e., by factor substitutions. In order to measure net savings in all inputs and, thus, changes in productive efficiency as such, we have attempted to relate real product in the economy and in thirty-three major industry groups [including chemicals] to total factor input, as well as to labor and to capital (including natural resources) separately."[3]

Over the years capital has been increasingly substituted for labor or utilized for technological reasons. The most meaningful measurement of productivity, therefore, is one that is based both on labor and capital inputs. Unfortunately, these comprehensive data are available only for the period ending either in 1948 (for chemicals) or in 1953 (for chemicals and allied products). Major emphasis will be given, therefore, to the traditional indexes of output per manhour or per employee.

Trends in the United States

Data Available

Data for output per manhour for chemicals are not published on any regular basis. At various times and on different bases estimates have been published as indicated below.

A series showing annual changes in output per manhour was prepared for the period 1919 to 1940 by the U.S. Bureau of Labor Statistics. This series originally was prepared by the National Research Project of the Work Projects Administration for the years 1919 to 1935. It was based on two Census industries—"chemicals, not elsewhere classified" and "compressed and liquefied gases", which together comprised chemicals. The output was based on production for sale or interplant transfer of chemicals chosen because of their relative value and significance in the industry. The major groups were: (1) organic and inorganic acids (hydrochloric, nitric, sulfuric acids, etc.); (2) nitrogen and fixed-nitrogen compounds (anhydrous ammonia); (3) sodium compounds (caustic soda, sodium bicarbonate, silicate, etc.); (4) potassium compounds (potassium bitartrate); (5) alums and other aluminum compounds (aluminum abrasives and aluminum sulphate); (6) coal-tar products (dyes); (7) plastics and pyroxylin products; (8) compressed and liquefied gases (acetylene, carbon dioxide, chlorine and oxygen); (9) miscellaneous organic and inorganic compounds (calcium chloride, carbon tetrachloride, refined glycerin, ferro-alloys, etc.). The employment data were derived from Census statistics while the manhours series was based on an annual series of actual hours worked per week derived from three National Industrial Conference Board (NICB) publications. Although the production and labor indexes were not completely identical, they were very similar.[4]

The National Research Project series was extended through 1940 by the U.S. Department of Labor, Bureau of Labor Statistics. Some revisions were made in the data beginning in 1933.[5]

The most comprehensive data for changes in productivity are those prepared by John W. Kendrick.[6] These data cover selected Census years between 1899 and 1957 (See Appendix Table 27). Data were estimated for chemicals and allied products for the period 1899 to 1957. For chemicals, n.e.c., rayon, and gases (chemicals), estimates were prepared for the period 1899 to 1954. Kendrick prepared separate estimates for output per manhour, output per person, output per unit of capital input, and total factor productivity. Total factor productivity is estimated by relating capital formation plus labor used to the resulting output.[7]

In recent years, manmade fibers is the only chemical product group for which BLS has prepared estimates of output per manhour. These data are for 1939 and 1947 through 1966.[8]

The author has derived estimates for output per manhour for chemicals and chemicals and allied products since 1947. Output based on the Federal Reserve Board index of production was divided by manhours derived by multiplying total employment by production worker weekly hours to yield estimates of output per employee manhour. Production worker employment was multiplied by the average number of hours per week of those workers to yield total production worker manhours. The employment data and weekly hours are those reported in BLS (See Tables VIII-1 and VIII-2).

Chemicals & Allied Products

1899-1957: There has been a phenomenal growth in output of chemicals and allied products since the turn of the century and particularly since 1937. Output far outdistanced employment so that *output per employee* rose 481% between 1899 and 1957 for chemicals and allied products, as compared with 204% for all manufacturing; between 1937 and 1957 the increases were 151% and 61%, respectively (See Appendix Table 20).

This gain in output per employee was exceeded on a manhour basis as hours of work have been reduced significantly over the past six decades. *Output per manhour* for chemicals and allied products increased by 684% between 1899 and 1957, as compared with 311% for all manufacturing. Thus, over the long term, output per manhour for chemicals and allied products has increased well over twice as much as for all manufacturing. Virtually all of this gain in efficiency came after World War I. Output per manhour for chemicals and allied products in 1919 was somewhat less than in 1909 and only a little greater than in 1899. Between 1919 and 1937, in contrast, it nearly tripled—and then increased two and a half times between 1937 and 1957.

Much of the gain in output per manhour for chemicals and allied products reflects the more rapid increase in the use of capital, horsepower, fuel, and energy than in labor input as the industry grew in size. In the early 1960s, for example, it was the third largest consumer of fuels and electric energy among major manufacturing groups, exceeded only by primary metals and petroleum and coal products.[9]

Chemicals and allied products accounted for only 4.5% of all manufacturing employment and about 5.3% of all manufacturing payrolls in 1962. On the other hand, this industry's share of total energy used in manufacturing was 14.1%.

Total factor productivity is the best measure of change in productivity for chemicals and allied products since the relatively high output per manhour figures are corrected for the application of greater amounts of capital. *Total factor productivity* for chemicals and allied products increased 372%, as compared with 191% for all manufacturing for the 1899-1953 period. On an annual basis, the increase for chemicals and allied products was 2.9%, as compared with 2.0% for all manufacturing and 1.7% for the entire private economy.[10]

1958-1968: In the period since 1957, chemicals and allied products continued to show greater gains in productivity than all manufacturing industries. Between 1958 and 1968 output per manhour for all employees increased by 73.2% for chemicals and allied products or nearly twice the increase of 38.8% for all manufacturing; the annual rates of increase were 5.7% and 3.4%, respectively. Clearly, output per manhour has risen much more markedly for the combination of industries grouped under chemicals and allied products than for all manufacturing industries during the past decade, as it has throughout the Twentieth Century. A similar pattern of gain is shown for output per employee (See Table VIII-1).

Using changes in *value added per production worker* as a crude measure of the trend of productivity, the U.S. Department of Commerce found that productivity for all manufacturing advanced at an annual rate of 5.3% from 1958 to 1966. The corresponding annual growth rate for total chemicals was 6.8%, or nearly a third higher than that for all manufacturing. Productivity gains in chemicals were most pronounced for industrial gases (average annual rate, 10.5%) and for organics (7.5%).[11]

Chart VIII-1

Annual Increase In Output
Per Manhour, 1947-1968

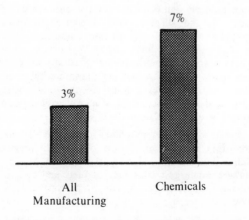

TABLE VIII-1

Indexes of Output Per Manhour and Output Per Employee For All Employees: Chemicals and Products and all Manufacturing, 1958-1968

(1958 = 100)

	Output Per Manhour		Output Per Employee	
	Chemicals & Products	All Manufacturing	Chemicals & Products	All Manufacturing
1958	100.0	100.0	100.0	100.0
1959	110.5	105.7	112.5	107.7
1960	115.0	107.5	116.7	107.9
1961	121.4	110.0	123.5	110.8
1962	130.1	116.5	132.9	116.3
1963	139.6	121.2	142.3	123.0
1964	147.3	127.1	150.6	130.1
1965	153.8	132.3	158.4	136.4
1966	161.5	134.1	166.6	139.1
1967	164.9	135.1	168.5	138.3
1968	173.2	138.8	177.9	NA
Per Cent Increase				
1958-68	73.2	38.8	77.9	38.3*
Annual Rate	5.7	3.4	5.9	3.7*

NA - Not available
*1958-67

Sources: Derived from Board of Governors of the Federal Reserve System, *Industrial Production 1957-59 Base,* Washington, D.C., 1962, pp. S-58, S-150; *Industrial Production Indexes,* 1961-1965, Washington, D.C., 1966, *passim; Federal Reserve Bulletin,* various issues; U.S. Department of Labor, Bureau of Labor Statistics, *Employment and Earnings Statistics for the United States, 1909-68,* Bulletin No. 1312-6, Washington, D.C., 1968, pp. 48, 51, 639, 641; *Employment and Earnings,* March 1969, pp. 56, 60, 87, 95; *Economic Report of the President,* January 1969, p. 266.

Chemicals

The above average productivity gain noted for chemicals and allied products was due in large measure to the outstanding performance of chemicals. Thus, between 1899 and 1948 output per manhour increased by 626% for chemicals as compared with 371% for all chemicals and allied products groups; clearly the allied products lagged far behind chemicals.[12]

The major part of the increases in chemical productivity developed largely after 1919. Kendrick estimated the annual rate of increase in output per manhour for chemicals (chemicals, n.e.c. plus rayon and gases) at 4.3% between 1899 and 1954. Only four of the eighty industries for which he made estimates showed a higher rate of gain. Included among the 80 industries were nine allied chemical products group, all of which showed smaller gains than chemicals in output per manhour.[13]

Fertilizers	3.3
Tanning and dyeing materials	2.8
Carbon black	2.6
Salt	2.1
Soap and glycerine	2.1

Explosives	1.9
Paints and allied products	1.9
Wood distillation	1.8
Gum naval stores	0.7

Clearly, the chemical industry was among the leaders in gains in output per manhour during the first half of the present century.

1947-1968: The gigantic increase in output per manhour that characterized the period through 1948 has contined in the subsequent years. During the postwar years, 1947 to 1968, output per manhour for chemicals increased by by 348%, or an annual rate of 7.0% as compared with 3.0% for all manufacturing industries (See Chart VIII-1). This was the largest annual rate of increase for any period excepting only 1919-29, when the total rate of gain was affected by the relatively low rate of output per manhour at the end of World War I. Output per manhour has continued to increase at high rates since 1963, with increases of 8.5% in 1964, 8.3% in 1965, 7% in 1966, 4% in 1967, and 9% in 1968. There is as yet no evidence of a slowdown in the superior productivity performance of the chemical industry (See Table VIII-2).

Man-made Fibers: The U.S. Bureau of Labor Statistics has published estimates for changes in *output per employee* and per manhour for man-made fibers.[14] Between 1939 and 1966, output per employee increased by 622% or 7.6% annually. Between 1947 and 1966, the increase was 255% or about 6.9% annually. This was a smaller rise than recorded for all chemicals for which output per employee increased by 313% or 7.8% annually during the same period.

TABLE VIII-2

Indexes of Output Per Manhour and Per Employee
For All Employees, Chemical Industry, 1947-1968
(1957-1959 = 100)

Year	Output Per Manhour	Output Per Employee
1947	50.7	49.7
1948	55.0	54.4
1949	59.1	57.5
1950	71.1	70.4
1951	71.1	71.1
1952	70.1	69.6
1953	72.7	72.3
1954	75.2	73.9
1955	87.5	87.3
1956	90.1	90.1
1957	94.2	93.8
1958*	95.0*	94.3*
1959	112.2	113.6
1960	117.8	119.3
1961	128.0	129.9
1962	145.1	147.3
1963	159.0	161.3
1964	172.5	174.5
1965	186.8	191.0
1966	199.8	205.6
1967	207.8	211.5
1968	226.9	233.1

Note: *New Series (with 1958 = 100) rebased by linking with 1958 at 95.0 with 1957-1959 = 100 for output per manhour and with 94.3 for output per employee.

Sources: Derived from National Industrial Conference Board, *Chemicals and Allied Products: IV,* New York, 1960, p. 8 (output on base of 1957 = 100); Board of Governors of the Federal Reserve System, *Industrial Production of 1957-59 Base,* Washington, D.C., 1962, p. S-59; *Federal Reserve Bulletin,* various issues; U.S. Department of Labor, Bureau of Labor Statistics, *Employment and Earnings Statistics for the United States, 1909-68, Bulletin No. 1312-6,* Washington, D.C., 1968, pp. 639, 641, 643, 644, 649, 650; *Employment and Earnings,* March 1969, pp. 60, 95.

Output per all employee manhour for man-made fibers increased by 263% as compared with 294% for all chemicals between 1947 and 1966; this was 7.0% and 8.4% respectively (Derived from Appendix Table 21).

Research and Development

The record rates of expenditures for basic and applied research sustained over decades provide the primary explanation for the superior productivity performance of the chemical industry. It has been this increasing search for new ways to fabricate or to process old materials in order to improve quality or to lower costs combined with emphasis upon the development of new products, processes, and materials that have placed the chemical industry in the forefront of technological progress. The new products, particularly the burgeoning list of synthetics, serve to meet existing needs at lower cost and to generate new demand, thereby expanding volume and offering even greater gains in efficiency through the economies of scale.

The unique advantages of conducting research in the United States have been summarized as follows:

"With a homogeneous, wealthy market about six times larger than that of any single European Country, with high volume, high wages and special Government needs creating technological demands unique in the world, especially in such areas as space, nuclear power, armaments, communications, electronics, mass transportation and health, the United States can indulge in extensive product innovation."[15]

"Test tube competition" has been a vital competitive force in the chemical industry. Research and development provides a more dynamic and a more powerful form of nonprice competition in chemicals than in any other industry except possibly the closely related drug industry. Because the chemical industry is research-oriented, the industry turns out many new products. Emphasis on research has also resulted in the improvement of present processes and the development of new uses for existing products.

Simon Whitney has pointed out:

"The real competition in the chemical industry goes beyond the manufacture of the same chemical from the same raw material by the same process - although this, too exists, as in alkalies, chlorine and heavy acids. Competition is more characteristically found in the search for different raw materials and processes to make the same product, for different chemicals to perform altogether new functions, and for new uses for established chemicals. . ."[16]

The pattern of development of the chemical industry reflects the impact of competition on the technological front. One result has been that the products of the chemical industry are among those with the highest growth rates. The extensive interindustry and interproduct competition previously noted testify to the effectiveness of these research efforts which have added a significant dimension to competition in this industry.

The ability of any chemical company to grow, irrespective of size, is dependent upon its ability to invent or to innovate. Each company knows that its products are constantly exposed to competition by other producers seeking to create ways to make the same chemical more cheaply, or to design a substitute that will satisfy similar end uses. Not only have potential sources of supply been steadily broadened domestically, but foreign producers also have stepped up their rate of innovation to gain deeper penetration into world markets.[17]

The extent to which productivity and record expenditures for research and development have been closely linked in the chemical industry long has been recognized. In a 1942 report, the United States Bureau of Labor Statistics noted that for the chemical industry:

"Much of the increase in productivity . . . is attributable to improvements in processes and equipment. . . Progress in technology offers a partial explanation of the 45 percent advance in output per manhour and the indecisive trend of unit labor cost. Many of the changes, however, were directed not so much toward the reduction of labor cost (which is a less important element of total cost than in many other industries) as towards the reduction of other operating costs (as of raw materials, through increased yields and solvent recovery) and capital costs (through lengthened average life of equipment). In general, the period of 1929-1940 was characterized by improvements in unit processes, the refinement of of techniques, the development of alternative manufacturing processes, improvements in equipment design, construction materials, and auxiliary equipment, and further progress in instrumentation and continuous-production methods."[18]

The chemical industry is no late-comer to the newly-found "industry of discovery." Decades ago, it recognized the high yield that would flow from investment in technology and in basic research. Chemicals and allied products firms spend about as much for research, including basic and applied research, as they do for development. For example, in 1967 total expenditures for R & D were divided as follows for chemicals and allied products:[19]

	Industrial Chemicals	Allied Products	Total
		(millions)	
Basic research	$ 130	$ 62	$ 192
Applied research	375	223	598
Total research	505	285	790
Development	501	274	775
Total	$1,006	$559	$1,565

Basic and applied research accounted for somewhat more than half of total R & D both for industrial chemicals and for allied products.

This research orientation of the chemical industry has been placed in fitting long-term perspective by the National Science Foundation:

"The chemicals and allied products industry has a relatively long history of reliance on science and technology. The first organized research laboratories were introduced into the industry at the turn of the present centruy, as contrasted with most industries in which R & D activities on an organized scale gained prominence only within the last decade or two. The chemical industry is dependent upon research and development to accomplish its commercial objectives. It is among those industries that rely heavily upon advances in scientific knowledge for growth and progress. Othe types of industries, in which the end products and productive processes are substantially fixed, are based not so much on science as on the traditional empirical arts."[26]

Total expenditures for R & D by chemicals and allied products were $1,565 million in 1967; the total increased by 122% between 1957 and 1967. Similarly, R & D expenditures in the chemical industry were $1,006 million in 1967 as compared with $503 million in 1956. Chemicals in 1967 accounted for 64.3% of all R & D expenditures by chemicals and allied products. (Appendix Table 22) R & D expenditures for drugs and medicines were $354 million and for other chemicals $206 million.

In 1967, the U.S. Department of Commerce explained the large R & D expenditures for industrial chemicals and drugs as follows:

"In the drugs and industrial chemicals fields new wonder drugs are constantly being developed for the benefit of mankind, and scientists are prying into areas such as pesticides and other agricultural chemicals. These and other factors explain the surge in scientific manpower in drugs and industrial chemicals. The paradox is that there has been a decrease in the scientific manpower requirements of other chemical industries, especially plastics. Trade sources indicate that a substantial effort is being made in other chemicals but evidently without increasing dependency upon scientific and engineering personnel."[21]

The total R & D expenditures for all industry reached $16.4 billion in 1967.[22] This growth has been heavily concentrated in defense-related activities. Nevertheless, the chemical industry's outlays have more than held their own in this armament-swollen total. In 1967, the industry accounted for 9.5% for all R & D outlays. As space technology has emerged, chemical industry research has been expanded to deal with the development of liquid and solid propellants for rockets and missiles.[23]

The chemicals and allied products industries spend more of their own money on R & D than any other industry except electrical equipment and communication. Of the $8,032 million in company funds spent by all industry for R&D in 1967, $1,353 million was accounted for by chemicals and allied products. Thus, these industries accounted for 16.8% of all company-financed research or close to twice their share of total industry expenditures for research (including that publicly financed). (See Table VIII-3).

In 1967 the chemical industry's research expenditures from company funds averaged 3.7 cents per dollar of net sales in contrast to 2.1 cents for all manufacturing.[24]

TABLE VIII-3

Expenditures From Company Funds For Research and Development By Major Industries, 1967

	Million	Per Cent of Total
Electrical equipment and communication	$1,567	19.5
Chemicals and allied products	1,353	16.8
Machinery	1,085	13.5
Aircraft and missiles	1,058	13.2
Motor vehicles and other transportation equipment	988	12.3
(Chemicals)[1]	(823)	(10.2)
Petroleum refinery and extraction	431	5.4
Professional and scientific instruments	317	3.9
Primary metals	237	3.0
Food and kindred products	167	2.1
Rubber products	165	2.1
Fabricated metal products	152	1.9
Stone, clay, and glass products	145	1.8
Nonmanufacturing industries	142	1.7
Lumber, wood products and furniture	14	0.2
Total	$8,032	100.0

[1]Included in chemicals and allied products.

Note: Data for textiles and apparel, paper and allied products and other manufacturing industries are not separately available but included in the total.

Source: National Science Foundation, "Research and Development in Industry, 1967," *Reviews of Data on Science Resources,* February 1969, p. 3.

Chemicals and allied products had attracted 41,000 scientists to its laboratories, or slightly more than one-tenth of all scientists so engaged in private industry. (See Table VIII-4) Chemicals alone had 23,600 scientists in January 1968, an increase of 4,800 since January 1958. A growing proportion of the employees on chemical payrolls are R & D scientists and engineers. As of January 1958 this group accounted for 43 of every 1,000 employees; by January 1968, the figure had risen to 46. This increase reflects the continuing interest in R & D by the chemical industry. The average cost for R and D per scientist in the chemical industry was about $40,000 in 1967.

Other industries have benefited from the research efforts of the chemical industry. The National Science Foundation concluded:

"The benefits derived from the development of new and improved products and processes by chemical companies spread across numerous industries, since many industries rely on chemical products in their manufacture. For example, new and improved fertilizers and insecticides developed within the laboratories of chemical companies have made significant contributions to the efficiency of production in agriculture."[25]

For Imperial Chemical Industries it has been reported that ". . . of the 6000 technical graduates employed by ICI in 1967, about half were employed on research and development."[26]

TABLE VIII-4

Employment of Research and Development Scientists and Engineers: All Industry, Chemicals and Allied Products, and Chemicals, 1957-1968

January	All Industry	Chemicals and Allied Products	Chemicals
	(in thousands of full-time equivalents)		
1957	229.4	29.4	18.0
1958	243.8	31.0	18.8
1959	268.4	33.5	20.2
1960	292.0	36.3	21.9
1961	312.1	37.3	23.1
1962	312.0	36.7	21.9
1963	327.3	38.6	23.3
1964	347.5	39.4	24.2
1965	346.3	41.1	26.2
1966	354.7	42.0	26.7
1967	367.2	38.7	22.7
1968	387.9	41.0	23.6

Note: Industry only; employment in government, educational and non-profit institutions excluded.

Source: "Basic Research, Applied Research, and Development in American Industry, 1964," *op. cit.,* p. 11; "Research and Development in Industry, 1966," *op. cit.,* p. 12; "Research and Development in Industry, 1967," *op. cit.,* p. 8.

One observer has warned that it is difficult to compare R & D costs for different companies:

". . . Unfortunately, it is impossible to accurately compare the dollar expenditures made by the different companies since no two companies seem to agree as to what to include in research costs—and many companies do not publish any figures. Some companies include all technical work including pilot plant expenditures, patent department, market research, sales service and any activity even remotely related to research. Others exclude process development work done at plant laboratories and only include the technical effort at the principal research laboratories."[27]

Foreign companies also have been investing heavily in R & D as is shown by the following data for 1966:[28]

Company	1966 Research & Development Expenses (000,000)	% 1966 Sales
Bayer	$51	4.9
Hoechst	62	4.3
BASF	46.5	5.1
CIBA (group)	45	9.2
Sandoz (group)	27	8.4

For Imperial Chemical Industries (ICI), it was reported that in 1967 expenditures were "of the order of 4 to 5 percent of our total sales income" in the United Kingdom.[29]

But R&D is not all a plus. The cost has been rising sharply as companies have had to bid for the limited number of personnel against a background of general inflation and increasingly sophisticated (and costly) techniques of research. Often it is difficult to relate investment in R&D and the return earned.

The payoff on R&D and to develop a product commercially often has taken many years. Thus, "It took 18 years and $43 million before earnings from dyes which Du Pont first produced in 1917 offset the operating losses accumulated in learning how to make them."[30]

However, the amount of lead time available has been reduced markedly as new products, which are successful, are immediately adopted by competitors. Thus, within four years after the introduction of Corfam, "Goodrich was marketing Aztran, Kurashki Rayon of Japan and Clarino, Georgia-Bonded Fibers had Sir-Pell and several other companies had indicated they would soon be in this market."[31]

The enormous expenditures for R & D have yielded great benefits to the economy. New products have proliferated, more economical processes have been developed, and the industry's productivity has risen remarkably.

Capital Invested

The nature of the chemical industry is such, particularly because of the continuous flow processes involved, that it lends itself to automatic controls which require a high capital input. In addition, the industry's record rate of research and development outlays has contributed toward the acceleration of scientific discoveries which in turn also, have required a large volume of new investment.[32] The industry's activities to reduce pollution also have required large capital investments.[33]

The intensive competition in the industry also contributes to high dollar expenditures for new plant and equipment. This was demonstrated by the enormous expansion in ammonia plant capacity in the mid and late 1960s. Many companies got into the act with the consequent development of a large amount of overcapacity which resulted in heavy pressure for lower prices as well as the retirement of older facilities.

In 1967, capital expenditures for chemicals aggregated $2,159 million and an additional $674 million was invested by the allied products industries; this was a total investment of $2,833 million. In that year, the chemicals and allied products industries accounted for 14.0% of the new capital investment but only 4.4% of the total employment in manufacturing industries.[34] Clearly, this a sector of the economy that uses capital very intensively.[35]

As is true of so many key economic variables, available statistics do not permit identification of the total amount invested in chemical plant and equipment. Data for investments in chemical plants by producers in other industries are especially inadequate because their chemical and other investments rarely are reported separately.

Table VIII-5 shows the FTC-SEC data for total assets of all manufacturing companies and for chemicals and allied products. In 1968, the total for chemicals and allied products was $45.6 billion or more than double the amount in 1958. A significant part of this increase has reflected the reinvestment of profits.[36] Total assets of chemicals and allied products companies have increased more rapidly than those of all manufacturing. In 1951, chemicals and allied products accounted for 8.6% of the total assets in all manufacturing; by 1967 the proportion had increased to 9.9%; in 1968 it was 9.4%.[37]

TABLE VIII-5

Total Assets: Chemicals and Allied Products and All Manufacturing, by Years, 1951-1968

Fourth Quarter	All Manufacturing (except newspapers)	Chemicals and Allied Products	Per Cent Relationship
	(in billions)		
1951	$158.1	$13.6	8.6
1954	175.1	15.6	8.9
1958	225.4	20.9	9.3
1963	302.6	28.7	9.5
1967	437.2	43.9	9.9
1968	485.9	45.6	9.4

Source: Federal Trade Commission-Securities and Exchange Commission, *Quarterly Financial Report for Manufacturing Corporations, Washington, D.C.,* (various issues).

TABLE VIII-6

Capital Invested Per Worker in Manufacturing Industries, 1964

	Per Production Worker	Per Employee
	(in thousands)	
Petroleum*	$152.6	$103.8
CHEMICALS	49.0	29.5
Tobacco	46.2	40.2
Motor vehicles	39.6	30.5
Primary metals	28.6	23.3
Food and beverages	24.8	16.4
ALL MANUFACTURING	23.1	17.1
Paper and products	21.9	17.1
Nonelectrical machinery	21.2	14.7
Instruments	20.8	13.2
Transportation equipment	20.8	13.2
Stone, clay and glass	20.7	16.7
Printing and publishing	17.7	11.2
Rubber and miscellaneous plastics	17.3	13.3
Electrical machinery	16.5	11.1
Fabricated metals	15.7	12.1
Lumber and wood products	14.2	12.5
Textile-mill products	12.2	10.9
Miscellaneous manufacturing**	10.2	6.7
Furniture and fixtures	8.4	6.9
Leather and products	7.0	6.2
Apparel	5.9	5.3

Notes: *Consists of petroleum refinery, extraction, and pipe-line transportation.

**Includes ordnance and accessories.

Source: National Industrial Conference Board, *Road Maps of Industry,* No. 1579 October 1, 1967.

The growth in total assets in chemicals and allied products was 235% between 1951 and 1968; it was greater than the increase in employment or total man-hours. Thus, each worker has been backed up by an increasing investment in new plant and equipment, more horsepower, and other tools which have helped to step up his productivity. Capital investment per worker is exceptionally high in chemicals. In 1964 each worker in the industry was provided with an average of almost $30,000 in "toolpower" or about one and three quarters times the amount available to the average worker in all manufacturing industries. (See Table VIII-6)

The investment requirements vary widely within the industry. In 1963, the investment per production worker ranged from $83,788 for organic chemicals to $46,010 for plastic materials and resins and only $2,802 for non-cellulosic fibers. With such a wide range, the capital requirements of individual companies will be significantly influenced by their product mix. (See Table VIII-7)

TABLE VIII-7

Investment Per Production Worker, Chemical Industries, 1963

Organic chemicals	$83,788
Synthetic rubber	53,314
Plastic materials & resins	46,010
Pharmaceutical preparations	25,381
Toilet preparations	9,737
Non-cellulosic fibers	2,802

Source: U.S. Department of Commerce, *Growth Pace Setters In American Industry, 1958-1968*, Washington, D.C., October 1968, pp. 70, 96, 105, 113, 148, 157.

High capital costs reflect the large capacity required to obtain maximum efficiency in the production of many chemicals, the state of technology which permits production to be achieved with a relatively high input and a low labor input, the intricate nature of the equipment which makes it expensive to produce, the continuous processes utilized and the large volume of equipment required, and the rapid obsolescence[38] and depreciation of the equipment used as new techniques and new products emerge from the research laboratory. Equipment also wears out quickly because of high temperatures, pressures, and corrosion.[39]

With investment opportunities of almost three billion dollars annually, chemicals and allied products have provided one of the major outlets for investment funds. The high growth rate of the industry has reflected this large scale investment.

Productivity In Other Countries

Output per manhour is significantly lower overseas than in the United States. However, in recent years productivity for chemicals and allied products has been increasing more rapidly abroad for several reasons: (1) the relatively lower base from which the gains are measured, (2) the installation of many modern large size plants, and (3) the greater increase in volume overseas.[40]

Crayton K. Black of Du Pont has noted that overseas companies "are building giant chemical complexes larger, cheaper, and every bit as efficient as anything we have here in this country."[41] As one illustration, Imperial Chemical Industries built an ethylene plant with a capacity of 450,000 long tons per year, a plant larger than most American ethylene plants.[42]

Estimates of changes in *output per employee* for chemicals and allied products in the United States and in several exporting countires between 1958 and 1967 are shown below:[43]

	Increase in Output Per Employee, 1958 to 1967
Italy	116.3%
West Germany	112.7
France	102.9
United States	68.8
United Kingdom	60.0

Output per employee increased 68.8% in the United States or at a significant smaller rate than in West Germany, France, and Italy. These relationships are similar to those for all manufacturing where the gains in the U.S. also have been smaller than abroad.[44]

Some additional scattered evidence also shows a greater increase in chemical output per manhour abroad during the post-World War II period. A study by C. T. Saunders showed that between 1954-1955 and 1960-61 *output per employee* for chemicals and allied products recorded an annual rate of increase of 6.3% for the United States as compared with 6.8% for France and 6.6% for West Germany.[45]

For West Germany, it has been estimated that *output per person employed* rose 96% between 1950 and 1961 while *output per operative hour* increased by 144%.[46] For chemicals and allied products in the United States, output per employee increased by 72.3% and output per employee manhour increased by 71.4% in the same period.

German productivity also appears to have expanded more rapidly than in the United States between 1957 and 1967 as measured by *sales per employee*. The increase was from $10,417 to $18,954 or 83% for four German companies (Bayer, BASF, Hoechst, and Cassella). For five large American companies (Du Pont, Dow, Monsanto, Allied Chemical and Union Carbide) the average increased from $22,556 to $28,802[47] or 27%. In 1957, the American company sales per employee were more than twice as large as for the German companies while in 1967 they were only about one and a half times as large.[48]

These greater gains abroad reflect the fact that "the European companies were building many new, large, efficient plants and closing down smaller units."[49] In addition, the level of productivity in European plants was so much lower that larger percentage gains were more easily achieved.

Despite the larger increases in output per manhour, the level in this country is still significantly greater than abroad. Two rough indications are found in the data for sales per employee and value added per employer.

Table VIII-8 compares the *sales per employee* in 13 Western European countries, Canada, Japan, and the United States in 1967. The sales data, which include chemicals and allied products, have been converted from local currencies to dollars by the OECD. Differences among the countries are af-

TABLE VIII-8

Sales of Chemicals and Allied Products Per Employee, Leading Countries, 1967

Country Western Europe	Sales (millions)	Total Employment (number)	Sales Per Employee	Per Cent of U.S.
Austria	$ 455	34,800	$13,075	30.6
Belgium	1,030	56,880	18,108	42.3
Denmark	320*	28,000	11,429	26.7
France	6,585	266,000	24,856	57.9
Germany (F.R.)	8,685	463,000	18,758	43.9
Ireland	110*	7,100	15,493	36.2
Italy	5,855	236,365	24,771	57.9
Netherlands	1,715	76,600	22,389	52.4
Norway	335*	19,100	17,539	41.0
Spain	1,950	138,200	14,110	33.0
Sweden	790	34,900	22,636	52.9
Switzerland	900	50,000	18,000	42.1
United Kingdom	6,945	406,000	17,106	40.0
Total Western Europe	35,675	1,816,945	19,635	45.9
Other Areas				
Canada	2,075	74,775	27,750	64.9
Japan	8,070	415,000	19,446	45.5
United States[1]	42,375	991,000	42,760	

*Sales estimated for 1967.

[1]According to U.S. Bureau of Labor Statistics, total employment was 1,002,400 in 1967 while the Bureau of the Census reported total shipments of $42.2 billion or an average of $42,099 per employee. U.S. Department of Labor, Bureau of Labor Statistics, "Employment and Earnings Statistics for the United States, 1909-68." *Bulletin 1312-6,* Washington, D.C., 1968, p. 639 and Bureau of the Census, *1967 Census of Manufactures,* General Statistics for Industry Groups and Industries, Preliminary Report, MC67(P)-1, Washington, D.C., April 1969, p. 7.

Source: Organisation for Economic Co-operation and Development, *The Chemical Industry, 1967-68,* Paris, 1969, pp. 146, 147.

fected by the varying proportions of chemicals and allied products, by differences in product mix, by differences in price levels among countries, by the differences in purchasing power parity among countries,[50] by the relative size of plants, by the availability of equipment, and by differences in the amount of duplication contained in the aggregate data for sales or shipments.

Sales per employee in the United States are much greater than those in any of the Western European countries or the average for all of them combined. The OECD study shows total sales in the United States in 1967 were $42.4 billion or almost 19% more than the $35.7 billion total for Western Europe.[51] Nevertheless, the American chemical industry employed only about half as many workers to produce this larger output. As a result, average sales per employee were about 2-1/4 times as large in the United States as in Western Europe and 2-1/2 times as large as in the United Kingdom.[52] For the reasons cited above these relationships must be considered to be very rough ones rather than precise measurements.

CHART VIII-2

**Sales of Chemicals And Allied Products Per Employee,
Selected Countries, 1967**

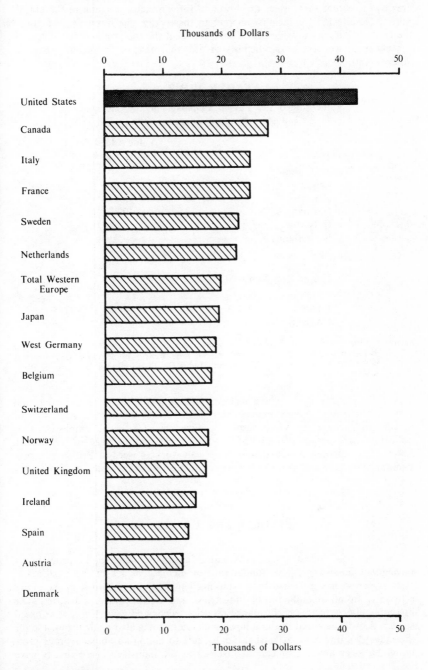

Thousands of Dollars

Thousands of Dollars

In terms of *value added per person*[53] employed in the chemical industry there is also a wide disparity. The average for the United States was $27,477 in 1967 as compared with $10,890 in Germany, $7,700 in the United Kingdom and $8,980 in Japan. (See Table VIII-9).

In real terms, the differences may be narrower than shown by the dollar figures to the extent that prices are lower in foreign countries than in the United States. Despite the limitations inherent in these data, the disparity in favor of the United States is so wide that it seems evident the the productivity of American chemical workers is significantly greater than that of their counterparts in other countries.[54]

TABLE VIII-9

Value Added Per Person Employed in the Chemical Industry, Leading Countries, 1967

Country	Value Added Per Person Employed
Western Europe	
Belgium	$7,210
France	8,610
Germany	10,890
Italy	8,840
Netherlands	9,010
Spain	4,380
Sweden	11,600
United Kingdom	7,700
Other Areas	
Japan	8,980
United States	27,477

Source: Organisation for Economic Co-operation and Development, *The Chemical Industry, 1967-68,* Paris, 1969, p. 30; *1967 Census of Manufactures,* General Statistics For Industry Groups and Industries, Washington, D.C., April 1969, p. 7.

A British study team which examined the experience in both British and American chemical plants concluded that American companies used 40 employees to produce the same output produced by 100 British employees thus indicating that output per employee was 2-1/2 times as large in the United States. They also estimated that if American workers were in British size production units it would take 64 employees to turn out that amount of output.[55]

Summary and Conclusions

The chemical industry has experienced dramatic increases in productivity throughout its history. The annual rate of increase of 7% in the post-World War II period has exceeded by a wide margin the gains recorded in the entire economy, in all manufacturing industries, and in the allied industries. The favorable effects of this performance on price trends and wage levels were noted earlier. As will be noted in the following chapter, it has also made it possible for the industry's investors, at least through 1966, to obtain an above average profit on the large amount of capital invested in the industry. These results have made chemicals a prime illustration of the benefits that flow from large-scale investment in research and development and intensive use of capital.

Every industry cannot equal the performance of chemicals which to a large extent has developed substitutes for other products rather than created entirely new types of goods. However, this industry's history does indicate the sustained high yield to be obtained by exploring new frontiers in the research laboratories.

The chemical industry is one of the largest providers of capital per employee in American industry. Its share of total fixed assets used in manufacturing industries has increased substantially over the years. It has provided major opportunities for new investments both within its own industry and among major industries using the materials it has created. This large scale use of capital also has contributed significantly to the industry's productivity performance.

On the basis of scattered data, it appears that output per manhour in this country far exceeds the levels overseas. However, the expanding size of overseas markets has made possible the introduction of large plants with the latest technological advances. As a result, output per manhour has been increasing more rapidly abroad in the past decade.

Although the productivity advantage of this country is still enormous, our relative margin is being reduced. In earlier years, the relatively higher productivity performance in the United States helped to offset the markedly lower hourly labor costs of chemical producers abroad. To the extent that productivity rises more sharply abroad than at home the offset to higher labor costs obtained from technological advantages will be narrowed.

[1]Adam Smith, *An Inquiry Into the Nature and Causes of the Wealth of Nations,* Modern Library Edition, Random House, New York, 1937, p. 326.

[2]U.S. Department of Commerce, "A Look at Chemical Productivity and Wages" *Chemicals,* September 1966, p. 6.

[3]John W. Kendrick, *Productivity Trends in the United States,* Princeton University Press, Princeton, N.J., 1961, p. 6.

[4]Work Projects Administration, National Research Project, *Production, Employment, and Productivity in 59 Manufacturing Industries,* Part Two, 1919-1936, Washington, D.C., pp. 36, 37, 42, 43.

[5]U.S. Department of Labor, Bureau of Labor Statistics, *Productivity and Unit Labor Cost in Selected Manufacturing Industries, 1919-40,* Washington, D.C., February 1942, pp. 22, 23.

[6]Kendrick, *op. cit.,* pp. 161-62, 471, 478-79, 484.

[7]*Ibid.,* Chapters 1 and 2.

[8]U.S. Department of Labor, Bureau of Labor Statistics, *Indexes of Output Per Manhour for Selected Industries, 1939 and 1947-67,* Washington, D.C., December 1968, pp. 57-59.

[9]Vivian E. Spencer, *Working Paper No. 6, Raw Materials in the United States Economy: 1901-1961,* U.S. Bureau of Census, Washington, D.C., 1963, pp. 134, 136.

[10]The same picture of greater efficiency in resource use for chemicals and allied products than for all manufacturing emerges from the Spencer study for the period 1939 to 1954. In that study, the index of total productivity was derived by combining production per employee weighted by payrolls and production per horsepower weighted by cost of fuels and purchased electric energy and current capital expenditures. This index increased 57% for chemicals and allied products and 32% for all manufacturing. The annual rates resemble those for total factor productivity as estimated by Kendrick. Spencer, *op. cit.,* pp. 48, 138.

[11]"Chemicals," *op. cit.*, p. 7.

[12]Total factor productivity increased 534% for chemicals and 285% for chemicals and allied products. Kendrick, *op. cit.*, pp. 478, 484.

[13]*Ibid.*, pp. 161-62.

[14]United States Department of Labor, Bureau of Labor Statistics, *Indexes of Output Per Manhour for Selected Industries, 1939 and 1947-61,* Washington, D.C., October 1962, pp. 28, 43; also "Indexes of Output Per Man-Hour, Selected Industries, 1939 and 1947-67," *op. cit.*, pp. 57-58.

[15]Sir Peter Allen, "The Chemical Industries of the U.K. and North America: Lessons and Opportunities," *Chemistry and Industry,* August 3, 1968, p. 1038.

[16]Simon Whitney, *Antitrust Policies,* Twentieth Century Fund, New York, 1958, p. 237.

[17]A. M. Schwieger, "Europe's New Industry: Threat or Promise?" *Industrial Research,* December-January 1960-1961, p. 47.

[18]"Productivity and Technological Changes in the Chemicals Industry, 1929-1940," *Monthly Labor Review,* July 1942, pp. 53, 55.

[19]National Science Foundation, "Research and Development in Industry, 1967," *Reviews of Data on Science Resources,* February 1969, p. 5.

[20]"Research and Development in the Chemicals and Allied Products Industry, 1956-61." *Reviews of Data on Research and Development,* Number 42, National Science Foundation, September 1963, p. 2.

[21]*Chemicals,* March 1967, p. 3.

[22]For 1968, the total was estimated at $17.6 billion for all industries and $1,643 million for chemicals and allied products. McGraw-Hill Publications Company, *Business Plans for Research and Development Expenditures, 1969-1972,* New York, May 16, 1969, Table I.

[23]General Electric in its 1964 report told its shareholders: "Space age metals and chemicals, many of them originally developed for use in our own products, are a fast-growing business. Lexan plastic, for example, is so tough that it is replacing metals in many applications." *General Electric in 1964,* p. 6.

[24]National Science Foundation, "Research and Development in Industry, 1967," *Reviews of Data on Science Resources,* February 1969, p. 7.

[25]"Research and Development in the Chemicals and Allied Products Industry, 1956-61," *op. cit.,* p. 2.

[26]Allen, *op. cit.*, p. 1042.

[27]C. P. Neidig, "Financial Comparison of World Chemical Companies," *Financial Analysts Journal,* January-February, 1968, p. 10.

[28]*Ibid.*

[29]Allen, *op. cit.*, p. 1042.

[30]Du Pont, *Better Living,* May/June 1967, p. 5.

[31]Du Pont, *Management Letter,* December 1967, p. 3. A study of R & D spending in 1964 by 22 chemical and petroleum companies concluded: "the bulk of the R and D projects are expected to be finished and to have an effect on profits in five years or less." Edwin Mansfield, "Industrial Research and Development: Characteristics, Costs, and Diffusion of Results," *The American Economic Review,* Papers and Proceedings, May 1969, p. 66.

[32] It has been estimated that 30 to 35% of the capital investment in the chemical industry in 1964 was "allocated for new products." *The Chemical Industry,* Bache & Company, New York, June 1964, p. 8.

[33] The investment required to control air and water pollution was estimated at $266 million for the five year period, 1962-1966 and projected at $405 million for the five year period, 1967-1971. Manufacturing Chemists Association, *Toward A Clean Environment,* 1967, p. 2.

[34] U.S. Department of Commerce, Bureau of the Census, *1967 Census of Manufactures, Summary Series,* Preliminary Report, General Statistics for Industry Groups and Industries, April 1969, pp. 3, 7.

[35] The relatively high investment is characteristic in other countries as well, In 1966 the chemical industry accounted for 15.6% of the total investment in manufacturing industries in the United Kingdom, 11.7% in Germany, 9.3% in France, 9.0% in Canada, and 10.4% (1965) in Japan. Organisation for Economic Co-operation and Development, *The Chemical Industry, 1967-1968,* Paris, 1969, p. 30.

[36] Between 1955 and 1965, for example, undistributed profits for chemicals and allied products aggregated $6.1 billion according to the U.S. Department of Commerce while assets increased by $17.9 billion.

[37] Daniel Creamer has prepared estimates of the *net fixed capital* of all manufacturing industries (including noncorporate firms) in real terms (eliminating price changes) for selected years since 1900. Between 1900 and 1937, the share accounted for by chemicals rose from 5.0% to 6.7%. See Raymond W. Goldsmith, *The National Wealth of the United States in the Postwar Period,* Princeton University Press, Princeton, N.J., 1962, p. 76.

[38] For example, Alathon polyethylene resins were first processed by Du Pont in 1948. The company has reported that "By 1956, this extruder for Alathon was obsolete; new machines had five times the capacity," *Better Living,* November-December 1963, p. 5.

[39] Under Treasury guidelines, chemicals and allied products equipment may be depreciated in 11 years. U.S. Treasury Department, Internal Revenue Service, "Depreciation, Guidelines and Rules," *Publication No. 456,* Revised, Washington, D.C., August 1964, p. 7.

[40] Between 1958 and 1967 output of chemicals and allied products increased by 113% in the United States as compared with 155% in Germany, 77% in the United Kingdom, 133% in France, and 279% in Japan. "The Chemical Industry, 1967-1968", *op. cit.,* p. 145.

[41] Crayton K. Black, "A U.S. Producer Looks At Foreign Competition," *Chemical Engineering Progress,* January 1967, p. 36.

[42] *Chemical & Engineering News,* February 10, 1969, p. 40 and *Chemical Week,* November 26, 1966, pp. 37-38.

[43] Derived from Organisation for Economic Co-operation and Development, *The Chemical Industry in the European Member Countries of OECD, 1953-1962,* Paris, 1964, p. 71 and "The Chemical Industry," 1967-1968, *op. cit.,* pp. 9, 64, 145, 147. U. S. Department of Commerce, Office of Business Economics, *Business Statistics 1967,* Washington, D.C., 1967, pp. 16, 69 and *Survey of Current Business,* March 1969, pp. S-4, S-13.

[44] Between 1958 and 1966, *output per manhour* increased 35.8% in the U.S., 50.6% in West Germany, 47.5% in France, 33.0% in the United Kingdom, 79.2% in Japan, and 92.8% in Italy. Derived from *National Institute Economic Review,* November 1968, pp. 71, 78.

[45] "International Comparisons of Productivity Growth in the 1950's," *Journal of the Royal Statistical Society,* Series A (general), Vol. 126, Part 2, 1963, p. 231. Data for the United States estimated by the present author by using U.S. Bureau of Labor Statistics employment data and Federal Reserve Board production index for chemicals and allied products.

[46] Gerhard Meier, "Productivity Statistics for German Industry," *Productivity Measurement Review,* November 1962, p. 30.

[47]The average sales per employee are lower than the average for the entire chemical industry shown in Table VIII-8 because the company totals do not include intracompany shipments which are included in the Census reports for the entire industry. With substantial amounts of captive production in the chemical industry, the totals on a company basis are significantly lower.

[48]Table VIII-8 shows the U.S. total at 2.3 times the German total because of the larger American sales per employee described in the preceding footnote.

[49]Neidig, *op. cit.*, p. 13.

[50]It has been noted that comparisons between sales per employee in the United Kingdom and in Italy are affected because the "purchasing power parity in Britain in 1960 was 4 per cent higher than the international quotation of the pound, whereas in Italy it was 10 per cent lower than the official rate of the lira. The purchasing power of the lira is therefore considerably less than that of the pound. This, in practical terms, means that Italian turnover and net values are lower than they appear to be when converted into foreign currency at the official rate of exchange." H. Wittmeyer, "Comparative Productivity in the Chemical Industries of the United Kingdom and the German Federal Republic and in the United Kingdom and Italy."*Productivity Measurement Review,* February 1964, p. 64.

[51]It must be kept in mind that the Census totals for shipments include in the United States extensive duplications so that the average figures derived tend to be higher than reported for individual companies. The averages for the largest chemical companies in the United States are much lower than the industrywide composite. Thus, in 1966, sales per employee were estimated at $28,200 for the ten largest companies as compared with the industry composite of $38,700. *Chemical & Engineering News,* May 20, 1968, p. 29.

[52]In a study of the relationships prevailing in 1950, it was found that the *physical output per worker* in the United States was three and a half times as large as in the United Kingdom for chemicals and allied products. Deborah Paige and Gottfried Bombach, *A Comparison of National Output and Productivity of the United Kingdom and the United States,* Organisation for European Economic Cooperation, Paris, 1959, p. 159. A study of 20 major items showed that for basic industrial chemicals, including fertilizers and plastics materials, output per worker in the United States was 3.72 times as large; for rayon, nylon and silk it was 2.22 times as large. *Ibid.*, pp. 37, 138, 159.

[53]The OECD has warned that "Care should be taken in making intra-country comparisons of value added per person employed since it is not possible to take into account the different structure of the industry and range of products manufactured as well as other factors, such as differences in purchasing power from one country to another in making the calculations." "The Chemical Industry, 1967-1968," *op. cit.*, p. 29.

[54]The 1962 Little Report suggested that "in expanding capacity abroad, the latest plant designs and advanced instrumentation are employed which means that employee productivity in the newer plants will compare more favorably with the typical U.S. operation." It then estimated "apparent productivity" in the United Kingdom, German, France, and Italy at 75% and Japan at 50% of the United States level. Arthur D. Little, Inc., *The Impact of Proposed U.S. Tariff Changes on Organic Chemical Imports,* Report to Synthetic Organic Chemical Manufacturers Association, May 1962, p. 28. These ratios are considerably higher than shown by the sales per employee data. The latter reflect the productivity of the entire chemical and allied products industries while the Little Report estimates are confined to the productivity of the *newer plants.*

[55]National Economic Development Office, *Manpower in the Chemical Industry,* Her Majesty's Stationery Office, London, 1967, p. 50. The products studied were chlorine and caustic soda, ethylene, formaldehyde, phosphoric acid, resin moulding powders, styrene and polystyrene, and titanium oxide. *Ibid.*, p. 59. The same study concluded that "On average, each American [plant] has only 80% *of the numbers employea* in the average British [plant] but nearly *twice as much capital* invested and produces over three times as much." *Ibid.*, p. 53.

Chapter IX

Employment and Wages

The chemical industry is one of the most intensive users of capital and inanimate energy and one of the least intensive users of labor and human energy.[1] As a result, the capital investment per employee is among the largest in American industry while the relative cost of direct labor is much lower in this industry than in most others. The exceptional growth rates in the chemical industry have been accompanied by expanding employment and tremendous gains in output per manhour. Similarly, the concentrated emphasis upon research and development and the central importance of the laboratory has meant that a shrinking proportion of the industry's labor force has been production workers. These internal institutional factors undoubtedly have influenced and conditioned the pattern of development of labor unions in the industry.

In the following pages there are examined the growth in employment and the pattern of unionization and the trends of wages and non-wage benefits as compared with the experience in other industries. The trend of labor costs as related to total shipments and the trends of unit labor costs are then examined.

Employment

Data for employment are published by the U.S. Department of Labor, Bureau of Labor Statistics, the U.S. Department of Commerce, Bureau of the Census and the National Income Unit. The BLS and Commerce data are collected by the Bureau of Employment Security and hence are similar.

For *chemicals,* Census data are available since 1899 for production workers and since 1947 for all employees; BLS data are available for both groups since 1939. For *chemicals and allied products,* Census data are available since 1899 and BLS data since 1939 for all employees and for production workers. Commerce data have been published since 1929.

Census totals usually are smaller than those reported by BLS as is shown below for 1967:[2]

Employment In Chemical Industries, 1967

	Bureau of Labor Statistics	Census of Manufactures
	(thousands)	
Chemicals and Allied Products		
All workers	1,002	854
Production workers	592	544
Chemicals		
All workers	520	429
Production workers	309	285

The most important reason for the difference shown is that Census data usually do not include employees in administrative and auxiliary establishments (e.g. central offices, garages, repair shops, sales offices, sales service laboratories, etc.) Thus, in 1963, Census reported total employment of 737,414 plus 115,707 in administrative and auxiliary establishments for a total of 853,121 for chemicals and allied products.[3] In the same year BLS reported total employment of 865,300. The spread was about 12,000 after the above adjustment is made.[4] A similar breakdown is not reported for the chemicals segment.

Growth in Employment

The growth rate of the chemical industry has been far greater than that of the national economy or of all manufacturing industries. It is not surprising, therefore, that the number of job opportunities created by the industry also has expanded more rapidly. Between 1899 and 1939, the number of chemical production workers increased from 18,000 to 123,000, or from 0.4% to 1.6% of the total for all manufacturing.

Chemical employment of production workers also increased much more rapidly than for the allied industries; its proportion increased from 13.5% of chemicals and allied products in 1899 to 48.8% in 1939.

Between 1939 and 1968, total employment in industrial chemicals also increased much more—both relatively and absolutely—than for allied products (See Appendix Table 23).

Total Employment
(thousands)

	Chemicals	Allied Products	Total
1939	158	213	371
1947	299	350	649
1954	400	353	753
1958	422	372	794
1963	455	411	866
1968	532	500	1,032

Source: U.S. Department of Labor, Bureau of Labor Statistics.

Total employment in chemicals increased from 158,000 in 1939 to 532,000 in 1968 or by 237%. For allied products employment increased from 213,000 to 500,000 or by only 135%.

Only ordnance and accessories, rubber and plastic products, and electrical equipment have recorded a greater rise in employment than chemicals. For all manufacturing industries, the increase was only 92%.

If the changes are measured between 1947 and 1968 the pattern is the same. The increases of 78% for chemicals and 43% for allied products compared with an increase of only 27% for all manufacturing industries in the same period. Although chemicals and allied products accounted for 4.2% of the total number of jobs in manufacturing industries in 1947, the proportion increased to 5.2% in 1968—with the major contribution made by chemicals, particularly fibers, plastics, and rubbers.

192

Table IX-1 shows the changes in total employment as reported by the Bureau of the Census for various groups of chemical products between 1947 and 1967. Despite the large increase in total employment in the chemical industry, the trends of employment were very diverse. As compared with the increase of 44.8% for industrial chemicals, the increases were 88.5% for organic chemicals, n.e.c. and 88.6% for inorganic chemicals, n.e.c. In contrast, employment declined sharply for cyclic intermediates and crudes and remained about unchanged for alkalies and chlorine. One of the most marked relative increases in employment was recorded for plastics.

The widely disparate trends reflected the different rates of growth and productivity for the several groups of chemical products.

TABLE IX-1

Per Cent Changes in Number of Employees, Chemicals and Allied Products, 1947 to 1967

	1947	1967	Per Cent Change
	(thousands)		
Industrial chemicals	174	252	44.8
Alkalies and chlorine	20	20	0
Industrial gases	9	10	11.1
Cyclic intermediates & crudes	35	28	-20.0
Inorganic pigments	14	13	-7.1
Industrial organic chemicals, n.e.c.	52	98	88.5
Industrial inorganic chemicals, n.e.c.	44	83	88.6
Plastics materials & synthetics	NA	177	NA
Plastics materials & resins	29	74	155.2
Synthetic rubber	8	13	62.5
Cellulosic manmade fibers	NA	28	NA
Organic fibers, noncellulosic	NA	62	NA
Drugs	81	119	46.9
Biological products	3	6	100.0
Medicinals & botanicals	13	6	-53.8
Pharmaceutical preparations	65	107	64.6
Soap, cleaners & toilet goods*	NA	NA	NA
Toilet preparations	27	40	48.1
Gum & wood chemicals	8	5	-37.5
Agricultural chemicals*	NA	NA	NA
Fertilizers	20	22	10.0
Fertilizers, mixing oil	24	15	-37.5
Miscellaneous chemical products*	NA	NA	NA
Adhesives & gelatin	8	9	12.5
Explosives	10	24	140.0
Printing ink	20	10	-50.0
Carbon black	3	3	0

*Industries are excluded from the broader industry group since data were not available for 1947.

Sources: U.S. Department of Commerce, Bureau of the Census, *Census of Manufactures, 1963,* Vol. II, Industry Statistics, Part 1, Major Groups 20 to 28, Washington, D.C., 1966, pp. 28A-8-9, 28B-5, 28C-4, 28D-5, 28F-4, 28G-6 and *1967 Census of Manufactures,* General Statistics for Industry Groups and Industries, MC67(P)-1, Washington, D.C., 1969, pp. 7-8.

In line with the trend in American industry generally, an increasing proportion of employees in the chemical industry and in all chemicals and allied products are non-production workers. In 1968 about 40% of all chemical employees were in this category; in 1939 and in the early postwar years the proportion was close to 25%. For all manufacturing industries the percent of non-production workers was 26% in 1968 as compared with 19% in the earlier year. Thus, non-production workers are much more important in the chemical industry and have been increasing in relative importance more rapidly than for all manufacturing industries during the past two decades. The trend is shown below:

Employment, Chemical Industry

(thousands)

	Production Workers	Other Employees	Total	% Other Employees
1939	119	39	158	24.7%
1947	234	65	299	21.7
1954	275	125	400	31.3
1958	263	159	422	37.7
1963	278	177	455	38.9
1968	317	215	532	40.4

Source: *Employment and Earnings and Monthly Report on the Labor Force,* various issues. U.S. Department of Labor, Bureau of Labor Statistics.

Thus, about 4 out of of every 10 employees in chemicals are in administrative, scientific, sales and clerical positions. This trend is likely to continue as the pace of technology in the chemical industry steps up. The result will be an expanded demand for workers with new and improved skills and a more substantial amount of education and training.

Unionization

Unions have played a lesser role in the chemical industry than in most mass production industries. In contrast to steel, automobiles, and rubber no single union occupies a dominant role. Four separate groups have endeavored to organize chemical workers: District 50, formerly of the United Mine Workers of America (Ind.); International Chemical Workers Union, AFL-CIO (ICWU); Oil, Chemical and Atomic Workers Union, AFL-CIO (OCAW);[5] and numerous independent unions that have no affiliation with a national or international union. No one union has obtained a dominant position.

In 1967, the ICWU was estimated to have 93,000 members while the OCAW had a membership of 165,000, a significant part of which were in this industry.[6] District 50 was reported to have about 110,000 workers in the chemical industry in 1968.[7]

Most companies must deal with several unions. For example, both District 50 and the ICWU have locals at Monsanto. Union Carbide deals with District 50 and the OCAW.[8] The ICWU also has locals at Hercules, American Cyanamid and Davison Chemicals Division of W.R. Grace, the OCAW at Parke, Davis and Lever Brothers, and District 50 at Dow, Allied, and Celanese.

Unionism came to the chemical industry after the birth of the CIO in 1935. By the early 1940s, membership of chemical workers in District 50 of the United Mine Workers and in the National Council of Chemical and Allied Industries

Union (AFL), the two largest unions, still was relatively small. For example, the latter group had only 20,000 members in 1940. Thus, a study by the Twentieth Century Fund [survey] concluded that "union organization in this basic industry is still of small proportions."[9]

During the ensuing twenty years union membership expanded only moderately in the chemical industry. Currently, a far smaller per cent of workers are in unions (both national and independent) than in such industries as steel, rubber, automobiles, and aluminum.

The development of independent local unions at Du Pont is an unique part of the pattern of labor relations in the industry. At Du Pont the national unions play a very minor role. As of the end of 1960, about 6% of the eligible workers were members of locals of national unions, slightly more than one-third were unorganized, and close to 60% were in 37 independent local unions.[10]

This approach of Du Pont toward unionism has been well summarized by G. G. Mitchell, Assistant Director of its Employee Relations Department, who has pointed out that Du Pont "does everything possible to operate its plant in such a manner that employees will not feel the need for representation."[11] Du Pont has had a pension program in effect since September 1, 1904 and an insurance program since 1919.

What has inhibited the growth of unionism in this industry in contrast to the experience of other mass production industries? In chemicals, the forward march of technology has reduced the relative need for production workers. As was noted earlier, the relative importance of salaried employees has been increasing steadily and is significantly greater than for other manufacturing industries. Since production workers are the core of the mass production industry unions, this development has affected the size of the potential union membership.

The location of many chemical plants in the South and Southwest also has played a role. In many of these localities there has been active opposition to unionism.[12] Further, many chemical plants have been located in smaller labor markets, where there is little competition for the current supply of labor because one employer occupied a dominant position.

G. G. Mitchell has noted:

"The comparatively isolated locations of many of these plants undoubtedly has allowed us a better opportunity to put our employee relations philosophy into practice than has been the case with many of the so-called basic industries operating large plants in highly industrialized communities."[13]

Moreover, the managements of most chemical companies have successfully pursued a program of bargaining with unions on a local basis and of wooing employees by paying liberal benefits and high wages. It may be seen why, therefore, the pattern of labor relations in this industry is substantially different from that found in most other manufacturing industries.

Wage Trends

Wages and non-wage benefits have been rising steadily in the postwar American economy. Chemical workers have shared fully in these trends with increases greater than those received by the average worker in manufacturing industries. The above average increase in employment opportunities and in output per manhour, therefore, have been accompanied by an average increase in economic benefits to employees.

Wage Data

The U.S. Bureau of Labor Statistics reports weekly hours and weekly and hourly earnings for production workers[14] in the chemicals segment and chemicals and allied products. The present series is available since 1947. BLS does not publish similar data for white-collar workers. Thus, the BLS data show the trend only for production workers who account for a declining proportion of chemical employment.

Wages, hours, and employment data are obtained on an establishment basis. Each establishment is assigned to a particular industry on the basis of its principal product as measured in dollar volume.[15] The Bureau of Labor Statistics obtains payroll data and the number of manhours paid for. The payroll total includes overtime pay, holiday pay, vacation pay, shift differentials, sick leave, and similar payments. The reported totals do not include the costs of pensions, welfare funds, Social Security, workmen's compensation, and similar non-wage benefits. Manhour data cover production by non-supervisory employees and include the hours paid for holidays, vacations, sick leave, etc. Average hourly earnings are determined by dividing the total payroll by the number of production worker manhours, so that they reflect the influence of overtime pay, shift differentials, holiday premiums, incentive wages, etc.

The average hours worked per week are obtained by dividing the total number of manhours for a week by the number of production and related workers. Weekly earnings are then determined by multiplying average hourly earnings by the average number of hours worked per week.

Since BLS does not report a combined figure for chemicals (SIC 281 plus 282), the data reported for these separate categories since 1947 have been combined on the basis of production worker employment in each period[16] (See Appendix Table 24).

The U.S. Department of Commerce has published estimates of average annual earnings per full-time employee since 1929. These estimates are obtained by dividing total wages and salaries by the number of full-time equivalent employees. According to the Department of Commerce, "Full-time equivalent employment measures man-years of full-time employment of wage and salary earners and its equivalent in work performed by part-time workers. Full-time employment is defined simply in terms of the number of hours which is customary at a particular time and place."[17] The annual earnings do not include non-wage benefits. Data are available for chemicals and allied products but for none of the component industries.

Average Hourly Earnings

Average hourly earnings (excluding non-wage benefits) were $3.36 for chemicals and allied products as compared with $3.11 for all manufacturing in December 1968.[18] The average varies widely among the industries that comprise this group as is shown below:

Average Hourly Earnings, December 1968

Industrial chemicals (SIC 281)	$3.73
(Chemicals) (SIC 281 and 282)	(3.53)
Plastics materials & synthetics (SIC 282)	3.30
Other chemical products	3.25
Soap, cleaners & toilet goods	3.27
Paints & allied products	3.18

Drugs...............................	3.12
Agricultural chemicals..................	2.81
All manufacturing......................	3.11

Only agricultural chemicals had lower average hourly earnings in December 1968 than the average for all manufacturing industries. Because of the higher skills required in many of its operations,[19] average hourly earnings for chemical workers have been higher than for the allied products.

Average hourly earnings of chemical workers increased from $1.33 in 1947 to $3.53 in December 1968 or by $2.20 an hour. This rise was greater than that recorded for all manufacturing industries, for which the increase was from $1.22 to $3.11 or $1.89 an hour. The percentage increases were 165% and 155% respectively (See Appendix Table 25).

Average Hourly Earnings

	Chemicals	All Manufacturing	Spread In Favor of Chemicals
1947	$1.33	$1.22	$ .11
1954	2.07	1.78	.29
1958	2.48*	2.11	.37
1963	2.92	2.46	.46
Dec. 1968	3.53	3.11	.42

*Starting in 1958, weighted average of industrial chemicals and plastics materials and synthetics.

The spread in favor of chemical workers as compared with all manufacturing increased from 11 cents an hour in 1947 to 29 cents in 1954, 38 cents in 1958, and 46 cents in 1963. Between 1963 and December 1968, average earnings for all manufacturing rose 4 cents more per hour than the composite for chemical workers. This disparity reflected the smaller hourly increases in plastic materials and synthetics as is shown below:

	Increase in Hourly Earnings, 1963 to December 1968
	(cents)
Industrial chemicals...............	66
Plastic materials & synthetics........	59
Chemicals (composite)..........	61
All manufacturing.................	65

In December 1968 average hourly earnings of chemical workers were $3.53. This average was exceeded in 59 industries out of 254 for which data are reported by BLS. The chemical workers were in the top quarter of manufacturing industries. The pattern for average weekly earnings and for annual earnings was similar (See Appendix Table 26).

Real Hourly Earnings

Data for money wages alone do not reveal the changes in the economic well-being of workers. During the postwar years there has been a considerable rise in consumer prices. From 1947 to December 1968, the consumer price index rose by 59.0%. However, average hourly earnings in chemicals rose by 165% or much more rapidly than prices.

Real Average Hourly Earnings

	Chemicals	All Manufacturing
1947	$1.71	$1.57
1954	2.21	1.90
1958	2.47	2.10
1963	2.74	2.31
Dec. 1968	2.85	2.51

After adjusting for the changes in the consumer price index, real average hourly earnings increased from $1.71 (in 1957-59 dollars) in 1947 to $2.85 in December 1968; this was a rise in real earnings of $1.14 an hour or 66.7 per cent. These data understate the total improvement experienced by chemical workers because they do not reflect the significant improvement in non-wage benefits and in leisure time discussed below.

For all manufacturing industries, real average hourly earnings rose from $1.57 to $2.51 an increase of 94 cents, or 59.9 per cent. Thus, the living standards of chemical workers have improved at a greater rate than for workers in all manufacturing industries. However, all of this relative gain had been achieved by 1963. During the price inflation starting in 1965, the real gains of chemical workers lagged behind those of workers in all manufacturing (See Appendix Table 27).

Non-Wage Benefits[20]

During World War II and in subsequent years, non-wage benefits have increased in relative importance in all industries. Among these benefits are: pensions; health and welfare plans; payments for time not worked, including holidays, extended vacations, and rest periods; and programs designed to cushion the effects of unemployment. Data for non-wage benefits generally are available only for the broad group, chemicals and allied products.[21]

Total Costs

For chemicals and allied products, total wage supplements[22] reported by the U.S. Department of Commerce increased from $139 million in 1947 to $1,288 million in 1967, a rise of 827 per cent; for all manufacturing, the increase was 817 per cent for the same period.[23] The exceptional growth in private pension and welfare funds was largely responsible for this tremendous increase in the costs of non-wage benefits.

Aggregate payments are affected by the total volume of employment which has risen more rapidly for chemicals and allied products than for all manufacturing industries. A better picture of the gains obtained by chemical workers, therefore, is shown by the change in relative importance of wage supplements as a percentage of total wages and salaries and by the trend of wage supplements per employee. Between 1947 and 1967, wage supplements increased in relative importance from 6.2 per cent of total wages and salaries to 15.8 per cent for chemicals and allied products. During the same period, the increase for all manufacturing industries was from 4.8 per cent to 13.9 per cent (See Appendix Table 28).

Wage Supplements As Per Cent of Total Wages and Salaries

	Chemicals & Allied Products	All Manufacturing
1947	6.2%	4.8%
1954	9.7	7.7
1958	11.3	9.6
1963	13.5	12.2
1967	15.8	13.9

Source: *Survey of Current Business,* July issues. U.S. Department of Commerce, Office of Business Economics.

In 1947, *wage supplements per employee* were $192 for chemicals and allied products as compared with $134 for all manufacturing industries. By 1967, the totals had risen to $1,287 and $958 respectively. Thus, the gap in favor of chemical workers had widened considerably from $58 to $329.

Wage Supplements

	Chemicals & Allied Products	All Manufacturing	Spread
1947	$ 192	$134	$ 58
1954	478	312	166
1958	678	452	226
1963	984	659	325
1967	1,287	958	329

Source: *Survey of Current Business,* July issues. U.S. Department of Commerce, Office of Business Economics.

The total wage supplements paid per employee by chemicals and allied products ranked eighth among the seventy-eight industries for which the Department of Commerce reported data; the industry ranked fifth among twenty-one manufacturing industries, exceeded only by products of petroleum refining, motor vehicles, primary metals, and tobacco manufactures. For a 2,080-hour work year, $1,287 for pensions, welfare funds, and related payments, is equal to 62 cents an hour. The failure to reflect these non-wage benefits means that average hourly earnings sharply understate hourly labor costs and the improvement chemical workers have experienced in living standards in the postwar period.

Time Paid for but Not Worked

The above data do not show separately the cost of vacations, holidays, and other time off with pay. Such benefits also have added to labor costs while increasing the leisure time of chemical workers in the post-World War II years. Moreover, such payments have become an increasing item of cost to most companies. A three-week vacation plus nine paid holidays, for example, equals 192 hours out of a 2,080 hour year.[24] Other time paid for but not worked includes sick leave, jury duty, voting time, and military leave.[25]

The Bureau of Labor Statistics last published estimates of the proportion of manhours of paid leave to total plant manhours for production and related workers in 1958.[26] For chemicals and allied products, paid leave was 7.4 per cent of total hours paid for; for all manufacturing industries it was 6.0 per cent. Only three of the other twenty industries had a higher ratio than chemicals (products of petroleum and coal, rubber, and primary metals); ordnance and instruments had the same ratio as chemicals. For each of the major types of paid leave, chemicals and allied products had a higher proportion of hours than all manufacturing industries.[27]

Paid Leave, Per Cent of Manhours, 1958

	All Manufacturing	Chemicals Allied Products
	(per cent)	
Vacations	3.6	4.1
Holidays	2.2	2.6
Sick leave	0.2	0.7
Other	0	0.1
Total	6.0	7.4

The overwhelming proportion of paid leave is accounted for by vacations and holidays. The further liberalization of vacation plans and holidays since 1958 increased the proportion of paid time off by chemicals and allied products to 9 per cent of the hours paid for. For 1967, the Chamber of Commerce of the United States estimated the cost of these benefits at 28.8 cents an hour or 9.0% of total payrolls paid by chemicals and allied products; for all manufacturing the totals were 22.3 cents an hour or 7.3% of their payrolls.[28]

Labor Costs

Total wages and non-wage benefits by themselves do not reveal the significance of labor costs to a company or to an industry. To determine their relative importance, labor costs must be examined either in relationship to shipments or sales or to units of output (unit labor costs). The available data on both bases are reviewed below:

Labor Costs as a Per Cent of Shipments

The relative importance of direct labor costs in any company or industry is influenced by many factors, including the extent to which materials, energy, or components are purchased rather than produced. Because their costs include larger payments for labor and less for purchased materials, vertically integrated companies tend to utilize a relatively higher proportion of the sales dollar for direct labor costs than companies which are not integrated.

Despite the large increases in average hourly earnings discussed earlier, the relative importance of total labor costs for operating manufacturing establishments in the chemical industry has declined during the postwar years.[29] Between 1947 and 1967, the labor cost ratio declined from 21.2% to 15.9%. The average for 1967 was at the lower end of the postwar range[30] (Table IX-2). Sharply expanding volume, heavy capital investment and mechanization, and

TABLE IX-2

Total Payrolls and Shipments For
Chemicals, Selected
Years, 1947-1967

	Shipments	Total Payrolls	Per Cent Relationship
	(in millions)		
1947	$ 4,143	$ 879	21.2
1954	8,906	1,709	19.2
1958	11,780	2,143	18.2
1963	16,579	2,737	16.5
1967	21,523	3,424	15.9

Sources: U.S. Department of Commerce, Bureau of the Census, *U.S. Census of Manufactures:* 1958, Vol. II, Industry Statistics, Part I, Major Groups 20 to 28, Washington, D.C., 1962, pp. 10-13; *1963 Census of Manufactures,* Vol. II, Industry Statistics, Part I, Major Groups 20 to 28, Washington, D.C., 1966, pp. 28-29; *1967 Census of Manufactures,* Preliminary Report, General Statistics for Industry Groups and Selected Industries, Washington, D.C., April 1969, p. 7.

large increases in output per manhour have acted to offset above average increases in wages and non-wage benefits. In connection with these trends, it should be kept in mind that the magnitude of the decline is probably overstated to a small extent because the Census payroll costs do not reflect the relative increase in administrative and auxiliary personnel.[31]

These data tend to understate the relative importance of labor costs for several reasons: (1) the payrolls as reported by the Bureau of the Census do not include employees in administrative and auxiliary establishments;[32] (2) the Census data do not include research and development which is relatively more important for chemicals than for industry generally and hence the understatement in labor costs shown in the Census data is greater; (3) the large amount of intra-industry shipments for chemicals probably results in a large amount of duplication in the Census shipments total which is not matched by the labor cost figures and hence acts to reduce the reported ratio of labor costs.

Census data also show the relative importance of labor costs among the allied products and for different groups of chemicals. Table IX-3 presents the labor cost ratios derived from data reported for operating manufacturing establishments by the Bureau of the Census. These data are subject to the limitations described above and hence are useful primarily to identify the product groups with higher labor costs rather than to provide a precise indication of the relative importance of labor costs in each instance.

Payroll costs vary in importance among the major groups included in chemicals and allied products. In 1967, payrolls were 15.9% of shipments for chemicals as compared with 10.5% for agricultural chemicals, 17.2% for paints and varnishes, 18.0% for drugs, and 15.0% for all allied products. For each of these allied industries, the ratio was lower than for all manufacturing (23.7%).

Within the chemical category, there was a wide range of experience. The highest ratios were reported for cellulosic man-made fibers (22.0%) and alkalies and chlorine (21.8%) while the lowest ratios were synthetic rubber (12.0%) and industrial organic chemicals, n.e.c. (13.2%). There was a similar disparity in the relative importance of labor costs for production workers alone.

Of the 21 groups for which data are reported by the Bureau of the Census, only food and kindred products, tobacco products, and petroleum and coal products had a lower ratio of labor costs than chemicals and allied products in 1967.

Unit Labor Costs

It is impossible to determine the level of unit labor costs for specific products from the published data because of the many thousands of items produced by the chemical industry and by most chemical companies. However, by comparing the changes in average hourly labor costs (average hourly earnings plus non-wage benefits) and output per manhour,[33] a broad picture is obtained of the general trend of unit labor costs.

Average hourly labor costs for chemicals increased from $1.40 in 1947 to $4.06 in 1968 or by 190%. The increase in output per manhour in the same period was 348%. On the basis of these data, unit labor costs *declined* 35.2% in the postwar years (See Appendix Table 29).

Unit Labor Costs

	Chemicals	Chemicals and Allied Products	All Manufacturing
		(1957 - 59 = 100)	
1947	100.0	98.4	73.9
1958	104.8	101.8	102.2
1963	75.7	89.3	99.7
1968	64.8	90.0	110.3

Two important qualifications should be noted in connection with these estimates: (1) average hourly labor costs make no allowance for the increased cost of vacations, holidays, and other time paid for but not worked, and (2) the increase in labor cost per manhour does not reflect the increasing importance of non-production workers. Production workers decreased in relative importance from 78.3% of chemical employment in 1947 to 59.6% in 1968. Because of this change in the employment mix, allowance for the higher average wage paid to non-production workers would probably mean that the rise in average hourly labor costs would be greater for all employees than for production workers alone. As a result the decline in unit labor costs was probably somewhat less than 35.2% in the postwar years.[34]

The decline in unit labor costs in the chemical industry is in marked contrast to the rise of 49.3% which took place in all manufacturing industries during the same period.

Actually all of the decline in chemical unit labor costs developed between 1958 and 1968. The index of unit labor costs for chemicals was close to its postwar peak in 1958 and 4.8% *higher* than in 1947. (Between 1947 and 1958, unit labor costs rose 34.9% for all manufacturing and 3.5% for chemicals and allied products).[35] However, since 1958 there has been a dramatic *decline* in unit labor costs which fell 38.2% for chemicals as compared with an increase of 7.9% for all manufacturing. This sharp decline resulted primarily from the phenomenal increase of 139% in output per manhour which in turn reflected the 180% rise in chemical output during the same period.[36]

The disparity in the trend of unit labor costs in the chemical industry and in all manufacturing was particularly marked during the price inflation which started in 1965. The rising rate of advance in consumer prices was accompanied by even larger increases in hourly labor costs as labor sought to keep pace with the price inflation. For all manufacturing industries, unit labor costs had remained relatively unchanged between 1958 and 1965. As hourly labor cost increases accelerated and output per manhour increases remained about the same, unit labor costs began to rise rapidly. In contrast, the increase in output per manhour in the chemical industry continued to outpace the rise in hourly labor costs so that unit labor costs continued to decline.

	Unit Labor Costs	
	All Manufacturing	Chemicals
	(1957-59 = 100)	
1965	99.1	68.7
1966	101.2	67.1
1967	106.5	68.0
1968	110.3	64.8
% Change 1965 to 1968	+11.3%	-5.7%

However, the effect of the general price and labor cost inflation was to slow down the rate of decrease in chemical unit labor costs.

Unit Labor Costs, Chemical Industry

Period	Decline in Unit Labor Costs
1959 to 1962	-14.0%
1962 to 1965	-14.3
1965 to 1968	- 5.7

Nevertheless, thanks to the continuing sharp rise in output per manhour the experience of the chemical industry was in marked contrast to the behavior of unit labor costs generally.[37] Through most of this period, chemical prices were also declining as was noted earlier. This sharp decline in unit labor costs provided some offset to the pressure on profit margins created by lower chemical prices.

It should be noted that the decline in unit labor costs between 1947 and 1968 took place although average hourly labor costs rose more for chemicals (190%) than for all manufacturing industries (174%). The major reason for the decline in unit labor costs for chemicals was the much larger increase in output per manhour which rose 348% or almost four times as much as the rise of 88% for all manufacturing.

Summary and Conclusions

The chemical industry is not a labor-intensive industry. Nevertheless, it has provided a steadily increasing proportion of the total jobs available in manufacturing industries. In 1968, it provided more than one million jobs, about equally divided between the chemical industry and its allied product industries. Because of its great dependence upon technology, an increasing proportion of the chemical workers are skilled. Only three chemical workers out of five are blue collar workers as compared with three out of four for all manufacturing industries.

TABLE IX-3

Relative Importance of Labor Costs: All Manufacturing and Chemicals and Allied Products, 1967

| | Per Cent of Shipments | |
	All Payrolls	Production Workers Payrolls
All manufacturing	23.7	14.6
Chemicals and allied products	15.4	8.5
Chemicals	15.9	9.5
Industrial chemicals	15.0	8.8
Alkalies and chlorine	21.8	13.2
Industrial gases	13.2	6.0
Cyclic intermediates & crudes	16.0	9.7
Inorganic pigments	17.8	11.7
Industrial organic chemicals,n.e.c.	13.2	7.7
Industrial inorganic chemicals,n.e.c.	16.1	9.2
Plastics materials and synthetics	17.7	10.9
Plastics materials and resins	16.5	9.6
Synthetic rubber	12.0	7.3
Cellulosic manmade fibers	22.0	16.3
Organic fibers, noncellulosic	20.6	12.7
Allied products	15.0	7.4
Drugs	18.0	7.6
Soap, cleaners, and toilet goods	10.8	5.4
Paints and allied products	17.2	7.9
Gum and wood chemicals	15.2	10.7
Agricultural chemicals	10.5	6.1
Miscellaneous chemical products	20.3	11.9

n.e.c. - not elsewhere classified

Sources: Derived from U.S. Department of Commerce, Bureau of the Census, *1967 Census of Manufactures,* MC67(P)-1, Washington, D.C., 1969, pp. 3, 7, 8.

Chemical workers occupy a pre-eminent position in the hierarchy of American labor. In the postwar years, they have experienced greater increases in wages than the average worker in all manufacturing industries. As a result, their real wages and their living standards also have risen more. Thus, the lesser role of unions in this industry has not placed its workers at a disadvantage. On the contrary, the gains of chemical workers have been above average.

Non-wage benefits have been more liberal and have risen more rapidly for chemicals and allied products than in most other industries (separate data have not been reported for chemicals alone). Pensions, welfare funds, and other wage supplements were equal to 15.8% of wages and salaries of chemicals and allied products in 1967 as compared with 13.9% for all manufacturing. Similarly, time paid for but not worked (vacations, holidays, etc.) is relatively higher in this industry than in all manufacturing.

Despite the above average increases in hourly labor costs, unit labor costs have been sharply reduced. This decline reflected the phenomenal rise in output per manhour. Unit costs have declined persistently since 1958 with the net decline a dramatic 38.2% for the decade. Despite the pressures which developed in the economy after the Viet Nam War was escalated, unit labor costs in the chemical industry continued to decline, although not as rapidly as in the preceding years.

The intensive use of capital and the great investment in research and capital equipment, which are hallmarks of the chemical industry, contributed significantly to the increase in output per manhour. The extraordinary increase in chemical productivity in turn made possible higher wages and non-wage benefits to workers without increasing the net unit labor cost to chemical companies.

---

[1]However, the industry is an intensive user of scientists and related personnel.

[2]U.S. Department of Labor, Bureau of Labor Statistics, *Employment and Earnings Statistics for the United States for 1909-68*, Bulletin No. 1312-6, Washington, D.C., 1968, pp. 639, 640, 643, 644, 649; U.S. Department of Commerce, Bureau of the Census, *1967 Census of Manufactures*, Preliminary Report, General Statistics for Industry Groups and Industries, Washington, D.C., April 1969, p. 7.

[3]U.S. Department of Commerce, Bureau of the Census, *Census of Manufactures: 1963*, Vol. II, Industry Statistics, Part 1, Major Groups 20 to 28, Washington, D.C., 1966, p. 45.

[4]BLS totals cover two categories, industrial chemicals and plastics materials and synthetics.

[5]In 1955, the United Gas, Coke, and Chemical Workers, with a membership of more than 70,000, most of them in chemicals, merged with the Oil Workers International Union, almost solely in the petroleum industry. The merger of these two former CIO unions resulted largely because of the dire financial straits of the United Gas, Coke, and Chemical Workers. Melvin Rothbaum, *The Government of the Oil, Chemical and Atomic Workers Union*, John Wiley & Sons, Inc., New York, 1962, pp. 10, 31.

[6]U.S. Department of Labor, "Directory of National and International Labor Unions In the United States 1967", *BLS Bulletin No. 1596*, Washington, D.C., 1968, pp. 21, 28.

[7]*Chemical Week*, March 16, 1968, p. 32.

[8]*Chemical Week*, March 2, 1968, p. 34, December 9, 1967, p. 40, March 16, 1968, p. 32.

[9]Philip Taft, "Chemicals," in *How Collective Bargaining Works*, Harry A. Mills, editor, The Twentieth Century Fund, New York, 1942, p. 914.

[10]Julius Rezler "Labor Organization at Du Pont: A Study in Independent Local Unionism," *Labor History*, Spring 1963, p. 181.

[11]Cited in *ibid.*, p. 187.

[12]Weber pointed out that: " . . . In many firms, chemical unions have had to cope with an additional handicap imposed by the presence of a sizable enclave of unorganized workers. And when a concern for local autonomy within specified unions has been superimposed on this generally divisive picture, the problem of mobilizing effective bargaining power has become increasingly difficult." Arnold R. Weber, "Competitive Unionism in the Chemical Industry," *Industrial and Labor Relations Review*, October 1959, p. 33.

[13]Cited in Rezler, *op. cit.*, p. 190.

[14]Production and related workers are defined as working foreman and all non-supervisory workers (including lead men and trainees) engaged in fabricating, processing, assembling, inspection, receiving, storage, handling, packing, warehousing, shipping, maintenance, repair, janitorial, watchman service, products development, auxiliary production for the plant's own use (e.g. power plant, recordkeeping, and other services closely associated with the production operations).

[15]In contrast, profits, sales, and net worth data usually are on a company-wide basis, with the industry classification determined by the principal products in terms of sales volume. Prices usually are for products.

[16]"Employment and Earnings Statistics for the United States, 1909-68," *op. cit.,* p. iv.

[17]U.S. Department of Commerce, *U.S. Income and Output,* Washington, D.C., November 1958, p. 211, fn. 1.

[18]Average hourly earnings include the effects of overtime pay. Excluding overtime pay, the average was $3.23 for chemicals and allied products and $2.97 for all manufacturing industries in December 1968. *Employment and Earnings,* March 1969, p. 98.

[19]One indication of the importance of semi-skilled workers is found in the proportion of women employed. In January 1968, women accounted for only 13% of the total employment in chemicals in contrast to 39% in drugs and 38% in soap, cleaners, and toilet goods. *Employment and Earnings Statistics for the United States, 1909-68, op. cit.,* pp. 643, 649, 657, 661.

[20]For a discussion of the types of non-wage benefits and of data available from various sources, see Jules Backman, *Wage Determination,* D. Van Nostrand Co., Princeton, N.J., 1959, Chapter 5.

[21]Continuous data are available from two sources for the costs of non-wage benefits: the U.S. Department of Commerce and the Chamber of Commerce of the United States.

[22]Wage supplements include mainly legally required social insurance and workmen's compensation and employer contributions to private pension and welfare funds. They do not include payments for time not worked, such as paid vacations and paid holidays. The annual data are published in the *Survey of Current Business,* July issue each year.

[23]U.S. Department of Commerce, Office of Business Economics, *U.S. Income and Ouput,* Washington, D.C., 1958, pp. 200-201; *Survey of Current Business,* July 1968, p. 43.

[24]Late in 1965, chemical companies had 8 or 9 paid holidays. "Typical vacation provisions were: 1 week's pay after 1 year of service, 2 weeks' after 2 years, 3 weeks' after 10 years, and 4 weeks' after 20 years." *Monthly Labor Review,* September 1966, p. 997.

[25]"Chemical plants employing slightly more than nine-tenths of the workers had formal provisions for paid funeral leave and paid jury duty leave." *Ibid.,* p. 998.

[26]The data included all types of payments except for severance pay, supplementary unemployment benefits (SUB), coffee breaks, lunch time, and reporting pay, and were reported separately for each of twenty-one manufacturing industries. L. Earl Lewis, "Composition of Payroll Hours in Manufacturing, 1958," *Monthly Labor Review,* July 1960, pp. 686-92.

[27]*Ibid.,* p. 687.

[28]Chamber of Commerce of the United States, *Fringe Benefits 1967,* Washington, D.C., pp. 12-13.

[29]Data are available for total wages of production workers and shipments for chemicals since 1899. Between 1899 and 1947, the ratio of their labor costs for production workers generally was between 14% and 16%; in 1947 it was 15%. By 1954, it had declined to 11.9% and in 1966, it was 9.4%, the lowest for the entire period. This decline reflected in part the decreasing importance of production workers to total employment and in part a reduction in relative labor costs.

[30]Between 1947 and 1967, the relative importance of labor costs increased for cyclic coal-tar crudes and inorganic pigments and fell for alkalies and chlorine, industrial gases, intermediate coal-tar products, synthetic rubbers, organics n.e.c., inorganics n.e.c., and plastics materials.

[31]Data are available only for 1954, 1958, and 1963. Between these years the payments to these employees increased from 10.7% to 14.3% to 17.4% of the total payroll. *U.S. Census of Manufactures, 1963, op. cit.,* p. 45.

[32]Of the 5.6 percentage point spread between Commerce (21.2%) and Census data (15.6%) in 1963 for relative labor costs for chemicals and allied products, 3.3 percentage points were accounted for by the exclusion of employees in administrative and auxiliary establishments from the Census data.

[33]The figures are only approximate. For chemicals hourly labor costs are based on average hourly earnings of production workers plus average wage supplements paid to all workers in chemicals and allied products. Thus, these data do not reflect the growing importance of non-production workers. The data for output per manhour are for all employees.

[34]For chemicals and allied products, hourly labor costs increased by 201% as compared with a rise of 229% in output per manhour; thus unit labor costs were reduced by 8.5% between 1947 and 1968.

[35]Levinson found similar relationships for the 1947-58 period for all manufacturing and chemicals and allied products. Harold M. Levinson, "Postwar Movement of Prices and Wages in Manufacturing Industries," *Study Paper No. 21,* Joint Economic Committee, Congress of the United States, Washington, D.C., January 30, 1960, pp. 28, 37. For the period 1948-56 chemicals and allied products had the smallest rise (5.0%) in unit labor costs, except for textiles, among twenty manufacturing industries. The major reason for this small rise in unit labor costs was that chemicals and allied products had by far the largest increase in output per manhour (57% as against 36% for textiles, the second largest increase). Charles L. Schultze and Joseph L. Tryon, "Prices and Costs in Manufacturing Industries," *Study Paper No. 17,* Joint Economic Committee, Congress of the United States, Washington, D.C, January 25, 1960, p. 43.

[36]The two qualifications noted earlier would have less significance for the period since 1958 than for the entire postwar period.

[37]For the entire private economy, labor cost per unit of gross product increased by 10.9% between 1965 and 1968. *Business Conditions Digest,* February 1969, p. 74.

Chapter X

Profits

Profits reflect the interaction and effects of many factors including the volume of sales, changes in selling prices, labor costs, productivity, raw material costs, research and development expenses, accounting conventions for the treatment of inventory profits and depreciation, changes in product mix, and changes in corporate income tax rates. Profits usually are the most volatile share of the sales dollar. Small changes in volume may result in large changes in profits.

In earlier chapters, the trends of prices, productivity and labor costs were discussed. The relatively high rates of gain in productivity and the above average increases in wages and non-wage benefits were noted. Selling prices were shown to have risen less or declined more than the average for all wholesale prices. In this chapter, the levels and trends of chemical company profits are reviewed.

Industry-wide profit totals represent a composite of varying degrees of success and failure. In a profit-and-loss economy, there is no common pool of profits upon which the unsuccessful or the below-average profits company can draw. The most successful companies in terms of profits tend to be those which meet or create an expanding demand and help to develop mass markets for their products or who lead in innovation and command a premium for their new products until their competitors catch up. Price policy may play an important role in their success. Many chemical companies, usually smaller ones, often operate at a loss.

The level of profits also may influence future costs. This is reflected in the tendency to be less concerned about costs in periods of prosperity and a greater drive for economy during periods of recession. Mounting profits also can induce excessive investment with the attending overcapacity as a number of companies independently decide to enter a specific market. One result can be the costs of maintaining relatively idle plant and equipment.

Profits play a vital role in connection with decisions to introduce new products or to expand the output of old ones. At best, only a very rough approximation of the profitability of specific products can be determined for a multi-product company. Allocations of overhead expenses necessarily involve assumptions which are useful for internal operating purposes but do not provide the basis to determine the profitability of each product. Even though the precise profitability may not be determined, it is possible to indicate the contribution made by each product to general overhead and then to give priority to those which make the greatest contribution on the assumption that they yield the largest profits. However, data are not publicly available to indicate the relative profitability of each product. In any event, total company profits are far more readily determined and meaningful than the "guesstimates" for individual products or product lines.

In the following pages profit trends and levels will be reviewed first in terms of dollars and in terms of their relationship to sales (the profit margin) and to net worth (or net assets). Each of these measures of profitability is useful to answer particular questions about a company or an industry. The stockholder, for example, is interested in the total dollars earned as well as the return on net assets. The price executive is concerned with the margin of income before taxes to sales as well as the other two measures.

Profits Data

Profits data are available for chemicals and chemicals and allied products industries from several sources. These data show the results of all of a company's activities and hence include profits from non-chemical activities where they are carried on.[1] On the other hand, there are excluded from these totals the profits earned by companies in other industries (e.g. petroleum) which are substantial producers of chemicals. As a result, the profits data are not directly comparable with Census data for shipments, payrolls, or value added, all of which are obtained on a plant basis rather than for the company as a whole.

Comprehensive data have been published by the Internal Revenue Service based upon the income tax reports filed by all companies. IRS assigns all of the profits of a company to only one group.[2]

The IRS data are available for earnings before and after income taxes and for companies reporting profits and for those reporting losses. IRS publishes gross receipts and net worth for the companies classified as chemicals and allied products. It takes a considerable period to compile these data, so that the latest figures are always several years old. Data can be calculated for chemicals and allied products since 1929 showing profit margins as a per cent of sales.

The U.S. Department of Commerce publishes total income before taxes and profits after taxes for chemicals and allied products as part of its annual estimates of national income.[3]

The First National City Bank of New York publishes each April profits as a per cent of sales and of net worth[4] for four groups of companies in this industry; chemical products,[5] paint and allied products, drugs and medicines, and soap, cosmetics, etc. These data have been available since 1925 for return on net worth and since 1934 for margin on sales. The profits data are reported only on an after-taxes basis.

The Federal Trade Commission and the Securities and Exchange Commission have published data on profits before and after taxes as a percentage of sales and stockholders' equity[6] for a selected group of industries, including chemicals and allied products, since 1947; data have been published separately for chemicals since 1956.[7] These data are published quarterly but not annually. Annual ratios can be obtained by averaging the quarterly figures. Since these are unweighted averages they may differ fractionally from the actual earnings.

Fortune magazine each year publishes a tabulation of profits as a percentage of sales and of invested capital[8] for the 500 largest industrial corporations. Included in this group are many chemical companies.[9]

The IRS tabulation covers all companies, large and small, profitable and unprofitable. On the other hand, the First National City Bank confines its sample to leading companies. The FTC-SEC tabulations attempt to secure representation of the smaller companies as well as the larger ones. Moreover, the composition of the samples used by First National City Bank and the FTC-SEC changes over time so that the trends do not reflect the record of an identical group of companies. Similarly, the IRS and Commerce data are affected by changes in the Standard Industrial Classification (SIC) for which adjustments cannot be made retroactively.

Trends of Profits and Losses

Ours is a profit-and-loss economy. Even in years of high level activity, many companies operate at a loss. This is true in the chemical industry as well as in the economy generally. The comprehensive data available from the Internal Revenue Service for 1965 are shown in Table X-1.

TABLE X-1
Number of Companies, 1965

	Total	Without Net Income	Per Cent Without Net Income
All active corporations	1,423,980	508,669	35.7
All manufacturing	185,924	54,587	29.4
Chemicals & allied products	10,804	3,902	36.1
Chemicals	2,783	1,023	36.8

Source: Internal Revenue Service, *Statistics of Income, 1965, Business Income Tax Returns,* Washington, D.C., 1968, p. 237.

More than one-third of all corporations and 29.4% of all manufacturing corporations reported no taxable net income in 1965. Similar high ratios prevailed for chemicals and allied products and chemicals. (Detailed data for the allied products are shown in Appendix Table 30)

The companies with losses were generally the smaller ones. This is indicated by the fact that the companies with losses accounted for a relatively small proportion of total compiled receipts. (Table X-2)

TABLE X-2
Total Receipts, 1965

	Total	Without Net Income	Per Cent Without Net Income
	(billions)		
All active corporations	$1,194.6	$114.9	9.6
All manufacturing	514.7	42.5	8.3
Chemicals & allied products	41.3	1.5	3.6
Chemicals	18.6	0.4	2.2

Chemical companies fared better than the average for all industry—only 2.2 per cent of the sales were by companies operating at a loss, as compared with 9.6 per cent for all corporations and 8.3 per cent for manufacturing industries.

There has been a large number of new entrants into chemicals and allied products since the end of World War II. The total number of corporate tax returns increased from 6,186 in 1945 to 10,569 in 1966. (See Appendix Table 31)

There has been a broad sweep forward both in sales volume and in taxable profits for the two past decades. During each postwar recession, sales volume had declined or stabilized to be followed by a forward surge to new high record levels.

Total receipts increased for chemicals in every year between 1948 and 1965 with two exceptions (1949 and 1960-61). In 1965, the total was more than five times as large as in 1948. But income before taxes has not shown a similar trend. The total doubled between 1948 and 1955 or about in line with the rise in receipts. In the succeeding decade, pre-tax income increased only two-thirds although the volume of business almost tripled. (See Appendix Table 32) As a result the profit margin on sales declined sharply as will be noted later.

Profit Margins

The profit margin, the ratio of reported profits to sales volume, is significant in connection with pricing. Do higher dollar profits reflect price increases or changes in volume? The ratio of income before taxes to sales gives us a first approximation to the answer.

In the absence of any offsetting increases in other unit costs, it would be expected that profit margins would widen when sales volume rises.[10] An unchanged profit margin under conditions of rising volume may indicate that other costs have risen or that prices have declined or some combination of both.

That change in volume is a major factor in determining the profits in any year is clearly demonstrated by the changes in profits from good years to poor years, and vice versa. Changes in sales usually are accompanied by much greater changes in profit. The experience during recessions in the past three decades provides ample demonstration of this point (See Table X-3).

The proportionate decline in profits after taxes has tended to be significantly greater than the decline in sales.[11] A similar pattern prevails during periods of expansion, when percentage increases in profits far outstrip those recorded for sales. Thus, in examining the profits of a company or the industry over time, care must be taken to compare years in a similar phase of the business cycle or the comparison will not be meaningful as to trend.

TABLE X-3

Changes In Sales and Profits, Chemicals and Allied Products, During Recessions, 1929-1961

Period	Sales	Profits After Taxes
1929-1932	-46.1%	-77.7%
1937-1938	-10.5	-24.8
1948-1949	- 6.2	- 2.6
1953-1954	+ 1.2	+21.4
1957-1958	- 1.4	-14.1
1960-1961	+ 8.2	- 2.0

Source: Derived from U.S. Department of Commerce, *The National Income and Product Accounts of the United States,* 1929-1965, Washington, D.C., 1966, pp. 126-29, 142-45.

Turnover of Capital

The profit margin on sales required to earn any designated return on net worth or net assets is determined by the volume of sales in relationship to net worth, that is, the turnover of capital. Turnover may be calculated from the First National City Bank data.[12] The capital turnover ratio varies widely among industries. There usually is an inverse relationship between the turnover ratio and the margin on sales. Thus, in 1968 meat packing had the lowest profit margin on sales, 1.0 per cent, and the highest turnover ratio, 8.2 times. In contrast, for cement the profit margin on sales was 6.2 per cent and the turnover ratio was only 1.2 times.[13] The net effect of the margin on sales and of the turnover ratio is shown in the return on net worth.

Chemical products had a turnover ratio of 1.81 times as compared with an average of 2.30 times for all manufacturing. This meant that the chemical industry had $1.81 in sales for every $1.00 of net worth in 1968. Thirty-five out of the other 40 manufacturing industires for which data were reported had a higher turnover ratio. The profit margin on sales for chemicals was 6.3 per cent, as compared with 5.7 per cent for all manufacturing industries. There were 33 manufacturing industries with a lower profit margin and 7 with a higher margin in 1968.[14]

The efficiency with which *total assets* or total investment has been used has declined "substantially" in recent years. According to Sciancalepore:

> "This has been due to the fact that new equipment costs have risen, while selling prices have either risen very slightly or have suffered substantial erosion because of existing overcapacity in many areas and the entry of new producers, compounding the problem of overcapacity. In addition, the industry branched out into more complex, highly processed areas such as petrochemicals, where the investment is large. Also, capital investment in recent years has been relatively higher because of the trend toward backward ingegration. Finally, the incremental cost of product quality improvement has increased; each upgrading step has become more expensive."[15]

However, Sir Peter Allen has observed that " . . . it is clear that chemical companies, including Imperial Chemical Industries, operating in Europe do not match U.S. companies in the ratio of sales to investment, however you choose to define the capital employed."[16]

Profit Margins Within the Industry

Comparisons of profit ratios as a per cent of sales (margin on sales) usually are more meaningful within an industry than among industries. However, even within an industry such comparisons may not be too significant when the product mix differs widely among companies.

The profit margin on sales varied widely within the chemical industry. For the 27 chemical companies (excluding Celanese) included in the *Fortune* survey in 1968. The average profit margin was 6.3%; excluding Du Pont (10.7%) the ratio was 5.5%. The margins for these companies ranged between 1.3% and 10.7%. However, the margin exceeded 10% for only one company and was between 8% and 10% for four others; it was below 4% for six companies. Margins vary between these companies for a number of reasons including: differences in product mix,[17] impact of price declines, timing of start-up expenses, productive efficiency, and extent of integration (See Appendix Table 5).

Trend of Profit Margins

Profit margins in the 1960's were below those prevailing in the earlier post-World War II years and before World War II. The First National City Bank reported profit margins ranging between 6.3% and 8.6% for chemicals in the 1960's in contrast to generally higher levels in the earlier post-World War II years.

Number of Years

Profits As % of Sales	1934-40	1946-60	1961-63	1964-68
above 10%	4	3		
9-10	1	4		
8-9	1	5		3
7-8		3	3	
6-7	1			2

Actually, profit margins were at their lowest postwar levels in 1967 and 1968, even lower than during the Korean War years (1951 and 1953), when corporate excess profits taxes were in effect (See Chart X-1).

During the postwar years, the percentage margin on sales was 10% or higher in three years (1949, 1950, and 1955) and between 9% and 10% in four years (1947, 1948, 1951 and 1956). Only two of the years with an average of above 9% on sales were after 1951. The level of 10% reached in 1955 occurred in a year when chemical sales rose 19.9% reflecting primarily an expansion in volume since their prices rose only 0.5%. Subsequently, the margin declined to 7.3% in 1961 then recovered to 8.6% in 1965; in 1968 the margin fell to 6.3% (See Appendix Table 33).

Reasons For Declining Profit Margins

The decline in chemical profit margins from 1955 usually has been attributed to foreign competition, intensive competition from new producers, declining prices and excess capacity.[18] These factors undoubtedly have played a role in connection with specific products. However, from 1955 through 1966 the effects of these developments on total profitability usually were offset in whole or in part by expanding volume, the development of new products which in their early history may have above average profit margins, and lower prices of chemicals purchased by chemical companies for further processing. In 1967 and 1968, however, pretax profit margins declined sharply because expanding volume could not offset the impact of higher costs and the erosion of prices. As compared with the early postwar years, higher depreciation charges also contributed to lower pretax margins.

Pretax Margins: Pretax margins reflect all of the cost-price relationships affecting a company or an industry. Such margins are reduced when price cuts are not matched by lower unit costs or when depreciation charges increase in relative importance. Unfortunately, comprehensive data are not available to show the pretax margin for chemicals over any extended period. However, data have been published by FTC-SEC since 1947 for chemicals and allied products for which the pattern of margins was similar to that for the chemicals segment.

The pretax margin for chemicals and allied products averaged 13.8% in 1947-49 and then increased to 18.6% in 1950. It was 16.4% in 1951 and 15.7% in 1955. Although the average pretax margin declined after 1955, the only years it fell below 13.6% were 1958 (12.7%), 1967 (11.9%), and 1968 (12.5%). Despite the price erosion, the average pretax margin between 1957 and 1966 was equal on the average to that prevailing in the early postwar years for chemicals and allied products.

However, in 1967 and 1968, the pretax margin fell sharply.

	Average Pretax Margin	Average After Tax Margin
1947-49	13.8%	8.6%
1955-57	15.1	8.0
1958-60	13.8	7.4
1961-63	13.8	7.4
1964-66	13.9	7.9
1967	11.9	6.9
1968	12.5	6.8

CHART X-1

Per Cent Profit Margin on Sales, Chemical Products, 1934-1968

Per cent

It seems clear, therefore, that the decline in after tax margins for all chemicals and allied products between 1955 and 1963 as compared with 1947-49 was due to the higher corporate tax rates which were enacted during the Korean War—and continued until 1964 when a small reduction was made effective. This tax reduction resulted in a small increase in the after tax margin for 1964-66. In 1968, this tax reduction was more than cancelled when the 10% surtax increased the effective rate to above the 1963 level. It appears that these higher tax rates have been borne by the companies rather than passed on to the consumer.

The record for the chemicals segment has been less favorable than for chemicals and allied products. The FTC-SEC data for this group first became available in 1956. The trend in pretax margins since that year is shown in Table X-4.

TABLE X-4
Pretax Margins, 1956-1968

	Chemicals	Chemicals and Allied Products
	(per cent of sales)	
1956	18.2	15.1
1957	17.4	14.4
1958	13.5	12.7
1959	17.5	14.8
1960	15.0	13.8
1961	14.6	13.6
1962	15.4	13.9
1963	15.3	14.0
1964	15.2	14.1
1965	14.4	13.9
1966	13.6	13.6
1967	11.0	11.9
1968	11.1	12.5

Source: Securities and Exchange Commission - Federal Trade Commission.

Between 1956 and 1968, the pretax margins for the chemical segment fell by 7.1 percentage points as compared with a drop of 2.6 percentage points for the broader group. From a pretax margin which had been averaging about 3 percentage points *greater* than for the broader group, the chemical industry rate fell to 1.4 percentage points *below* the other total in 1968; in 1967 it was 0.9 percentage points below. In other words, the allied products had larger pretax margins than the chemical industry.

For six of the seven companies in Table X-5, the pretax margin in 1967-68 was lower—usually sharply lower—than in the earlier post-war years. For Du Pont, the pretax margin in 1967-68 was 20.2% as compared with an average of about 25% between 1955 and 1963. For Monsanto the average of 10.6% compared with 12.9% and higher in the earlier periods. Dow, with a lower margin in the 1961-63 period, was the only company for which the pretax margin was not at a new post-World War II low in 1967-68. Dow's relatively smaller interest in fibers contributed to this result.

TABLE X-5

**Profits Before and After Taxes, Depreciation, and Pretax Margin
Plus Depreciation as a Per Cent of Sales, Leading
Chemical Companies, Selected Years, 1946-68**

Company and Years	Profits Before Taxes As Per Cent of Sales	Profits After Taxes As Per Cent of Sales	Depreciation as a Per Cent of Sales	Pretax Margin Plus Depreciation as Per Cent of Sales*
Airco				
1946-1949	11.4	6.7	4.5	15.9
1955-1957	17.1	8.5	5.5	22.6
1958-1960	15.0	7.2	4.9	19.9
1961-1963	11.1	5.6	5.1	16.2
1964-1966	10.8	6.4	4.7	15.5
1967-1968	7.1	4.0	5.4	12.5
Allied Chemical				
1946-1949	15.4	9.0	3.7	19.1
1955-1957	12.5	7.2	7.6	20.1
1958-1960	11.8	6.4	7.6	19.4
1961-1963	13.1	7.2	8.2	21.3
1964-1966	12.5	7.5	8.1	20.6
1967-1968	5.6	3.6	9.4	15.0
Dow				
1946-1949**	17.3	10.9	8.2	25.5
1955-1957**	17.6	9.0	13.7	31.3
1958-1960	16.8	9.0	11.5	28.3
1961-1963***	13.6	7.8	10.9	24.5
1964-1966	15.3	9.2	9.5	24.8
1967-1968	14.8	8.8	9.7	24.5
Du Pont				
1946-1949	21.8	11.8	5.7	27.5
1955-1957	27.8	14.1	6.2	34.0
1958-1960	23.5	12.3	7.0	30.5
1961-1963	24.6	12.2	7.7	32.3
1964-1966	26.0	14.2	8.1	34.1
1967-1968	20.2	10.5	8.9	29.1
Hercules				
1946-1949	14.8	8.8	4.9	20.7
1955-1957	16.7	7.8	5.8	22.5
1958-1960	16.4	7.9	6.1	22.5
1961-1963	14.7	7.0	5.9	20.6
1964-1966	14.8	7.9	5.5	20.3
1967-1968	13.4	7.3	6.1	19.5

Continued on next page

Continued TABLE X-5

Company and Years	Profits Before Taxes As Per Cent of Sales	Profits After Taxes As Per Cent of Sales	Depreciation as a Per Cent of Sales	Pretax Margin Plus Depreciation as Per Cent of Sales*
Monsanto				
1946-1949	17.3	10.7	4.7	21.9
1955-1957	13.9	7.0	7.0	20.9
1958-1960	12.9	6.9	7.8	20.7
1961-1963	13.9	7.2	9.4	23.3
1964-1966	13.7	7.9	9.1	22.8
1967-1968	10.6	6.2	9.8	20.4
Union Carbide				
1946-1949	24.2	15.2	3.8	28.0
1955-1957	21.4	10.8	8.7	30.1
1958-1960	19.8	10.4	8.6	28.4
1961-1963	17.4	9.5	9.3	26.7
1964-1966	15.7	9.6	8.2	23.9
1967-1968	10.1	6.3	8.8	18.9

Notes: *Includes amortization and depletion

       **Until 1961 the year ended May 31.

       ***In 1961 the year end was changed to December 31.

Sources: 1968 Annual Reports of Union Carbide, Monsanto, Allied, Air Reduction, (Airco) Dow, Hercules, Du Pont; *Moody's Industrials—1964,* pp. 1447, 1482, 1635, 1675; 1963, p. 2843; 1962, pp. 107, 527, 1003, 1008, 1033, 1271, 1462, 1534, 2292, 2605, 2895.

The table also shows the wide variations in pretax margins among chemical companies ranging from an average of 20.2% for Du Pont to 5.6% for Allied and 7.1% for Airco in 1967 and 1968. These results reflect largely the different product mixes of these companies and varying rates of introduction and development of new products.

It appears that for the entire industry, the *net* decline in the after tax profit margins through 1966 as compared with the 1946-1949 period reflected largely two developments: (a) relatively larger depreciation charges and (b) higher corporate taxes. The significance of these two factors is measurable for chemicals and allied products, but not for the chemical industry alone. However, data where available are shown for 7 chemical companies in Table X-5.

Depreciation Charges: Depreciation charges represent the cost of the plant and equipment used up or worn out in producing current output. It is just as much a cost of doing business as labor, raw materials, advertising, etc. In the 1946-49 period, income before taxes was 12.6% of sales for chemicals and allied products, while in the 1962-66 period, the ratio was 11.2%. Thus, between these two periods, the margin before taxes declined 1.4 percentage points. However, between these two periods, depreciation charges rose sharply so that the ratio increased from an average of 2.0% to 5.0% of sales or by 3.0 percentage points. Depreciation charges increased 1.6 percentage points *more* than the decline in pretax margins. (Derived from Appendix Table 34)

The increase in total depreciation reflected a combination of several factors:[19] (1) large expansion in total plant and equipment;[20] (2) the rise in cost of replaced plant and equipment; (3) the liberalization of depreciation to permit larger charges in the earlier years of the life of plant and equipment (e.g. sum-of-the-year's-digits or double rate declining balance methds of depreciation);[21] (4) changes in Schedule F of the Internal Revenue Service which shortened the useful life of depreciable assets.[22] The last two factors affect short term rather than long term rates of depreciation since they affect the timing of depreciation charges.

The pretax margin plus depreciation[23] increased from 14.6% in the 1946-49 period to 16.0% in the 1961-63 period and to 16.1% in 1964-66 for chemicals and allied products. It should be noted that these figures already reflect all changes in wages, prices, and volume between the two periods.[24] Because of the liberalization of depreciation allowances the quality of chemical industry profits in the early 1960s was much better than in the earlier postwar period when part of the reported after tax profits had to be used to compensate for the inadequacy of accumulated depreciation to replace retired plants at the higher prices prevailing after World War II. In other words, in those earlier years the full cost of the plant and equipment used in production was not reflected in the total costs of most companies.

When allowance is made for more realistic depreciation allowances (but not for depreciation on the enlarged volume of investment) it is probable that pretax margins for chemicals and allied products in the early postwar years were not much different from those in the 1961-63 period. It was possible to achieve this record, despite cost increases and more intensified competition, because total sales more than doubled ($12.8 billion annual average for 1946-49 to $30.2 billion for 1961-63). The FTC-SEC data suggest that profit margins were lower in 1967-68 because the continuing expanding volume of sales did not fully overcome the price cutting experienced in that period.

Comprehensive data are not available for the chemicals segment. Because they account for about half of the chemicals and allied products group, it is probable that the decline in profit margins for chemicals reflected the same factors. Sales of chemicals increased more rapidly and prices have declined more, so that there were some differences for that group as compared with allied products.

However, enlarged depreciation charges have been of significance as indicated earlier in Table X-5. Depreciation charges for four of the seven companies were equal to a record percentage of sales in 1967-68. For Union Carbide, it was below the 1961-63 level but higher than in earlier years and for Airco it was lower than in 1955-57. Only for Dow was depreciation in 1967-68 relatively smaller than in several of the preceding periods.

A comparison of the experience in the 1967-68 period as compared with 1964-66 indicates that the decline in pretax margins reflected only in small part an increase in depreciation. Thus, for example, for Du Pont depreciation increased by 0.8 percentage points as compared with the decline of 5.8 percentage points in the pretax margin. For Airco, the changes were +0.7 and -3.7 respectively. As compared with the early post-war years, however, the depreciation factor was important in explaining the difference in pretax margins.

Role of Corporate Taxes: The imposition of the 10% surtax in 1968 contributed to the narrowing of after tax profit margins in that year. However, this tax was not in effect in 1967 when the major decline in profit margins took place. If the surtax had not been imposed, the profit margin would have been almost a half percentage point higher in 1968. That factors other than the surtax have been of primary importance in the decline in profit margins is shown by comparing the 1968 margin with that in 1961-63 when tax rates were similar. In the earlier period, the corporate tax was 52% while in 1968 the effective rate was 52.8%.[25] In 1961-63 the profit margin for chemical companies was 7.5% while in 1968 it was 6.3% according to the First National City Bank data.[26] Thus, with approximately the same tax rates, profit margins were more than one percentage point lower in 1968 than in 1961-63.[27]

Comparisons over the longer term are affected by changing federal corporate tax rates as the post-World War II experience clearly shows. Thus, prior to the Korean War (1946-49), federal corporate tax rates were 38% as compared with 47% in 1950 and 52% from 1951 to 1963. In the 1946-49 period, the chemical profit margin averaged 9.7% as compared with 7.5% in 1961-63. This was a sizeable decline in the after tax profit margin. Although comprehensive data are not available for the earlier period for chemicals, the SEC-FTC data show that the pretax profit margin was the same for 1947-49 and 1961-63 for chemicals and allied products. Thus, for the broader group the entire decline in the after tax profit margin was equal to the higher taxes. If tax rates had remained unchanged at the pre-Korean War level, profit margins would have equalled the earlier postwar level despite the significant rise in depreciation charges noted earlier. Of course, these factors cannot be treated mechanically since lower tax rates may have affected other business decisions with accompanying changes in the pretax margins.

The chemical industry has not always been able to pass on higher tax costs to its customers. This has been particularly true in the 1960s when it has had to reduce many prices because of the increasingly intensive competitive environment in which it has been operating. The small cut in corporate tax rates in 1964 provided a little relief from this price squeeze and as a result the profit margin increased by 0.5 percentage points in the 1964-66 period. But it was quickly offset by price weakness and by the higher depreciation charges in 1967-68 and the surtax in 1968.

In other words, although changes in volume, prices, and labor costs affected the profitability of individual companies, it is interesting to note that for the entire industry these factors tended to be offsetting through 1966 so that the net decline in profit margins was about equal to the increases in federal taxes and depreciation charges.[28] For 1967-68, price erosion was the major factor cutting profit rates.

Return on Net Worth

In terms of incentives, it is the relationship of dollar profits to the amount invested that is important. The resulting ratio - the return on net worth or stockholders' equity[29]—reflects the combined effect of the profit margin and the turnover ratio. However, because they may be distorted by price inflation, the reported figures do not always show what can be earned on new commitments of capital. It is useful, therefore, to consider the manner in which price inflation has affected reported profits before reviewing the trend of return of net worth.

Significance of Price Inflation

Reported profits reflect the accounting conventions that have gained acceptance during any period. But these conventions change from time to time. Thus, for example, changes in the methods of handling depreciation charges over the years have influenced reported profits. Similarly, the treatment of replacement costs for inventories (last in-first out,[30] first in-last out, average cost, etc.) and for capital equipment affect the significance of reported profits.

Conventional accounting procedures are well suited to years of relative price stability. However, problems arise during a period of price inflation, such as that experienced during and after World War II.[31] Companies in this country were permitted to count as a cost for tax purposes depreciation based on the actual cost of the assets rather than on their replacement value. As a result reported profits were overstated.[32]

Some companies informed their stockholders of this situation. For example, Du Pont has included statements such as the following in its annual reports:

> "Many of the company's plants and facilities were built when construction costs were considerably lower than those existing now. This investment is carried on the books substantially at cost. If operating investment were stated at estimated present replacement costs, *the return on investment would be substantially less* than is shown . . . and operating investment per employee would be greater."[33](Italics added)

In foreign countries, companies are permitted to revalue their assets on a replacement cost basis and to take this factor into account in estimating their profits. Thus, Montecatini, the largest chemical company in Italy, reported in 1961 that the gross replacement value of its property, machinery, and equipment was 422.1 billion lire. The balance sheet also showed a surplus of 30.5 million lire arising from revaluation of assets. The result of these adjustments was to yield lower reported profits than recorded under the American system of accounting.[34]

Clearly, price inflation and the accompanying inadequacy of depreciation charges[35] result in a fictitious return on net worth for companies including those in the chemical industry. Returns on net worth for such periods largely reflect a comparison of *overstated* reported profits with *understated* net worth.

The increase in depreciation charges has acted to reduce this fictitious element included in reported profits and hence to improve the quality of profits as compared with the earlier postwar years.

However, the re-emergence of price inflation starting in 1965 could create new problems in this area. The use of various methods to accelerate depreciation reduced the impact of this new inflation as compared with the earlier post-World II years because larger proportions of new plant and equipment are charged off immediately.

Trend of Return on Net Worth

The returns on net worth or its equivalent reported for chemicals and allied products and chemicals vary depending on the source as the following data for 1965 show:

Return on Net Worth, 1965

	Chemicals	Chemicals and Allied Products
	(per cent)	
First National City Bank	15.4	NA
FTC-SEC	14.3	15.3
Internal Revenue Service	NA	13.9

NA—not available.

The highest return was reported by the First National City Bank which confines its sample to leading chemical corporations; the lowest return usually is reported by the Internal Revenue Service because it records the profit experience of all corporations, profitable and unprofitable, large and small. (See Appendix Table 35) In the following discussion, the First National City Bank data will be used because this series is continuously available since 1925. It should be kept in mind, however, that the returns it shows are probably one or two percentage points higher than those earned by all chemical companies.

A sharp rise in return on net worth in early postwar years and a steady decline during the early 1950s developed both for chemicals and for all manufacturing.[36] The decline in return on net worth during the 1950s reflected in part the sharp rise in the value of net worth as an increasing proportion of total assets represented new investment or the replacement of assets at the higher price levels prevailing during that period.

Thus, the total capital invested (fixed assets less government securities and obligations of other corporations) in chemicals and allied products increased from $9.3 billion in 1949 to $24.1 billion in 1963.[37] More than three-fifths of the gross assets were acquired in the 1950s and early 1960s and there was a considerable replacement of some of the lower cost assets which had been acquired earlier. As a result, the significance of price inflation as a factor contributing to the over-statement of reported returns became steadily less important. Clearly, some part of the decline in reported returns on net worth after 1950 reflected this factor.

The return on net worth for chemicals reached a post-Korean War peak in 1955 when the First National City Bank reported the return was 17.7%. This ratio had been exceeded only twice (18.0% in 1929 and 21.3% in 1950) and equaled only once (1948) since the tabulation was started in 1925. The average return moved downward sharply to 11.1% in 1958. The ratio rose in 1959 and 1960 and then declined again in 1961 to just above the 1958 level. Between 1955 and 1961, the return on net worth fell from 17.7% to 11.8%.[38] The return on net worth increased to 15.4% in 1965. It then declined again to 11.5% in 1967 and 11.4% in 1968. This latter decline reflected the narrower margin earned on sales (6.3% compared with 10.0%).

Diversity of Earnings

The 1968 *Fortune* tabulation included 28 predominantly chemical companies. The average after tax return on invested capital for 27 companies[39] in 1968 was 10.8% or 0.6 percentage points *less* than for the First National City Bank group. These data show the wide variations in profit performance which combine to make up the industry average—the range was from 2.1% to 14.6%; for five companies the return was 7% or lower and for nine companies it was 12% or higher. These data also suggest that there was little relationship between the size of a company and its rate of earnings in 1968. (See Appendix Table 5)

Comparison with Other Industries

Since 1925 the return on net worth has been greater for chemicals than for all manufacturing, with five exceptions: 1925, 1926, 1948, 1967 and 1968. In 1968, the return was 1.7 percentage point *lower* than for all manufacturing as compared with an average spread of 1.4 percentage points for the entire postwar period (1946 to 1968) in favor of chemicals and an average favorable spread of 4.9 percentage points for the 1929-39 period. (See Appendix Table 36 and Chart X-2)

221

In most years, the chemical industry reported among the highest returns for the forty-one manufacturing industries in the First National City Bank tabulation. In 1968, however, 26 out of 40 manufacturing industries reported higher returns on net worth.[40]

CHART X-2

Per Cent Returns on Net Worth: Chemical and
All Manufacturing, 1925-1968

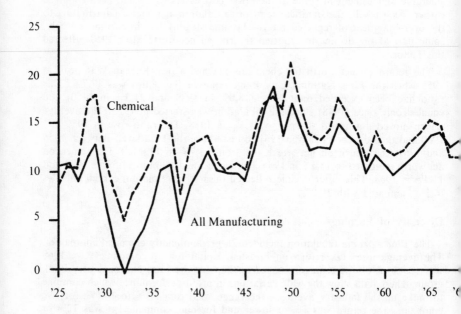

Historically, returns on net worth have been higher for chemicals than for all manufacturing industries. The widest spread occurred between 1928 and 1935, when the return for chemicals was more than five percentage points greater than that earned by leading companies in all manufacturing industries. In the post-World War II years, the average return on net worth earned by chemical companies was as much as three percentage points greater than for all manufacturing in only one year (4.2% in 1950). In most of these postwar years, the spread has been less than two points in favor of chemicals.

The U.S. Department of Commerce concluded in 1966 that "Chemical profits have been moderately higher than the average for all industries. A higher rate of return has enabled chemical companies to pay better dividends, finance with retained earnings and invest heavily in order to meet the virtually insatiable demand for their products."[41]

The sharp drop in earnings in 1967 and 1968 reduced the ability of chemical companies to finance their investment needs through retained earnings.

The narrowing spread between profit returns in the chemical industry and in all manufacturing in recent years has been attributed to three factors:

> "(1) it is getting harder and harder to make patents and proprietary positions last, (2) pressure on margins . . . from international competition; and (3) more and more outsiders want a piece of the action."[42]

In the light of fabulous records of productivity and of growth, the spread in favor of chemicals before 1967 would appear to be a modest premium for investments in this industry. The decline recorded both for chemicals and all manufacturing since the early postwar years—1946 to 1950—reflected primarily an improvement in the quality of earnings as the inadequate depreciation charges and inventory profits of the earlier period were gradually reduced in importance, if not almost completely eliminated. Such decline in returns that developed apart from these factors reflected primarily the higher corporate tax rate in the period after 1950. However, the decline in the chemical profit rate in 1967 and 1968 reflected primarily the price erosion which took place in those years.

Disposition of Profits[43]

Funds for expansion may be obtained from internal sources or from external sources. The major internal sources are undistributed profits and depreciation allowances. The main external sources are the sale of new securities and borrowing from financial institutions. Actually, depreciation allowances are used largely to replace existing plant and equipment rather than to finance a net expansion although the technical efficiency of the replacements would tend to be higher. In the earlier post-World War II period part of the undistributed profits was required to compensate for the inadequacy of depreciation allowances to replace plant and equipment at the prevailing higher prices, as discussed earlier, and hence was not fully available to finance growth.

Corporate profits may be paid as dividends or retained for reinvestment in the business. There is no "normal" percentage which should be paid as dividends; the experience varies widely among industries. Ordinarily, dividend payments do not fluctuate as much as profits. As a result, they tend to be a larger proportion of profits in poor times than in good times. The increases in the ratio of payment in such recession years as 1938, 1949, 1954 and 1958 should be noted. (See Chart X-3)

Dividend payouts as a percentage of profits after taxes were relatively smaller for all manufacturing than for chemicals and allied products in most of the postwar years. In 1965, the ratios were 40.8 per cent and 50.9 per cent respectively.[44]

The U.S. Department of Commerce reported the proportion of dividend payout for twenty-one manufacturing industries in 1965. In only one of these industries, (tobacco manufactures) was the dividend payout relatively higher than for chemicals and allied products.

The proportion of profits paid as dividends fell below 50 per cent and was unusually low from 1946 to 1951. This low ratio reflected the fact that reported profits were inflated by inventory profits and inadequate depreciation allowances during these years. It was necessary for many companies to use part of their overstated reported profits after taxes to compensate for those developments.

From 1950 to 1965, chemicals and allied products retained $8.5 billion, or 37.6 per cent of the total profits of $22.6 billion to finance the expansion of the industry.[45] These retained earnings have been used to finance the new plant and equipment which has been so important in the growing chemical industry.

Reasons for Higher Profits in Chemical Industry

The basic reasons for the above average profits performance of the chemical industry through 1966 were: (1) the high growth rate which has a leavening effect on profits,[46] and (2) the tremendous investment in research and development with the accompanying ever-increasing flow of new products, many of which yielded high profits to the innovating company or companies.[47]

By examining the record of companies he classified as innovators and as imitators, Chaplin Tyler of Du Pont has shown that innovation is associated with higher profits.

> ". . . 24 companies in the chemicals and allied products industry were divided into two groups of 12 each, one group being classed arbitrarily as innovators and the other as imitators. For the year 1959 the innovator group earned a net return of seven per cent on the average gross capital employed. This was twice the return achieved by the imitator group.

> "The comparison was then restricted to four companies, all of which are among the largest in the industry. Two of these were classed as innovators and two as imitators. Again, the net return on the average capital employed was twice as much, eight per cent in 1959, as for the imitators. Moreover, the average research expenditure as a percentage of sales was twice as much, roundly three per cent, for the innovators as for the imitators."[48]

Roland P. Soule has suggested that formerly "the bulwarks of its high profit margins" included "restricted raw materials, secret processes, complex technology, and large capital needs to obtain competitive costs."[49] However, the industry has "lost" these "bulwarks" because of intensified competition from non-chemical companies which have "invaded" the industry and because of foreign competition.

R & D may have a twofold impact on profits. A company's own discoveries add to its profitability[50] while the development of similar products by competitors act to reduce profitability. However, the lead time between these developments has been shrinking. The increasing number of new products acts to offset in whole or in part the shorter period during which an individual product may yield high profits. Thus, the pace of innovation has become the key to good profits. If new products can be developed to offset the lower profitability that develops as competitors enter the market then total profit margins can be maintained; otherwise they tend to erode.

The maintenance of above average profit margins requires the continuous discovery of new products and specialties on which high profit margins[51] may be earned while the former products in that category evolve into commodity chemicals with lower margins.[52] A company which has a high proportion of specialties and new products in its mix will tend to have higher profits than those which are highly concentrated in commodity chemicals.

The chemical industry experience is not unique. Profits must be high enough to induce the risks of product obsolescence and to attract new capital. At the same time, they attract new companies into the industry as has been so evident in the post-World War II experience of the chemical industry.

Prices and Profits

Selling prices affect the total revenues of a company and hence may influence its overall profitability. The intensive competition in the chemical industry in the 1960s was accompanied by price declines for many organic chemicals, including the synthetics. As a result, there have been frequent references in the annual reports of chemical producers to the adverse effect of declining prices upon profits.

Allied Chemical reported in 1967 that "lower selling prices [for fibers] reduced profits."[53] Airco reported that "During 1968, sales of chemicals were up encouragingly, but earnings fell slightly below 1967 levels, reflecting aggressive price competition from other producers, particularly in polyvinyl chloride and polyvinyl alchol."[54] Monsanto estimated in 1968 that operating earnings were reduced by 66 cents a share because of lower prices. It reported that "price erosion, which particularly affected ammonia and many plastics, was again the major challenge to profitability."[55]

The factors affecting Monsanto's earnings per share are summarized in Table X-6. The difficulty of pinpointing the relationship between prices and profits is well illustrated by this tabulation. Thus, for example, higher sales volume added $1.09 a share to earnings. But there is no way to determine the extent to which the decline in prices may have led to greater volume and thus provided an offset in whole or in part to the "losses" experienced because of the lower prices. Dow reported a 2.0% rise in earnings in 1968 despite a decline of more than 4% in prices.[56] Du Pont reported a 12% rise in earnings despite a 2% decline in prices in 1968.[57]

A decline in chemical prices is not entirely an adverse factor. Chemical companies buy large quantities of chemicals from each other. Hence, to some extent lower buying prices may provide a partial offset to lower selling prices. Monsanto reported savings of 8 cents a share because of lower raw material prices.

Companies reacted in a variety of ways to the price cutting described earlier. The policies followed included: cut costs, discontinue unprofitable lines, close down marginal facilities, and seek greater volume.

Cut Costs: The pressure created by price cuts also has been offset to some extent by "production efficiencies"[58] and "improvements of existing processes." Celanese reported in 1968 that "process improvements have permitted maintenance of our profit margins in the face of lower polyester and nylon prices."[59] In Table X-6, Monsanto noted that its savings in manufacturing costs in 1968 were equal to 31 cents a share. Olin reported in 1968 that for fertilizers "We managed to offset 75% of the full effect of price declines and cost increases. We achieved that through increased market penetration, improvements in distribution, greater operational efficiencies, higher production yields, and some cost reductions. We shut down two obsolete facilities, an old ammonia plant . . . and a low-strength phosphoric acid plant. . . ."[60]

Costs may be reduced in various ways. One method is to find a more efficient way to produce the item. For example, Air Reduction was reported to be replacing a number of small plants producing industrial gases by a few plants which were larger and more efficient.[61] The large scale investment in production facilities in recent years often has had as one objective a reduction in costs.

TABLE X-6
Impact of Selected Factors on per Share Earnings, Monsanto Chemical Company, 1968

Year 1967 earnings			$3.19
Deduct - sale of investment in Mobay			.19
			3.00
Additional operating earnings resulting from:			
Higher sales volume	1.09		
Manufacturing cost savings	.31		
Lower raw material prices	.08		
	1.48		
Reductions in operating earnings caused by:			
Lower selling prices	$ .66		
Higher selling, administrative. research, development and other expenses	.29		
	.95		
Increase in operating income		.53	
Deduct:			
Higher income taxes	.21		
Higher income charges	.02	.23	.30
Year 1968 earnings as reported			3.30

Source: Monsanto Chemical Company, *1968 Annual Report,* p. 1.

Discontinue Low Profit Lines: When price cutting becomes too severe, companies sometimes have discontinued production of the affected items. FMC Corporation reported, that "As a consequence [of severely competitive market conditions] several low-profit plasticizers were eliminated from this product line" in 1962.[62] Du Pont and Celanese discontinued the production of rayon because profits were not satisfactory. Edward J. Bock, president of Monsanto, has announced that "Any product that can no longer pull its own weight will be phased out."[63]

Close Down Marginal Facilities: Where the price reductions were preceded by a large expansion in capacity, older marginal plants have been closed down. The dramatic increase in capacity to produce ammonia after 1965 led to overcapacity and price cutting. Late in 1968 it was reported that "Since January 1, 1967, an estimated 20 small ammonia plants have closed shop." The new 1,000 ton per day or larger plants had much lower costs than the "old technology" plants of 400 tons per day or less.[64] The sharp cuts in phenol prices in 1967 led some producers to close down their smaller operations.[65] Celanese discontinued its viscose fiber operation in Rome, Georgia in 1966.[66] Airco sold its two vinyl fabric plants in 1968 "because we were unable to attain an acceptable level of profit."[67]

Seek Greater Volume: With greater output, fixed overhead is spread over more units thus reducing total unit costs, and bringing them back into line with prices. If the demand for a product is elastic in the short run, so that total demand is increased substantially at the lower price, producers can share in the larger volume at the lower price. On the other hand, if demand is inelastic then a company can only be successful in increasing its volume at a lower price at the expense of other companies.

It is clear that there has been no simple relationship between price declines and profits for chemicals. The relationship will vary among companies and will depend upon the impact of price declines on sales volume, the product mix, and the ability of management to effect offsetting economies.

Summary and Conclusions

The profits picture changed dramatically in the chemical industry in 1967 and 1968. From a position with above average returns on net worth, the industry's return fell below the average in manufacturing industries. This loss of position developed despite a continued increase in production by about 10% a year, a rise in output per man-hour averaging about 7% a year, continued large expenditures for R & D, heavy capital investment, and further declines in unit labor costs.

In the past, the combination of these factors yielded a healthy rate of profits which provided both the incentive for new investment and the means of financing it. But this was not true in 1967 and 1968. These favorable factors were more than offset by the continued erosion of prices. With many costs rising as a result of the general price inflation during this period, the chemical industry experienced a profit squeeze. Profit margins declined and returns on net worth followed a similar pattern. The large expansion in capacity and the intensification of competitive pressures were key factors in the decline in prices for organics and synthetic materials.

While it is difficult to disentangle the various factors affecting profit margins on sales, it appears that the changes in sales volume, prices, and labor costs between 1946-49 and 1966 were about offsetting so that the pretax margin plus the cost of depreciation during the 1961-66 period showed only small changes as compared with the early postwar years. The decline in profit margins after taxes reflected higher corporate taxes and rising depreciation charges.

Profit margins vary widely among chemical companies for several reasons, including differences in product mix, varying impact of price declines, differences in productive efficiency, extent of integration, and timing of start-up expenses.

Average profits earned by leading chemical companies were moderately higher than those earned by leading companies in all manufacturing industries through 1966. The spread in return on net assets was 1.6 percentage points for the 1946-66 period. Profits were higher in the chemical industry for two fundamental reasons: (1) the higher growth rate and (2) the tremendous investment in research and development.

The steady flow of new products from the chemical industry's laboratories contributed both to growth and to profits. Often it is possible to earn higher rates of profit in the early stages of a product's life cycle. However, competitors quickly bring out equivalent products with the resulting pressure on prices and on profit margins. This is the traditional operation of our competitive economy. Thus, the pace of innovation is the key to maintaining good profit margins because unless there is steady replacement of high profit items, the average profit necessarily will decline as products move from specialty to commodity status. This tendency places a great premium upon the development of specialty products.

The experience in 1967 and 1968 indicated that the major problem faced by the industry is the behavior of its prices. And that even when other factors are favorable to good profit performance, they can be more than offset by price declines. Of course, there is no way in which the industry can legally prevent price cutting.

An intensification of programs designed to cut costs, discontinue low profit lines, and close down marginal facilities will help to maintain levels of profits. If these developments take place on a broad enough scale they could reduce the pressure on prices by removing part of the excess capacity. But so long as each company seeks to protect its market position in the future by expanding capacity today, the problem of excess capacity will continue to arise and to plague the industry for some of its products.

---

[1] For example, chemical products accounted for 55% of the total sales of W. R. Grace & Company in 1968, *Annual Report, 1968*, p. 23. For Olin-Mathieson, chemicals accounted for 30% of total sales in 1968, *Annual Report, 1968*, p. 2.

[2] According to the Bureau of Internal Revenue: "Each *return* was classified according to the *principal* business activity of the corporate unit(s) represented. A principal industry was that which accounted for the *largest portion of total receipts*, even though the return may have been filed for a company engaged in numerous different business activities, or may have been a consolidated return filed for members of a legally-defined affiliated group of corporations." U.S. Treasury Department, Internal Revenue Service, *Statistics of Income-1965, Corporation Income Tax Returns*, Washington, D.C., 1969, p. 233.

[3] *Survey of Current Business*, July issue of each year. The Department of Commerce publishes a tabulation annually in which it reconciles its estimates of total corporate profits with those published by the Internal Revenue Service. See Table 7.S, *Survey of Current Business*, July 1968, p. 48.

[4] "Net worth at the beginning of each year is based upon the excess of total balance sheet assets over liabilities; *the amounts at which assets are carried on the books may not represent present day values*." (Italics added) First National City Bank of New York, *Monthly Letter on Business and Economic Conditions*, New York, April issue of each year.

[5] In 1968, 78 companies were included in chemicals. While it is questionable whether some of these companies should be included, it appears that the overall results are representative for the leading chemical companies.

[6] "Stockholders' equity consists of capital stock, capital surplus, earned surplus and surplus reserves and reserves not reflected elsewhere (the bulk of the last item is surplus reserves because not all companies include such reserves with earned surplus as called for on the report form)." Federal Trade Commission-Securities and Exchange Commission, *Quarterly Financial Report for Manufacturing Corporations*, Third Quarter 1968, Washington, D.C., 1968, p. 60.

[7] The Federal Trade Commission published estimates of rates of return for the four largest industrial chemical companies (Du Pont, Union Carbide, Allied Chemical, and Dow), for 23 other chemical companies, and for five rayon companies for the years 1940 and 1947 to 1952. Federal Trade Commission, *Report on Rate of Return (After*

Taxes) for 516 Identical Industrial Companies in 25 Selected Manufacturing Industries, 1940, 1947-1952, Washington, D.C., 1954, pp. 3, 13.

[8]Invested capital includes capital stock, surplus, and retained earnings at the year's end. *Fortune,* May 15, 1969, p. 168.

[9]Tabulations of profits also are reported by other sources (for example the Federal Reserve Board, *The Wall Street Journal, The New York Times,* etc.). However, they are not as comprehensive as the other series.

[10]Near or at cyclical peaks, however, profit margins may shrink despite rising volume because high cost marginal equipment is brought into use with an accompanying rise in unit costs.

[11]Between 1919 and 1920, income *before* taxes as a percentage of sales fell from 15.0 to 10.9 per cent for large chemical companies. Ralph C. Epstein, *Industrial Profits in the United States,* National Bureau of Economic Research, in cooperation with the Committee on Recent Economic Changes, New York, 1934, p. 280. These data are available only before taxes. Since the corporate income tax was relatively small at that time, the picture would be substantially the same on an after tax basis.

[12]Actually, all assets, whether representing debt or ownership, are used to obtain sales. If data were available for total assets, the turnover ratios cited would be lower by varying amounts, depending upon the proportion of debt involved in the different industries. Thus, the First National City Bank data are useful primarily as evidence of the general relationship between turnover and profit margins.

[13]First National City Bank of New York, *Monthly Letter on Business and Economic Conditions,* April 1969, p. 41.

[14]For paint and allied products, the profit margin was 4.7% and the turnover ratio 2.40 times, for drugs and medicines 9.5% and 2.11 times, and for soap, cosmetics 6.6% and 2.83 times.

[15]Sciancalepore, *op. cit.,* p. 19.

[16]Allen, *op. cit.,* p. 1038.

[17]*Ibid.*

[18]See, for example, Conrad Berenson, *The Chemical Industry: Viewpoints and Perspectives,* Interscience Publishers, New York, 1963, p. 24.

[19]Robert Lindsay and Arnold W. Sametz, *Financial Management: An Analytical Approach,* Richard D. Irwin, Inc., Homewood, Ill., 1963, pp. 212-14, and Robert E. Graham, Jr. and Jacquelin Bauman, "Corporate Profits and National Output," *Survey of Current Business*, November 1962, pp. 19-27.

[20]According to the compilations prepared by the FTC-SEC; *total assets* for chemicals and allied products increased from $8.7 billion in 1947 to $45.6 billion in the fourth quarter of 1968; for chemicals the First National City Bank shows an expansion from $2.8 billion in 1947 to $14.4 billion at the beginning of 1968. Because the composition of these samples has varied over time, the data cited are significant primarily as an indication of the general, rather than the precise, magnitude of expansion in assets.

[21]These methods of depreciation were estimated to add $1 billion to total permitted depreciation for all companies in 1956 and in 1957. *Survey of Current Business,* September 1957, p. 12.

[22]It was estimated that this change would permit all companies to increase their depreciation charges by $4.7 billion. *Economic Report of the President,* January 1963, Washington, D.C., 1963, pp. 136-37.

[23]It must be repeated that depreciation is a cost, not part of profits. The only reason for treating the figures together is to demonstrate how the increase in this cost has affected income before taxes.

[24]U.S. Department of Commerce, Office of Business Economics, *The National Income and Product Accounts of the United States, 1929-1965,* Washington, D.C., 1966, pp. 119-21, 139-41, 143-45, and *Survey of Current Business,* July 1968, pp. 44-46.

[25]Corporate income taxes were reduced to 50% in 1964 and 48% in 1965; the latter rate remained in effect until 1968.

[26]The FTC-SEC averages were 7.4% for 1961-63 and 6.8% for 1968.

[27]Part of this decline reflected the 7% investment tax credit which was enacted in 1962 and hence was in operation in only two of the three earlier years. In addition, the volume of capital investment was considerably lower in 1961-63 than in 1968.

[28]For an examination of the interplay of these forces in reported profit rates for the entire economy and in manufacturing industries see Jules Backman, "Is the Profits Squeeze Behind Us?", *Challenge,* February 1964, pp. 7-10.

[29]The First National City Bank and Internal Revenue Service data are for return on net worth and the FTC-SEC for return on stockholders' equity. Both concepts yield a similar base against which to measure profits.

[30]Lifo "has not been generally adopted by chemical companies," W. Warmeck, "Principles Governing Handling of Financial Data," in *The Chemical Industry,* a series of lectures presented by Allied Chemical at the invitation of The New York Society of Security Analysts, 1959, p. 97.

[31]Ralph Coughenour Jones, *Effects of Price Level Changes on Business Income, Capital, and Taxes,* American Accounting Association, New York, 1956, pp. 80, 81. It has been pointed out that in the early post-World War II period ". . . depreciation charges were low relative to the price of current output and the replacement costs of capital goods which had risen sharply." As an indication of the "abnormally low level of capital consumption," it was estimated that such allowances "accounted for 8-1/2 percent of corporate gross product in 1929 and 1939, but amounted to only 5-1/2 percent in 1948. . . ." Graham and Bauman, *op. cit.,* p. 26.

[32]Some rough estimates of the effect of price inflation are contained in George J. Stigler, *Capital and Rates of Return in Manufacturing Industries,* Princeton University Press, Princeton, N. J., 1963, pp. 127-31, 182-83. For example, in 1948 the return based on book values was 10.47% for chemicals and allied products; when depreciation was adjusted to a current basis the return was only 7.12%. These data are based on the errata sheet issued by Professor Stigler to correct errors appearing in the volume.

[33]E. I. du Pont de Nemours & Company, *Annual Report 1968,* p. 50.

[34]In 1961, this revaluation surplus was transferred to capital and the number of shares held by stockholders was increased by a one for five distribution. *Montecatini, Reports and Balance Sheet, 1961,* Milan, Italy, April 18, 1962. Imperial Chemical Industries, Limited, also showed on its balance sheet an amount for "revaluation of fixed assets - increment," *Annual Report for the Year 1962,* pp. 27, 28.

[35]For all manufacturing establishments it has been estimated that the replacement cost of plant and equipment averaged above 1.53 times the original cost for the years 1947 to 1952. *Survey of Current Business,* November 1956, p. 11.

[36]A similar pattern is shown for chemicals and allied products.

[37]"The Economic Almanac, 1967-68," *op. cit.,* p. 272.

[38]FTC-SEC data, which have been published since 1956, showed a similar pattern. In addition, the Federal Trade Commission published a series for 25 identical chemical companies. The return on stockholders' investment was 14.7% in 1940, 17.2% in 1947, 24.0% in 1950, 20.2% in 1955, and 13.9% in 1961. In 1967, data were reported for 30 identical companies for which group the return on stockholders' investment was 14.9% in 1958, 16.5% in 1965, and 13.3% in 1967. Federal Trade Commission, *Report on Return for Identical Companies in Selected Manufacturing Industries, 1940, 1947-1961,* Washington, D.C., 1962, p. 15 and *Rates of Return for Identical Companies in Selected Manufacturing Industries, 1958-1967,* Washington, D.C., 1968, p. 17.

[39]Excluding Celanese which had large writeoffs in 1968.

[40]In the decade prior to 1929, chemicals and allied products reported a somewhat lower average return than all manufacturing industries. Thus, for the period 1919 to 1928, Ralph Epstein reported that 210 large identical chemicals and allied products companies averaged 10.2 per cent before taxes on capitalization and before interest payments on permanent debt as compared with 10.8 per cent for 2,046 identical large manufacturing companies. For a sample of non-identical small chemicals and allied products companies, a simple average of the annual data for the ten-year period was 13.5 per cent; for small manufacturing companies, it was 12.6 per cent. Epstein, *op. cit.*, pp. 241-42, 278-82, 365, 414.

[41]"A Look at Chemical Productivity and Wages," *Chemicals,* September 1966, p. 7.

[42]John Davenport, "The Chemical Industry Pushes Into Hostile Territory", *Fortune,* April 1969, p. 162.

[43]For an excellent discussion see Lindsay and Sametz, *op. cit.,* Chapters 11-13. See also John Lintner, "Distribution of Incomes of Corporations Among Dividends, Retained Earnings, and Taxes," *American Economic Review, Papers and Proceedings,* May 1956, pp. 97-113.

[44]This was similar to the experience between 1924 and 1928: Epstein's group of 20 large chemicals and allied products companies paid 68.1 per cent of their incomes in cash dividends, as compared with 59.4 per cent for large manufacturing companies in general.

[45]In 1968 retained earnings as a per cent of profits were as follows: Du Pont, 28.9%; Union Carbide, 23.0%, Dow, 46.7%; Monsanto, 50.4%.

[46]For synthetic rubber, one detailed study concluded that although it was a "growth industry" and a "a successful innovator," its earnings level "has been both relatively stable and low," Charles F. Phillips, Jr., *Competition in the Synthetic Rubber Industry,* The University of North Carolina Press, Chapel Hill, N.C. 1963, p. 214. Marris concludes ". . .the relationship between growth rate and profit rate becomes direct." Robin Marris, *The Economic Theory of Managerial Capitalism,* Macmillan and Co., Ltd., London, 1964, p. 251.

[47]". . .it is plausible enough—and can be rigorously proved—that the faster the rate of technical progress the higher the rate of return." Robert M. Solow, *Capital Theory and the Rate of Return,* North-Holland Publishing Co., Amsterdam, 1963, p. 46.

[48]Chaplin Tyler, *New Horizons—Chemistry,* an address before the Twelfth National Mutual Fund Dealers' Conference, Washington, D.C., September 13, 1960, p. 9. The returns shown in this quotation are lower than cited elsewhere in this study since they are related to gross assets for operating properties which are much larger than net assets or net worth because in effect they also include long term debt and depreciation reserves.

[49]Roland P. Soule, "Chemical Industry's Problem: Slowing Profits," *Chemical & Engineering News,* August 14, 1961, p. 103.

[50]Dexter M. Keezer and Associates, *New Forces in American Business,* McGraw-Hill New York, 1955, p. 34.

[51]In its *1967 Annual Report,* Olin stated: "A larger proportion of the research budget in 1967 was directed toward specialty chemicals which promise a higher return." (p. 7)

[52]It has been pointed out that "Synthetics producers . . . are now relying on high-priced specialties to bring new markets and profits." *Chemical Week,* December 15, 1962, p. 37. That profits will tend to be smaller for old line chemicals is illustrated by Sheets' comments regarding profits on chlorine. "Chlorine, a charter member of the heavy chemical family with its classically established production methods and a finite technology, offers monetary satisfaction only to those firms satisfied with profit margins lower than those popularly associated with the chemical process industries. It is significant, perhaps, to note that chemical firms showing the highest rates of return on investment are not in the merchant chlorine business." Theodore Sheets, Jr., "Trends in the Chlor-Alkali Industry," *Chemical Engineering Progress,* October 1952, p. 482.

[53]Allied Chemical Corporation, *Annual Report 1967*, p. 11. See also Phillips Petroleum Company, *Annual Report, 1963*, p. 22; Union Carbide, *Annual Report 1968*, p. 2; Dow, *Annual Report 1967*, p. 5; Wyandotte Chemicals Corp., *Annual Report 1968*, pp. 2, 4, 5.

[54]*Airco Annual Report 1968*, p. 11.

[55]*1968 Annual Report*, Monsanto Company, p. 1.

[56]"President's Letter," Herbert D. Doan, The Dow Chemical Company, *1968 Annual Report*, p. 3.

[57]*Annual Report, 1968*, p. 6.

[58]Monsanto Company, *1967 Annual Report*, p. 2; Olin *Annual Report 1967*, p. 7.

[59]*Celanese Annual Report 1968*, p. 3.

[60]*Annual Report 1968*, p. 17.

[61]*Chemical Week*, June 8, 1963, p. 23.

[62]Annual Report 1962, p. 4; see also Kawecki Chemical Company, *1962 Annual Report*.

[63]Monsanto Company, *1969 First-Quarter and Annual Meeting Report*, May 2, 1969, pp. 9-10.

[64]*Chemical Engineering*, September 23, 1968, p. 100. See also Allied Chemical Corporation, *Annual Report 1968*, p. 8.

[65]*Chemical Week*, November 4, 1967, p. 29.

[66]*Celanese Annual Report, 1966*, p. 6.

[67]*Airco Report to Stockholders*, Second Quarter and Six Months Ended June 30, 1968.

Chapter XI

Foreign Trade in Chemicals and Allied Products

Competition from foreign produced goods has been increasing for an expanding number of American industries and products. As Europe and Japan have risen from the ashes of World War II, their producers have become increasingly active in international trade, first to regain their prewar position and then to expand further. Hundreds of productivity teams were sent to this country and were exposed to the most efficient American production techniques. As a result, new foreign factories often reflect the latest advances in technology and represent enormous advances in efficiency as compared with those destroyed during the War.

One of the most dramatic developments affecting European competitive ability has been the organization of the Common Market. The six country area creates an economic unit whose population and working force are similar in size to those in the United States although its national income is slightly more than two-fifths as large. Nevertheless, this new trading area is of such dimensions that additional plants which can benefit from the economies of mass production have become economically feasible. These plants replace the fragmentation which characterized the productive capacity of the six countries taken individually.

In this chapter there are reviewed the trends and magnitude of American exports and imports in relationship to domestic sales, to total foreign trade, and to world trade in these products. The extent to which chemicals and allied products are contributing to the nation's export surplus and the changes in the composition of foreign trade are examined.

Attention is then directed to available data for chemical wages and non-wage benefits, total unit costs, and prices here and abroad. Although these data usually are inadequate and incomplete, they do indicate general relationships which are of interest even though they may not always be controlling.

The dollar volume of American foreign trade has expanded vigorously during and since the end of World War II. Initially this expansion reflected our participation in the reconstruction of war-torn areas and the gap created when Japan and European countries could not supply former customers. However, later it represented our participation in the burgeoning volume of trade which has accompanied economic growth throughout the world. Chemicals and allied products have shared in this expansion with the dollar value of both imports and exports reaching new record levels each year.

The relatively favorable foreign trade record of chemical companies has been attributed to its research orientation. It was one of five such industries identified as having a strong position in this area:

> "The figures show that the five industries with the strongest research effort accounted for 72.0 per cent of the nation's exports of manufactured goods, though they were responsible for only 39.1 per cent of the nation's total sales of such goods. The same five industries were also responsible for 89.4 per cent of the nation's total R&D expenditures and 74.6 per cent of the company-financed R&D expenditures. The five industries concerned, therefore, represent both the

heart of U.S. export strength in manufactured products and the heart of its industrial research effort. . . ."[1]

Exports provide a substantial number of jobs in the United States. A study by the U.S. Bureau of Labor Statistics reported that for chemicals 87,000 jobs and for allied products 15,000 jobs were attributable to exports of merchandise in 1965. The export employment was 14% of total private employment for chemicals while for allied products the ratio was 5%. The ratio for chemicals was one of the highest for any manufacturing industry.[2] These are gross figures against which must be offset the loss of any jobs because of imports.

Competition from imports has become an increasingly important factor to American firms producing chemicals and allied products. This competition is met within the United States as well as in many foreign countries. Modernization of foreign plants, acquisition of American "know-how," and relatively lower wages abroad have made it possible for foreign companies to undersell American companies in the United States for an increasing number of products.

In some instances, the increase in imports has begun to affect domestic prices. Included in this group are acrylic fiber, citric acid, perchloroethylene, trichloroethylene, polyvinyl chloride, dicalcium phosphate, dyes, and methylene chloride. As imports continue to expand, their impact on prices will become steadily greater.

Size of Foreign Competitors

Foreign competitors for chemicals and allied products usually are among the largest companies in their own countries. Appendix Table 37 lists 56 foreign companies which produce and sell chemicals and allied products included in the *Fortune Directory* as being among the 200 largest foreign industrial corporations in 1968. Several of these companies such as Royal Dutch and Unilever obtain only a small share of their revenues from chemicals while others are major producers of chemicals:

> Six companies whose prime business is chemicals had sales in excess of $1 billion—Imperial Chemical Industries, the largest privately owned company in Great Britain, $2,970 million; three German companies, Farbenfabriken Bayer, $1,731 million, Farbwerke Hoechst, $1,907 million, and BASF, $1,395 million; and two French companies, Pechiney, $1,275 million and Rhone-Poulenc $1,201 million.

> Seven other companies producing chemicals as well as other products had total sales over $1 billion.

> Nineteen companies had sales of $500 million to $1 billion.

> Twenty-four had sales between $250 million and $500 million.

Clearly, there are many big companies competing in the chemical business throughout the world. Since foreign companies usually have a large proportion of their volume in foreign trade, it is evident that American companies must face strong competitors in this country and throughout the world.

Statistical Data For Imports and Exports

Trends of foreign trade are difficult to analyze because of changes in the methods of compilation and differences in the statistical classifications used in the United States and elsewhere and those used for foreign trade and domestic statistics. There are four statistical categories now in use:

1. Standard Industrial Classification (SIC)

2. Standard International Trade Classification (SITC)

3. Tariff Schedules of the United States (TSUS)

4. The Brussels Tariff Nomenclature (BTN)

The nature of each series is described briefly below:

Standard Industrial Classification

The Standard Industrial Classification (SIC) is used in the United States by most statistical collecting agencies. By using the same classification system meaningful comparisons can be made between various economic series. The SIC classifies establishments by their type of activity. It divides all such activities into broad industrial divisions. Each division in turn is broken down into major industry groups (two digits), industry groups (three digits), the industry (four digits), product class (five digits), and the product (seven digits).

The categories for chemicals and allied products are illustrated below:

SIC Code	Designation	Name
28	Major industry group	Chemicals and allied products
281	Industry group	Basic chemicals
2812	Industry	Alkalies and chlorine
28121	Product class	Chlorine compressed or liquefied
28121-11	Product	Chlorine gas

Data are reported to the Bureau of the Census in terms of detailed products and then the broader classifications are built up.

"In essence, the system seeks to establish spheres of economic activity which are unique and distinguishable from other spheres because of a composite of similar characteristics which they have in common. These characteristics include similarity of products in terms of their uses and the bringing together of plants which specialize in making these products and account for a significant proportion of their shipments. They also include similarity of processes, similarity of materials used, and the bringing together of a group of plants which are economically significant. . . ."[3]

Formerly, United States foreign trade statistics were compiled within the SIC framework thus facilitating comparisons with domestic data for output and shipments. But in 1963, the Bureau of the Census shifted to the SITC classification for imports and exports to make the U.S. international trade data comparable with those for other countries.

Standard International Trade Classification (SITC) Revised

In 1950, a Statistical Commission of the United Nations established the Standard International Trade Classification in order to have a uniform basis for collecting statistics of imports and exports for each country. Originally the classifications of the SITC did not correspond completely to the BTN used for tariff purposes by many countries. Revisions were made so that the BTN and SITC could be related. The resulting system is the SITC Revised, which is now used to compile international trade statistics by all leading countries.

The SIC and SITC Revised cover almost identical items. However, the SITC section on chemicals includes photographic and cinematographic supplies which is part of the category photographic equipment (3861) in the SIC. Although the major categories for the allied products are similar in both systems, the classifications used for basic chemicals are different because of practices developed over the years.

The shift to the SITC classification by the United States resulted in somewhat larger totals for exports and imports as the following data for 1963 show:

| | U.S. Trade Data | | |
	SIC	SITC	Difference
	(*millions*)		
Exports	$1,943	$2,009	+66
Imports	558	701	+143
Export surplus	$1,385	$1,308	-77

In 1965, Schedule B export commodity classifications were designed

" . . . to achieve substantial comparability to (1) the Standard International Trade Classification (SITC). and (2) commodity classification based on SIC. . . . Comparability to SITC was the primary consideration. The Schedule B structure, numbering system, and arrangement were adapted from the SITC. However, within the SITC framework, SIC-based commodity building blocks were developed to provide comparability in terms of commodity classifications related to the origin of production. Thus, convertibility to SITC at various levels (5-digit, 4-digit, etc.) is practically complete."[4]

Tariff Schedules of the United States (TSUS)

The TSUS is the congressionally approved official schedule according to which duties are levied in the United States. It contains more than 6,300 different product identifications which are used to determine the duty status of imports.

The U.S. Department of Commerce has published a tabulation matching up the comparable categories in the SIC and the TSUSA.[5] Thus, for example, SIC 28121 (chlorine) corresponds to TSUSA 415.20 and SIC 28123 (sodium hydroxide) corresponds to TSUSA 421.08.

The Brussels Tariff Nomenclature (BTN)

Over the years other countries also had developed different national schedules for tariffs. Because the variations among countries created considerable confusion and often difficulty in determining appropriate tariffs, there was finally adopted in 1955 the Brussels Tariff Nomenclature (BTN).

"The BTN consists of about 1,100 four-digit headings arranged in 99 chapters, which are themselves grouped into 21 sections. . . . It is specifically designed for customs tariff purposes, and each country using the agreed classification is free to employ subheadings under the agreed headings to accommodate national needs."[6]

Growth in Foreign Trade

The postwar years may be divided into three periods to evaluate the significance of trends in foreign competition for chemicals and related products: 1946-1950, 1951-1955, and since 1955. In the 1946-1950 period, American companies met relatively unimportant foreign competition as Europe and Japan reconstructed their war-torn economies; the United States was virtually the only major world supplier of many chemicals and allied products. During that period, the United States was able to achieve technical product advantages because research in Europe was very small as a result of the war and the needs of reconstruction. Now, as is noted later, America must once more compete with new technical developments abroad. The dollar value of imports of chemicals and related products into the United States generally was moderately higher than in the prewar years but U.S. exports of these products rose substantially. (See Appendix Table 38)

The 1951-1955 period was marked by emerging competition from producers in Western European countries and Japan as their output continued to expand and as their local needs were more fully met. American imports of chemicals and related products rose to between $244 and $300 million in each of those years as compared with $80 million before World War II. Exports continued to rise and reached $1.3 billion in 1955 as compared with $163 million in 1939. (See Appendix Table 38)

The period since 1955 has been characterized by vigorous and expanding competition from foreign producers.[7] The formation of the Common Market, the full recovery of Europe and Japan[8] the expansion of foreign research, the building of modern plants, and the availability of American technology[9] all contributed to this development.

Despite the increasing competition from foreign producers there has been a significant increase in U.S. exports of chemicals and related products since 1956. (The data since 1956 are not comparable with those of earlier years because of changes in the classifications used.) By 1963, the volume exceeded $2.0 billion and in 1968 reached about $3.3 billion. (See Chart XI-1)

Imports of these products rose from $541 million in 1956 to $760 million in 1962. After recording moderate changes in the next three years the total expanded rapidly to $1.1 billion in 1968.[10] (See Appendix Table 39) These totals reflected the situation before the Kennedy round of tariff adjustments became operative. It was not until the mid-1960's that the full effect of competition from the restored economies of Europe and Japan began to make itself felt on a significant scale.

A special study by the U.S. Department of Commerce projected the probable trends of foreign trade. For chemicals, exports were projected to increase at an annual rate of 6.9% and imports by 10.2% in the five year period ending 1973.[11] Chemical exports were "expected to grow more slowly . . . than in the 1962-67 period."[12]

Relationship to Total Sales

Foreign trade in chemicals and allied products account for a smaller proportion of total sales in the United States than in other leading exporting nations. In 1967, total exports were equal to only 8% of sales in the United States as compared with 9% for Japan, 12% for Italy, 21% for Canada, 20% for France, 21% for the United Kingdom, 33% for Germany and 56% for Belgium.[13] Foreign producers rely much more heavily upon foreign trade than do those in the United States and hence they pursue such trade quite vigorously.

CHART XI-1

Chemicals and Related Products: Exports and Imports, 1929 to 1968

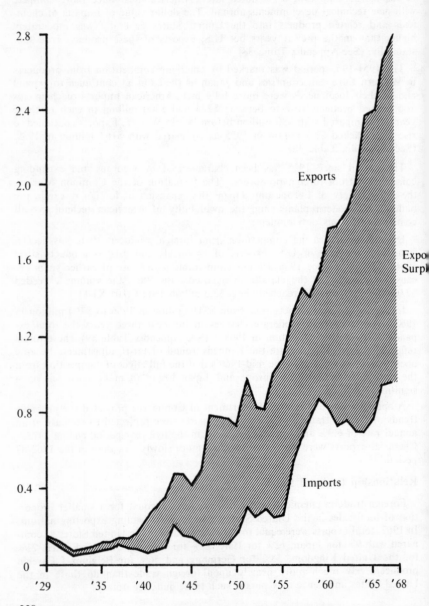

Billions of Dollars

Exports

Expo
Surp

Imports

2.8

2.4

2.0

1.6

1.2

0.8

0.4

0

'29   '35   '40   '45   '50   '55   '60   '65 '68

After World War II, U.S. exports increased in relative importance as compared with the prewar period. Exports of chemicals and allied products were equal to 3.8% of sales in 1929 and 1939, 5.6% in 1948 and in 1956. The new series showed a ratio of 6.4% in 1957 and unimportant changes have taken place in this ratio since that year.[14] (See Chart XI-2)

Imports (new series) were 2.5% of total sales in 1956 and then rose to 3.5% in 1958. A decline in imports while total sales were rising between 1959 and 1964 resulted in a drop in their relative importance to 2.0% in the latter year. (See Appendix Table 40) However, the sharp rise in imports since 1964 increased the ratio to slightly above 2% in 1968.

CHART XI-2

Imports and Exports as a Percentage of Total Sales of Chemicals and Allied Products, Selected Years, 1929 to 1965

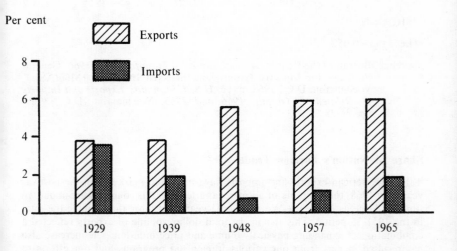

For major groups of chemicals and allied products, imports in 1966 averaged less than 2-1/2% except for gum and wood chemicals (5.7%). For one important category, namely, cleaning and toilet goods, the ratio was only 3/10 of 1% while for paints and allied products imports were virtually non-existent (See Table XI-1).

The nature of an average is such that imports and exports of some products are relatively more important than indicated by the averages for broad groups of products. Thus, although imports of basic chemicals etc. were only 2-1/2% of total domestic shipments, for intermediate coal-tar products (SIC 2815) the ratio was 6.8% and for inorganic pigments (SIC 2816) it was 6.5% while for alkalies and chlorine (SIC 2812) it was only 0.8%.

It seems clear, therefore, that the chemical industry owes only a small part of its extraordinary growth to sales abroad and that the tremendous growth rate of the industry through 1968 had not been impeded to any significant degree by imports.

TABLE XI-1

Relative Importance of Imports to Shipments for Chemicals and Allied Products, 1966

	Shipments*	Imports*	%
	(*millions*)		
Agricultural	$ 2,611	49	1.9
Cleaning and toilet goods	6,108	20	0.3
Drugs	4,826	107	2.2
Paints and allied products	2,970	1	**
Gum and wood chemicals	209	12	5.7
Basic chemicals, fibers, plastics, rubber and miscellaneous	24,073	603	2.5
Total	40,797	792	1.9

*SIC Code

**Less than 0.05%

Sources: Bureau of the Census, *Annual Survey of Manufactures: 1966*, General Statistics for Industry Groups and Selected Industries (M66(AS)-1, Washington, D.C., 1968, p. 12; *U.S. Commodity Exports and Imports as Related to Output, 1966 and 1965*, Washington, D.C., 1968, pp. 35-38.

Share of Nation's Foreign Trade

Total American exports and imports have increased markedly in the postwar years. By 1968, total exports of all merchandise from this country were about ten times as large as in the pre-World War II years and more than double the total in the 1951-55 period. This rise in the total dollar volume of exports reflected a combination of expanding physical volume and price inflation. The increase also has resulted in part from our various foreign aid programs and our efforts to reduce agricultural surpluses. But basically, it has reflected the demands of an expanding world economy.

Chemicals and related products contributed significantly to this expansion through 1959 since the exports of these products rose more rapidly than the total for all industries. During the 1930s, chemical exports generally averaged between 4% and 5% of total national exports. As a result of the large rise in the past two decades, the proportion exceeded 9% in 1959, and remained at that relative level through 1967; in 1968 the proportion increased to 9.8%.

The rise in total imports lagged in the earlier post-World War II years. Chemicals and related products were particularly affected by World War II since several of the belligerents were the leading factors in the world markets for these products.

In the pre-World War II years, 1936 to 1939, imports of chemicals and related products averaged 3.3% of total imports. By 1947 and 1948, the ratio was about half as large. The relative importance of imports of these products moved irregularly upward to 2.7% in 1951 and 1953, and then drifted lower. In 1956, as a result of the change in the classification of imports of chemicals and related products, the ratio jumped markedly to 4.2% of total U.S. imports and then rose to 6.2% in 1958. Between 1958 and 1968, imports of chemicals and related products rose less rapidly than total imports so that their relative importance declined to 3.4%. (See Appendix Tables 41 and 42)

Share of World Trade

During World War II and the early postwar years, American exports increased sharply as this country met the war-induced vacuum created by the loss of supplies from belligerents. As compared with about 14% of total world exports in 1937-38, the U.S. share increased to 31.5% in 1947. From this abnormally high war-induced proportion, the share dropped rapidly to 17.7% in 1950 as the revived war participants began to increase their volume of exports. Between 1951 and 1956, the U.S. share of world trade fluctuated around that proportion. Since the latter year there has been a fairly steady erosion to 15.8% in 1968. Despite this decline, the U.S. share of total world trade is still moderately higher than in the pre-World War II years. Foreign nations have almost completely recovered the loss in relative position experienced during World War II and in the early postwar years. A continuation of recent trends, however, would rapidly return their share to the prewar proportions.

Unfortunately, the data for world trade in chemicals and related products on a consistent basis are available only since 1956, so that prewar comparisons cannot be made. It is probable that the U.S. proportion of world trade in these products in the late 1950s and early 1960s was considerably higher than in the prewar period. In 1956 the proportion was 25.3%; it receded to 19.6% in 1966 as foreign exports rose more rapidly than those from the United States. The decline in the relative importance of American exports of chemicals and related products as a share of world trade since 1956 has been about in line with that recorded for all U.S. exports.[15]

Figures on total world trade tell only part of the story. In broad terms, the United States exports to two groups of countries: (1) those which can produce the same or similar products and hence compete with the U.S. (EEC, United Kingdom and Japan) and (2) third markets for which the U.S. competes with companies in the first group. The trends in both areas may be illustrated by exports of plastics and resins which aggregated 1,313 million pounds with a value of $473.3 million in 1967. The U.S. exported 431 million pounds or one-third the total volume and $193 million or two-fifths the total value to the EEC, United Kingdom and Japan where competition is met from locally based companies. The balance was sold in third markets where foreign producers compete with the United States for the business. The trends between 1963 and 1967 for exports of plastics to third markets were as follows:[16]

Exports of Plastics To Third Markets

(*1000 metric tons*)

	1963	1964	1965	1966	1967
United States	246	357	358	359	367
EEC	491	634	744	876	1,068
United Kingdom	206	236	248	267	301
Japan	79	92	167	260	309
Total	1,022	1,319	1,517	1,762	2,045

241

In the years 1964 to 1967, the volume of U.S. exports of plastics to third markets remained about unchanged[17] while exports from competing countries continued to expand significantly.

The shift in world trade reflects the recovery of Europe and Japan and the movement of their economies to new record levels of activity. Foreign capacity to produce chemicals and allied products has been rising rapidly and has been reflected in their vigorous competitive efforts in world markets.

Export Surplus For Chemicals and Allied Products

Exports of chemicals and allied products from the United States have exceeded imports by a wide margin. In 1939, the export surplus for these products was $83 million, in 1947 it was $678 million, in 1961 it exceeded $1 billion, and in 1968 was a record high of $2.2 billion. Table XI-2 shows that, except for dyeing and tanning extracts, synthetic dyestuffs, essential oils, and explosives and pyrotechnic products,[18] exports from the United States in 1967 exceeded imports for every major category of chemicals and related products. To a large extent, the export surplus reflected large exports of medicinal and pharmaceutical products, synthetic resins, mass produced organics, and specialty products.

The export surplus reflected the development of many new products and aggressive selling of these products abroad. Thus, both at home and abroad, the chemical industry owes much of its growth to the steady flow of new products from the research laboratories.

Chemicals and related products have contributed importantly to the total merchandise export surplus in U.S. foreign trade. For example, in 1963 chemicals and related products contributed 25.9% of the total merchandise export surplus of $5,057 million.[19] In 1966 and 1967, chemicals and related products accounted for more than two-fifths of the total trade surplus. In 1968, when the total U.S. trade surplus fell to $626 million, there would have been a net deficit if it had not been for the surplus of $2,154 million for chemicals and related products. (Appendix Table 44) (Chart XI-1)

The intensification of foreign competition in the United States and abroad has developed against the background of a major shift in the U.S. balance of payments. As postwar reconstruction was completed abroad, the dollar shortage of the early postwar years gave way to a dollar surplus. In 1968, thanks to an inflow of funds to our securities markets, there was a small surplus in the balance of payments.

In each of the ten years 1958 to 1967, the adverse balance of payments was between $1.3 billion and $3.9 billion. One result was a reduction in the U.S. gold stock from $22.9 billion to $10.9 billion. The substantial outflow of gold focused public attention upon the dramatic change in the balance of payments and upon the large increase in dollar credits held by foreigners in America.

The magnitude of this problem—which was serious enough—would have been intensified if it had not been for the large amount of dollars earned by net exports of chemicals and related products. During this critical period (1958 to 1968), annual exports of chemicals increased by $1.9 billion and imports by almost $600 million or a net increase of more than $1.3 billion in the export balance. In 8 of the 11 years, the export surplus of chemicals and related products exceeded one billion dollars and increased steadily. (See Appendix Table 39) The aggregate export surplus from 1958 to 1968 was $16,337 million. If the export balance of $779 million for chemicals and related products in 1958 had remained unchanged, in the following ten years this country would have earned an aggregate of $7,768 million *less* than it did on international account. Such a reduction in the export surplus would have seriously intensified the balance of payments problems.

Despite the continuing expansion of chemical exports and in the size of the export surplus through 1968, several factors which have contributed to this development appear to be weakening.

1. American companies had an advantage in the development of products because of our lead in research over European and Japanese competitors whose efforts in this area were disrupted by World War II.[20] The patents American companies obtained "have been a most important contribution in our exports of pharmaceuticals, medicinals, animal drugs, and agricultural chemicals such as herbicides, pesticides, fungicides, etc."[21] Research efforts by foreign producers have been increased substantially. New process technology (e.g. polyolefins) as well as new products are now being developed in Europe and Japan.

A comprehensive survey of European technology in 1969 concluded "there is now some evidence that Europe is more than holding its own in chemical technology."[22]

An OECD study concluded: "No important gap exists in invention, originating innovations or the production of bulk plastics" and that for pharmaceutical products there were "No general and deep-rooted differences in inventive capacities."[23] Karl Winnacker, chairman of Farbwerke Hoechst has stated "In chemistry, there is no technological gap."[24]

2. The development of the Common Market has improved the competitive advantage of companies located within the six countries for sales within that area, as well as increased their exports to third markets. In 1968, all tariff barriers were finally removed between EEC countries thus giving companies located there an advantage as compared with imports. The enormous expansion taking place in capacity for many chemical products in EEC countries appears to be far in excess of local demand, thus assuring intensified competition with American companies in third markets.

3. The discrimination against imports and the inducements offered to foreign companies to build local plants also affect trade in many areas. In addition, American companies have been increasing their overseas investments because local plants can provide better service, supply lines are shortened, and they can produce items suited to the local market. Dow has stated that "Much of our foreign sales growth will come from capacity now under construction in foreign countries."[25]

4. To the extent that the tariff reductions under the Kennedy Round open up greater opportunities for imports into the United States than they stimulate exports, the export surplus will be adversely affected. In the first stage for chemicals and related products, most tariffs are to be reduced by 50% with an average of 43% in the U.S. as against a reduction of about 20% in the EEC. However, the full cut in American tariffs in the first stage will not be effective until 1972 while the overseas tariffs were reduced as of July 1, 1968. Thus, the 1968 increase in exports probably reflected in part the benefits of lower tariffs overseas but the full impact is yet to be experienced for imports. Price competition from imports will intensify as the 10% annual tariff cuts cumulate. If the second stage of the Kennedy Round becomes effective, EEC tariffs will be reduced further so that the total cut is 46%, other foreign tariffs would be reduced by smaller amounts, the American Selling Price valuation system for benzenoids would be eliminated in the United States and further cuts in duties would become effective. (See Chapter XII)

5. The increase in border taxes scheduled for the EEC countries (except France) will create new barriers against imports in that important area.

6. To the extent that exports of chemicals and related products have been financed by the foreign aid program (Agency for International Development— AID), the cutback in such aid will adversely affect total exports. In the period July 1967 through March 1968, for example AID-financed expenditures included fertilizers $145.7 million, medicinal and pharmaceuticals $25.1 million, DDT $7.0 million, and pesticides and agricultural chemical specialties $7.1 million.[26]

7. Curbs on direct investment overseas may adversely affect exports of intermediates for further processing and restrain shipments to affiliates involving credit since the latter counts as part of the total direct investment permitted.[27]

As against these factors which would adversely affect chemical exports, the world market is expanding rapidly thus creating enlarged opportunities for trade. However, as shown in Appendix Table 43 the United States has been getting a declining share of world markets. While the relative share of these markets is declining, the total in dollars can continue to expand as it has in recent years. Nevertheless, it should become increasingly difficult to continue to increase the export surplus for chemicals and probably in time some reduction will develop.

Changing Composition of Foreign Trade

As new products have been developed and as the pattern of production abroad has changed, there have been major shifts in the composition of imports and exports of chemicals and related products.

Appendix Table 45 shows the changes in exports between 1958 and 1967, a period when the total about doubled. Organic chemicals, which accounted for 26.7% of the exports in 1967 as compared with only 11.7% in 1958, have been increasing at a rate more than twice as rapidly as total exports. Synthetic resins, regenerated cellulose and plastic materials, the second most important group, accounted for one-sixth the total in 1967. Manufactured fertilizers also have increased in relative importance. The greatest loss in position was experienced by medicinal and pharmaceutical products for which the total dollar volume of exports was about the same in 1958 and 1967 so that their relative importance fell from 19.7% to 10.3%. Other categories which have declined in relative importance have been soaps, cleansing, polishing and finishing preparations, explosives, essential oils, perfume, and flavor materials, and the miscellaneous group.

Total imports increased from $367 million in 1958 to $963 million in 1967. The largest rise was recorded by organic chemicals which increased in relative importance from 11.5% to 22.8%. In contrast, imports of inorganics declined from 31.4% to 22.4%. Synthetic organic dyes, natural indigo, color lakes and toners increased from 2.5% of total imports in 1958 to 3.8% in 1967 while dyeing and tanning extracts fell from 3.5% to 1.0%. (See Appendix Table 46)

Costs and Prices

The flow of foreign trade is significantly affected by relative export prices here and abroad. As foreign competition has intensified there has developed considerable interest in comparative costs of production in the various countries and in the composition of such costs, particularly wages, as well as in export

TABLE XI-2

Total Imports and Exports, Chemicals and Related Products, 1967
(*millions of dollars*)

SITC		Exports	Imports	Net Exports (+) Net Imports (–)
512	Organic chemicals	$748.5	$218.7	+529.8
513	Inorganic chemical elements: oxides and halogen salts	191.2	167.0	+ 24.2
514	Other inorganic chemicals	107.7	48.8	+ 58.9
515	Radioactive and associated materials	50.6	16.0	+ 34.6
521	Mineral tar, tar oils, and crude chemicals from coal, petroleum and natural gas	28.9	8.8	+ 20.1
531	Synthetic organic dyestuffs, natural indigo color lakes and toners	31.7	36.9	– 5.2
532	Dyeing and tanning extracts, and synthetic tanning materials	2.7	10.0	– 7.3
533	Pigments, paints, varnishes and related materials	74.3	5.7	+ 68.6
541	Medicinal and pharmaceutical products	288.0	71.7	+216.3
551	Essential oils, perfume and flavour materials	44.4	49.1	– 4.7
553	Perfumery and cosmetics, denti- frices and other toilet prepara- tions (except soaps)	26.5	12.7	+ 13.8
554	Soaps, cleansing and polishing preparations	69.8	6.9	+ 62.9
561	Fertilizers, manufactured, and fertilizer materials	230.6	142.3	+ 88.3
571	Explosive and pyrotechnic products (including hunting and sporting ammunition)	18.5	41.0	– 22.5
581	Synthetic resins, regenerated cellulose and artificial resins	473.3	60.3	+413.0
599	Chemical materials and products, n.e.c.	415.9	67.4	+348.5
		2,802.5	963.1	+1,839.4

SITC - Standard International Trade Classification.

Sources: U.S. Department of Commerce, Bureau of the Census, *United States Export Statistics,* Report FT 450, 1967 Annual, Washington, D.C., 1968, pp. 7-10; *U.S. Imports-General and Consumption, Schedule A Commodity and Country,* Report FT 135, December 1967, Washington, D.C., 1968, pp. 5-7.

prices. Comparisons based on wage rates or average hourly earnings alone are not too meaningful because of differences in the scale and volume of operations, the variations in fringe benefits among countries, differences in output per manhour, and differences in other components of costs.

It is virtually impossible to measure differences in costs or in prices among countries with any precision because of the inadequacy of the available data. "Proper measurement of price competitiveness would require indices of 'delivered' prices by market. Such indices would measure—in addition to changes in basic export prices—changes in transportation and distribution costs and in tariffs. *However, no such measure is currently available.*"[28] (Italics added) At best rough comparisons can be made by using one or more of three types of data: unit labor costs, unit values of exports, and wholesale prices.

For the chemical and allied products industries the problem is further complicated because even such indexes are not published for all important exporting countries and usually are not available on a continuous basis. The usefulness of such data also is limited by differences of coverage in the index for different countries.

It is widely asserted that, as a result of their higher wages, American manufacturers operate under a considerable handicap when competing with foreign producers. However, if high-priced American labor cannot compete with low wage labor abroad, why is the United States the world's largest exporter? Why did it persistently sell abroad so much more than it bought until 1968?

These questions suggest that differences in wages between countries may be less important than often stated, particularly for items produced in large volume by continuous process. In fact, it has been demonstrated that wages are relatively high (by U.S. standards) in the principal export industries and that industries most affected by imports tended to pay below-average wages.[29]

Average Labor Costs

Comprehensive labor cost data are not available on a continuous basis for all leading countries for the chemical industry. Generally, data are available for wage workers (production workers) and/or salary workers. In some countries these data include fringe benefits but in the U.S. they do not. For some large companies an average labor cost figure can be derived by dividing total labor compensation by the total number of employees. Such data provide only a rough picture of average compensation per employee because they usually include salaries of executives and high paid research personnel whose relative importance varies among companies. The average also may be affected by varying numbers of part time employees. Moreover, such annual averages conceal the differences in the numbers of hours worked annually.

Average hourly earnings show only part of the cost incurred for labor. Consideration also must be given to nonwage benefits. Hourly labor costs abroad are much lower than in this country. With less capital available, the scale of operations generally has been much smaller. As a result, smaller quantities of goods have been produced per employee or per manhour than in American companies. The United States possesses the combined advantages of abundant natural resources, unequaled capital resources, and unexcelled management and marketing "know-how." Equally important, wherever mechanical production systems can be used, unit costs are reduced sharply because of the economies of large-scale production.

Even under the most favorable conditions, labor cost comparisons are difficult to make. Within a nation, the average wage rate in any industry varies depending on the jobs to be filled. For the same occupation, there are variations between different areas of the country, different firms in the same locality, and different plants within a firm, depending on the race, sex, seniority, and skill characteristics of the employees. The proportions of wage and salary workers also vary. International comparisons are further complicated by variations in coverage and in non-wage benefits, which generally comprise a much larger relative share of a wage earner's total compensation abroad, and by the limitations which attend the conversion of their labor costs into dollar equivalents.[30]

Average hourly labor costs in the United States in 1966 were about twice as large as in West Germany, France, and Belgium.[31] (See Table XI-3) Hourly labor costs abroad for other industries similarly are much lower than those paid in the United States, so that the goods and services bought by foreign chemical companies also are less costly. These comparisons do not tell the full story because they do not reflect the higher wages paid to salaried employees than to production workers.

Average annual cost per employee also is substantially higher in the U.S. than overseas. In the United States annual labor costs averaged $8,748 to $9,571 in 1966. The Japanese companies are at the other extreme, with annual compensation usually below $2,500. The German companies are reported to incur about half the labor cost shown for American companies while Imperial Chemical is about two-fifths the American average.[32]

In recent years, chemical wage costs have been rising relatively more rapidly abroad than in the United States. Between 1959 and 1966 average hourly labor costs increased by less than one-third in the United States as compared with 90% in Italy and 70% in France and 128% in the Netherlands. (See Table XI-4 and Chart XI-3).

CHART XI-3

Increase in Hourly Labor Costs, Chemicals and Pharmaceutical Products, in Leading Countries, 1959 to 1966

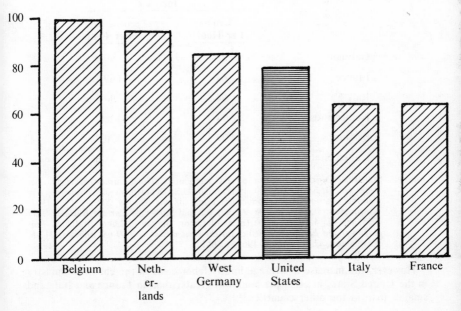

TABLE XI-3

Average Hourly Labor Costs For Chemicals and
Allied Products, 1966
(*in American Dollars*)

	Plastic Materials	Artificial and Synthetic Fibers	Chemicals and Allied Products	Basic Chemicals
Germany	$1.32	$1.70	$1.80	$1.94
France	1.19	1.80	1.55	1.74
Italy	1.10	1.37	1.35	1.40
Netherlands	1.13	1.79	1.68	1.82
Belgium	1.30	1.68	1.81	1.87
United States		3.65	3.69*	3.86*

*BLS average hourly earnings in 1966 and Chamber of Commerce fringe benefits for 1967.

Source: U.S. Department of Labor, Bureau of Labor Statistics, *Labor Developments Abroad,* January 1969, p. 18 and Chamber of Commerce of the United States, *Employee Benefits, 1967,* Washington, D.C., 1968, p. 13.

TABLE XI-4

Changes In Hourly Labor Costs For Chemicals and
Pharmaceutical Products, Selected Countries,
1959 to 1966

	Increase	
	Cents Per Hour	Per Cent
Germany	85	90.8
France	64	69.7
Italy	64	90.1
Netherlands	94	128.3
Belgium	99	120.7
United States	79	28.6

Source: Statistical Office of the European Communities, *The Common Market: Ten Years On,* Brussels, May 30, 1968, p. 86. U.S. Department of Commerce, *The National Income and Product Accounts of the United States, 1929-1965,* Washington, D.C., 1966, pp. 93, 97, 105 and *Survey of Current Business,* July 1968, pp. 41, 42; U.S. Department of Labor, Bureau of Labor Statistics, *Employment and Earnings Statistics for the United States,* 1909-68, Bulletin 1312-6, Washington, D.C., August 1968, p. 641.

However, the increase in average hourly labor costs in the chemical industry in the United States in cents per hour was greater than in France and Italy and smaller than in the other countries.[33]

The data for annual compensation show a similar pattern. For the five year period 1961-1966, each of the American companies recorded increases of less than 20% in contrast to increases of 40% for many large chemical companies in Europe and increases as high as 60-80% in Japan.[34]

Total labor costs of the chemical industry in the United States are considerably higher than in other countries.

Unit Labor Costs

Comparisons of *hourly labor costs* alone overstate by a wide margin the difference in *unit labor costs* in the chemical industry here and abroad. To a large extent higher wages in the United States reflect the higher productivity of the American chemical industry—a pattern which is similar to that found for other American industries. (See Chapter IX) An extremely rough picture of unit labor costs can be obtained by comparing the relationship between sales per employee in the United States and abroad and the relationship between hourly labor costs.

It should be emphasized that there are many limitations to these relationships. Differences in the product mix and in the number of hours paid for per year would affect the significance of the results shown. Lack of comparability of coverage for sales and labor costs and inadequacies in the underlying data are significant. The results also are affected by the upward revaluation of the mark which has resulted in a lower ratio of American to West German labor costs when converted to dollars and by the devaluation of the franc which resulted in a higher ratio of American to French labor costs.

Although precise measurement is not possible with the available data, the American sales per employee are so much greater than in the other countries, that it seems clear that on the average a very substantial part of the difference in labor costs per hour is offset by the higher productivity of the American chemical industry. This conclusion does not apply to all products, particularly those made by batch processes.

The relative importance of employee costs to total sales in 1967 is shown in Table XI-5 for five American and five European companies. The significance of such data is influenced by the product mix which varies among companies. Nevertheless, these data indicate that relative labor costs are significantly lower overseas than in the United States but by a much narrower margin than suggested by average hourly wage costs alone. Thus, for five large American chemical companies labor costs averaged 30% of sales in 1967 as compared with 22.7% for five European companies. To state it differently, $3.33 in sales for the five U.S. companies required one dollar in total employment costs while for the five European companies the relationship was one dollar for $4.30 in sales. The disparity is even wider with Japan.

It is also clear that despite larger labor cost increases than in the United States, their relative importance declined for many foreign companies between 1961 and 1966 as it did for most American companies. Despite the relatively low levels for Japan, the labor cost ratios fell for each of the four companies in that five year period as is shown in Table XI-6.

The differences in total labor cost per unit of output in the chemical industry appear to be considerably narrower than suggested by wage or labor cost data alone.

TABLE XI-5

Relative Labor Costs, American and European Chemical Companies, 1967

Five U.S. Companies

	Sales	Personnel Expenses	Per Cent
	(*millions*)		
Allied*	$1,243	$ 329	26.4%
Dow*	1,383	362	26.2
Du Pont	2,940	1,118	38.0
Monsanto*	1,632	398	24.4
Union Carbide*	2,126	592	27.9
Total	$9,324	$2,799	30.0

Five European Companies

	Sales	Personnel Expenses	Per Cent
BASF	$ 912	220	24.1
Bayer	1,082	255	23.5
Hoechst	1,400	286	20.4
CIBA	192	62	32.4
Pechiney*	225	44	19.5
Total	$3,811	867	22.7

*Companies reporting consolidated data

Source: Annual Reports, 1967.

Comparative Total Unit Costs

High unit labor costs do not necessarily mean high end product prices in world markets for American chemical manufacturers. The impact of unit labor costs on total unit costs hinges upon the relative importance of labor costs. Total costs are determined by the cost of materials, capital costs, management methods and overhead as well as labor costs. Labor cost differentials can have their greatest significance where they account for a large share of the sales dollar unless this factor is offset by markedly higher productivity.

Relative labor costs may vary considerably among chemical products. Thus, they would tend to be lowest for basic chemicals such as salts, acids, and alkalies which are produced in large quantities. As these products are subject to further processing, labor costs tend to increase as intermediates are created and modified to meet customer specifications. Finally, the intermediates are converted into finished chemicals which require relatively more labor input to meet differing specifications of purchasers.

TABLE XI-6

Total Employee Costs Relative To Sales, 1961 and 1966

	1961	1966
Du Pont	31.6%	31.9%
Union Carbide	28.0	25.7
Monsanto	24.0	23.3
Dow	29.4	25.6
*ICI	26.7	24.6
Bayer	-	24.2
*Hoechst	20.7	21.7
BASF	24.9	24.4
Ugine Kuhlmann	-	22.1
Pechiney-St. Gobain.	-	20.4
*CIBA	30.8	32.3
*Geigy	24.7	26.6
Sandoz	30.7	30.2
Toyo Rayon	9.0	7.7
Asahi	12.0	9.0
Mitsubishi	9.3	7.1
Sumitomo	16.3	13.1
Union Carbide of Can.	19.2	20.5

*Groups

Source: C. P. Neidig, "Financial Comparison of World Chemical Companies," *Financial Analysts Journal,* January-February 1968, p. 12.

Until recently, the economies of scale arising from the huge dimensions of America's domestic market enabled chemical producers to spread their fixed costs over a much larger number of units than was possible abroad. The application of a greater amount of electric energy and of machine power also contributed to rising productivity which helped to offset higher wage costs.

Foreign chemical companies use many chemicals as raw materials and can purchase some of these chemicals at lower prices abroad.[35] This is also true for petroleum.[36] (See section on oil import quotas, Chapter XII).

Total costs also may be influenced by tax burdens directly borne by producers, by the level of capital costs,[37] and by government subsidy. It must also be kept in mind that transportation,[38] insurance, and related costs are incurred in overseas trade.[39]

The relative position of American producers of chemicals and allied products in international markets, therefore, is seen in better perspective when viewed in terms of total unit costs of production—for identical items and for identical volume, where this is possible. Although such data are far more difficult to assemble than comparisons of wage costs alone, some scattered data are available to permit some broad comparisons.

The National Industrial Conference Board made a detailed analysis of the cost of production of identical products produced by American manufacturers here and in their foreign plants in 1960-1961. For the chemical industry, 50 product reports were analyzed, reasonably well distributed among the major geographical areas. *Total unit costs* were lower than in the U.S. for half the products, the same for 14%, and higher for 36%.[40] For the Common Market, it was found that for 5 of the 8 chemical products surveyed, *total manufacturing costs* were less than in the United States. The contrast was even more marked for the United Kingdom, where 7 of the 8 chemical industry product reports revealed lower total unit costs.[41] The NICB study showed that costs of materials generally were higher for the overseas plants than for those in the United States.

A special study by American Aniline in 1964 concluded that the *total cost of production* in a European *dyestuff* plant was more than one-fifth lower than in an American plant as shown below:[42]

	U.S.	Europe
	(*thousands*)	
Materials	$ 6,210	$5,161
Manpower	2,740	1,678
Other	1,050	930
Total	$10,000	$7,769

William F. Christopher of Hooker Chemical reported in 1964 that for polyvinyl-chloride plants with the same scale of operations "the foreign producer has approximately a 15% cost advantage."[43]

For *organic chemicals,* Arthur D. Little, Inc., estimated in 1962 that *total unit costs* in West Germany, the United Kingdom, France, Italy, and Japan averaged between 80.8% and 84.6% of the American average. The differences in costs were accounted for mainly by estimated lower costs for labor, plant overhead, and administrative costs.[44]

However, the Little Report also found that *base manufacturing costs* for organic chemicals were *lower* in the United States than in the United Kingdom and West Germany for 12 out of 15 products, lower than in France for 16 out of 17 products, lower than in Japan for 9 out of 15 products, and lower than in Italy for 9 out of 19 products. Only for phthalic anhydride and Naphthol A S were base manufacturing costs higher in the United States than in each of the other countries for which data were reported.[45] For indigo,[46] costs were higher than in each of the countries except Japan.

On the basis of *marginal manufacturing costs,*[47] the Little Report estimated that the lowest cost country abroad could have a landed cost on the East or Gulf Coast that was lower than the American price based on full costs plus a 10% return on total investment for 6 out of 15 products studied.[48] In terms of full costs, however, the relative position of even the lowest cost foreign producers would have been less favorable.

In a 1966 study of the relative cost of producing petrochemicals, Arthur D. Little, Inc. found that for crude *hydrocarbons,* costs were between 18% and 22% lower in the United Kingdom, France, Germany, Italy and Japan than in the United States, for *organic intermediates* 5.8% to 19.5% lower, for *fibers* 13.5% to 17.2% lower, and for *detergents* 14.4% to 17.5% lower. For *plastics* costs were higher overseas under some assumptions and lower under others—the range was between 17.9% lower and 8.2% higher.[49]

William F. Christopher reported in 1968 that production costs for *condensation polymers* (e.g. phenolics, epoxies, polyesters) "are typically lower in other major producing countries than those in the U.S." because they are batch produced and because raw material costs often are lower than in the U.S. On the other hand, for *large-volume thermoplastics* (e.g. polyethylene, polystyrene, polypropylene) "the U.S. has historically had an advantage in scale of production and, therefore, in the costs of producing these materials." Current trends suggest that in the years ahead these historic cost advantages may be equalized. He also reported that "Research and development costs, application engineering costs, and the costs of technical assistance to customers are considerably higher in the U.S. than in foreign countries."[50]

A study by Robert B. Stobaugh, Jr. estimated that the cost of manufacture for dyes in West Germany in 1963 was a maximum of 17% lower than in the United States. The difference was due to lower costs of labor and of raw materials.[51]

The available studies of comparative total unit costs show mixed results. Total unit costs appear to be lower abroad although there are exceptions to this generalization. Lower costs for energy,[52] the economies of scale, and greater productivity in the United States offset to a major degree the wide disparity in labor costs. It must also be kept in mind that costs are incurred in shipping products from overseas. The situation for each product in each country must be examined separately in order to obtain meaningful comparisons.

Prices: United States and Abroad

Data for unit labor costs and total unit costs should not be confused with prices and price trends. Although costs may influence prices, they do not determine them.[53] In fact, there may be little relationship between them as is shown below:

> "A notable divergence of price and cost trends occurred in Japan, where the index of unit labor costs rose by 14 per cent [from 1953 to 1963], while wholesale prices remained roughly constant and export unit values declined by 13 per cent."[54]

Exports also contribute to total output and hence to the economies of scale. Thus, they may help to reduce unit costs at home. In light of the transportation, insurance, and other charges incurred on overseas trade, export sales often can be made only if they yield a lower net price than sales in the home market.

American companies must face the fact that they sell in overseas markets in which prices and local purchasing power are much lower than in the United States. Unless they meet those lower prices, sales cannot be made for competitive products; for non-competitive products, prospective buyers will be unwilling and unable to pay American prices. The alternatives are to meet those price levels or to do little or no business.

Comprehensive data are not available to compare actual prices for imports and domestic products either within the American economy or within the foreign countries to which it exports.[55] Table XI-7 summarizes the data reported by *European Chemical News* for prices in the United States and in six European countries in January 1969.

It must be recognized that these comparisons are based on list prices for small volume. Large volume transactions often are made at different prices both here and abroad. Moreover, such list prices appear to have less meaning abroad than in this country.

A total of 1001 comparisons were made with U.S. prices. For 622 comparisons the foreign prices were lower while for 365 the foreign prices were higher; prices were the same in 14 instances. In the six countries the price was lower than in the United States in two-thirds of the instances.

The products which had higher prices in the United States than in any of the other countries included: acetic acid (glacial), calcium carbide, carbon tetrachloride, caustic soda (solid), perchloroethylene, trichloroethylene, urea, stearic acid and isobutyl acetate.

The products which had lower prices in the United States than in any of the other countries included: sulfuric acid, ammonium sulfate, carbon black, phosphoric acid, polyethylene, and styrene monomer.

Price indexes are available for several leading countries but their levels are not directly comparable. However, such price indexes are useful as an indication of the extent to which prices are rising or falling.

TABLE XI-7

European Prices Compared With American Prices, January 1969

	Lower	Same	Higher
United Kingdom	115	5	67
France	91	1	65
Germany	114	3	73
Italy	116	1	62
Belgium	119	1	64
Netherlands	67	3	34
Total	622	14	365

Source: Derived from *European Chemical News,* January 3, 1969, pp. 22, 25, 26, 28.

The relatively larger increase in labor costs and in price levels in foreign countries than in the United States in recent years has caused some observers to conclude that foreign products will become less competitive in international markets. However, there has been little visible support for this proposition. Western Europe experienced a larger price inflation than the United States between 1958 and 1967 as Table XI-8 shows.

Between 1958 and 1967, the wholesale price level rose 5.7% in the United States as compared with increases ranging from 8.0% in West Germany to 22.0% in France. These data, however, refer to the price changes in local currency.

TABLE XI-8

Per Cent Changes, 1958 - 1967

	All Whole-sale Prices	Chemicals and Allied Products
	(*per cent*)	
United States	5.7	−2.0
West Germany	8.0 (13.4)	−4.7 (0.1)
France	22.0 (3.7)	13.2 (−3.8)
United Kingdom	9.0	2.3
Italy	13.0	4.4
Japan	11.0	−11.8

Note: Figures in brackets adjusted for changes in value of the currency.

Source: U.S. Department of Labor, Bureau of Labor Statistics, mimeographed sheets (for United States price data); International Monetary Fund, *International Financial Statistics,* April 1968 (for all wholesale price data in foreign countries). Organisation for Economic Co-operation and Development, *The Chemical Industry* (for chemicals and allied products data in foreign nations).

Allowance must be made for changes in the external value of the currency for Germany and France. Thus, the upward revaluation of 5% in the West German mark in March, 1961[56] meant that the increase in German prices to an American buyer was 13.4% instead of 8.0%.[57] On the other hand, because of the devaluation of the French franc by 15% in December, 1958,[58] the cost of French products to Americans increased by only 3.7%. On balance, it seems that the general level of wholesale prices rose much more abroad than in the United States during the 1958-67 period.

The above pattern, however, does not apply to chemicals and allied products. These prices either declined or their rise was smaller than for wholesale prices. When allowance is made for the devaluation of 15%, the prices of French chemicals declined by 3.8%.[59] In the United Kingdom, prices of chemicals and allied products rose 2.3% (compared with the increase of 9.0% for all wholesale prices) between 1958 and 1967. These trends have developed despite the larger relative increases in hourly labor costs abroad.

On the average, it appears that, except for Japan, there has been little relative change between these foreign countries as a group and the United States in the prices of chemicals and allied products in contrast to the relative improvement in our average position for products of other industries.

Although foreign domestic prices generally have risen somewhat more than prices in the U.S., average export prices did not follow the same pattern for the 1958-67 period except for the United Kingdom.[60] (See Appendix Table 47.)

Changes In Export Prices, 1958-1967

	1958-1967	1963-1967
	(*per cent*)	
United States	12	10
United Kingdom	15	10
West Germany	10	2
France	5	7
Italy	−5	1
Japan	1	1

Of course, these are averages which may conceal significant variations but the general conclusion still appears to hold.

The fact that both U.S. imports and exports of chemicals and allied products continue to expand each year suggests that the factors which influence the volume of trade—price relationships, economic growth, development of new products, etc.—have on balance been favorable. Of course, the increase in imports has disadvantaged some American producers while the increase in U.S. exports in some instances has been at the expense of sales by its foreign competitors. All of the increases in imports of chemicals and allied products do not represent a diversion from home producers—either here or abroad. Sometimes they reflect the expansion in total demand for the product affected.

Summary and Conclusions

Exporters of chemicals and allied products have been meeting increasing competition abroad from foreign companies which are growing rapidly in size. Thus, while total American exports of these products have continued to expand significantly, the world markets have grown so much more rapidly that the American share of those markets has declined from more than one quarter in 1956 to less than one-fifth in 1967.

Exports and imports of chemicals and allied products have risen sharply since the end of World War II. Although the *percentage increases* have been much larger for imports, the *dollar increases* have been greater for exports.

Exports of chemicals and allied products have accounted for a larger proportion of total sales of American companies in the post-World War II years than before the war. In contrast, imports have been a smaller proportion of total sales. Export trade represents a relatively smaller share of total sales of chemicals and allied products in the United States than in most leading countries. In recent years, exports have been equal to about 8% of total sales.

Exports of chemicals and allied products have been increasing more rapidly than total exports of merchandise from the United States. Although chemical imports lagged in the earlier post-World War II years, they have been increasing more rapidly than total merchandise imports in recent years.

The excess of exports over imports (export surplus) has been growing and has made significant contributions to the international balance of payments.

In the eleven years 1958 to 1968, chemicals and allied products earned an export surplus of more than $16 billion. In 1968, the export surplus of $2,154 million for chemicals and allied products was $1.5 billion *greater* than the entire trade surplus. Clearly, this group of industries has made a major contribution in this area.

Among the developments which can act to reduce the export surplus in the years ahead are: the reduction in American technological advantage, the development of the Common Market making possible larger companies and the economies of large scale production, growth in American plants abroad, the delayed effects of tariff reductions under the Kennedy Round, the erection of non-tariff barriers abroad, foreign export incentives, and the cutback in American foreign aid.

The composition of exports has been changing with plastics and resin materials, fertilizers, and organics increasing in relative importance. Dollar exports of medicinals and pharmaceuticals, pigments, paints, and varnishes, and soaps and cleaners also have increased but not so rapidly as total exports. As a result their relative importance has declined.

For imports, the major changes in recent years have been the sharp rise in organic chemicals, synthetic resins, and synthetic organic dyes; inorganics have been declining in relative importance although increasing in dollar volume.

The available data for chemical costs and prices yield a few facts which are not disputed although varying interpretations may be placed on their significance.

1. Average hourly labor costs are two to four times as high in the United States as in Europe and an even wider spread as compared with Japan but labor costs have been rising much more rapidly abroad in recent years.

2. Productivity in the United States averages considerably higher than abroad for chemicals and allied products as a group, but productivity is now rising *relatively* more rapidly abroad. (See Chapter VIII)

3. Unit labor costs appear to be significantly lower abroad; they are especially low in Japan.

4. Energy costs in the United States are lower than abroad.

5. The large size of the American economy creates opportunities for economies of scale which act to hold down total unit costs.

There is considerable disagreement concerning some aspects of the current cost situation. This is indicated by the following questions:

1. Are chemical raw material costs higher in the United States? The record is mixed.

2. Are total unit costs for chemical products higher or lower in the United States? The conclusion seems to be that they are higher but there appear to be some exceptions.

3. Are foreign chemical export prices increasing or decreasing relative to American prices in export markets? During the past decade, the rise appears to have been greater for U.S. export prices except as compared with the United Kingdom.

4. Are the differences in foreign costs reflected in comparable differences in their export prices?

Unfortunately, satisfactory data are not available to answer these questions definitively. It does appear, however, that much of the discussion concerning costs does not come to grips with the real question, namely relative prices. Costs do not determine prices and this is particularly true in foreign trade. Accordingly, studies of total costs here and abroad would not be too meaningful even if they were more adequate.

---

[1] William Gruber, Dileep Mehta, and Raymond Vernon, "The R&D Factor in International Trade and International Investment of United States Industries," *The Journal of Political Economy,* February 1967, pp. 24-25, 30.

[2] Chemicals included chemicals and selected chemical products and plastics and synthetic materials. Allied products covered drugs, cleaning and toilet preparations and paints and allied products. Daniel Roxon, "Domestic Jobs Attributable to U.S. Exports," *Monthly Labor Review,* December 1967, p. 14.

[3] Senate Subcommittee on Antitrust and Monopoly, *Concentration Ratios In Manufacturing Industry, 1963,* Washington, D.C., 1966, Part 1, p. xii.

[4] *U.S. Commodity Export and Imports as Related to Output, 1966 and 1965,* U.S. Department of Commerce, Bureau of the Census, September 1968, p. 122.

[5]U.S. Department of Commerce, Bureau of the Census, *U.S. Imports For Consumption and General Imports SIC-Based Products and Area,* FT 210, 1967 Annual, Washington, D.C., pp. 272-318.

[6]Harold J. Heck, *The International Business Environment,* American Management Association, New York, 1969, p. 180.

[7]A number of other industries including cotton textiles, steel, cameras, and electrical machinery, also have experienced the impact of greater foreign competition for important lines of products.

[8]Japan's petrochemical industry "did not really get on stream until 1958 but [in 1964] it is tied with West Germany for second place in the manufacture of synthetic resins and plastics and is surpassed only by the United States in synthetic fiber output." *Japan,* First National City Bank, New York, August 1964, pp. 1, 15.

[9]It has been estimated that " . . . competitive processes satisfactory for the manufacture of nearly 90% of [Du Pont's] output are available to our foreign competitors." Letter from Crawford H. Greenewalt to the Senate Finance Committee, August 2, 1962, p. 5.

[10]The trend of imports has been significantly influenced by the inclusion of uranium oxide imports. In 1962, total imports were $766 million but excluding uranium oxide the total was only $514 million. In 1967, the reported totals were $963 million and $947 million respectively because uranium oxide imports had declined to only $16 million. Thus, a significantly higher rate of increase is shown if uranium oxide imports are excluded. Testimony of Robert C. Barnard in *Foreign Trade and Tariff Proposals,* Hearings before the Committee on Ways and Means, House of Representatives, 90th Cong., 2nd Sess., Part 10, Washington, D.C., 1968, p. 4513.

[11]U.S. Department of Commerce, *U.S. Foreign Trade, A Five Year Outlook With Recommendations For Action,* Washington, D.C., April 1969, p. 57.

[12]*Ibid.,* p. 64.

[13]For all countries, exports of chemicals and allied products have been increasing in relative importance. In 1958, the ratios were: Belgium 52%, France 14%, Italy 8%, United Kingdom 19%, Canada 16%, and the United States 6%. Data are available for Japan only since 1963 when the ratio was 7%. Organisation for Economic Co-operation and Development, *The Chemical Industry, 1967-1968,* Paris, 1969, p. 36. In 1961, exports of plastics were estimated to be 12% of production in the United States as compared with 29% in West Germany and in Italy, 31% in the United Kingdom, 6% in Japan, and 81% in the Netherlands. C. Freeman, A. Young, and J. Fuller, "The Plastics Industry: A Comparative Study of Research and Innovation," *National Institute Economic Review,* London, England, November 1963, p. 25.

[14]This ratio is based on SITC 5 and hence is less than the 8% figure reported by the OECD which includes synthetic rubber (SITC 231.2) and photographic and cinematographic supplies (SITC 862) in its export total.

[15]For dyes, exports from the United States accounted for 65% of world exports in 1947. By 1955, the ratio had declined to 9.3%; in 1962 the ratio was 6.7%. *Chemical and Engineering News,* August 24, 1964, p. 72.

[16]Derived from tables included in testimony of William F. Christopher, "Foreign Trade and Tariff Proposals," *op. cit.,* Part 7, pp. 3103-4 and United Nations, *1967 World Trade Annual.*

[17]Third markets include all areas outside the exporting countries.

[18]Five years earlier (1962), we had an export surplus for each of these categories except dyeing and tanning extracts. On the other hand, import surpluses for radioactive and associated materials and other inorganic chemicals in 1962 had shifted to large export surpluses in 1967.

[19]Dr. Lewis E. Lloyd of Dow Chemical has pointed out that our total export surplus in 1963 resulted in part from $3.6 billion of military grant-aid and other government financed shipments and that the chemical proportion of commercial trade export surplus alone was about 60%. *Chemical and Engineering News,* August 24, 1964, p. 67.

[20]In connection with plastics, it has been pointed out that Germany led prior to World War II. After the war, the United States " . . . was able to draw ahead, when German industry was dislocated and disorganized. But in the last five or six years the successor firms to I. G. Farben in Germany have again been prominent in patents and innovations. Britain's research effort in plastics has been very much greater since the war than before it." Freeman, Young, and Fuller, *op. cit.,* p. 43.

[21]Statement of Lewis E. Lloyd before the Trade Information Committee, Washington, D.C., January 29, 1964, p. 4 (mimeo).

[22]Peter Ellwood, "European Chemical Technology," *Chemical Engineering,* February 10, 1969, p. 113.

[23]*Ibid.,* p. 116.

[24]*Forbes,* May 1, 1968, p. 64.

[25]*Chemical Week,* January 11, 1969, p. 26.

[26]*Chemical and Enginnering News,* November 11, 1968, p. 36.

[27]Michael G. Duerr, "U.S. Foreign Production vs U.S. Exports", *The Conference Board Record,* December 1968, p. 42.

[28]For an analysis of the statistical inadequacies of the data available to make international price and cost comparisons see Helen B. Junz and Rudolf R. Rhomberg, "Prices and Export Performance of Industrial Countries, 1953-63," *International Monetary Fund Staff Papers,* July 1965, pp. 230-34. See also Morton Ehrlich and John Hein, *The Competitive Position of United States Exports,* National Industrial Conference Board, New York, 1968, pp. 21-28.

[29]Irving B. Kravis, "Wages and Foreign Trade," *Review of Economics and Statistics,* February 1956, pp. 14-30. See also N. Arnold Tolles assisted by Betti C. Goldwasser, *Labor Costs and International Trade,* Committee for a National Trade Policy, Washington, D.C., 1961, p. 31 and Yale Brozen, "The New Competition—International Markets: How Should We Adapt?," *The Journal of Business,* October 1960, p. 324.

[30]These limitations include: (1) official rates of exchange do not always reflect actual currency values; (2) currency devaluation or upward revaluation; and (3) annual changes in equivalent dollar wage rates may bear little, if any, relation to changes in wages paid in terms of a local currency. From 1956 to 1958, for example, hourly wages in the chemical industry in France *increased* from 2.08 to 2.50 francs or by 20%. Because of the devaluation of the franc, however, the equivalent hourly wage in American currency *declined* from 59 to 51 cents. While this reduction in equivalent dollar wage rates improved the international competitive position of French producers as compared with the United States, to some extent it was offset by an increase in the cost of imported materials.

[31]A study by one large chemical company of its average hourly labor costs in the United States and abroad showed that for operator labor the cost in this country was more than three times as large as in Italy, Germany and the United Kingdom.

[32]C. P. Neidig, "Financial Comparison of World Chemical Companies," *Financial Analysts Journal,* January-February 1968, p. 14.

[33]For one large chemical company the increase was $1.21 an hour from 1959 to 1966.

[34]Neidig, *op. cit.,* p. 14.

[35]A study by Arthur D. Little, Inc., concluded that " . . . many items can be purchased abroad at equivalent or lower prices than in the United States for comparable volume requirements." *The Impact of Proposed U.S. Tariff Changes on Organic Imports,* Report to Synthetic Organic Chemical Manufacturers Association, May, 1962, p. 25. Out of 79 comparisons for 17 raw materials in five other countries, a lower cost to the foreign country was shown in 31 instances, *Ibid.,* p. 26.

[36]James G. Tewksbury, "The Kennedy Round and the Chemical Industry", *Equity Research Associates,* New York, September 1967, p. 11. See also testimony of Carl Gerstacker, chairman of the board of Dow Chemical, "Hearings on Foreign Trade and Tariff Proposals" (1968), *op. cit.,* Part 10, p. 4595.

[37]It has been estimated that a 100 million pound per year ethylene plant cost 85% as much to build in Germany as in the United States; a 200 ton per day nitric acid plant cost 87% as much. General George H. Decker, *Brief Submitted by the Manufacturing Chemists' Association before the Trade Information Committee of the Special Representative for Trade Negotiations,* Washington, D.C., January 21, 1964, p. 27. The Little Report estimated that "for a comparable continuous-process high-volume chemical plant, construction costs in France and the United Kingdom were 90% of U.S. costs, in Germany and Italy were 85%, and in Japan was 80% in 1962." *op. cit.,* p. 23.

[38]Transportation costs are relatively highest for low cost basic chemicals and relatively lowest for higher priced finished chemicals.

[39]William C. Shelton and John H. Chandler, "The Role of Labor Cost in Foreign Trade," *Monthly Labor Review,* May 1963, pp. 485-90.

[40]Theodore R. Gates and Fabian Linden, *Costs and Competition: American Experience Abroad,* Studies in Business Economics No. 73, National Industrial Conference Board, New York, 1961, pp. 207, 218.

[41]The pattern is quite different for Latin America. There, despite sharply lower wage costs, 11 of the 21 observations of chemical products yielded higher total operating costs than in the U.S.

[42]*Request of American Aniline Products, Inc., for Reservation of Synthetic Organic Dyes, Pigments and Intermediates From Trade Agreement Negotiations,* before the United States Tariff Commission, Washington, D.C., January 1964, p. 44, (mimeo).

[43]*Statement by William F. Christopher* before the United States Tariff Commission and the Trade Information Committee, Washington, D.C., January 29, 1964, p. 3.

[44]"The Impact of Proposed U.S. Tariff Changes on Organic Chemical Imports," *op. cit.,* p. 37.

[45]*Ibid.,* p. 41.

[46]Du Pont abandoned production of indigo in 1963. This action was attributed to "increasing foreign competition," *Chemical Week,* September 14, 1963, p. 43.

[47]Total manufacturing cost plus a 10% return on investment in raw materials facilities minus fixed costs. "The Impact of Proposed U.S. Tariff Changes on Organic Chemical Imports," *op. cit.,* p. 45.

[48]*Ibid.,* p. 48.

[49]Arthur D. Little, Inc., *Oil Import Quotas and the U.S. Balance of Payments in Petrochemicals,* Report to the Dow Chemical Company and Monsanto Company, March 1966, p. 74.

[50]Testimony before the House Ways and Means Committee, (1968) *op. cit.,* Part 7, p. 3102.

[51]Testimony of Robert B. Stobaugh, *Ibid.,* Part 10, p. 469.

[52]However, Thomas F. Willers, President of Hooker Chemical Co., has reported "improving energy costs for foreign producers." "The Outlook For Chemicals," An Address before the National Industrial Conference Board 1969 Sales Management Conference, Los Angeles, California, May 8, 1969, p. 8.

[53]William F. Christopher of Hooker has pointed out that "In export markets, prices are encountered lower than normal domestic prices in the exporting country. Marginal costing and incremental income appear to be adequate incentive for foreign producers to market their materials in other countries. Incremental income as an incentive for export sales certainly is not unknown. In such a competition it is clear, however, that the advantage lies with the low-cost producer." Statement before the U.S. Tariff Commission, 1964, *op. cit.,* p. 4. In connection with synthetic fibers in the United Kingdom, it has been pointed out that "Differential pricing policy is generally pursued by exporters of synthetic fibers . . ." D. P. O'Brien, "Patent Protection and Competition in Polyamide and Polyester Fibre Manufacture," *The Journal of Industrial Economics,* Oxford, England, July 1964, p. 229.

[54]Junz and Rhomberg, *op. cit.,* p. 230.

[55]See Irving B. Kravis and Robert E. Lipsey, *Comparative Prices of Nonferrous Metals In International Trade,* Occasional Paper 98, National Bureau of Economic Research, New York, 1966, pp. 1-3.

[56]In March, 1961, the West German mark was revalued upward from 4.2 to the $1 to 4.0 to the $1.

[57]Prices in marks, were 8.0% higher and it took 5% more in dollars to buy a mark.

[58]The French franc was devalued from 350 to 420 to the dollar in August, 1957 and then further devalued to 493 to the dollar in December, 1958. In January, 1960, 100 old francs were converted into one new franc.

[59]Prices rose by 13.2% and it cost an American 85% as much to buy a franc; 113.2 times 85 equals 96.2 or a decline of 3.8%.

[60]International Monetary Fund, *International Financial Statistics,* December 1959, p. 38, June 1966, p. 30, and August 1968, p. 3.

Chapter XII

Tariffs and Non-Tariff Barriers

Tariffs have played a vital role in the establishment of the U.S. chemical industry. The chemical industry has received tariff protection since early in our history.[1] In 1823, duties were increased substantially on the products already covered and protection was extended to a larger group of chemicals. In the 1870's, dyes were made subject both to a specific duty and to an *ad valorem* duty.[2] It has been reported that partly because of this protection at least ten new dye firms were established. In 1883, however, the specific duty was eliminated although the *ad valorem* duty was retained. Within two years, half of the firms in the industry were reported to have failed.[3]

In 1897, the Dingley Act reduced the *ad valorem* duty on coal-tar dyes from 35% to 30%. Although the Payne-Aldrich Tariff raised the duties for many products in 1909, most duties were lowered for chemicals. The rate was cut 50 per cent for finished organic chemicals; 80 of the 97 chemical raw materials were placed on the free list while duties were increased on most of the others.[4]

The Underwood Tariff Act in 1913 reduced many chemical duties; sodium phosphate and potassium cyanide became free goods. However, the duties on cellulose products were raised and a 5% *ad valorem* duty was established for benzene, toluene, xylene, and naphthalene.[5]

Despite the tariff protection, the organic chemicals industry was virtually non-existent in this country prior to World War I. Thus, for example, there were only seven establishments with 528 employees in the wartime vital dye industry.[6] The loss of German supplies, therefore, was a serious blow. German companies had dominated the industry and allegedly engaged in "determined underselling" whenever new competition developed.[7]

To induce an expansion in output in this country, the Revenue Act of 1916, also called the Emergency Tariff of 1916, provided for 15% *ad valorem* duties plus 2-1/2 cents per pound on coal-tar intermediates and duties of 30% *ad valorem*, plus 5 cents per pound for finished products; coal-tar crudes all were duty free. This Act provided protection for a 5 year period, and then the rates were to be reduced 20 per cent annually. It also provided that if, at the end of five years, American companies did not produce at least 60% of any dye or medicinal, the tariff on that product would be eliminated. The U.S. Tariff Commission was established to collect an annual census of coal-tar chemical output in order to carry out this provision.

The combination of these tariffs and the lack of availability of German supplies led to a great growth in the industry in a short period of time. By 1918, 128 companies were producing coal-tar intermediates, 78 companies manufactured dyes, and 31 were making synthetic medicinals.[8]

However, the end of the war brought a renewed threat of competition from Germany. With the recent experience in mind, a consensus quickly developed that the new industry had to be given adequate protection to assure its survival because of its key role in national defense. To give Congress time to enact a permanent law, which was done in 1922, the Dye and Chemical Control Act of 1921 imposed a six month embargo on products "for which a comparable domestic product was available on reasonable terms."[9]

Prior to 1922, the general rule had been that the dutiable value of imports should be determined by the selling price in the country of exportation. Under the new act, for imports of coal-tar products *only,* there was substituted two alternative bases of valuation, namely, American Selling Price for competitive imports and United States value for non-competitive products. Since these dutiable values generally were higher than the foreign value,[10] the effective tariff for coal-tar products was higher than the reported duties indicated. As one observer has pointed out:

> "The avowed policy of building an American dye industry after World War I required for its implementation substantial protection without effecting a complete embargo. Inasmuch as chemical using and processing industries required essential chemicals not available in this country the valuation methods adopted made it possible to import the items listed . . . on the basis of United States value in the absence of comparable domestically produced products"[11]

Although the Smoot-Hawley Tariff Act in 1930 raised many tariffs, the duties on coal-tar intermediates, dyes and chemicals generally were not changed; the American Selling Price was retained in that law.

Since 1934, American policy has been directed to a progressive lowering of tariff barriers. In that year, the Trade Agreements Act authorized the President to negotiate reductions of up to 50% in prevailing duties by agreements with other countries. Reductions negotiated with any country were to be extended to other countries with which the U. S. had most favored nation agreements. Chemical tariffs were reduced along with tariffs on other products.

By 1945 the maximum reductions in tariffs permitted under the 1934 Act generally had been effected and Congress enacted a new law under which tariffs could be reduced an additional 50% below the January 1, 1945 levels.

In 1955, additional rate reductions up to 15 per cent of the 1955 level were authorized over a three year period. In addition, any *ad valorem* rates which were above 50 per cent could be reduced to that level. Then in 1958, an additional reduction of 20% from the July 1, 1958 level was authorized. Finally, the Trade Expansion Act of 1962 permitted further reductions in tariffs of 50% (the so-called Kennedy Round).

The role of tariffs is markedly different for heavy chemicals and for the various organics. For heavy chemicals relative labor costs are low but relatively high transportation charges make importing uneconomical. As a result, heavy chemicals are either on the free list or are subject to low duties. In 1954, for example, the average tariff was estimated to be 5.3% for alkalies and chlorine, while there was no tariff for cyclic crudes (benzene, toluene, naphthalene, xylene).

On the other hand, the average tariff has been much higher for organic chemicals. In 1954, the highest average duty was levied on cyclic intermediates (phenol, styrene, phthalic anhydride, chlorobenzene, etc.) for which it averaged 21.4%. For plastics materials the average was 17.1%, for synthetic rubber 10.0%, and for synthetic fibers 15.4%.[12]

Tariff Reductions Since 1934

Under the laws enacted and agreements negotiated since 1934, tariff rates for chemicals and allied products had been reduced by more than 50%.[13] Some typical reductions for chemicals below the tariff levels in effect in 1930 and scheduled reductions under the Kennedy Round are shown in Table XII-1.

TABLE XII-1

Tariff Rates for Selected Chemicals, 1930, and Before and After Kennedy Round

TSUSA Item	Article	1930	Prior to Kennedy Round	1969	1970	1971	1972
427.74	Butyl alcohol (lb.)	6.0¢	2.5¢	2.0¢	1.7¢	1.5¢	1.2¢
415.20	Chlorine (lb.)	25%	10½%	8.0%	7.0%	6.0%	5.0%
427.88	Ethyl alcohol (gal.)	15¢	6¢	4.8¢	4.2¢	3.5¢	3¢
403.40	Phenol (lb.)	3½¢+17%	3½¢+20% (ASP)	2.4¢+13.5%	2.1¢+11.5%	1.8¢+10%	1.5¢+8.5%
416.30	Phosphoric acid (lb.)[1]	2¢	1¢	0.8¢	0.5¢	0.5¢	0.5¢
403.08	Phthalic anhydride (lb.)	2.4¢+14%	7¢+40% (ASP)	1.9¢+11%	1.68¢+9.5%	1.44¢+8%	1.2¢+7%
445.45	Polyvinyl chloride (lb.)	6.0¢+30%	2½¢+12½%	2¢+10%	1.7¢+8.5%	1.5¢+7%	1.25¢+6%
421.08	Sodium hydroxide (caustic soda) (lb.)[1]	¼¢	¼¢	0.2¢	0.15¢	0.15¢	0.1¢
403.10	Styrene (lb.)	2.8¢+18%	7.0¢+45% (ASP)	2.24¢+14%	1.9¢+12.5%	1.65¢+10.5%	1.4¢+9%
446.15	Synthetic rubber (lb.)	20%	6½%	5%	4.5%	3.5%	3.0%
429.42	Trichloroethylene (lb.)[1]	30.0%	7½%	6%	5%	4%	3.5%
428.68	Vinyl acetate (lb.)	6¢+30%	1¼¢+6¼%	1¢+5%	0.87¢+4%	0.75¢+3.5%	0.6¢+3%

Note: Tariff rates shown for phthalic anhydride, phenol, and styrene for 1970, 1971 and 1972 are contingent upon the elimination of ASP. If this is not approved by the Congress, the 1969 rates of duty will remain in effect.

[1] In accordance with general note 3(f) to Schedule XX (Geneva—1967), the rates of duty for this item in the columns headed 1970, 1971, 1972 will become effective unless the European Economic Community and the United Kingdom do not proceed with certain reductions provided for in their respective schedules annexed to the Geneva (1967) Protocol to the GATT. If these two participants do not so proceed, the President shall so proclaim, and the rate of duty in the column headed 1969 will continue in effect unless or until the President proclaims that they have agreed so to proceed.

Source: United States Tariff Commission, *Tariff Schedules of the United States, Annotated, 1969,* TC Publication 272, Washington, D.C., 1969, *passim.*

For coal-tar finished products generally, duties were reduced from 45% of the American Selling Price plus 7 cents a pound to 14% to 22-1/2% of ASP plus 2.4 to 3-1/2 cents a pound. The reductions shown in the table for styrene took place in four steps (1951, 1958, 1962 and 1963), for vinyl acetate in three steps (1939, 1947, and 1958), and for trichloroethylene in three steps.

Between 1934 and 1953, there were similar reductions in duties collected as a percentage of the value of dutiable imports for all merchandise and for chemicals, oils, and paints as is shown below:[14]

	1934	1945	1953
	-----(per cent)-----		
All dutiable imports	24.4	17.9	12.2
Chemicals, oils, and paints	25.1	20.0	12.4

Between 1953 and 1960, the average duty for all dutiable imports recorded only minor changes.[15]

Foreign Tariffs

The average duties on various categories of chemical products in the United States and abroad in 1961 prior to Kennedy Round are shown in Table XII-2. A number of important chemicals are duty free in the United States (e.g. benzene, toluene, calcium chloride, sulfuric acid, and hydrochloric acid.)

It has been reported that in 1961 Japan did not impose tariffs on 13% of the $178.6 million of chemicals and allied products imported from the United States while we permitted 49% of the $18.6 million of imports of these products from Japan to enter this country duty free.[16] The average tariff on dutiable chemical imports from Japan was 15% f.a.s. in the United States as compared with an average of 16.9% c.i.f. by Japan on dutiable chemical imports from the United States.[17]

The development of the Common Market involved significant tariff changes which are disadvantageous to the United States. External tariffs have been equalized[18] for the six Common Market countries. Since varying levels were in effect, the net result was to raise tariffs substantially for important customers such as the three Benelux countries and to some extent for West Germany, while tariffs were lowered for Italy and France. Thus, on balance, these changes were unfavorable to the United States. But an even more important advantage to foreign competitors located within the Common Market has been the gradual elimination of tariffs between the six countries. This favors local producers and diverts business away from companies in other countries. The reduction of tariff rates between Common Market countries has been accompanied by a significant increase in the volume of trade among these countries. Thus, total intra-EEC imports increased from $6,790 million in 1958 to $24,161 million in 1967 or by 256%. In contrast, total imports by these countries from the United States increased from $2,808 million to $5,858 million or by only 107%.[19] The establishment of plants within the Common Market countries by American companies is intended in part to overcome this handicap.

TABLE XII-2

Average Tariffs on Key Chemical Categories, 1961
(tariffs expressed on per cent of value of
dutiable and free goods)

	United States	United Kingdom	Germany	France	Italy	Benelux	Japan
Organic chemicals	19%	23%	9%	24%	18%	5%	20%
Inorganic chemicals	6	20	10	15	9	2	20
Pharmaceuticals	12	10	13	16	18	9	20
Pigments and paints	12	15	10	22	17	6	22
Manufactured fertilizers	0	16	4	1	11	1	0

Source: *Trade Restraints in the Western Community,* Subcommittee on Foreign Economic Policy of the Joint Economic Committee, Washington, D.C., 1961, pp. 6-7.

Note: Average tariff is f.a.s. (free alongside the vessel) for the United States and c.i.f. (cost, insurance, and freight) for all other countries. The latter provides a higher total cost against which a tariff is levied.

The Kennedy Round

The Kennedy Round of tariff negotiations was brought to a conclusion on June 30, 1967 after three years of bargaining by over 50 countries. This was the Sixth Round of Trade Negotiations under the General Agreement on Tariffs and Trade (GATT).

The major results of the Kennedy Round were:

1. Tariff concessions encompassing around $40 billion of trade. The United States granted concessions on $8.5 billion of trade. The lower tariffs are to take place in five equal instalments, between January 1, 1968 and January 1, 1972.

2. Tariff reductions of 50% were made on numerous nonagricultural commodities. Smaller reductions were agreed upon for many additional items. Approximately two-thirds of the lower duties were set on an across-the-board basis (involving such countries and areas as the United States, European Economic Community, Great Britain and Japan) and involved cuts of at least 50%.

3. The reductions for farm products were generally smaller than for non-agricultural items.

For chemical products the agreement had two parts. The first, was an unconditional reduction in the tariffs for numerous chemical products in the U. S. and abroad.

United States tariffs were to be reduced 50 percent on most items with rates above 8 percent and 20 percent on most items with duty rates of 8 percent and below. The reductions were scheduled to be 10% a year starting January 1, 1968. It was estimated that these reductions would average about 43%.

In return the EEC reduced its tariffs by an average of 20%, Japan by 44%, and Switzerland by 49%.

The second part of the chemical package is based upon the elimination of the American Selling Price (ASP) valuation system for benzenoid chemicals. It was to be replaced by the regular valuation methods ("converted rates") established by the U. S. Tariff Commission. "Converted" rates "provide an equivalent amount of duty when applied on the valuation basis normally used for other United States imports." "Converted" rates would generally be reduced, by stages, by 50 percent or to an *ad valorem* equivalent of 20 percent, whichever is lower. Major exceptions to this formula are dyes, duties on which would be reduced to 30 percent rather than 20 percent. The "converted" rates have been severely criticized as involving reductions in tariffs because of the procedures used in converting from the ASP approach to the new rates.[20]

The United States would also reduce the rates that were 8 percent and below which are subject to a 20 percent reduction in the first part of the package by an additional 30 percent. The two stages would result in a combined weighted average cut of 47 percent for all United States chemical tariffs.

In return, EEC chemical tariffs would be reduced to a maximum of 12-1/2% for most items to achieve a combined Kennedy Round reduction of 46%.

Further tariff reductions would also take place in the United Kingdom, Switzerland, Austria, and the Scandinavian countries. The EEC would also modify road-use taxes so as to eliminate discrimination against American-made automobiles.[21]

American Selling Price

When *ad valorem* duties are imposed, the tariff that must be paid by an importer reflects two factors: the tariff rate and the price against which the duty is calculated. Usually, American tariffs are applied to the foreign export value at point of origin. But in some instances a different basis may be used. The American Selling Price (ASP) basis of valuation has been in effect since 1922 for competitive coal-tar (benzenoid) products.[22]

Under ASP, the selling price in the U.S. is ascertained and the duty is then determined based on that price. The duty is a combination of a designated number of cents per pound and an *ad valorem* rate. Based on this combination of rates a dollars and cents duty is calculated and then applied to all imports of that product irrespective of its foreign value.

The use of a value basis other than export values is not unusual. European countries often relate the tariff to the price, including insurance and freight at the point of importation. An *ad valorem* duty applied to such a base necessarily will yield a higher effective tariff than that applied to a price excluding the cost of insurance and freight.[23]

The "arm's length" clause and the "would fetch" clause in the Brussels System as sometimes applied in European countries results in a valuation basis similar to ASP. When the European customs official suspects a close relationship between the importer and U.S. exporter, he may deny the landed cost and choose a valuation equal to or similar to their domestic price.

In 1967, only $82.6 million or 8.6% of total chemicals and related products imports of $963 million in the U.S. were of a type which were eligible for assessment on the ASP basis if competitive; only $43.1 million or 4.5% was designated as competitive and hence subject to ASP treatment. The proportion of imports of benzenoids subject to ASP has increased from 2.0% in 1959 to 4.5% in 1967 as is shown below:[24]

Imports

	All Chemicals and Related Products	All Benzenoid Products Value	% of Total	Competitive Benzenoid Products Value	% of Total
	------(millions)------			(millions)	
1959	$ 874	$ 35.9	4.1%	$17.7	2.0%
1961	726	38.2	5.3	15.0	2.1
1963	701	43.6	6.2	21.2	3.0
1965	769	65.0	8.5	31.0	4.0
1967	963	82.6	8.6	43.1	4.5
1968	1,135	107.3	9.5	NA	NA

NA-Not Available

Of the total imports in 1967, $28.2 million were intermediates, $23.4 million were dyes and azoics, and the balance was other finished benzenoids.[25]

The ASP basis of valuation does not apply to all benzenoids. Thus there is no tariff on benzenoid crudes or on benzenoid elastomers or synthetic rubbers. Nor does ASP apply to benzenoids produced from natural animal or vegetable products. In the categories affected by ASP, it does not apply to noncompetitive products. For such noncompetitive products, United States value is used. This is derived by subtracting from the wholesale price of the product in this country most of the expenses incurred in importing and selling it.

Imports of benzenoid products have usually involved very large numbers of products with relatively small volume. From year to year the mix of imports changes dramatically. Thus "of 2,400 items imported in 1963, about 1,350 were items of a type that had not been imported in 1961. On the other hand, there were about 1,600 items which had been imported in 1961, but were not imported in 1963."[26] Such dramatic changes in the mix of imports have accentuated the problem of valuing them and of determining whether or not they are competitive with American products.

The U.S. Tariff Commission reports the relative importance of competitive and noncompetitive items each year. In 1966 about half of the total value of benzenoid imports was classified as competitive. Thus, the ASP basis of valuation was used for less than 5% of the value of imports of chemicals and related products; the ratio in the preceding years was similar.

Exports of benzenoids are many times as large as imports. In 1966, the total was estimated to be about $600 million or almost 7 times the volume of imports. This was more than 15% of the total benzenoid sales in that year. The exports of benzenoids consist largely of mass produced tonnage items such as styrene, phenol and synthetic resins. In contrast, most of the benzenoid imports are dyes, intermediates, and pharmaceuticals.

ASP for many domestic products will tend to be higher than the invoice value of an imported item—often by a significant margin. According to a study by SOCMA:

"Of the 51 intermediates for which reliable foreign price information is available, foreign producers have a competitive price advantage on 28 products—after paying shipping and insurance costs and U.S. duty. Of the 51 products, U.S. manufacturers had a price advantage on only 17, with U.S. and foreign prices virtually equal on 6 others."[27]

Thus, for many products the tariff will be higher on the ASP basis than when determined by the relationship to prices at point of origin. For example, if the *ad valorem* duty is 25%, the ASP 40 cents a pound, and cost at the point of origin is 20 cents, the tariff will be 10 cents when based on ASP and only 5 cents when based on point of origin cost. The net effect of use of ASP, therefore, is to raise the effective rate on the products to which it is applied. The arguments which have been advanced in favor of ASP include:

1. To give greater protection to coal-tar chemicals because they are basic to many other products and are vital to our national defense. Many of these products are particularly susceptible to foreign competition because they are produced in small quantities and hence cannot develop large increases in productivity as an offset to materially lower foreign wages and labor costs. Nevertheless, because of the benzenoid definition , ASP also applies to large-volume products such as phtahalic anhydride, styrene, and phenol.

2. According to the Synthetic Organic Chemical Manufacturers Association (SOCMA): "Because of the nature of the molecular structure of benzenoid chemicals it is necessary to produce and to sell all of a series of benzenoid co-products, all of which may not be in demand, with the result that some products provide the bulk of the income and others are available at extremely low prices." The importation of a key co-product at low prices could break the "necessary economic balance and make an entire line of products uneconomical."

3. The relatively large advantage in productivity held by American companies may be non-existent for products which are made in small "batches", such as many dyes and fine chemicals, and hence do not benefit from the economies of mass production and continuous processing. The batch process has been described as follows:

> "In this type of chemical manufacturing, the basic chemical raw materials to be processed are subjected to a variety of physical and chemical changes, carried out consecutively in equipment suited for bringing about the desired change, such as kettles, vats, autoclaves, grinding and pulverizing mills, filter presses, cooling tanks, ovens and driers. . .

> "Unlike continuous processing of high volume chemicals, where relatively few production workers are required, batch processing depends upon the skilled labor and judgment of chemists and technicians to set up the batch by 'charging' the equipment with the precise amounts of raw materials, setting the conditions for the chemical and physical changes to be achieved, and controlling the reactions and processing, so that the chemical synthesis or physical change does not go beyond the stage required at each step in the processing cycle."[28]

A special study found that for organic intermediates labor costs accounted for 41% of total costs for products made by batch process as against only 22% for those made by continuous process.[29]

Lower wages abroad for such products are more significant in terms of unit costs than for the commodity type chemicals where the application of large amounts of capital and continuous processing reduce the relative importance of labor and make possible large increases in output per man-hour. Of course, it must also be recognized that the batch process products are high cost chemicals which often sell for $1 or more per pound in contrast to basic chemicals which sell for 2 to 5 cents a pound and intermediates which range from 4 to 15 cents a pound.

Crayton Black has stated that ". . . foreign producers can make most benzenoid chemicals much cheaper than we can. The more sophisticated the chemical the greater the advantage since these, in general, are batch produced, high labor content products. We have collected a great deal of data on foreign prices in third countries. In most instances these are much lower than our prices and frequently, are below our costs."[30]

4. It is often difficult to determine overseas prices because price schedules are not published and because prices vary widely among countries. According to J. E. Hull there are:

". . . no dependable foreign price data covering any of the 1,200 commercially important dyes and thousands of intermediates now dutiable under the American Selling Price provision . . . if the products were dutiable on foreign values, foreign producers would be in a position to manipulate the values for duty purposes."[31]

Thus, low values might be used to obtain lower effective tariffs. Dumping is facilitated under these conditions. U.S. based subsidiaries of foreign companies also can benefit by importing materials at low cost from their parent companies. These problems are overcome by use of ASP.

The arguments advanced against ASP include the following:

1. The use of ASP creates a great deal of uncertainty for the foreign exporter because he "cannot know at the time he signs a contract or ships the product whether it will be subject to ASP, or what the ASP will be until it has passed through our Customs."[32] Importers also face delays in clearing customs while these problems are being resolved. Moreover, the importer sometimes doesn't know at the time of the shipment whether or not the product will be declared to be competitive when it arrives here and hence subject to ASP valuations. Although importers can obtain pre-importation rulings, they are reluctant to do so.

Several proposals have been made by SOCMA to correct the foregoing criticisms of the administrative procedures: (1) have U.S. producers file prices quarterly with the Customs officials, (2) Customs should announce the competitive status of imports in advance, and (3) an arbitration board of experts should be established to determine the competitive nature of imports.[33] These proposals are offered to eliminate some of the uncertainty that may surround the ASP basis of valuation.

2. ASP also is criticized as being inconsistent with the General Agreement on Trade and Tariff (GATT) which provides that "The value for customs purposes of imported merchandise should be based on the actual value of the imported merchandises. . . ," (Art. VII. Sec. 2 (a)) Accordingly, it is claimed that this method of valuation should be abandoned. If this is done and the special valuations used in Europe also are abandoned, the valuations would be on a uniform basis in all the affected countries.

3. The use of ASP clearly establishes a much higher tariff than indicated by the rates levied alone. According to Ambassador Roth ". . . the system clearly disguises the degree of protection it provides. There is no way of knowing how high rates can go. . . ."[34] Moreover, because of the method used to determine ASP, one importer has pointed out that "any rise in domestic prices raises the cost of imports. Thus, the direct effect of a domestic inflation would be to raise the level of protection."[35] During such a period, the tariff in cents per pound increases but as a percentage of costs decreases.

4. It is also charged that "when there are relatively few producers any ability to set or vary prices becomes under the ASP system the further ability to

determine a product's own level of tariff protection. This, in turn, can further restrain competition, both domestically and internationally."[36] In support of this statement a study was prepared which showed that in 1966, 2,282 out of 3,910 ASP products were produced by one firm, 654 by two firms, 330 by three firms, and 644 by more than three firms. Thus, three quarters of the products were produced by only one or two firms.[37] Of course, it must be recognized that domestic prices are set at a level which is justified by market conditions not at levels designed to increase "tariff protection."

Foreign producers have been very critical of this basis of valuation because it limits their opportunities in the American market both for existing products and for some new products.

Benzenoids accounted for $3.8 billion in shipments in 1966 or about 10% of the American chemical market. Imports of these products were $88 million or slightly more than 2% of benzenoid shipments. The volume of imports subject to ASP was equal to a little more than 1% of total shipments of benzenoids.

The insistence of foreign negotiators upon the elimination of ASP and the fact that the entire Kennedy Round almost foundered on this issue suggest that overseas producers expect to increase their sales of these products significantly in the U.S. market. The fact that more than half of the 50% cut in chemical tariffs abroad was held back pending the abandonment of ASP also supports this conclusion. It gives support to the expressed concern of American producers that imports will make great inroads in the American market. Whether foreign producers hope that the claimed blow to domestic research will give them future advantages in the timing and frequency of new product development is not clear. But this, too, could be a factor. By the vehemence on both sides it appears that the stakes are high.

Effect of Tariffs

How effective have the tariffs been in holding down imports of chemical products into this country? A study by Arthur D. Little, Inc. concluded they have been a major factor for organic chemicals:

> ". . . with no tariffs, many items can be landed in the United States at a cost competitive with U.S. producers. Taking into account the factors which tend to inhibit import opportunities, and recognizing the cost differentials that exist, we estimate that organic chemical imports could reach a level of about 10% of annual sales; this compares with a current import volume of 2% of industry turnover. Some categories such as dyes, flavouring and perfume chemicals and other highly upgraded products should show even higher potential losses. Secondary effects from import competition with organic chemical end products, such as raincoats made from vinyl plastic or textile fabrics of synthetic fiber, could increase the total impact of imports on the U.S. organic chemical industry to 20% of sales volume."[38]

These estimates suggest that the pre-Kennedy Round tariffs prevented a veritable flood of imports of organic chemicals. The Little Report recognized that part of the projected increase in imports might be supplied by U.S. producers with factories in Europe and Japan. As is noted in Chapter XIII, such sales in the U.S. are now relatively unimportant. However, these companies "could play an important role in expanding exports to the United States since they have direct access to U.S. consumers through established marketing organizations."[39] Thus, the loss in volume to U.S. companies would be smaller than the projected increase in imports. Nevertheless, an increase in imports of chemical products regardless of the source, without a compensating increase in exports of chemicals or other products, would aggravate our balance of payments problem which already is precarious.

The impact of such tariff changes would vary among companies because of differences in the product mix. Those companies with a larger proportion of products subject to import competition would be hurt while those with greater interest in products demanded abroad would benefit.

The competitive pattern of chemicals in the United States market may be affected by foreign competition and the tariffs designed to limit it. Two types of pressures may be distinguished: (1) the competition of foreign products in the United States market and (2) the increasing supplies available here when our exports are reduced because foreign capacity is expanded (displaced exports).

That large sections of the chemical industry have not been directly affected by foreign supplies is suggested by the overall trend of foreign trade in chemicals. Both imports and exports have expanded markedly in the postwar years with the dollar volume of total exports outstripping total imports by a wide margin.

Tariffs have not prevented the development of excess capacity and intensive competition for many of these products in the American market with the accompanying downward pressure on prices.[40] For some products, foreign supplies have affected the domestic market directly. Among the products for which imports have played a role are methylene chloride, acrylic fiber, sodium bichromate, citric acid, phosphorus, perchlorethylene, polyvinyl alcohol, ferrochrome, and trichlorethylene.

Reichhold Chemicals Inc. discontinued melamine production because "lower prices of imported melamine make competitive production impractical."[41] In 1968, Monsanto stated it had discontinued producing H-acid, a dye intermediate, caffeine, and cyclamates due to import competition.[42]

The expansion of capacity in foreign countries also may create competitive pressures in our market. This is particularly so when our exports of the affected product are reduced thus increasing the supply that must be sold in the domestic market. As a result of a large expansion in foreign capacity, for example, phenol exports as a percent of production declined from 7.6% in 1956 to 1.5% in 1962. A similar situation has developed for other products.

Foreign competition affects the American market to varying degrees for different chemical products. That tariffs have not permitted American producers to avoid intense competition is evident from the experience with various plastics, resins, and synthetic fibers. American producers have built excessive capacity behind these tariff walls with the resulting intense competitive pressures in recent years. It is not clear to what extent this capacity was built because of any illusion of security created by the existence of tariff walls.

Non-Tariff Barriers Abroad

In addition to tariffs, imports into many countries have been surrounded by a variety of onerous restrictions and regulations which act to hamper the free flow of trade and often place American exporters at a disadvantage in countries which are important producers of chemicals; they place all exporters at a disadvantage in third markets. According to the U.S. Department of Commerce "A non-tariff barrier is defined as any law, regulation, policy, or practice of a government, other than the import duty proper, which has a restrictive impact on imports."[43] For many products, the non-tariff measures provide a higher barrier to imports than do tariffs.

The U.S. Department of Commerce has listed the following non-tariff barriers:[44]

A. Customs Law

(1) Regulations governing the right to import

(2) Valuation and appraisement of imported goods

(3) Classification of goods for customs purposes

(4) Marking, labeling, and packaging requirements

(5) Documentary requirements (including consular invoices)

(6) Measures to counteract disruptive marketing practices, e.g., antidumping and countervailing duties

(7) Penalties (for example, fees charged for mistakes on documents)

(8) Fees assessed at customs to cover cost of processing (handling) goods

(9) Administrative exemptions (for example, administrative authority to permit duty-free entry of goods for certain purposes)

(10) Treatment of samples and advertising material

(11) Prohibited and restricted imports

(12) Administration of customs law provisions (delay in processing goods, inadequate or delayed publication of customs information)

B. Other legislation specifically applicable to imports, under which restrictions are applied prior to entry of goods

(1) Taxes

(2) Balance of payments restrictions (including quantitative import restrictions, licensing fees, prior deposit requirements, import surcharges, credit controls on import transactions, multiple exchange rates)

(3) Restrictions imposed to protect individual industries (including measures to protect infant industries)

(4) Taxes applied to imports to compensate for indirect taxes borne by comparable domestic goods (European turnover taxes)

(5) Restrictions applied for national security reasons (other than under Customs Law)

(6) State trading (or the operation of enterprises granted exclusive or special import privileges)

(7) Sanitary regulations (other than under Customs Law)

(8) Food, drug, cosmetic, and pharmaceutical regulations

(9) Patent, trademark and copyright regulations

(10) Shipping and insurance regulations

C. Other legislative and administrative trade barriers

(1) Government purchasing regulations and practices

(2) Domestic price control regulations

(3) Restrictions on the internal sale, distribution and use of products

  (a) Screen quotas and other restrictions affecting motion picture film and television program material
  (b) Specifications, standards, and safety requirements affecting such products as electrical equipment, machinery and automobiles
  (c) Internal taxes that bear more heavily on U.S. goods than on domestic products (for example, automobile taxes in Europe based on horsepower rating)

(4) Restrictions on advertising of goods
(5) Restrictions on display of goods at trade fairs and exhibitions

Import licenses are required in Italy (citric acid and oxide calcium nitrate), Belgium (textile fibers and chemical fertilizers), Brazil (caustic soda and phthalic anhydride), India (all commercial imports), Netherlands (some industrial chemicals, penicillin, artificial textile fibers, fertilizers), and Japan (chemicals and drugs). Argentina, Turkey, Greece and Japan among others require *prior deposits* in local currency. In Great Britain, starting November 27, 1968 importers had to keep half of the value of imports on deposit for six months. *Quantitative restrictions* on imports are in effect in Japan (chemicals and drugs), Turkey (some chemicals, paints and pharmaceuticals), Finland (coal tar distillation products), Austria (antibiotics) and Italy (tetraethyl lead). Some countries like Chile have a complete embargo on imports of some products.

In Finland two state owned companies control imports of fertilizers, in India state trading affects caustic soda, soda ash and fertilizers, and in Tunisia a state owned company imports all pharmaceuticals. *Prior authorization* is required in Peru for many pharmaceuticals. *Health, sanitary and safety regulations* affect imports of pharmaceutical products into France. *Government procurement favors local purchases* in many countries including Belgium, Denmark, and Greece.

Special taxes are levied on imports in many countries including Belgium, the Netherlands, France, West Germany and Italy. These taxes are as high as 25%. *Exchange restrictions* have been in effect in Brazil, Indonesia, Iran, India, and Yugoslavia. India requires the formation of an Indian subsidiary for some products. Sweden has *cumbersome customs procedures.*[45]

A special study of cost of entry in 1965 was made for 14 chemical products.[46] The EEC and UK tariff rates for these products averaged 13.3% as compared with 18.7% in the United States. However, shipping costs,[47] border taxes, c.i.f. valuation, and special taxes applying to specific products in specific countries added 43.2% to the cost of entry into the EEC countries and the United Kingdom as against 17.1% into the U.S. The combined impact of tariffs and nontariff barriers was a cost of 56.5% on U.S. shipments to the EEC and the U.K. as against 35.8% on EEC and U.K. shipments to the U.S. All rates of increase were measured against the selling price in the country of origin.

The difference of 26.1 percentage points for costs other than the tariff reflected primarily the use of c.i.f. methods of valuation and border taxes for the EEC countries and the UK. The use of c.i.f. for levying duties was estimated to yield an average increase of 8.5 percentage points as compared with an f.a.s. base.[48] The balance of the difference reflected largely the impact of border taxes.

W.F. Christopher estimated the impact of the Kennedy Round (both stages) reductions and the planned harmonization of the TVA (tax on value added) at

14.7% on the costs of entry for the same 14 chemicals, While the EEC and UK tariff rate will be reduced to 6.6% and the American tariff rate to 9.3%, the other costs of entry become 49.2% for the EEC and UK and 12.8% for the U.S. The net result is a total cost of entry of 55.8% into the EEC and UK—or about the same as before the tariff cut while the cost of entry into the U.S. declines from 35.8% to 22.1%. In other words, because of the operation of TVA, the cost of entry disadvantage of the U.S. increased from 20.7 percentage points (56.5% - 35.8%) before these adjustments to 33.7 percentage points (55.8% - 22.1%) after the adjustments.[49] Clearly, other barriers are more important in other countries and are greater barriers to trade than tariffs. In the U.S. the reverse is true.

The extent to which border taxes may offset changes in tariffs has been described by Thomas P. Turchan, president of SOCMA, as follows:

> "In Germany, for example, the average chemical tariff is on the order of 12%, and this was reduced by less than 3 percentage points as a result of the Kennedy Round agreement. Yet, even before these 3 percentage points were cut from our costs of entry, the Germans increased their border tax by 6 percentage points. . . As a consequence, it now costs us more to sell in the German chemical market than it did before the Kennedy Round began."[50]

Border taxes are indirect taxes in contrast to income taxes which are direct taxes. Exporters from EEC countries receive a tax remission of such taxes thus improving their competitive cost position in sales to third countries vis à vis U.S. companies who get only minor rebates of sales and excise taxes.

William B. Kelly, Jr. has pointed out that the impact of non-tariff barriers can be significantly increased when tariffs are lowered.

> "Existing nontariff measures that may only marginally affect trade when coupled with tariff protection could become formidable obstacles it tariffs were eliminated or further reduced. More important, in order to compensate domestic producers for loss of tariff protection, it is likely that many nontariff measures, now dormant, would be rigorously applied, new measures introduced, and old ones amended to make them more effective in restricting trade . . . ."[51]

> "Estimates of the trade effects of nontariff barriers must be based in most instances on the educated guesses of commodity or other specialists who have a 'feel' for the subject."[52]

Some nontariff barriers, such as customs regulations, licenses, etc. may create uncertainty because of the difficulty of determining how they will be applied. While the precise impact cannot be measured, it seems probable that these nontariff barriers place obstacles to some exports, add to costs, and in general act as a restraining force on American foreign trade in many countries.

Oil Import Quotas

In 1959, the Mandatory Oil Import Program was established by Presidential Proclamation.[53] The program was intended to "preserve to the greatest extent possible a vigorous, healthy petroleum industry" because of the "requirements of our national security."[54] The quotas apply to imports of crude oil and its products and derivatives.

For purposes of administering the Oil Import Program, three geographical areas have been established;

1. Districts I-IV, encompassing those states east of the Rockies.

2. District V, those states west of the Rockies, plus Alaska and Hawaii.

3. Puerto Rico.

For Districts I-IV allowable imports have been set at 12.2% of domestic production of petroleum and natural gas liquids, although actual imports have sometimes exceeded this level by small amounts.

Import quotas were allocated among petroleum companies until 1966 when small quotas were assigned to petrochemical producers. Increases in the quotas to chemical companies were made in each of the following years. Early in 1969, this part of the oil quota was 77,690 barrels per day[55] as compared with total permitted oil imports of 1,152,412 barrels a day. The quota for each chemical company was equal to 11.2% of its input of these feedstocks—estimated at 693,669 barrels a day.[56]

For the area west of the Rockies, an amount can be imported equal to the difference between estimated production and total demand in that area.

Special provision was made for oil quotas for Puerto Rico and for imports from the Virgin Islands so that refinery and petrochemical complexes could be established in those areas to provide employment opportunities for their inhabitants.

A major effect of the import quotas has been to keep prices of crude oil in this country above the world market price. In 1968, it was estimated that crude oil "averages $1.25 per barrel higher in price in the United States than elsewhere in the world. This is a differential of 3 cents a gallon, or 60 percent above the world price."[57] It has been estimated that "the net cash benefit to the economy from the removal of oil import restrictions might be $2.7 billion annually."[58]

A detailed study by Standard Oil Company (New Jersey) estimated that the oil quota system would cost consumers $3,310 million in 1970. However, a number of offsets aggregating $3,080 million must be considered including taxes of $600 to $800 million received by state and federal governments. The net cost to the economy, therefore, was estimated at $230 million.[59]

Mr. Kenneth H. Hannan, Vice-Chairman of the Board of Union Carbide, has testified that:

". . . raw material costs amount to more than 50 percent of the cost of production of ethylene, the most widely used basic petrochemical. The $1.25 per barrel differential between the price of domestic and foreign crude oil can add about 12 percent to the current price of ethylene and 5% to the cost of polyethylene. This is about equivalent to the 6.7 percent margin of profit on sales earned by the chemical industry in the first quarter of 1969."[60]

On the other hand, a study published by petroleum companies concluded that:

"Even if a differential of 20 percent existed between costs of foreign and domestic petrochemical feedstocks, this hypothetical differential would be reflected only as a difference of generally less than 2 percent of the delivered selling price of the major ethylene derivatives and even less in more highly processed products."[61]

The price of naphtha has been lower overseas[62] because of the lower cost of crude oil and because petroleum is converted primarily into heating oil overseas and hence there is a larger volume of naphtha as a by-product. The end result is a large supply and lower prices. In the United States, on the other hand, petroleum is used mainly to make gasoline. The naphtha by-product is relatively small and thus prices are higher.

However, the major feedstock in the United States is natural gas liquids, the cost of which is competitive with naphtha overseas. Thus, in 1969, the chemical companies were not yet experiencing any significant competitive disadvantage. In addition, it would require further investment to facilitate wide use of naphtha in the United States since the processes now used are based overwhelmingly upon other feedstocks. Nevertheless, concern has been expressed because it is anticipated that the supply of natural gas liquids will not be adequate in the years ahead.[63]

The petrochemical industry uses several feedstocks including ethane, propane, naphtha, and natural gas liquids. However, these feedstocks do not yield the same combinations of petrochemical products. According to an Arthur D. Little study, naphtha yields "a much broader spectrum of products" than other feedstocks. "By cracking naphtha, it is possible to make available at one location most of the key petrochemical raw materials such as ethylene, propylene, butylene, butadiene, benzene, toluene, and xylene."[64]

Although naphtha is not yet a key raw material in this country, "recent technical developments involving 'high severity' cracking of naphtha . . . have made naphtha an attractive raw material for petrochemical production in the future." The study concluded that "Unless the U.S. petrochemical industry has access to key raw materials at world prices, its competitive position will be impaired over the next ten years."[65]

In contrast to these claims, petroleum companies point out:

> "Plants and associated facilities to process naphtha cost more than plants which crack ethane and propane."

> "Traditionally, about a third of the products from naphtha cracking find outlets only in fuels markets.

> "Naphtha cracking results in multiple products, only some of which have ready markets at suitable prices."[66]

To avoid a feedstock cost problem in the future, it has been proposed that restrictions should be modified or removed for oil imports used for the manufacture of petrochemicals so that the full benefit of world-competitive costs can be obtained. This type of liberalization has been vigorously opposed by the petroleum industry which claims it would undermine the entire quota system.

In 1969, President Nixon set up a Cabinet Task Force on Oil Import Control under the chairmanship of George P. Shultz to review U.S. policy in this area.

Summary and Conclusions

Tariffs played a vital role in the development of the American chemical industry, particularly after World War I. However, starting in the early thirties, tariff rates were reduced significantly for chemicals and allied products as well as for other products. By 1960, tariff rates had been cut in half. Despite this reduction, exports continued to exceed imports by an ever-widening margin.

In the Kennedy Round of tariff negotiations, agreement was reached to cut tariffs on chemicals and products here and abroad in two stages. In stage one U.S. tariffs were to be reduced an average of 43% over a five year period starting in 1968, while the EEC cut its tariffs by about 20%. In the second stage, the American Selling Price (ASP) basis of valuation used for benzenoid chemicals was to be eliminated and certain other rates were to be cut; in return further reductions would take place in EEC tariff rates to make the total reduction 46%.

ASP is much higher than the export value at point of origin for many products. The result is a considerably higher effective duty on those products when *ad valorem* rates are used. The elimination of this basis of valuation would reduce considerably the level of effective duties. Although ASP has caused considerable irritation abroad, it actually has affected less than 5% of our imports and a little more than 1% of total shipments of benzenoids.

ASP has been criticized because it provides a value base which often is indefinite and uncertain to the foreign exporter. This problem can be overcome by advance notice of the competitive status of benzenoids and by having domestic producers of the affected products file their prices periodically with Customs officials.

Although ASP is criticized as being inconsistent with GATT, European countries base their tariffs on cost, including insurance and freight (c.i.f.). The use of the c.i.f. increases their effective rates about 10% over the level which would apply to export value at point of origin. And this basis of valuation applies to practically all imports in contrast to the relatively small volume subject to ASP. In defense of ASP it is emphasized that the affected products are vital to national defense, they are produced in small batches and hence involve high labor costs and low productivity gains, and their overseas prices are difficult to determine.

The United States is not alone in providing tariff protection to its chemical industry. The organization of the Common Market with its uniform external tariff operates to the disadvantage of American exporters because it raised the tariff for the Benelux countries and West Germany, important purchasers of U.S. chemicals and allied products, and created a six country tariff-free area for producers located in those countries.

Other trade tariff barriers also act to restrict the flow of American exports of chemicals and related products. Import licenses, required prior deposits in local currency, taxes, quantitative restrictions, exchange restrictions, and other measures have placed obstacles to our exports and add to their cost abroad.

These measures may provide a higher barrier to imports than do tariffs. Such measures add much more to the cost of entry abroad than they do to entry into the United States. Programs to encourage the flow of trade must include modification or elimination of non-tariff barriers as well as tariffs.

An important trade barrier in the United States is the oil import quota system. The quotas, which have been adopted for reasons of national defense, have added to the cost of petroleum in the United States. This is particularly important to the chemical industry because it cuts off low cost raw materials from abroad and hence is expected by the industry to affect the relative competitive position of the industry in sales overseas in the future.

---

[1] In 1789, revenue tariffs were levied on gun powder and indigo. Williams Haynes, *American Chemical Industry*, D. Van Nostrand Company, Inc., New York, 1954, Volume 1, p. 434.

[2] A specific duty is levied in terms of cents per unit while an *ad valorem* duty is levied as a percentage of some designated value.

[3] Haynes, *op. cit.,* p. 311.

[4] *Ibid*, Volume II, p. 11.

[5] *Ibid.,* pp. 13, 128.

⁶U.S. Tariff Commission, *Census of Dyes and Coal-Tar Chemicals, 1917,* Tariff Information Series No. 6, Washington, D.C., 1918, p. 41.

⁷Synthetic Organic Chemical Manufacturers Assocation, *Trade, Strength and Security,* prepared for the Commission on Foreign Economic Policy, December 1953, pp. 71-72.

⁸U.S. Tariff Commission, *Census of Dyes and Coal-Tar Chemicals, 1918,* Tariff Information Series No. 11, Washington, D.C., 1919, p. 11.

⁹"Trade, Strength, and Security," *op. cit.,* pp. 77-83.

¹⁰The American Selling Price was "the price at which a *comparable domestic article* is freely offered to all purchasers in the principal market of the United States. United States value was the price at which the *imported merchandise* is offered for sale in the principal market in the United States, less duty, transportation costs, insurance, commissions and other expenses and an allowance for profit." Percy W. Bidwell, *What The Tariff Means To American Industries,* Harper and Brothers, New York, 1956, p. 189.

¹¹R. Elberton Smith, *Customs Valuation in the United States,* University of Chicago Press, Chicago, Illinois, 1948, p. 227.

¹²Beatrice N. Vaccara, *Employment and Output in Protected Manufacturing Industries,* The Brookings Institution, Washington, D.C., 1960, p. 91.

¹³U.S. Congress, House Committee on Ways and Means, *Trade Expansion Act of 1962,* Hearings, Washington, D.C., 1962, p. 3306.

¹⁴The U.S. Tariff Commission has warned that: "These estimates understate tariff levels in 1934 (and therefore understate the reduction since 1934) because they are based on 1952 imports. The ratio of duties collected in 1934 to 1934 duties would be higher than the ratio shown here because 1934 prices were lower than1952 prices." U.S. Tariff Commission estimates reproduced in *United States Commercial Policy; A Program for the 1960's,* Subcommittee on Foreign Economic Policy of the Joint Economic Committee, 87th Cong., 1st Sess., Washington, D.C., 1961, p. 4.

¹⁵"United States Commercial Policy: A Program for the 1960's," *op. cit.,* p. 7.

¹⁶For imports of chemicals and allied products from all countries, 46% were duty free in 1961. This total included items "which were specially exempted from duty such as imports by the U.S. Government," "Chemical and Rubber Industry," *Chemical and Rubber,* May 1962, p. 8.

¹⁷*Tariffs in United States, - Japan Trade, A Comparative Analysis,* United States - Japan Trade Council, Washington, D.C., 1964, pp. 4, 9.

¹⁸In calculating the new average tariff, the average for the EEC was raised by considering member countries with no tariff as having a tariff of 3%.

¹⁹Statistical Office of the European Communities, *The Common Market: Ten Years On,* Brussels, May 30, 1968, pp. 58, 60.

²⁰"Converted" rates have been criticized because (1) they are set at a given point in time and hence do not provide protection equivalent to ASP under which the rates change as the price changes, (2) "the quantity and the reliability of the data used for making the conversion are insufficient to provide a reliable statistical base," (3) "a substantial portion of U.S. import transactions are between related companies . . . [and] do not represent arms-length transactions" thus making it possible for them "to control the basis of valuation," (4) because competitive and noncompetitive products were put into the same "basket" for 27 TSUS items thus treating unlike situations as being the same (for example, for all dyes the converted rate was 48% but if competitive dyes had been treated separately the rate would have been 72%). (5) because of their nature export value provides an "unreliable basis of valuation for benzenoid chemicals." Testimony of Robert C. Barnard representing SOCMA, House Ways and Means Committee, *Foreign Trade and Tariff Proposals* (1968), 90th Cong., 2nd Sess., Washington, D.C., 1968, part 10, pp. 4519-22 and William F. Christopher, chairman of the Society of Plastics Industry Tariff Committee, "Kennedy Round Agreement on Chemicals and Plastics," August 10, 1967, pp. 4-5 (mimeo).

[21]Office of the Special Representative for Trade Negotiations, "General Agreement on Tariffs and Trade, 1964-67 Trade Conference," *Report on United States Negotiations*, Volume 1, pp. 173-76.

[22]It is also used for rubber soled footwear, low priced wool knit gloves and mittens, and clams, except razor clams.

[23]It has been estimated that the EEC method of c.i.f. valuation results in a duty of 11% higher than the use of f.o.b. valuation. Committee for Economic Development, *Comparative Tariffs and Trade*, Supplementary Paper, No. 14, Vol. 1, March 1963, p. XIII. This is a little lower than the 17% cost of insurance and freight included in U.S. imports of chemicals and related products in 1964. U.S. Tariff Commission, *C.I.F. Value of U.S. Imports*, February 7, 1967, p. 9 (mimeo).

[24]*U.S. Tariff Commission, Imports of Coal Tar Products, 1959*, Washington, D.C., 1960, pp. 7, 27-28; *Imports of Coal Tar Products, 1961*, 1962, pp. 7, 32, 33; *Imports of Coal Tar Products, 1963*, 1964, pp. 4, 27-28; *Imports of Benzenoid Chemicals and Products, 1965*, Washington, D.C., 1966, pp. 4, 26-27; *Imports of Benzenoid Chemicals and Products, 1967*, 1968, pp. 4, 25-26.

[25]"Imports of Benzenoid Chemicals and Products," *op. cit.*, pp. 5, 24.

[26]Yale L. Meltzer, *Chemical Guide to GATT, The Kennedy Round and International Trade*, Noyes Development Corporation, Park Ridge, N.J., 1968, p. 139.

[27]Synthetic Organic Chemical Manufacturers Association, *American Selling Price — The Illusory Trade Barrier*, New York, 1964.

[28]*Request of American Aniline Products, Inc., for Reservation of Synthetic Organic Dyes, Pigments and Intermediates From Trade Agreement Negotiations*, before the United States Tariff Commission, Washington, D.C., January 1964, pp. 3, 4 (mimeo).

[29]Crayton K. Black, *Memorandum of the Synthetic Organic Chemical Manufacturers Association of the United States In Opposition to Further Reductions in Existing Rates of Duty*, before the United States Tariff Commission, Washington, D.C., February 13, 1964, p. 21.

[30]Crayton K. Black, "A U. S. Producer Looks At Foreign Competition," *Chemical Engineering Progress*, January 1967, p. 39.

[31]J.E. Hull, "The United States Chemical Industry and Import Competition," *Foreign Trade Policy, Compendium of Papers on United States Foreign Trade Policy*, Subcommittee on Foreign Trade Policy, House Committee on Ways and Means, 88th Cong., 2nd Sess., Washington, D.C., 1958, p. 1035.

[32]Roth, *op. cit.*, pp. 471, 473.

[33]*Chemical and Engineering News*, February 10, 1964, p. 28.

[34]Roth, *op. cit.*, p. 470

[35]Hans Lautenschlager, "A Chemical Importer Views the Competition," *Chemical Engineering Progress*, January 1967, p. 34.

[36]Roth, *op. cit.*, p. 471.

[37]Hearings on "Foreign Trade and Tariff Proposals," *op. cit.*, Part 2, p. 601.

[38]Arthur D. Little, Inc., *The Impact of Proposed U.S. Tariff Changes on Organic Chemical Imports*, Report to Synthetic Organic Chemical Manufacturers Association, May 1962, p. 2.

[39]*Ibid.*, p. 54.

[40]In December 1968 the wholesale price indexes for organic chemicals and for plastics were 12.4% and 19.5% respectively below the 1957-59 average.

[41]*The Journal of Commerce*, August 22, 1968.

[42]Testimony of John Gillis, vice president Monsanto, Hearings on "Foreign Trade and Tariff Proposals," *op. cit.,* part 10, p. 4622.

[43]Cited in Lewis E. Lloyd, "The Economics of International Trade," *Ward's Quarterly,* Detroit, Michigan, 1968, p. 19.

[44]Reproduced in Lloyd, *op. cit.,* pp. 19-21.

[45]For a more complete list of the non-tariff barriers in 74 countries see General George H. Decker, *Brief Submitted by the Manufacturing Chemists' Association, Inc.* before the Trade Information Committee of the Special Representative for Trade Negotiations, Washington, D.C., January 21, 1964, Appendix I and "Hearings on Foreign Trade and Tariff Proposals," *op. cit.,* Part 1, pp. 123-307.

[46]The study was based on fourteen chemical products for which price and trade data were available: phosphoric acid, caustic soda, zinc oxide, titanium dioxide, soda ash, sodium cyanide, hydrogen peroxide, styrene monomer, ethylene glycol, phenol, acetone, vinyl acetate, phthalic anhydride, and ammonium sulfate. In 1964 these products accounted for $115.9 million of U.S. exports to the countries studied and $10.6 million of U.S. imports from them. While the fourteen products are not a scientifically representative sample of all chemical products, the data illustrate the great effect of c.i.f. valuation and border tax adjustments on costs of entry. *Comparative Cost of Entry Into United States and European Chemical Markets,* Horace J. dePodwin Associates, Inc., February 1966, p. 3.

[47]For the purposes of the study shipping and insurance costs were assumed to be the same in both directions so that differences in the total cost of entry reflect tariffs and non-tariff barriers. *Ibid.,* p. 20. However, shipping costs to the United States are much lower than shipping costs from the United States. See William F. Christopher, "Trade Barriers Against American Industrial Exports To Europe", an address before the Conference on Tariffs and Other Barriers to European-American Trade sponsored by the Federal Bar Association and Georgetown University Law Center, Washington, D.C., November 8, 1963, pp. 9-10.

[48]"Comparative Cost of Entry Into United States and European Chemical Markets," *op. cit.,* p. 8.

[49]Testimony of William F. Christopher, Hearings on "Foreign Trade and Tariff Proposals," *op. cit.,* Part 7, pp. 3107-8.

[50]*U.S. Trade Policy and the American Chemical Industry,* an address before the Chemical Marketing Research Association, New York City, May 3, 1968, p. 6, (mimeo).

[51]William B. Kelly, Jr., "Nontariff Barriers," in *Studies in Trade Liberalization,* edited by Bela Balassa, The Johns Hopkins Press, Baltimore, Maryland, 1967, p. 315.

[52]*Ibid.,* p. 317.

[53]*Proclamation 3279,* March 10, 1959.

[54]*Proclamation 3693,* December 10, 1965.

[55]This quota reflected a policy adopted by the Secretaries of Commerce and Interior to have two sectors of the oil import program—one for energy and one for petrochemicals. One objective of the program was to make sure that exports were not hampered by high-non-competitive feedstock costs.

[56]*Chemical Week,* February 15, 1969, p. 19.

[57]Statement by Herman K. Intemann, vice president of Union Carbide Corp., "Hearings on Foreign Trade and Tariff Proposals", *op. cit.,* Part 9, p. 4333. The differential was the same in the Spring of 1969. Monsanto Company, *1969 First-Quarter and Annual Meeting Report,* May 2, 1969, p. 5. See also, *The Petrochemical Industry and Oil Import Controls,* published by a group of chemical companies, March, 1969, p. 7.

[58]Statement by John H. Lichtblau before the Senate Subcommittee on Anti-trust and Monopoly, April 2, 1969, p. 12 (mimeo).

[59]*Response to Inquiry of Cabinet Task Force on Oil Import Control,* July 14, 1969, pp. 29-31.

[60]Testimony before Antitrust and Monopoly Subcommittee, Senate Judiciary Committee, July 22, 1969, p. 7 (mimeo).

[61]*Petrochemical Feedstocks and the Oil Import Program,* published by a group of petroleum companies, June 1969, p. 11.

[62]Early in 1969, the price of naphtha was 5 to 6 cents a gallon in Europe as compared with 8 to 9 cents in the United States. *Fortune,* April 1969, p. 162.

[63]Hannan, *op. cit.,* p. 5.

[64]Arthur D. Little, Inc., *Oil Import Quotas and the U.S. Balance of Payments in Petrochemicals,* Report to the Dow Chemical Company and Monsanto Company, March 1966, p. 5.

[65]*Ibid.,* p. 1.

[66]"Petrochemical Feedstocks and the Oil Import Program," *op. cit.,* p. 17.

Chapter XIII

Internationalization of the Chemical Industry

A major economic development during the 1960s has been the internationalization of industry. As Edward Littlejohn has observed: "The jet plane and electronic communications have created the world market, and the international company of many nationalities is there to serve it. It serves that market with capital resources, with technology, with management skills."[1] The result has been the multi-national company.

A number of large companies have had foreign subsidiaries for many years.[2] However, international investment has grown at a tremendous rate, particularly since the organization of the Common Market. Considerable public attention has been given to the American investments in Europe.[3] But the Organisation for Economic Co-operative Development (OECD) has estimated that worldwide direct foreign investments as of 1968 were $85 billion and that European and Japanese companies accounted for $31 billion of the total.[4]

Investment across national boundaries is not confined to Europe. The U.S. Department of Commerce reports that at the end of 1967, direct foreign investments in the U.S., amounted to almost $10 billion.[5] But as *Fortune* has pointed out this total ". . . understates the situation, since it is based on book value rather than current market value, and it encompasses only those U.S. corporations in which a foreign stockholder owns at least 25 percent of the common voting stock."[6] Investment across borders has become an important activity of large companies in all the major industrial countries.[7] And American companies have been playing an increasingly important role in this area.

Participation in the international market requires significant changes in attitudes toward foreign markets by American companies. Two Union Carbide officials have emphasized:

> ". . . *the absolute necessity of going global in their planning and operations.* The effects are apparent wherever one looks—in the frequent reorganization of international departments—in the significant changes in the self-image of corporations including name changes. In the past, most of our large chemical companies looked upon themselves as United States corporations with significant operations scattered around the world. The self-image is rapidly becoming one of multi-national chemical companies whose headquarters happen to be in the United States. Changes in names are reflecting the change in self-image. One large corporation recently dropped the appendage "-of America" from its name to eliminate this implied limitation. The global push is increased by competitive pressures at home and abroad. . . ."[8] (italics added).

Not only are the sellers becoming international but their customers are also moving in this direction. Monte C. Throdahl and Onnik S. Tuygil of Monsanto have noted:

> ". . . the basic chemical industry to which they are closely linked, are growing outside the United States, through subsidiaries, joint ventures, or acquisitions. They, too, are going through the throes of meeting the challenge posed by doing business on a world-wide scale. . . .
>
> "In fact, more and more often an overseas subsidiary wants to know specifically which product or service the parent company supplies to the

parent of a customer of theirs. The worldwide supplier is now meeting the international customer, whose requirements of supply, service and back-up are essentially the same outside the U.S. as inside."[9]

"The new breed of international customers, with their sophistication and instant communication systems, will deal only with suppliers who are equally sophisticated and fast on their feet. European and Japanese competitors have practiced the fine art of doing business on a world scale for many years, and many, particularly the Japanese, are now able to offer services which cannot be matched by most American-based companies. We must find some way of providing counterpart services within our free-enterprose system if we are to compete with these companies."[10]

As Thomas F. Willers, president of Hooker Chemical has concluded: "The successful firms will have truly developed an international perspective. Large firms will optimize on a world-wide scale."[11]

American chemical companies have been investing heavily abroad while to a lesser extent foreign chemical companies have been investing in this country as well as in others. The world market in which these multi-national companies are seeking to participate is an enormous one. In 1965, the value of world chemical output was estimated at $115 billion and in 1968 at $150 billion.[12]

American participation abroad is either by establishment of foreign plants, participation in joint ventures, or by licensing foreign companies to produce or to sell their products or processes. A National Industrial Conference Board Report has concluded that "exporting, licensing and direct investment are accepted as compatible and complementary ways of developing foreign markets."[13] The extent of activities in each of these areas and the reasons for the method used are reviewed as well as the trend of sales from overseas plants and their relationship to exports from this country. The growth of investments in the United States by foreign chemical companies also is examined. Although foreign chemical companies also have been investing in other countries, the extent of such investments has not been reviewed.

Foreign Investments by American Chemical Companies

American companies have made very substantial investments in plants they have opened in foreign countries during the post-World War II period. Foreign plants have been financed by (1) transfer of capital from the United States, (2) reinvestment of earnings from foreign operations, (3) reinvestment of depreciation reserves, and, since the imposition of controls on foreign investments, (4) by selling securities abroad. Historically, the main sources of financing have been through outflows of capital from the United States[14] and reinvestment of overseas earnings.

Companies often first probe the magnitude of foreign potential with exports[15] or by licensing foreign producers to sell their products. For all American manufacturing companies, total direct investments increased from $3,831 million in 1950 to $16,861 million in 1964, or by 440%. Chemicals and allied products companies have participated very extensively in this development with an increase from $512 million in 1950 to $3,068 million in 1964 or 599%. (See Table XIII-1)

Separate data for total direct investments abroad have not been published for chemicals and allied products by the U.S. Department of Commerce since 1964. However, data for annual expenditures for plant and equipment abroad show

TABLE XIII-1

Total Direct Investment Abroad: All Manufacturing and Chemicals and Allied Products, Selected Years, 1929-1964

	All Manufacturing	Chemicals and Allied Products	Per Cent of Total
	(millions)		
1929	$ 1,813	$ 138	7.6
1936	1,710	205	12.0
1940	1,926	221	11.5
1950	3,831	512	13.4
1957	8,009	1,378	17.2
1959	9,707	1,661	17.1
1960	11,152	1,902	17.1
1961	11,997	2,059	17.2
1962	13,250	2,260	17.1
1963	14,937	2,605	17.4
1964	16,861	3,068	18.2

Sources: Samuel Pizer and Frederick Cutler, *U.S. Business Investments in Foreign Countries.* A Supplement to the Survey of Current Business, Washington, D.C., 1960, p. 96; *Survey of Current Business,* September 1960, p. 22; August 1961, p. 24; August 1964, p. 13; September 1965, p. 27.

that direct investment in chemicals and allied products has continued to expand very markedly.

The gross new investment overseas in plant and equipment was $3,096 million in the three years 1965 to 1967 (see Table XIII-2) or an amount greater than the total foreign direct investment in chemicals and allied products at the end of 1964. Because of depreciation, the net increase in direct investment is smaller than the gross expenditures for new plant and equipment. Thus, in the six year period 1959-1964, new plant and equipment spending abroad aggregated $2,094 million but total direct investments increased by only $1,407 million or about two-thirds as much. If the same ratio prevailed in the 1965-1967 period, the net increase in direct investment would have been $2,081 million to a total of about $5.2 billion.[16]

Between the end of 1964 and 1967, direct investments abroad in all manufacturing industries increased by $7,263 million. In the three year period, chemicals and allied products accounted for 23.8% of expenditures for new plant and equipment in all manufacturing industries. If this same ratio is applied to the increase in direct investments, the total for chemicals and allied products would have increased by $1,729 million to about $4.8 billion.

For the three years 1965 to 1967, the capital outflow from the United States reported for chemicals and allied products aggregated $1,204 million.[17] In the preceding three years the total direct investment abroad increased by $1,009 million, (See Table XIII-1) while the capital outflow was $579 million, or 57.4% as large. If the same ratio prevailed in the 1965-1967 period, an increase of $2.1 billion in direct investments would be indicated.

These rough estimates suggest that by the end of 1967, the total direct investment overseas in chemicals and allied products was in the neighborhood of $5 billion. With plant and equipment expenditures of $1,318 million, a further large increase in the total direct investment took place in 1968. By 1969, total direct investments abroad probably exceeded $6 billion.

TABLE XIII-2

Annual Plant and Equipment Expenditures Abroad: All Manufacturing and Chemicals and Allied Products, 1957-1968

	All Manufacturing	Chemicals and Allied Products	Per Cent Chemicals of All Manufacturing
	(millions)		
1957	$1,347	$ 234	17.4
1958	1,180	261	22.1
1959	1,141	216	18.9
1960	1,337	237	17.7
1961	1,697	278	16.4
1962	1,941	308	15.9
1963	2,153	436	20.3
1964	3,007	619	20.6
1965	3,884	861	22.2
1966	4,583	1,040	22.7
1967	4,510	1,195	26.5
1968 (est.)	4,443	1,318	29.7

Source: House Ways and Means Committee, *Foreign Trade and Tariff Proposals,* Part 2, June 5 and 10, 1968, Washington, D.C., 1968, p. 547 and U.S. Department of Commerce, *Plant and Equipment Expenditures By Foreign Affiliates of U.S. Corporations,* Washington, D.C., March 25, 1969, pp. 5-6.

In addition, a large number of American companies which are not generally classified primarily as chemical in nature—such as petroleum companies—have made substantial investments in chemicals and allied products abroad so that the total direct investment is greater than the total cited above.

Of the total direct investment in foreign affiliates held by chemicals and allied products companies at the end of 1964, 33% was invested in Canada, 35% in Europe, and 22% in Latin America; only small amounts were invested in Africa, Asia and Oceania.[18]

This geographic pattern was similar to that for all American direct investments overseas. Europe reached first place as a result of the large investments in the 1955-65 decade; in 1955 Europe accounted for only 15% of our total direct investments overseas. Several factors combined to stimulate large scale investments in Europe: (1) the formation of the Common Market, (2) the removal of exchange controls for non-residents, and (3) the sharp rate of economic growth which resulted in markedly expanded consumer demand. Many of the new direct investments were made in the Common Market countries but expansion also was rapid in the United Kingdom and the other European countries.[19]

Plant and Equipment Expenditures

Annual expenditures for new plant and equipment by foreign affiliates and subsidiaries of American companies[20] have been increasing rapidly since 1959. For all manufacturing industries, the total increased from $1,141 million in 1959 to $4,443 million in 1968, or by 289%; for chemicals and allied products the total increased from $216 million to $1,318 million or by 510%.[21]

In 1968, the estimated expenditures for plant and equipment by chemicals and allied products were distributed among major geographical areas as follows:[22]

	millions
Canada	$ 166
Latin America	198
Common Market	319
Other European	235
Other areas	400
	$1,318

Investments overseas are used in part to establish new facilities and in part to expand existing ones. Between January 1961 and December 1967, American companies divided their activity as follows:[23]

	New Establishments	Expansion
Chemicals and allied products	645	240
Rubber and plastic products	87	46
All American companies	4,441	1,262

For chemicals and allied products a major portion of the activity was devoted to setting up new establishments. However, expansion of existing plants also was undertaken in many instances.

Sales by Overseas Plants

Sales by foreign affiliates have increased sharply as new plants have been established and as the volume in the older ones has expanded. Between 1957 and 1967, their sales of chemicals and allied products increased from $2,411 million to $9,000 million. Apparently this has been a much more rapid increase than the sales by the foreign affiliates of all manufacturing companies.[24]

Most of these sales are made within the foreign country in which the plant is established. Thus, out of $6,851 million in sales of chemicals and allied products by affiliates of American companies in 1965, $5,767 million or 87.1% were made locally. Only $171 million of their sales or 2.2% of the total represented exports to the United States. Most of this latter total was from plants in Canada.[25]

Total sales by American owned chemicals and allied products plants abroad have been rising more rapidly than exports of these products from the United States. (See Table XIII-3) Between 1957 and 1965, sales by foreign affiliates increased by about $4.4 billion or 180% while exports of these products from the United States increased by about $1 billion or 71%. Between 1965 and 1967, sales by U.S. plants abroad increased by about $2 billion or 30% while exports of chemicals and allied products from the United States rose by about $400 million or 17%.

In 1967, foreign sales by American companies (exports plus sales by overseas affiliates) were almost $12 billion as compared with domestic sales of $39.4 billion.[26] Clearly, overseas business has become of great importance to American chemical companies and further increases seem probable.

Foreign affiliates can play an important role in exports from the United States. A special study of the 1965 experience by the U.S. Department of Commerce showed that for the reporting companies with exports of $8.5 billion, $4.4 billion

TABLE XIII-3

Chemicals and Allied Products: Sales by American-Owned Plants Abroad and Exports From the United States, Selected Years, 1957-1967

	Sales by U.S. Plants Abroad	Exports from the United States	Total
	(millions)		
1957	$2,411	$1,376	$ 3,787
1959	2,950	1,558	4,508
1961	3,890	1,789	5,679
1963	5,130	2,009	7,139
1965	6,851	2,402	9,253
1967	9,000	2,803	11,803

Source: House Ways and Means Committee, *Foreign Trade and Tariff Proposals,* Part 2, June 5 and 10, 1968, Washington, D.C., 1968, p. 548.

or slightly more than half, was made through foreign affiliates. The chemical industry was among those which "channeled a large share of their exports through affiliates." For chemicals and allied products $756 million out of $1,468 million in exports by reporting companies was through affiliates; for chemicals alone the record was $611 million out of $1,256 million.[27]

Du Pont has reported that its overseas operations have stimulated its exports from this country.[28] Similarly, Hercules has reported ". . . exports tend to increase upon the announcement of a new [overseas] plant . . . . Often our overseas plants do not make a complete line of products . . . Usually, a Hercules foreign plant will supply the bulk of the products required in that country, but our customers also require specialty chemicals that are produced only here in the United States. The customers' need for a broad range of chemicals leads to increased exports from the United States."[29]

General George H. Decker, then president of the Manufacturing Chemists Association, testified in 1969 that "Over two-thirds of the exports of some chemical companies are shipped to their overseas affiliates. These exports involve raw materials, intermediates, and certain other materials marketed directly by these affiliated companies."[30]

Foreign plants usually produce a limited number of products. Yet the physical presence of the plant combined with company controlled sales and service efforts, storage facilities, and on the spot publicity probably facilitate the sale of the company's other products. The net result can be an expansion of American exports in many instances.

However, the experience of a single company or of a single industry gives only a part of the story. Direct investments overseas contribute to the rate of growth in the countries in which they are made. The accompanying rise in incomes creates opportunities for American companies in other industries to increase their exports. While it is impossible to determine all the effects of overseas direct investments on our foreign trade, it is important to keep these indirect benefits in mind.

Factors Affecting Investments Abroad

Investments abroad have been stimulated by a variety of factors including:[31] the desire to operate inside foreign tariff walls and thus equalize position with local producers, large profits available, desire to participate in growth abroad, provide an outlet for intermediate chemicals, relatively lower costs of production abroad, and because frequent interruptions to shipping from the United States add to costs and disrupt service.

Lammot du Pont Copeland, formerly President of Du Pont, has described the situation requiring foreign investments as follows:

> "We would much prefer to serve world markets from our United States plants. But this choice is governed to a large extent by factors out of our control. In the developed markets, the success of an export program sometimes leads to a level of business which justifies local manufacture, and customers become increasingly insistent on a local source of supply. Since there are other potential producers in each of our product lines, a competitor will build a plant there if we don't. In the developing countries, there are other factors—close government control of the economy which closes the border to imports when the first local producer is established, plus tariffs and other trade restrictions.
>
> *"The point is that the export business in both these areas will be lost in any event. But if we build a plant there, we lose the market to ourselves"* [32] (italics added).

Purchasers desire short lines of supply and on occasion nations restrict imports after a local supplier has been established. Thus, as an export market increases in size, the exporter must build a plant within the country or the market will go to the company that does construct one.

Investment has been particularly attracted to countries that have had an above-average rate of growth. This has been noticeably important "for American capital going to Europe, because the level of European incomes is now such that consumers are demanding the kinds of products which Americans like to produce and for which long experience has given U.S. manufacturers a comparative advantage."[33]

Investments in Japan have been limited because prior to 1967, foreign companies could not establish plants nor could they control more than 50% of a joint venture. In 1967, these restrictions were modified and guidelines were issued providing automatic approval for participation in joint ventures in Japan. Up to 50% could be invested by foreign companies in projects to produce the following chemicals and allied products: ammonia fertilizers, caustic soda, agricultural chemicals, vinyl chloride, medical and pharmaceutical products other than biological agents, and synthetic fiber spinning. In 1969, there was added to this list plastics derived from phenol, urea, and melamine and cellophane. Foreign companies may invest up to 100% in rayon and monosodium glutamate.[34]

However, in an examination of joint ventures, published under Japanese auspices, Herbert Glazer has stated "At the risk of oversimplifying, one may say that any foreign investment that directly or by implication carries management participation or control with it is not welcome in Japan."[35]

As against these advantages, a number of problems must be considered. An American company operating overseas must be concerned with a wide variety of local laws and customs with which it may not be familiar. In many countries it faces formidable local companies including some which are owned by the government (e.g. France and Italy)[36] Relationships with local governments often can be difficult and require considerable skill in communication. Periodically, anti-American campaigns develop which can lead to expropriation of American companies and their nationalization as experience in Cuba, Mexico, Peru, and other countries has demonstrated. Alternatively, it may place restrictions upon new investments thus holding down growth rate. Canada provides a recent illustration of this latter development after having been very hospitable to American investments for many years.

The South American experience with rampant and chronic inflation reflects another type of problem which adds to the risk involved in overseas investment. This has affected the magnitude and value of returns on investment and the ability to remit dividends to the United States. A closely related problem is that of foreign exchange control which limits the amount of funds that can be withdrawn from a country. The movement of funds into a country often can be readily undertaken but their withdrawal may become another matter. Similarly, devaluation of a currency may result in significant losses as became evident when the English pound was devalued from $2.80 to $2.40 in November 1967.

Another problem area is that of obtaining an adequate supply of local skilled labor and management talent. Countries vary widely in the degree of education of their citizens with the developing countries ranking particularly low in this respect. Staffing may thus be a difficult problem.

Not all overseas ventures are successful. Early in 1969, it was reported that Union Carbide had sold its interest in a joint venture in Sicily.[37] Celanese reported it was selling SIACE, its Sicilian affiliate, and British Paints, a United Kingdom affiliate. Both had been losing propositions.[38]

Pfizer reported that in 1968 it had discontinued production of plastics and related lines in the United Kingdom, Europe, and Brazil.[39]

After reviewing its foreign investments "with the objective of moving out of those where profit potential was determined to be below acceptable levels and writing down certain other investments to better reflect current values," Allied Chemical sold an Australian nylon plant and "action was taken to sell a Costa Rican oil refinery, and investments in various European and South African operations were written down."[40]

As the volume of overseas investment increases, the risks will become greater as competition intensifies and as more projects become marginal in their profit opportunities.

Controls Over Foreign Investments Since 1964

The free flow of capital abroad was inhibited as a result of programs adopted to redress the large and continuing deficit in our international balance of payments. In September 1964, an Interest Equalization Tax (IET) was adopted to reduce foreign portfolio investments by Americans. The act was retroactive to mid-1963 and provided for a graduated tax ranging from 1.05% to 15% on acquisition of debt on or before January 25, 1967. From January 26 through August 29, 1967, the tax ranged from 1.58% to 22.5%; starting August 30, 1967, the rate became 1.31% to 18.75% and on April 5, 1969, it was reduced to 0.79% to 11.25%. The tax on purchases of foreign stocks was 15% prior to January 26, 1967 when it was increased to 22.5%; on August 30, 1967, the rate became 18.75% and on April 5, 1969 it was cut to 11.25% It succeeded in lowering substantially the sale of foreign issues in this market[41] and in reducing the foreign portfolio investments held by Americans.

In February 1965, "voluntary" programs were put into operation to reduce the flow of funds for investment in overseas plants. About 500 large corporations with substantial direct investments abroad were asked to curtail new capital outflows for this purpose. In addition, they were informed it would be most helpful if they would depend on foreign financing for a larger share of their investments and if they would increase the return flow of dividends to this country. Late in 1965, these companies were asked to limit capital outflow plus reinvested earnings to 135% of the 1962-64 annual average. The net outflow of private capital declined significantly between 1964 and 1965, particularly, the movement of short-term capital.[42]

This program did not bring about the desired improvements in our balance of payments. Accordingly, in December 1965 new measures were adopted to contain further the outflows for direct investment abroad. The number of corporations affected was increased to about 900. They were asked to hold their combined 1965 and 1966 direct investment outflows to certain countries to a maximum of 90% of the total to those areas in 1962-1964; this two year period was equivalent to 135% of the annual average in the three earlier years. "A joint target was set for the years 1965 and 1966 in order not to penalize firms which had cut back in 1965, and in order to seek greater restraint by those which had invested more heavily that year."[43]

In December 1966, the suggested annual ceiling on direct investment plus overseas retained earnings for 1966-1967 was cut to 120% of the 1962-1964 average.

In January 1968, the voluntary program was made mandatory by an Executive Order issued by the President of the United States and the number of companies affected was increased to about 3,200. A moratorium was placed on new capital outflows to Western Europe and reinvestment of overseas earnings was limited to a maximum of 35% of the average total foreign direct investment in 1965 and 1966. For other developed countries—Canada, Japan, United Kingdom, Australia, and a few others—the maximum permitted was 65% of the annual average capital outflow plus reinvested earnings in 1965-1966. For less developed countries the ceiling was 110% of the average in 1965-1966.[44] In addition, companies had to repatriate earnings on overseas investments—the greater of the percentage repatriated in the years 1964 to 1966 or the amount in excess of permitted direct investment. However, a "minimum investment allowable" of $200,000 was permitted for new overseas investors and small companies. Short term financial assets held abroad had to be reduced to and held at the 1965-1966 average.[45] Direct foreign investments were reduced dramatically from $3.7 billion in 1967 to $1.5 billion in 1968 or "well under the 1968 target ceiling of $2.7 billion."[46] Since many companies did not use their full quota of direct investments in 1968, there was a "considerable backlog of unexpended foreign-borrowed funds and a substantial carry-forward of investment allowables from 1968 into 1969."[47]

In April 1969, the controls were relaxed effective January 1, 1969 so that companies were permitted an alternative method of computing their allowable investments, namely, 30% of their 1968 foreign earnings. In addition, the amount exempted from control was raised to $1 million and quarterly reporting requirements were abandoned for those companies. Special adjustments were also made for extractive industries and airlines. It was estimated that these changes theoretically would permit an increase of $400 million in direct investments overseas to a total of $3.35 billion.[48]

The U.S. Department of Commerce concluded that the decline in net capital outflow in 1967 was due in part to this voluntary program which "had a clear impact on foreign borrowing by U.S. companies to finance their foreign investments."[49]

There has been a sharp rise in foreign security placements in the Euro-bond market by companies incorporated in the United States:[50]

	millions
July-December 1965	$197
1966	600
1967	450

The sale of $450 million in securities in 1967 compared with capital outflow of $3,020 million and reinvested earnings of $1,578 million for direct investment in that year. Sales of securities abroad increased very substantially to $2.1 billion in 1968[51] after the mandatory controls went into effect and accounted for a larger proportion of direct investments than in earlier years.

Among the American chemical and allied products companies which have sold securities in the Euro-bond market are the following:[52]

Company	Date	Amount
		(millions)
Monsanto International Finance Co.	October 1965	$25
Du Pont Europa Holdings S.A.	October 1965	25
W. R. Grace Overseas Development Corp.	November 1965	20
Bristol-Myers International Finance	December 1965	20
Warner Lambert International Capital	February 1966	15
W. R. Grace Overseas Development Corp.	March 1966	15
Du Pont Europa Holdings S.A.	February 1967	25
Dow Chemical Overseas Capital Corp.	March 1967	11.4
Celanese International Finance Corp.	June 1967	20
Union Carbide International Capital Corp.	July 1967	50
Du Pont Europa Overseas Capital Corp.	October 1967	13.7
Revlon International Finance Corp.	May 1968	26
Miles International	June 1968	15
Warner-Lambert Overseas, Inc.	August 1968	20
Norwich Overseas, Inc.	December 1968	26

In addition, a number of rubber and oil companies, which are actively involved in the chemical industry, sold securities abroad. This large volume of overseas borrowing resulted in increasing the debt burden of many companies. The Acting Director of the Program stated early in 1969 that "We are aware of the rising debt-equity ratios of some companies which may soon reach a dangerous point . . . there is a foreseeable time when reliance on foreign debt to finance direct investment may no longer be an acceptable solution."[53]

Similarly, General G. H. Decker has pointed out that as a result of the control program, chemical companies have been "required . . . to take certain financial actions which are unsound from a business viewpoint and which otherwise would not have been taken. These include foreign borrowing at rates higher than in the U.S. and restricting of trade credits to foreign affiliates."[54] General Decker also reported "The excessive costs and time—clerical, accounting, financial, and executive—required to meet the periodic reporting requirements of the Office of Foreign Direct Investments and the time and costs required to prepare, submit, and defend specific authorizations impose a heavy burden on corporate management and prevent prompt, flexible responses to opportunities in the marketplace."[55]

The control program was designed to meet a short term balance of payments problem. But it could only do so at the expense of our long term balance of payments. The direct investment which is aborted today results in the loss of the reverse flow of interest and dividends tomorrow. Such investments are made when it is expected they will be profitable. One of the strong components of the balance of payments is the return flow of direct investment income which was about $3 billion in 1968. When the required funds are obtained overseas, the income earned will remain overseas. The price of any gains achieved in the short run, therefore, are self-defeating in the long run.

The program also acts to hold down exports. A U.S. Department of Commerce study reported that "U.S. manufacturing affiliates abroad generate a large market for U.S. exports which might be difficult to obtain in the same magnitude by other means. Excluding aircraft and automobile companies, the manufacturers interviewed for this study projected approximately one-half of their exports to their own affiliates."[56] Manufacturers "projected exports as about 2% less in 1973 on the assumption of continued controls."[57]

One price of any gains achieved in the balance of payments in the short run, therefore, is a smaller net inflow in the long run.

Joint Ventures

The use of joint ventures at the international level has increased substantially in recent years. Since 1957 a large number of companies in all manufacturing and in chemicals and allied products have been established as joint ventures by American and foreign concerns, either on a 50-50 ownership basis or, on occasion, with majority control in the hands of the overseas enterprise. The joint venture permits a combination of the products and mass marketing techniques of the American concerns and the intimate knowledge of the local market by the foreign firm.[58]

As Herbert Brownell has pointed out: "in the highly organized business economy of Western Europe, a United States business may prosper faster and more enduringly, if it can call on a local concern's knowledge and experience and, perhaps, its facilities."[59]

Under some circumstances, political considerations have necessitated that an American firm take in local citizens or partners. This is the only way that government approval will be forthcoming in such nations as Indonesia and Iraq. In some other countries, it is vital to create an image of local ownership or discriminatory legislation may be enacted. For example, Austral-Pacific Fertilizers Ltd. was organized in 1967 by Dow, Swift & Co., and local partners to market and produce nitrogenous fertilizers.[60]

Most joint ventures abroad have been started because of the resources that the local enterprise possesses in terms of experience, sales organization, facilities, and/or money. Sometimes, it is very difficult for an American concern to establish a plant in a foreign land. Thus, Monsanto pointed out that its establishment in Belgium would have taken a minimum of one more year to start without local investment. Mr. Onnik S. Tuygil, managing director of the joint venture, stated that the Belgians "helped us select the factory site, introduced us to government officials at all levels, assisted us with local building codes, and helped to establish union relations and hire people."[61]

Some Illustrations

Tennessee Eastman Company (a division of Eastman Kodak) and Chemische Werke Huels A. G. (West Germany) formed a joint venture, Fraserwerke Huels Gmb H., to manufacture and sell polyester fiber for the European textile market.

It was indicated that the new company "will bring together the long fiber experience of Tennessee Eastman and the well known chemical skill of Chemische Werke Huels and will bring to the textile industry in Europe an outstanding polyester fiber to meet the growing quality and quantity demands of the market. . . . "[62]

Other joint ventures include:

Pittsburgh Plate Glass with Rumianca, S.p.A of Italy to manufacture perchloroethylene, trichloroethylene, ethylene dichloride and glycerine by techniques developed by the American firm's chemical division.[63]

Hooker Chemical and Sumitomo Bakelite of Japan to manufacture industrial phenolic resin.[64]

Du Pont and Showa Neoprene, K.K. of Japan for the manufacture of neoprene synthetic rubber as well as acetal resins.[65]

National Petrochemical Co. of Iran and B. F. Goodrich to build Iran's first polyvinyl chloride plant and its first dodecyl benzene plant.[66]

Asahi-Dow Ltd. in Japan to produce acrylonitrile-butadiene-styrene (ABS) resins, styrene-butadiene latex, styrene monomer and other products.[67]

Petroquimica-Dow S.A. in Chile (30% owned by Petroquimica, a state owned corporation) in 1967 to produce vinyl chloride, polyethylene, and polyvinyl chloride.[68]

Konam, N. V. (Celanese and Koninklijke Zout-Ketzen N. V.) in The Netherlands produces acetic acid, vinyl acetate, formaldehyde, methanol and other products.[69]

Airco and the British Oxygen Company formed Airco/BOC "to design, construct and market throughout the world, air separation plants and other low temperature process equipment."[70]

Stauffer Chemical and Farbwerke Hoechst A. G. formed Stauffer-Hoescht to produce rigid (unplasticized) vinyl film and sheeting.[71]

Allied Chemical and National Petrochemical Company of Iran formed Shahpur Chemical Company, Ltd. to produce sulfuric acid, urea, ammonia, phosphoric acid and various fertilizer products.[72]

The diversity of joint ventures into which American chemical companies have increasingly entered indicates the ever-growing role of such types of operations throughout the world. Practically every chemical company, including the smaller ones,[73] has participated in joint ventures to some extent and some have done so to a major degree.

Foreign chemical companies also are involved in many joint ventures. It has been reported that "The European and Japanese chemical companies have been involved in more joint ventures than have the American chemical companies—this is especially true in France where Rhone Poulenc, for example, has at least 65 joint ventures."[74] Many of these joint ventures involve only foreign companies. (e.g. Bayer and British Petroleum, BASF and Shell).

Some Problems

Several financial and legal problems may arise in connection with joint ventures. The Chairman of the Federal Trade Commission, Paul Rand Dixon, has implied that our antitrust laws should be applied to foreign joint ventures. In his words:

" . . . it appears to be a particularly common practice for American companies to channel their activities into joint enterprises when they move abroad . . . . The claim is made that restraint of trade, if any, is confined exclusively to foreign countries and thus is beyond the jurisdiction of our antitrust laws. Again the implicit assumption is that the togetherness of joint ventures has rigidly defined boundaries; that corporations may stand as one in foreign countries or markets, but that within the territorial confines of the United States, they are vigorous rivals in the competitive struggle. This is an interesting matter for speculation, but what is needed to determine the answer are detailed facts of events and behavior."[75]

In the Imperial Chemical Industries case (1952), the court struck down joint ownership arrangements on the ground that they were established to implement a cartel agreement for the sharing of markets.[76]

If the partners have different philosophies toward expansion and the utilization of profits, problems may develop. For example, the American concerns that begin operations in overseas markets may desire to reinvest all of the profits in plant expansion, yet the foreign owners may prefer to receive dividends.

Despite the potential problems, joint ventures have proved to be a valuable approach to overseas investments. The blending of the financial resources and the technical skills of the partners has yielded substantial benefits. American firms have been able to participate in rapidly growing markets through the use of the joint venture.

Licensing Foreign Companies

A third method of participating in overseas markets is to license foreign companies to produce or to sell American products. It has been reported that " . . . foreign licensing is considerably more prevalent among U.S. manufacturing companies today [1969] than it was ten years ago." Chemicals and drugs and pharmaceuticals were identified "among the most active licensing groups."[77] There are many advantages to licensing:

It avoids the problems that may be incurred in overseas manufacture.

It permits entry into areas with unstable economies or with a questionable political climate where direct investments would be extremely risky.

It permits entry into smaller markets in which the establishment of a new plant could not be economically justified.

It permits entry into countries where it is difficult for foreigners to establish plants (e.g. India).

It may provide the opportunity to obtain licenses to manufacture in this country products developed abroad.[78]

It provides an opportunity to earn profits which are subject to lower tax rates since royalty income often is subject to lower taxes than profits earned in local plants owned by foreign companies.

It provides an inexpensive method of entering foreign markets because usually no capital must be invested by the American company and thus it is particularly attractive to smaller companies.[79]

It provides a method of testing the demand for these products in foreign markets at little cost.

It has "helped expand U.S. exports through the sale of component parts and complementary products of the U.S. licensor."[80]

On the other hand, it has been pointed out that:

> "The usual independent licensing agreement is confined to a specific process and too frequently does not create a relationship continuing beyond the first contract period, nor does it generally provide a strong foundation for technical flexibility. Further, compensation under licensing agreements is seldom deemed adequate to warrant the licensor's committing a great deal of time or energy to making such technical flexibility possible even if he were willing to do so."[81]

Sometimes licensing agreements precede and lead to the establishment of a joint venture.[82] For example, Wyandotte Chemicals licensed an affiliate of Etablissements Kuhlmann to produce several of its products starting in 1958. Then in 1963, the two companies formed Marles-Kuhlmann-Wyandotte to produce and sell propylene oxide and its derivatives.[83]

An American company also may enter into a joint venture to produce some products and license its foreign partner to produce others. For example, Celanese Corporation and Dainippon Celluloid Company (Daicell) established a company to produce Celcon and acetate film and sheet in Japan. At the same time, Daicell was granted a license to manufacture and to sell cellulose acetate flake and molding powder.[84]

Companies vary in their policies about licensing. It has been reported, for example, that: "Some companies lean heavily toward capital investment abroad (e.g. Dow Chemical), others seem to prefer to license (e.g. Reichhold). Others exhibit no particular preference."[85] In 1967, Union Carbide and Diamond Alkali were reported to have "switched to more liberal licensing policies."[86]

A survey of 16 chemical companies indicated that for products or processes requiring "conventional know-how" (no patent protection), "most companies will license regardless of kind of payment" although "A few insist on like value know-how in exchange." On the other hand, for those involving "unique know-how" (protected by patents and considered to be "significantly better than other processes"), "about half require more than monetary consideration."[87]

American companies license many foreign companies. J. P. Cunningham has reported that:

> "*The recent change of view towards licensing can be attributed first to the increased availability and attractiveness of the opportunities, but also to an appreciation of the constant threat of process obsolescence.* Modern enlightened self-interest, with its emphasis on the time value of money tends to *choose the course with the assured payout* and let the salesman handle the market problems as they occur."[88]

> " . . . Ethylene oxide, one of the earliest U.S. petrochemicals, had been traditionally manufactured from ethylene via ethylene chlorohydrin. As recently as 1961, the market was dominated by this process and by two major producers, although the direct oxidation of ethylene was known to be feasible and economically promising. Five years later, active licensing of the new process had completely altered the situation and a tabulation in *Chemical Week* indicated that of some *50 plants of all types throughout the world, 28 were to be operated by licensees.*"[89] (italics added).

Information concerning the magnitude of licensing generally is not available. A study by Touche, Ross, Bailey and Smart found that "twice as many chemical companies possess licensing agreements as hold capital investments abroad (although many do both) and the license-to-investment ratio is rising."[90] In 1966, Hooker reported it had 23 licenses in 37 countries.[91]

Booz, Allen and Hamilton reported that between January 1961 and December 1967, American companies producing chemicals and allied products concluded 150 agreements which involved "an exchange of proprietary rights with a foreign group"; an additional 45 agreements were made by rubber and plastics companies.[92]

A study of overseas plants built between 1940 and 1966 showed the relatively great importance of licenses.

> For styrene-butadiene rubber, 15 plants were built between 1950 and 1966; three were built by producers who owned licenses and 12 were built to use licenses granted by producers.

> For styrene, 51 plants were built between 1940 and 1966; 17 were built by producers, 20 to use licenses obtained from producers and 14 under licenses granted by engineering development companies.

> For nylon 66, 19 plants were built between 1938 and 1965; 14 were built by producers and 5 to use licenses obtained from producers.

> For nylon 6, 64 plants were built between 1938 and 1965; 1 was built by a producer who owned the license, 15 under licenses obtained from producers, 15 under licenses obtained from engineering firms and 33 under licenses obtained from machinery suppliers and caprolactam producers.[93]

Licensing is one way to capitalize on large scale R and D. It has been estimated that "Licensing fees or 'down' payments for an important process can run into the millions of dollars—a figure which doesn't include royalty payments which are usually based on the quantity of the product produced."[94]

A substantial income is derived from foreign licenses. Data compiled by the U.S. Department of Commerce show that receipts of royalties and license fees from abroad increased "from around $378 million in 1957 to an estimated $786 million in 1967." Total receipts in 1967 were derived as follows:[95]

	millions
Independent foreign firms	$347.7
Subsidiaries, affiliates and branches	438.0
Total	$785.7

It was estimated that total earnings from foreign licensing was more than $800 million in 1968 "with more than half of the income flowing from licenses to overseas affiliates."[96]

For royalties alone, it was estimated in 1965 that the United States earned about $140 million a year and paid out about $70 million. Projections for 1970 estimated receipts of $300 million and payments of $200 million.[97]

Data are not available to indicate the income derived by the chemical industry from licensing. However, some data have been made available for Imperial Chemical Industries. In 1965, ICI earned $37.8 million from patents and licenses. *Fortune* reported that " . . . The real lessons from ICI's experience with polyethylene and Terylene are that licensing only builds the foreign competition; such major breakthroughs are exceedingly rare. The new policy is to develop as many new products as possible—and exploit their uniqueness single-handedly."[98] In 1968, Sir Peter Allen, Chairman of ICI reported: "We have . . . earned about 40 million pounds [$96 million] so far out of polyethylene licenses and 'Terylene' has earned nearly as much in this way."[99]

Foreign Chemical Companies in the United States

The flow of capital has not been a one way street. The U.S. Department of Commerce has been seeking to encourage investments by foreign companies by its "Invest in the U.S." program.

> "This program is designed to provide contacts between U.S. companies and foreign investors for the purpose of promoting joint ventures, licensing agreements, and other types of investment in the United States. The program seeks to attract foreign investment in new U.S. plants and licenses from foreign firms to manufacture in the United States products that are now being imported."[100]

Foreign chemical companies have invested substantial sums in plants in the United States and have participated in many joint ventures in this country. A special study of foreign investments in the United States concluded that "Chemicals and related products have been a major field for investment for many years . . . ." In 1959, total direct investments in these industries were estimated at $465 million or about one-fifth of the total foreign investment in manufacturing industries in this country.[101] Earnings on this investment were $37 million.[102]

The total foreign investment in chemical plants in the United States was estimated at $921 million in 1963.[103] and at "approximately $2.5 billion" in 1968.[104] Robert B. Stobaugh, Jr. has reported that " . . . investment by foreign chemical companies in the United States is much higher in dye manufacturing than in other areas."[105] Similarly, SOCMA has reported that in dyes "foreign producers accounted for almost 30% of the total number of dyes produced in the United States by only one firm, almost 10% of the number of pigments produced by only one firm, and almost 12% of the total number of intermediates by only one firm."[106]

According to Du Pont: "Either through subsidiaries or through joint companies involving U.S. partners [foreign companies] participate in about 18 per cent of U.S. [non-cellulosic] fiber production."[107] In mid-1969, Dow Badische "brought onstream two 30-million-lbs. per year parallel production lines under one roof at Anderson, S.C.—one for polyester, the other for nylon-6." This development was described as a "gaint step" establishing the company as a "major factor" in the textiles fiber industry.[108]

Neidig has reported that " . . . U.S. ethical drug sales, exclusive of the hospital market, of Hoffman La Roche, a Swiss Company, are over $130 million [in 1966] ranking third behind only Lilly and Merck . . . . Other prominent European companies in the U.S. pharmaceutical market include: Ciba (14th largest), Geigy (22nd largest), Burroughs Wellcome (24th largest) and Sandoz (26th largest).[109]

Appendix Table 37 lists 48 foreign companies which *Fortune* identified as being involved in the chemical industry. A comprehensive study published in *Chemical Week* showed that 24 of these large foreign firms had a financial interest in companies in the United States. Table XIII-4 indicates the number of U.S. chemical companies in which these large overseas based companies have an interest.

TABLE XIII-4
Number of Companies Owned In United States By Foreign Firms: Chemicals and Allied Products, 1968

Country of Parent Company	Number of Companies	
	100% Owned	Less Than 100% Interest
Britain	9	8
West Germany	14	6
Canada	4	0
Netherlands	14	8
France	3	5
Switzerland	6	1
Belgium	2	0
Total	52	28

Source: Derived from *Chemical Week,* August 17, 1968, pp. 105-109.

These 24 foreign companies owned completely or had a substantial interest in 80 American companies. In addition, a number of chemical companies in this country are owned by large foreign firms not identified by *Fortune* as being in the chemical business (e.g. American Petrofina) or by smaller overseas companies. The total involvement in this country by overseas companies undoubtedly is greater than suggested above because there is no way to gather a complete list of such investments. Japanese[110] and Italian chemical companies are the only ones which have not sought to operate in the United States on any significant scale. Excluding those two countries, each of the ten largest overseas chemical companies has an interest in one or more companies in the United States.

Some of the foreign controlled companies are quite large.

Shell Chemical Company is a subsidiary of Shell Oil which is 69% owned by the Royal Dutch-Shell group (Britain and Netherlands). Shell Chemicals' sales in 1968 were $513 million.

American Petrofina which ranked 382 in the *Fortune* list of 500 largest industrials with sales of $185 million in 1967 is 64% owned by Petrofina (Belgium).

Lever Brothers which ranked 195 in 1967 with sales of $440 million is controlled by Unilever (Britain and Netherlands).

Beecham Inc., which had sales of $67 million in fiscal 1968, is controlled by the Beecham group (Britain).[111]

BASF Corporation, which had sales of $30 million in 1968, is 100% owned by Badische Anilin & Soda-Fabrik (Germany)[112] It was reported that BASF invested $40 million in the U.S. in 1967 and $35 million in 1968 and expected to invest $35 million in 1969.[113]

It has been pointed out that: "Hundreds of foreign companies have U.S. firms acting as their sales agents or representatives in this country, but these operations are not considered a part of the direct capital investment structure."[114]

Investments in the United States have been made by establishing wholly owned subsidiaries, by acquiring an existing firm, and by participating in a joint venture with an American company. Sometimes the plant has been financed with assistance from government units in this country.[115]

Many foreign companies have participated in joint ventures in the United States. Imperial Chemical Industries, for example, joined with Celanese in forming Fiber Industries, an important producer of synthetic fibers. Phillips Fibers is owned equally by Rhone-Poulenc (France) and Phillips Petroleum, Stauffer Hoechst Polymer by Stauffer and Farbwerke Hoechst (Germany), and Columbia Nitrogen by PPG Industries (51%) and Dutch State Mines (Netherlands).

Monsanto sold its 50% interest in Mobay to its partner Farbenfabriken Bayer (Germany) in 1967 after the Justice Department started a civil antitrust suit. Similarly, Pittsburgh Coke & Chemical sold out its half interest in Chemagro to Bayer its partner.

Investments in the United States have been motivated by the same reasons that have attracted U.S. companies to invest abroad: (1) the desire to combine foreign technological know-how with American experience in marketing;[116] (2) foreign companies with funds to invest have wanted to participate in the large American market and have concluded that the best way to do so was by producing in this country; (3) a desire to participate in the internationalization of the chemical industry;[117] (4) a desire to learn more about American operations and marketing methods.[118]

Summary and Conclusions

During the post-World War II period, the internationalization of chemical companies has been proceeding at a rapid pace. Activity by American companies overseas has been expanding steadily and is reflected in the significant annual increases in the volume of new investments, in licensing agreements, and in joint ventures. In 1969 direct investments probably passed $6 billion, exclusive of those made by petroleum companies. That overseas investments may be risky was illustrated by the large losses reported by several American companies when they withdrew from some foreign markets. The imposition of controls over foreign investments has acted to curtail the outflow of capital from the United States but has been offset to a large extent by increased borrowing abroad. The rising debt-equity ratios resulting from foreign borrowing became a matter of concern. As often happens, voluntary controls were replaced by mandatory controls which were extended to more companies and made more rigorous until a small start was made toward relaxing them early in 1969. While these controls help our balance of payments in the short run, they result in a smaller inflow of funds over the longer period.

Sales of American owned foreign plants—mainly in the countries in which located—have been increasing far more rapidly and are more than three times as large as chemical exports from the United States. Exports plus overseas production combined are equal to almost one-third of domestic shipments. Accordingly, the need to coordinate export sales from the United States and overseas operations has become increasingly important. As a result, officials charged with overseas operations have assumed a more vital role in the top councils of these companies.

Foreign plants have had a mixed impact on chemical exports from the United States, replacing some items but stimulating the flow of materials and of other chemicals and allied products. Because of measures instituted by foreign governments, in some instances the establishment of plants in those countries has become the only way for American companies to retain a share of those markets. A substantial amount of chemical exports is channeled through foreign affiliates.

Investments by foreign chemical companies in the United States also have been expanding very rapidly and were estimated at about $2.5 billion in 1968. Such investments have been particularly important for fibers, drugs, and dyes. Most of the large foreign chemical companies now have an investment in U.S. facilities. Sometimes, these investments involve joint ventures with American companies.

The trend toward internationalization of chemical companies is very strong and, continues despite current governmental restrictions on foreign investment. One result has been to expand the markets for many chemicals and allied products and competitive pressures from national to international dimensions.

---

[1]From an address before the National Industrial Conference Board, New York, February 20, 1969, p. 4 (mimeo).

[2]The entry of U.S. companies into overseas markets dates back to 1920 when "Monsanto bought a half-interest in a British coal-tar processor, which eventually was fully owned by Monsanto and became Monsanto, Ltd." *Chemical Week*, November 16, 1968, p. 142.

[3]Jean-Jacques Servan-Schreiber, *The American Challenge*, Atheneum, New York, 1968.

[4]Cited in *Fortune*, September 15, 1968, p. 100.

[5]*Survey of Current Business*, October 1968, p. 29.

[6]*Fortune*, September 15, 1968, p. 194.

[7]Several articles dealing with international activities appear in *Fortune*, September 15, 1968. See also John J. Powers, Jr., "The Multi-National Corporation," and G. A. Costanzo, "The Multi-National Executive," in *Preparing Tomorrow's Business Leaders Today*, edited by Peter F. Drucker, Prentice-Hall, Inc., Englewood Cliffs, N.J., 1969, pp. 171-79, 226-32.

[8]E. Edgar Fogle and George Forstot, "Organization For Marketing in a Large Integrated Company" in *Chemical Marketing: The Challenges of the Seventies*, American Chemical Society, Washington, D.C., 1968, pp. 39-40.

[9]"Sales In A World Market," *Ibid.*, p. 191.

[10]*Ibid.*, p. 194.

[11]"Sales Outlook For Chemicals", An address before a meeting of the National Industrial Conference Board, Los Angeles, Cal., May 8, 1969, p. 6 (*mimeo*)

[12]*Fortune*, April 1969, p. 112.

[13]*Appraising Foreign Licensing Performance*, Studies in Business Policy No. 128, National Industrial Conference Board, New York, 1969, p. 3.

[14]According to the U.S. Department of Commerce the data for capital outflows include overseas borrowings to finance investment in overseas affiliates. "When foreign-borrowed funds are transferred to a foreign affiliate, they are included in direct investment capital outflows, i.e., are reported with funds sent directly from the United States." Emil L. Nelson and Frederick Cutler, "The International Investment Position of the United States in 1967," *Survey of Current Business*, October 1968, p. 22.

[15]For a review of investments in England prior to World War II and in the first postwar decade see John H. Dunning, *American Investment In British Manufacturing Industry*, George Allen and Unwin, Ltd., London, 1958, pp. 41-2, 59-64. Dow has explained its policy as follows: "Our practice is to enter international markets with export materials and then, when local production will result in substantial sales increases at acceptable profit levels, to establish plants in or near major consumption areas." The Dow Chemical Company, *Annual Report for the Year 1963*, p. 18.

[16]Du Pont reported that at the end of 1968 its operating investment (total current assets plus plants and property before depreciation) of subsidiaries and affiliates outside the United States was "approximately $1,100 million". *Annual Report, 1968*, p. 8.

[17]*Survey of Current Business*, October 1968, p. 27.

[18]Samuel Pizer and Frederick Cutler, "Foreign Investments, 1964-65," *Survey of Current Business*, September 1965, p. 27.

[19]*The Morgan Guaranty Survey*, March 1969, pp. 8-14.

[20]" . . . the term 'foreign affiliate' applies to unincorporated foreign branches of U.S. firms, or foreign corporations in which U.S. companies have a directly held voting interest of 25 per cent or more. In practice, the voting interest is predominantly in the range of 75 per cent or more. The data used for each affiliate are taken for its entire operation . . . . This tends to inflate somewhat the U.S. interest in these firms," Frederick Cutler and Samuel Pizer, "U.S. Firms Accelerate Capital Expenditures Abroad," *Survey of Current Business*, October 1964, p. 11.

[21]Annual expenditures for plant and equipment in chemicals are in part for new capacity and in part for modernization.

[22]*Survey of Current Business*, March 1969, p. 15.

[23]Booz, Allen & Hamilton, Inc., *New Foreign Business Activity of U.S. Firms*, No. 14, Chicago, Illinois, 1968, pp. 2, 7.

[24]Data are available only through 1965 for all manufacturing. Between 1957 and 1965, sales by foreign affiliates of chemical companies increased by 184% as compared with 131% for all manufacturing. *Survey of Current Business*, November 1966, p. 8.

[25]"Chemicals Overseas Affiliates Grow Rapidly," *Chemicals*, U.S. Department of Commerce, Business and Defense Services Administration, March 1967, p. 7.

[26]Total shipments of $42.2 billion less exports of $2.8 billion.

[27]Marie T. Bradshaw, "U.S. Exports to Foreign Affiliates of U.S. Firms", *Survey of Current Business*, May 1969, pp. 36-37.

[28]Du Pont, *Annual Report, 1966*, p. 18.

[29]Joseph O. Bradford, "Hercules Circles The Globe", *Hercules Chemist*, September 1967, p. 8.

[30]Testimony before the Subcommittee on Foreign Policy of the House Committee on Foreign Affairs, March 27, 1969, p. 3 (*mimeo*). James G. Morton, former special assistant to the Secretary of Commerce, testified that "About 25 per cent of all U.S. exports are shipped to foreign subsidiaries and affiliates of American corporations. In fact, shipments to affiliates account for even more substantial percentages of the exports, up to 35 per cent or more, of some of our larger international companies." *Ibid.*, March 26, 1969, pp. 5-6 (*mimeo*).

[31]F. W. MacMullen, "Chemicals," in *American Enterprise, The Next Ten Years*, edited by Martin R. Gainsbrugh, The Macmillan Company, New York, 1961, pp. 58-59 and Michael G. Duerr, "U.S. Foreign Production vs U.S. Exports," *The Conference Board Record*, December 1968, pp. 40-43.

[32]*The General Electric Forum*, April-June 1964, p. 16.

[33]Walter S. Salant and others, *The United States Balance of Payments in 1968*, The Brookings Institution, Washington, D.C., 1963, p. 128.

[34]*Chemical & Engineering News*, February 17, 1969, p. 9.

[35]Herbert Glazer, "Capital Liberalization" in *Joint Ventures and Japan*, edited by Robert J. Ballan, Sophia University, Tokyo, 1967, p. 17.

[36] John Davenport, "The Chemical Industry Pushes Into Hostile Territory," *Fortune,* April 1969, pp. 108-14, 156-62.

[37] *The Wall Street Journal,* March 11, 1969, p. 36.

[38] *Celanese Annual Report 1968,* p. 2. See also *Chemical Week,* May 31, 1969, p. 13.

[39] *Annual Report 1968,* p. 16.

[40] *Annual Report 1968,* p. 9.

[41] Frederick L. Deming, Under Secretary of the Treasury reported in January 1969 that "only about $120 million of foreign issues subject to IET have been floated in the U.S. in the 5-1/2 years since the tax took effect." This compared with $356 million in 1962 and an annual rate of $700 million in 1963 for countries subject to the tax. Testimony before the Subcommittee on International Exchange and Payments of the Joint Economic Committee, January 15, 1969, pp. 36-37 (mimeo).

[42] The Board of Governors of the Federal Reserve System also set up guidelines for maximum limits on lending abroad by financial institutions. *Economic Report of the President,* January 1969, p. 144.

[43] *Ibid.,* January 1966, p. 167.

[44] These quotas together with specific relief granted made possible investments of $1.6 billion or 50% higher than the 1967 total for less developed countries. Dan D. Cadle, Acting Director of the Office of Foreign Direct Investments, U.S. Department of Commerce in an address before the National Industrial Conference Board, February 20, 1969, p. 4 (mimeo).

[45] *The New York Times,* January 2, 1968, p. 15.

[46] U.S. Department of Commerce, Office of Foreign Direct Investments, *News Release,* May 6, 1969, pp. 1-2 (mimeo).

[47] Cadle, *op. cit.,* p. 6 (mimeo).

[48] *The New York Times,* April 5, 1969, pp. 1, 39. The controls over bank lending abroad were also liberalized in April 1969.

[49] Emil L. Nelson and Frederick Cutler, "The International Investment Position of the United States in 1967," *Survey of Current Business,* October 1968, p. 22.

[50] *Survey of Current Business,* October 1968, p. 31.

[51] *The Morgan Guaranty Survey,* March 1969, p. 13.

[52] Yale L. Meltzer, *Chemical Guide to GATT, the Kennedy Round and International Trade,* Noyes Development Corporation, Park Ridge, N.J., 1968, pp. 321-24; Du Pont, *Annual Report 1967,* p. 25; Morgan Guaranty Trust Company, *World Financial Markets,* various issues. In addition, there has been considerable borrowing from overseas banks. In June 1969, Dow announced its German subsidiary had made a loan agreement to borrow about $250 million from a consortium of German banks. *The New York Times,* June 10, 1969.

[53] Cadle, *op. cit.,* p. 6.

[54] Statement Before the Subcommittee on Foreign Economic Policy, House Committee on Foreign Affairs, March 27, 1969, p. 5 (mimeo).

[55] *Ibid.,* p. 7.

[56] U.S. Department of Commerce, *U.S. Foreign Trade, A Five Year Outlook With Recommendations For Action,* Washington, D.C., April 1969, p. 29.

[57] *Ibid.,* p. 8.

[58]For an excellent discussion of the problems encountered in connection with foreign joint ventures see Fred C. Foy, *Policy Problems of the Jointly Owned Foreign Company,* an address before the Harvard AMP Symposium, December 8, 1966.

[59]Herbert Brownell, "American Business in World Trade," in *Antitrust in an Expanding Economy,* National Industrial Conference Board, New York, May 16, 1962, p. 55.

[60]*The Dow Chemical Co. 1967 Annual Report,* p. 19.

[61]*The Wall Street Journal,* May 9, 1962, p. 1.

[62]Eastman Kodak Company, *News Release,* January 1961.

[63]Pittsburgh Plate Glass Company, *News Release,* October 3, 1961.

[64]Hooker Chemical Corporation, *News Release,* September 3, 1963.

[65]*News Release,* May 31, 1962.

[66]*The B. F. Goodrich Company Annual Report 1968,* p. 4.

[67]The Dow Chemical Company, *1967 Annual Report,* p. 19.

[68]*Ibid.*

[69]*Celanese Annual Report, 1967,* p. 8.

[70]*Airco 1967 Annual Report,* p. 5.

[71]*Stauffer Chemical Company 1967 Annual Report,* p. 15.

[72]*Allied Chemical Corporation Annual Report 1967,* pp. 13-14.

[73]Atlas Chemical Industries has joint ventures in Canada, England, India, Japan, Mexico, Nicaragua, and Taiwan.

[74]C. P. Neidig, "Financial Comparison of World Chemical Companies," *Financial Analysts Journal,* January-February, 1968, pp. 3-4.

[75]Paul Rand Dixon, "Joint Ventures: What Is Their Impact on Competition," an address before the Economic Club of Detroit, Michigan, March 12, 1962, p. 16. Similar questions have been raised in connection with joint ventures within this country.

[76]*United States v. Imperial Chemical Industries, Ltd.,* 105F, Supp. 215, 238, (S.D.N.Y. 1952).

[77]"Appraising Foreign Licensing Performance," *op. cit.,* pp. 9-10.

[78]Lawrence J. Eckstrom, "Licensing in Foreign Operations," in *Case Studies in Foreign Operations,* International Management Association, Special Report No. 1, New York, 1957, pp. 205-11.

[79]*Chemical Week* reported that Foote Mineral, Alco Chemical, and Haveg Industries contemplated the licensing route because it would not tie up capital, May 30, 1964, p. 55.

[80]Vincent D. Travaglini, "Licensing U.S. Know-How Abroad Is Increasing," in *Foreign Business Practices,* April 1967.

[81]Charles E. Fiero, "The American Corporation in the Common Market," in *The Common Market: Friend or Competitor,* New York University Press, 1964, pp. 67-68.

[82]*Chemical Engineering,* September 25, 1967, p. 84.

[83]*News From Wyandotte,* September 9, 1963.

[84]*News About Celanese,* June 26, 1962.

[85]*Chemical Week,* May 30, 1964, p. 56.

[86]*Chemical Engineering,* September 25, 1967, p. 82.

[87]E. K. Stilbert and R. E. Peterson, "Licensing—Hazard or Bonanza" in *Chemical Marketing and Economics Papers,* September 1966, pp. 109-10.

[88]J. P. Cunningham, "The Challenge of Marketing for Inorganic and Heavy Chemicals," in "Chemical Marketing: The Challenge of the Seventies," *op. cit.,* p. 28.

[89]*Ibid.,* pp. 27-28.

[90]*Chemical Week,* May 30, 1964, p. 55.

[91]*Hooker Annual Report,* 1966, p. 9.

[92]"New Foreign Business Activity of U.S. Firms," *op. cit.,* p. 7.

[93]Stilbert and Peterson, *op. cit.,* pp. 111-14.

[94]*Chemical & Engineering News,* May 20, 1968, p. 62.

[95]Cited in "Appraising Foreign Licensing Performance," *op. cit.,* p. 5.

[96]David B. Zenoff and James A. Jepson, "How To Boost Profits From Your Foreign Licensing Agreement," *Business Abroad,* December 1968, p. 35.

[97]Louis Blecher, "It's a Small Competitive World, The World of Chemicals," *Chemical Marketing and Economics Papers,* September 1965, p. 181.

[98]Murray J. Gart, "The British Company That Found a Way Out," *Fortune,* August 1966, p. 182.

[99]Sir Peter Allen, "The Chemical Industries of the U.K. and North America; Lessons and Opportunities," *Chemistry and Industry,* August 3, 1968, p. 1042.

[100]*Survey of Current Business,* October 1968, p. 30.

[101]Samuel Pizer and Zalie V. Warner, *Foreign Business Investments in the United States,* A supplement to the Survey of Current Business, Washington, D.C., 1962, p. 7.

[102]*Ibid.,* pp. 8, 18.

[103]*Chemical and Engineering News,* February 24, 1964, pp. 83-85.

[104]*Chemical Week,* August 17, 1968.

[105]House Ways and Means Committee, Hearings on *Foreign Trade and Tariff Proposals,* 90th Cong., 2nd Sess., Washington, D.C., 1968, p. 4693.

[106]*Ibid.,* p. 4763.

[107]E. I. du Pont, *Management Newsletter,* January 1967, p. 1.

[108]*Chemical Week,* May 31, 1969, p. 18.

[109]Neidig, *op. cit.,* p. 2.

[110]Sekisui Chemical, a Japanese chemical company, built a polystyrene plant in Hazleton, Pennsylvania, an area with large unemployment. $1.2 million out of $1.7 million was provided by the Area Redevelopment Administration, the Pennsylvania Industrial Development Authority, and some private funds, *Chemical and Engineering News,* February 25, 1963, pp. 26-27 and February 24, 1964, p. 86. In 1967 this plant was sold to Instrument Systems, *Chemical Week,* August 17, 1968, p. 107.

[111]*Fortune,* September 15, 1968, p. 194.

[112]*Chemical Week,* August 17, 1968, p. 110.

[113]An address by H. Lautenschloger of BASF at Rutgers University, May 5, 1969.

[114]*Chemical and Engineering News,* February 24, 1964, p. 84.

[115]Hystron Fibers, a joint venture of Hercules and Farbwerke Hoechst, built a plant in Spartanburg, S.C. with the help of $75 million in tax exempt industrial revenue bonds. *Chemical Week,* August 17, 1968, p. 104.

[116]Several of the acquisitions of American companies by Farbwerke Hoechst were ascribed to a desire to build up a sales organization in this country, *Chemical Week,* June 18, 1960, p. 92.

[117]When Montecatini bought an interest in Minerals and Chemicals Phillipp Corp. in 1961, the latter's president stated "By associating ourselves with one of the strongest companies in Europe we now have a board of directors with international experience in chemicals." *Chemical and Engineering News,* July 17, 1961, p. 32.

[118]When Dynamit-Nobel A. G. acquired Rubber Corporation of America, the president of the latter company was reported to have stated: "Dynamit hasn't followed U.S. technical developments as it should. Now it's getting a window in the U.S." *Chemical Week,* June 11, 1960, p. 31.

APPENDIX A

Bureau of the Census Estimates for Chemicals and Allied Products

Chemicals and allied products were first included as a separate group in the Census of 1879. In succeeding yearrs the Bureau of the Census has changed its definitions of the chemical industry group[1] many times as the burgeoning industry developed new products and as the frontiers of the industry have been extended. These changes in classification have affected the consistency of the reported data and make it necessary to exercise considerable caution in using these data to measure long-term trends.

For example, when a major revision was made in the Standard Industrial Classification in 1957, the following industries were added to the chemicals and allied products group.[2]

	Value Added
	(millions)
Tall oil (old SIC 2611)	$ 11.3
Fireworks and pyrotechnics (old SIC 3985)	9.0

The following products were *removed* from this industry group:

	Value Added
	(millions)
Cottonseed oil mills	$ 63.6
Linseed oil mills	17.8
Soybean oil mills	139.9
Vegetable oil mills, n.e.c.	13.7
Grease and tallow	122.6
Animal oils, n.e.c.	24.0
Ink cartridges for ballpoint pens	1.9

The periodic changes in the Standard Industrial Classification have affected the number of industries for which separate data were reported for each Census year. In 1899, for example, there were 7 separate industries[3] while in 1958

---

[1] An industry grouping (2-digit SIC code) is composed of several industry classifications which cover plants or establishments producing related groups of products (4-digit SIC code). These industry classifications are broken down into product classes (5-digit SIC code) which in turn are broken down into more narrowly defined products (7-digit SIC code).

[2] U.S. Department of Commerce. Bureau of the Census, *U.S. Census of Manufactures: 1958, Vol. II, Industry Statistics, Part I Major Groups 20-28,* Washington, D.C., 1961, Appendix C, pp. C-9, C-10, and C-27.

[3] U.S. Department of Commerce, Bureau of the Census, *Census of Manufactures: 1914, Vol. II,* Reports for Selected Industries, U.S. Government Printing Office, Washington, D.C., 1919, p. 458.

there were 31 industries[4]; at times there have been even more. These changes have reflected the reclassification of the industry's establishments into new industry combinations, the creation of new industry categories, and the elimination of older ones. As a result, over the period 1899-1958 the data are not comparable for any of the chemical industry groups as currently defined.

In many instances, when the Bureau of the Census has revised its definitions, data also were revised for earlier years. However, this has not always been done. For example, the totals for chemicals and allied products for the years 1899 to 1954 have not been adjusted by the Bureau of the Census to conform with the 1957 SIC codes and thus are not comparable. However, for some subgroups within the industry, comparable data were reported back to 1935.

To obtain a series for chemicals and allied products for the 1899-1967 period, the following adjustments were made for the period prior to 1958:

Industry	Years Adjusted
Subtract:	
Cottonseed oil mills	1899-1954
Linseed oil mills	1899-1954
Grease and tallow	1899-1954
Oils, n.e.c.	1899-1937
Soybean oil mills	1937-1954
Vegetable oil mills	1939-1954
Animal oil mills, n.e.c.	1939-1954
Ferroalloys	1921-1937
Add:	
Fireworks and pyrotechnics	1899-1954

These adjustments do not yield a perfectly comparable series. For example, data for the number of establishments and value of product for ferroalloys were available only for the period 1921-1937; for the period 1899-1919, separate data were not reported for this industry. Despite such limitations, the revised data shown in Appendix Tables 1 and 2 do represent a fairly consistent series for the entire period since 1899.

The 1957 SIC changes in the Census of Manufactures had a major effect on the data for the chemicals and allied products industry group. On the basis of the new classification the 1958 totals were significantly lower than they would have been under the former classification as is shown in Table A-1.

The changes reduced the number of establishments by 891 or 7.3%, the number of employees by 30,689 or 4.2%, and value added by $374.3 million or 3.0%.[5]

The data for earlier years were affected to a relatively larger degree by the recomputations. In 1899, for example, the number of establishments was decreased by 11.3%, the number of production workers by 11.1% and value added

---

[4]U.S. Bureau of the Census, *Historical Comparability of Census of Manufactures Industries, 1929-1958*. Working Paper No. 9, Washington, D.C., 1959, p. 29.

[5]The 1958 data - new SIC - were subsequently revised. The most recent 1958 data are 11,372 establishments, 698.342 employees, and value added by manufacture $12,308.0 million. U.S. Department of Commerce, Bureau of the Census, *1963 Census of Manufactures*, Washington, D.C., 1966, p. 28-3.

by 11.4%. (See Appendix Tables 1 and 2) The effect of these recalculations is larger in the earlier years because: (1) the base is smaller and (2) the industries which were eliminated generally grew at a slower rate than the remaining chemicals and allied products during the 1899-1958 period.

There were no significant changes in the Census classifications for chemicals and allied products between 1958 and 1963. For all but two industries in SIC 28 the *1963 Census of Manufactures* notes: "The code number as well as the definition of this industry was unchanged between 1958 and 1963.[6] The only industries that had some differences in their composition were 2851 (paints, varnishes, lacquers, enamels, and allied products) and 2899 (chemical preparations, not elsewhere classified). In the former the Bureau of the Census indicates: "The code number for this industry in the Standard Industrial Classification Manual is unchanged, but the content of the industry has been slightly changed from the classification system used in 1958. The change in the composition of the industry as now constituted, compared with that under the classification system followed in the 1958 census, is due principally to the inclusion of industry 2852, Putty and Caulking Compounds, in 1963. Data shown for years prior to 1963 have been adjusted to include data for industry 2852, Putty and Caulking Compounds."[7] For SIC 2899, Census notes: "The code number for this industry in the Standard Industrial Classification Manual is unchanged, but the content of the industry has been slightly changed from the classification system used in 1958. The composition of the industry as now constituted, compared with that under the classification system followed in the 1958 census, is due principally to a change in definition of industry 2899 to include fatty acids and the subsequent reclassification of establishments formerly included in the old industry 2894, fatty acids to industry 2899."[8]

Revisions in Reported Data for Chemicals

It is impossible to derive consistent and complete data for chemicals (SIC 281 and 282) for the entire 1899-1967 period, because in many cases separate data are not available to make necessary corrections. In some instances, the data may be non-existent, while in others, the earlier totals were reported only as part of other series. However, a number of adjustments can be made. The total for all industrial chemicals is more complete than that for the component four-digit classes. To obtain data for the number of establishments, wages, employment, and value added for industrial chemicals the series shown on the next page were combined for the period indicated.

From the totals derived by combining these series, data for ferroalloys were subtracted for the years, 1921-1937.

The inability to make the following adjustments for all of the series covered results in some *understatement* of the totals for chemicals for the years indicated:

    1. In 1958, bone black and lamp black were shifted to organic pigments from carbon black and whiting was shifted to organic pigments from whiting and fillers. Complete, separate data were not available for prior years.

---

[6]U.S. Department of Commerce, Bureau of the Census, *1963 Census of Manufactures,* pp. 28A-2,-7, 28B-1-3, 28C-1-3, 28D-1-3, 28E-2, 28F-1-3, 28G-1-3.

[7]*Ibid.,* p. 28E-1.

[8]*Ibid.,* p. 28G-4.

SIC Code No.		Industry	Period
1958	2812	Alkalies and chlorine	1939-1966
1958	2813	Industrial gases	1927-1966
1958	2814	Cyclic crudes (coal-tar products)	1939-1966
1958	2815	Dyes, intermediates, lakes and toners	1939-1966
1958	2816	Inorganic pigments	1935-1966
1958	2818	Industrial organic chemicals, n.e.c.	1939-1966
1958	2819	Industrial inorganic chemicals, n.e.c.	1939-1966
1958	2821	Plastics materials	1939-1966
1958	2822	Synthetic rubber	1947-1966
1958	2823	Cellulosic man-made fibers	1958-1966
1958	2824	Organic fibers, non-cellulosic	1958-1966
1954	2825	Synthetic fibers (rayon and allied products)	1925-1954
1939	912	Colors and pigments	1937
1939	981	Coal-tar products, crudes and intermediates . . .	1937
1939	982	Plastics materials	1937
1939	999	Chemicals, n.e.c.	1899-1937
1909	—	Sulfuric, nitric, and mixed acids	1899-1909

The following data show the shipments of these products for earlier years:[9]

	1939	1947	1954
		(*000 omitted*)	
Bone black	$1,389	$3,731	$2,226
Lamp black	681	866	N.A.
Whiting[10]	765	871	1,306

N.A. - Not Available

2. Prior to 1935, separate data were not available for inorganic pigments. In 1935, total shipments were $67 million and value added by manufacture $31 million.

3. Chemical catalytic preparations were added to inorganic chemicals, n.e.c. in 1958 from chemical products, n.e.c. In 1954, total shipments were $34.7 million.[11] Complete, separate data were not available for prior years.

The inability to make the following adjustments results in some *overstatement* of the totals for chemicals for the years indicated.

1. Synthetic sausage casings were shifted from synthetic fibers to another industry group in 1954. Separate data were not reported prior

---

[9]U.S. Bureau of the Census, *Census of Manufactures: 1947, Volume II, Statistics By Industry*. Washington, D.C., 1949, pp. 416, 443, and "U.S. Census of Manufactures: 1958" *op cit.*, Volume II, Part I, pp. 28A-18, 19.

[10]Excludes precipitated calcium carbonate for the years 1939 and 1947.

[11]"U.S. Census of Manufactures: 1958," *op. cit.*, p. 2A-21.

to 1947 so that an undetermined amount remains in the synthetic fiber totals. In 1947, this industry had a value added of $12.9 million.[12]

2. Emulsifiers, penetrants, wetting agents, etc. were removed from industrial organic chemicals, n.e.c. in 1958. For prior years separate data were not available. The result is a small overstatement in the totals for years before 1958.[13]

3. Pyroxylin products were shifted from chemicals, n.e.c. to paints and varnishes in 1927. Separate data were not available for earlier years so that chemicals, n.e.c. could not be reduced.[14]

4. The use of the broad category chemicals, n.e.c. for the years 1899-1937 results in an overstatement for the years indicated because of the inclusion of the following industries:[15]

Medicinal chemicals, inorganic 1919-1937
Surface active agents, n.e.c. 1919-1937
Animal dips 1899-1937
Agricultural chemicals 1899-1937
Fatty acids 1899-1937

Data are not available to determine the extent to which the overstatements and understatements noted above offset each other.

TABLE A-1

The 1958 Census of Manufactures Data for the Chemicals and Allied Products Industry Group, Based on the New and Old SIC Code

	Number of Establishments	Number of Employees	Value Added by Manufacture, Adjusted (*millions*)
1958 Data—New SIC	11,309	699,166	$12,270.4
1958 Data—Old SIC	12,200	729,855	12,644.7
Per cent decrease from old to new	7.3%	4.2%	3.0%
Derivation of new from old data:			
Add:			
Fireworks and pyrotechnics	67	1,628	9.0
Tall oil	10	460	11.3
All other industries	62	3,008	67.7
Total additions	139	5,096	88.0
Deduct:			
Fats and oils	943	32,481	380.6
Ink cartridges for ballpoint pens	5	222	1.9
All other industries	72	3,082	79.8
Total deductions	1,030	35,785	462.3
Net Increase (decrease)	(891)	(30,689)	(374.3)

[12]U.S. Department of Commerce; Bureau of the Census, *U.S. Census of Manufactures: 1954, Industry Statistics, Part I, Major Groups 20 to 28*. U.S. Government Printing Office, Washington, D.C., 1957, Vol. II, Part I, p. 28B-4 and Appendix B, p. B-3.

Footnotes continued on next page

Footnotes continued from page 311

[13]"U.S. Census of Manufactures: 1958," *op. cit.,* pp. 28A-3, 4.

[14]U.S. Department of Commerce, Bureau of the Census, *Biennial Census of Manufactures: 1927,* U.S. Government Printing Office, Washington, D.C., 1930, pp. 673, 711.

[15]"Historical Comparability of Census of Manufactures Industries, 1929-1958," *op. cit.,* pp. 30-31.

APPENDIX B

Statistical Tables

APPENDIX TABLE 1

Establishments and Value Added: Chemicals and Allied Products Industries, 1899-1967

| | Establishments, Number | | Value Added by Manufacture[1] | |
	As Reported in the Census of Manufactures	Recomputed (Based on 1957 SIC Classification)	As Reported	Recomputed
			(millions)	
1899[2]	7,669	6,806	$ 212	$ 186
1904	8,370	7,169	286	252
1909	10,280	8,930	401	351
1914	10,698	9,282	457	402
1919	10,688	9,246	1,198	1,038
1921	8,208	7,077	834	773
1923[3]	8,253	7,258	1,185	1,097
1925	8,160	7,160	1,320	1,203
1927	8,594	7,600	1,474	1,358
1929	9,327	8,415	1,737	1,646
1931[4]	8,324	7,520	1,359	1,299
1933	7,297	6,569	1,121	1,073
1935	8,225	7,411	1,363	1,299
1937[5]	8,337[3]	7,494[6]	1,732	1,636
1939	8,839	7,945	1,819	1,732
1947	10,019	8,916	5,317	4,861
1954	11,074	10,154	9,547	9,185
1958[7][8]	11,372	11,372	12,308	12,308
1963	11,996	11,996	17,585	17,585
1967	NA	NA	23,440	23,440

NA - Not available.

[1]For the period 1954-1967, figures represent adjusted value added by manufacture and for earlier years, unadjusted value added. Adjusted value added is equal to value of shipments (including resales of finished products made by other manufacturing establishments) less cost of products, materials, supplies, fuel, electric energy and contract work, plus the net change in the value of finished products and work-in-process inventories between the beginning and end of the year. Unadjusted value added is equal to value of products (excluding resales of finished products) less cost of materials, supplies, fuel, electric energy and contract work; no adjustment is made for changes in inventories of finished products and work-in-process during the year. For 1899-1933, cost of contract work was not subtracted from value of products in calculating value added by manufacture.

[2]The figures for 1899 include data for establishments primarily engaged in manufacture of candles. Value added by manufacture for candles in 1904 was $0.9 million.

Footnotes continued on next page

Footnotes continued from page 313

[3]The figures for 1899-1923, but not for later years, include data for certain establishments primarily engaged in manufacture of rubber cement.

[4]The figures for 1899-1931 do not include data for establishments primarily engaged in manufacture of ethyl alcohol, included for these years in the figures for the "Food and kindred products" industries.

[5]The figures for 1899-1935 but not for later years, include data for establishments primarily engaged in mining of rock salt or in smelting and refining of aluminum. In 1937, the value added by manufacture for these industries was $28 million.

[6]The figures prior to 1939 include data for establishments primarily engaged in manufacture of electrometallurgical products, included from 1939 in the "Primary Metal" industries. The recomputed data for establishments exclude ferroalloys for the years 1921 to 1937. Separate data were not available for earlier years.

[7]Figures for years prior to 1958 do not include data for tall oil as no separate data was available.

[8]The figures for 1954 and prior years include data for ink cartridges for ballpoint pens.

Sources: U.S. Department of Commerce, Bureau of the Census, *U.S. Census of Manufactures: 1958, Vol. II, Industry Statistics, Part I, Major Groups 20 to 28,* Washington, D.C., 1961, p. 28-2; U.S. Bureau of the Census, *Annual Survey of Manufactures: 1959 and 1960,* Washington, D.C., 1962, pp. 34-37; *Annual Survey of Manufactures: 1962,* General Statistics for Industry Groups and Selected Industries (M62(AS)-1) Washington, D.C., 1963, pp. 10-13; Various volumes of *Census of Manufactures,* 1899 to 1954. U.S. Department of Commerce, Bureau of the Census, 1963 U.S. Census of Manufactures: Vol. II, *Industry Statistics, Part I, Major Groups 20 to 28,* Washington, D.C., 1966, p. 28-3; *1967 Census of Manufactures,* General Statistics for Industry Groups and Industries, Preliminary Report, MC67(P)-1, Washington, D.C., April 1969, p. 7.

APPENDIX TABLE 2

Number of Production Workers and Wages: Chemicals and Allied Products Industries, 1899-1967

| | Number | | Wages | |
	As Reported in the Census of Manufactures	Recomputed Based on 1957 SIC Classification	As Reported	Recomputed
			(*millions*)	
1899[2]	143,552	129,310	$ 51	$ 46
1904	158,410	138,025	65	57
1909	184,976	161,730	82	72
1914	207,654	178,625	106	98
1919	293,466	253,172	306	270
1921	212,264	187,293	218	195
1923[3]	264,297	240,626	286	263
1925	260,872	234,493	297	270
1927	278,053	249,972	319	289
1929	307,387	284,626	352	330
1931[4]	248,238	230,992	259	244
1933	254,011	234,645	217	206
1935	293,493[1]	272,974	282	267
1937[5]	303,291	276,986	366	344
1939	275,669	250,307	342	320
1947	464,144	432,375	1,236	1,159
1954	498,745	471,262	1,994	1,901
1958	453,112	453,112	2,242	2,242
1963	474,141	474,141	2,780	2,780
1967	544,000	544,000	3,579	3,579

---

[1]The figures for 1899-1935, but not for later years, include data for woods employees of the gum naval stores industry. Woods data in 1937 (for which data are not included in the figures) were reported as follows: Production and related workers, 30,880 and wages $9 million.

For notes 2 to 5—See Appendix Table 1.

Source: See Appendix Table 1.

APPENDIX TABLE 3

Selected Census Data: Chemicals, 1899-1967

	Number of Establishments	Production Workers Number	Wages	Value Added by Manufacture	Value of Shipments
				------------------(millions)------------------	
1899	350	17,519	$ 9	$ 26	$ 57
1904	329	22,294	12	37	84
1909	401	25,981	16	58	128
1914	427	35,375	24	77	173
1919	836	76,918	105	313	614
1921	708	49,138	62	212	403
1923	750	77,354	103	327	634
1925	746	77,018	107	375	643
1927	808	81,900	112	398	716
1929	915	104,695	145	528	911
1931	922	90,101	109	415	694
1933	883	100,259	101	391	654
1935	1,003	126,172	142	521	940
1937	1,138	148,779	202	738	1,312
1939	1,086	122,683	175	745	1,277
1947	1,362	214,405	622	2,058	4,143
1954	1,747	241,046	1,057	4,650	8,906
1958	2,105	243,824	1,322	6,214	11,780
1963	2,482	257,339	1,656	9,037	16,579
1967	NA	285,000	2,043	11,572	21,523

Note: Includes industrial chemicals (SIC 281) plus plastics materials and synthetics (SIC 282)

NA - Not available.

Sources: See Appendix Table 1.

APPENDIX TABLE 4

Shipments of Inorganic and Organic Chemicals, By Main Classes of Products, 1963

SIC Code No.	Inorganics	Amount (*millions*)	Per Cent of Total
28199	Reagent and high purity grades of inorganic chemicals and other inorganic chemicals, n.e.c.	$ 826	5.5
28191	Synthetic ammonia, nitric acid & ammonium compounds	588	3.9
28197	Potassium & sodium compounds (except bleaches, alkalies and alums)	513	3.4
28195	Aluminum oxide, except natural alumina	319	2.1
28161	Titanium pigments	277	1.8
28134	Elemental gases & compresssed & liquefied gases, n.e.c.	245	1.6
28123	Sodium hydroxide (caustic soda)	210	1.4
28193	Sulfuric acid	194	1.3
28192	Chlorine & other bleaching compounds	200	1.3
28121	Chlorine, còmpressed or liquefied	164	1.1
28194	Inorganic acids, except nitric & sulfuric	166	1.1
28163	Chrome colors & other inorganic pigments	152	1.0
28122	Sodium carbonate	124	0.8
28196	Other aluminum compounds	104	0.7
28132	Acetylene	93	0.6
28198	Chemical catalytic preparation	75	0.5
28162	Other white opaque pigments	50	0.3
28133	Carbon dioxide	50	0.3
28124	Other alkalies	28	0.2
28130	Industrial gases, n.s.k.	2	*
		4,380	28.9

Organics

SIC Code No.	Organics	Amount (*millions*)	Per Cent of Total
28182	Miscellaneous acylic chemicals & chemical products	3,154	21.0
28213	Thermoplastic resins & plastics materials	1,302	8.7
28220	Synthetic rubber (vulcanizable elastomers)	862	5.7
28151	Cyclic intermediates	759	5.1
28211	Unsupported plastic film, sheetings, rods, tubes & others	688	4.6
28242	Other noncellulosic synthetic organic fibers	473	3.1
28183	Synthetic organic chemicals, n.e.c. (except bulk surface active agents)	419	2.8
28214	Thermosetting resins & plastics materials	420	2.8
28232	Rayon yarn, viscose & cuprammonium process	399	2.7
28212	Regenerated cellulosic products, except rayon	328	2.2
28216	Synthetic resins for protective coatings	272	1.8
28231	Acetate yarn	250	1.7
28152	Synthetic organic dyes	243	1.6

Continued on next page

SIC Code No.	Organics	Amount (*millions*)	Per Cent of Total
28184	Pesticides & other organic agricultural chemicals (not formulations)	223	1.5
28217	Custom compounding of purchased resins	185	1.2
28181	Miscellaneous cyclic chemical products	201	1.3
28185	Ethyl alcohol & other industrial organic chemicals, n.e.c.	192	1.3
28153	Synthetic organic pigments, lakes & toners	112	0.7
28140	Cyclic (coal-tar) crudes	79	0.5
28219	Plastics & resin materials, n.e.c.	60	0.4
28215	Synthetic resin, adhesives	29	0.2
28180	Industrial organic chemicals, n.s.k.	12	0.1
28210	Plastics materials, synthetic resins & non-vulcanizable elastomers, n.s.k.	8	0.1
28150	Intermediate coal-tar products, n.s.k.	3	*
		10,673	71.1
	Grand Total	15,053	100.0

*Less than 0.05 percent.

n.s.k. - Not specified by kind.

n.e.c. - Not elsewhere classified.

Source: U.S. Department of Commerce, Bureau of the Census, *U.S. Census of Manufactures: 1963,* Vol. II, *Industry Statistics, Part 1, Major Groups 20 to 28,* Washington, D.C., 1966, pp. 28A-20-31, 28B-12-15.

APPENDIX TABLE 5

Chemical Companies Included Among the 500 Largest Industrial Corporations, 1968

Rank		Sales	Net Profit	Invested Capital	Profit As Per Cent of Sales	Profit As Per Cent of Invested Capital
		----------(millions)----------				
15	Du Pont (E. I. de Nemours)	$ 3,481	$ 372	$ 2,540	10.7	14.6
26	Union Carbide	2,686	157	1,701	5.8	9.2
41	Monsanto	1,793	109	1,126	6.1	9.7
45	Grace (W. R.)	1,738	33	598	1.9	5.5
50	Dow Chemical	1,652	136	1,010	8.2	13.5
65	FMC	1,376	75	549	5.5	13.7
73	Allied Chemical	1,278	18	724	1.4	2.5
75	Celanese	1,266	(77)	553	-	-
102	American Cyanamid	1,023	86	684	8.4	12.5
104	Olin Mathieson Chemical	1,002	75	586	7.5	12.9
137	Hercules	718	53	385	7.4	13.9
173	GAF	570	21	286	3.7	7.4
191	Diamond Shamrock	515	35	306	6.7	9.6
192	Ethyl	509	32	244	6.2	12.9
194	International Minerals & Chemicals	502	9	230	1.9	4.1
205	Stauffer Chemical	478	31	275	6.5	11.3
215	Koppers	449	15	189	3.4	8.0
220	Air Reduction	438	21	245	4.8	8.6
228	Rohm and Haas	423	35	318	8.2	10.9
236	Pennwalt	405	23	213	5.6	10.7
281	Interchemical	317	14	124	4.5	11.5
340	Chemetron	241	10	139	4.3	7.5
343	American Enka	239	20	139	8.2	14.1
371	Witco Chemical	221	11	86	4.8	12.4
388	Air Products and Chemical	202	12	125	5.8	9.4
436	Cabot	168	13	156	7.6	8.1
448	Reichhold Chemicals	161	7	73	4.1	9.0
494	Wyandotte Chemicals	147	2	88	1.3	2.1
		22,732	1,425	13,139	6.3	10.8

Note: Totals exclude Celanese.

Source: *Fortune,* May 15, 1969, pp. 168-85.

APPENDIX TABLE 6

Value Added by Manufacture, Value of Shipments, All Employees, Payroll, and Capital Expenditures, By Industry Groups, 1967

	Value Added by Manufacture[1]	Value of Shipments[2]	Pay-roll	All Em-ployees[3]	Capital Expendi-tures[4]
	----------(billions)----------			(000)	(millions)
Transportation equipment	$28.9	$70.5	$15.6	1,890	$1,717
Machinery, except electrical	27.7	49.1	14.3	1,872	1,739
Food and kindred products	26.4	81.7	10.0	1,654	1,601
Electrical equipment & supplies	24.9	43.6	12.9	1,884	1,462
Chemicals and allied products	23.4	42.2	6.5	854	2,833
Industrial chemicals	7.7	14.1	2.1	252	1,219
Plastics materials & synthetics	3.9	7.4	1.3	177	940
Primary metal industries	20.1	47.0	9.8	1,283	2,968
Fabricated metal products	17.1	33.2	9.0	1,307	1,009
Printing and publishing	14.2	21.7	7.3	1,064	821
Apparel & other textile products	9.7	20.8	5.2	1,363	198
Paper and allied products	9.7	20.9	4.4	643	1,426
Stone, clay, & glass products	8.4	14.8	3.9	605	722
Textile mill products	8.0	19.8	4.4	931	710
Rubber and plastics products n.e.c.	6.5	12.4	3.2	504	605
Instruments & related products	6.1	9.5	2.7	377	359
Petroleum & coal products	5.4	22.0	1.2	140	1,004
Ordnance and accessories	5.0	8.8	3.4	377	201
Lumber and wood products	4.8	10.9	2.8	563	394
Miscellaneous manufacturing industries	4.5	8.4	2.3	423	188
Furniture and fixtures	4.0	7.6	2.2	429	197
Leather and leather products	2.6	4.9	1.5	332	61
Tobacco manufactures	2.0	5.0	0.4	75	53
Total	259.3	554.6	131.7	19,388	20,268

Note: Administrative and auxiliary employees included in totals for all payrolls ($8.7 billion) and all employees (818,000).

n.e.c. - not elsewhere classified.

[1]Value added by manufacture, "represents value of products shipped (including resales of finished products produced by other manufacturing establishments) less cost of products, materials, supplies, fuel, electric energy, and contract work plus the net change in finished products and work-in-process inventories between the beginning and end of the year."

[2]Value of shipments data "include extensive duplication arising from shipments between establishments in the same industry classification."

[3]All employees figure is "an average of four monthly figures for the 'production workers' plus the March figure for all other employees."

[4]Excludes "expenditures for plants under construction and not yet in operation."

Source: U.S. Department of Commerce, Bureau of the Census, *1967 Census of Manufactures,* General Statistics for Industry Groups and Industries, Preliminary Report, MC 67(P)-1, Washington, D.C., April 1969, pp. 3, 7.

APPENDIX TABLE 7

Value of Shipments of Basic Chemicals, by Major Product Groups, 1935-1967

	Alkalies and Chlorine	Industrial Gases	Cyclic (Coal-tar) Crudes	Inter-mediate Coal-tar Products	Inorganic Pig-ments	Organic Chemicals n.e.c.	Inorganic Chemicals n.e.c.
			(*millions*)				
1935	NA	$ 42	NA	NA	$ 67	NA	NA
1937	NA	56	NA	NA	85	NA	NA
1939	$102	53	$ 33	$ 140	79	$ 237	$ 302
1947	209	94	61	474	287	973	623
1949	249	106	69	NA	270	NA	NA
1950	292	117	78	NA	364	NA	NA
1951	377	147	NA	NA	417	NA	NA
1952	355	162	90	NA	350	NA	NA
1953	396	180	97	NA	333	NA	NA
1954	414	201	79	743	389	2,245	1,978
1955	444	187	86	853	424	2,746	2,423
1956	476	202	105	910	454	3,004	2,766
1957	497	218	103	967	425	3,027	2,759
1958	504	277	117	817	418	3,098	2,754
1959	565	315	120	994	492	3,609	3,078
1960	577	344	124	1,004	487	3,735	3,114
1961	589	362	122	1,015	483	3,947	3,101
1962	628	382	120	1,032	488	4,430	3,259
1963	652	425	105	1,108	485	4,840	3,494
1964	712	507	93	1,197	548	5,265	3,727
1965	735	551	87	1,361	552	6,062	3,757
1966	783	550	73	1,483	582	6,541	3,845
1967	737	567	1,485		546	6,582	4,179

n.e.c. - Not elsewhere classified. NA - Not available.

Value of shipments data for 1958-1967 and 1954, "includes costs of products bought for resale without further manufacture, processing or assembly; for other years, excludes cost of products bought for resale." For 1939 and previous years data represent value of production.

Data for 1949-1953, 1955-1957, 1959-1962 and 1964-1967 "represent estimates derived from a representative sample of manufacturing establishments canvassed in the Annual Survey of Manufactures. These estimates, therefore, may differ from the results that would have been obtained for a complete canvass of all manufacturing establishments."

Sources: U.S. Department of Commerce, Bureau of the Census, *1963 U.S. Census of Manufactures,* Vol. II, Industry Statistics, Part I, Major Groups 20 to 28, Washington, D.C., 1966, pp. 28A-8-9; *Annual Survey of Manufactures: 1964 and 1965,* Washington, D.C., 1968, p. 39; *Annual Survey of Manufactures: 1966,* General Statistics for Industry Groups and Selected Industries (M6(AS)-1, Washington, D.C., 1967, pp. 12-13; *1967 Census of Manufactures,* General Statistics for Industry Groups and Industries, Washington, D.C., April 1969, p. 7.

APPENDIX TABLE 8

Value of Shipments of Fibers, Plastics, Rubbers, by Major Product Groups, 1925-1967

	Plastics Materials	Synthetic Rubber	Cellulosic Man-Made Fibers	Organic Fibers Non-Cellulosic	Cellulosic Plus Organic Fibers, Non-Cellulosic
			(*millions*)		
1925	NA	NA	NA	NA	$ 88
1927	NA	NA	NA	NA	110
1929	NA	NA	NA	NA	150
1931	NA	NA	NA	NA	133
1933	NA	NA	NA	NA	157
1935	NA	NA	NA	NA	185
1937	$ 67	NA	NA	NA	255
1939	83	NA	NA	NA	247
1947	478	$235	NA	NA	705
1949	592	185	NA	NA	920
1950	792	247	NA	NA	1,124
1951	1,081	484	NA	NA	1,204
1952	1,073	480	NA	NA	1,192
1953	1,255	442	NA	NA	1,251
1954	1,255	362	NA	NA	1,242
1955	1,499	515	NA	NA	1,479
1956	1,651	579	NA	NA	1,364
1957	1,775	609	NA	NA	1,457
1958	1,847	536	$723	$ 688	1,411
1959	2,236	703	782	875	1,657
1960	2,183	726	709	868	1,577
1961	2,125	696	644	1,040	1,683
1962	2,372	759	724	1,192	1,916
1963	2,571	764	732	1,403	2,135
1964	2,774	819	839	1,581	2,420
1965	3,118	848	903	1,843	2,746
1966	3,533	955	924	1,992	2,916
1967	3,584	927	735	2,181	2,916

NA - Not available.

Data for plastics materials for 1939 are not entirely comparable with 1937. Value of shipments data for 1958-1966 and 1954, "includes cost of products bought for resale without further manufacture, processing or assembly; for other years, excludes cost of products bought for resale." For 1939 and previous years data represent value of production. Data for 1949-1953, 1955-1957, 1959-1962, and 1964-1967 "represent estimates derived from a representative sample of manufacturing establishments canvassed in the Annual Survey of Manufactures. These estimates, therefore, may differ from the results that would have been obtained from a complete canvass of all manufacturing establishments."

Sources: See Appendix Table 1.

APPENDIX TABLE 9

Value of Shipments: Chemicals, 1939-1967

	Industrial Chemicals (SIC 281)	Plastics Materials and Synthetics (SIC 282)	Total Chemicals
	(*millions*)		
1939	$ 946	$ 330	$ 1.277
1947	2,719	1,419	4,138
1954	6,048	2,858	8,906
1955	7,163	3,493	10,656
1956	7,917	3,595	11,512
1957	7,994	3,841	11,835
1958	7,986	3,794	11,780
1959	9,175	4,597	13,772
1960	9,384	4,486	13,870
1961	9,618	4,504	14,123
1962	10,367	5,048	15,415
1963	11,109	5,470	16,579
1964	12,149	6,013	18,062
1965	13,042	6,712	19,754
1966	13,857	7,403	21,260
1967	14,096	7,427	21,523

Sources: See Appendix Table 1.

APPENDIX TABLE 10

Per Cent Relationship of Sales: Chemicals and Allied Products to Total Corporate and Manufacturing, 1929-1966

	Total Corporate Sales	Manufacturing Sales	Chemicals & Allied Products Sales	Per Cent Relationship of Chemicals and Allied Products Sales to:	
				Total Corporate	Manufacturing
	----------(billions)----------				
1929	$ 138.6	$ 70.3	$ 4.0	2.9%	5.7%
1930	118.3	58.5	4.9	4.1	8.4
1931	92.4	42.8	2.8	3.0	6.5
1932	69.2	31.0	2.2	3.2	7.1
1933	73.0	34.3	2.3	3.2	6.7
1934	89.6	40.1	2.7	3.0	6.7
1935	102.0	46.8	3.1	3.0	6.6
1936	119.5	56.0	3.8	3.2	6.8
1937	128.9	61.5	4.1	3.2	6.7
1938	108.6	50.0	3.7	3.4	7.4
1939	120.8	57.2	4.3	3.6	7.5
1940	135.2	65.8	4.8	3.6	7.3
1941	176.2	92.0	6.4	3.6	7.0
1942	202.8	116.3	7.2	3.6	6.2
1943	233.4	141.9	8.6	3.7	6.1
1944	246.7	151.0	9.8	4.0	6.5
1945	239.5	138.7	9.8	4.1	7.1
1946	270.6	136.8	10.6	3.9	7.7
1947	347.1	177.6	13.3	3.8	7.5
1948	388.1	196.0	13.2	3.4	6.7
1949	369.5	183.7	12.4	3.4	6.8
1950	431.1	216.1	15.4	3.6	7.1
1951	487.7	250.2	17.2	3.5	6.9
1952	498.5	256.1	16.9	3.4	6.6
1953	522.3	275.5	17.7	3.4	6.4
1954	515.7	264.9	17.9	3.5	6.8
1955	598.2	302.2	20.7	3.5	6.8
1956	631.1	314.8	21.8	3.5	6.9
1957	670.3	329.4	22.9	3.4	7.0
1958	656.9	321.9	22.6	3.4	7.0
1959	737.3	357.7	26.1	3.5	7.3
1960	763.2	364.6	26.3	3.4	7.2
1961	780.7	369.9	28.4	3.6	7.7
1962	849.1	399.7	29.6	3.5	7.4
1963	892.6	419.3	32.7	3.7	7.8
1964	961.6	453.2	34.5	3.6	7.6
1965	1,058.9	503.0	40.2	3.8	8.0
1966	1,158.3	557.3	43.6	3.8	7.8

Sources: U.S. Department of Commerce, Office of Business Economics. *The National Income and Product Accounts of the United States, 1929-1965,* Washington, D.C., pp. 142-145; *Survey of Current Business,* July 1968, p. 46 and July 1969, p. 44.

APPENDIX TABLE 11

**Per Cent Relationship of Value Added in Chemicals and
Allied Products and Chemicals to All Manufacturing,
1899-1967**

	All Manufacturing	Chemicals & Allied Products	Per Cent Relationship	Chemicals	Per Cent Relationship
	------------(*billions*)------------			(*billions*)	
1899	$ 4.6	$ 0.2	4.3%	$ *	0.6%
1904	6.0	0.3	5.0	*	0.6
1909	8.2	0.4	4.9	0.1	1.2
1914	9.4	0.4	4.3	0.1	1.1
1919	23.8	1.0	4.2	0.3	1.3
1921	17.3	0.8	4.6	0.2	1.2
1923	24.6	1.1	4.5	0.3	1.2
1925	25.7	1.2	4.7	0.4	1.6
1927	26.3	1.4	5.3	0.4	1.5
1929	30.6	1.6	5.2	0.5	1.6
1931	18.6	1.3	7.0	0.4	2.2
1933	14.0	1.1	7.9	0.4	2.9
1935	18.6	1.3	7.0	0.5	2.7
1937	25.2	1.6	6.3	0.7	2.8
1939	24.5	1.7	6.9	0.7	2.9
1947	74.3	4.9	6.6	2.1	2.8
1954	117.0	9.2	7.9	4.7	4.0
1958	141.5	12.3	8.7	6.2	4.4
1963	192.1	17.6	9.2	9.0	4.7
1964	206.2	19.2	9.3	10.0	4.8
1965	227.0	21.0	9.3	10.9	4.8
1966	251.0	22.8	9.1	11.7	4.7
1967	259.3	23.4	9.0	11.6	4.5

*Less than 0.05 billion.

Sources: See Appendix Table 1.

APPENDIX TABLE 12

Value Added by Manufacture: Chemicals, 1939-1967

	Basic Chemicals (SIC 281)	Fibers, Plastics, Rubbers (SIC 282)	Total Chemicals
	(millions)		
1939	$ 536	$ 208	$ 744
1947	1,330	728	2,059
1954	3,223	1,427	4,650
1955	3,946	1,830	5,776
1956	4,278	1,792	6,070
1957	4,313	1,916	6,230
1958	4,314	1,900	6,214
1959	5,075	2,395	7,413
1960	5,144	2,256	7,357
1961	5,298	2,287	7,520
1962	5,736	2,626	8,323
1963	6,170	2,866	9,036
1964	6,792	3,234	10,026
1965	7,297	3,603	10,900
1966	7,549	3,999	11,548
1967	7,685	3,887	11,572

Sources: U.S. Department of Commerce, Bureau of the Census, *1963 U.S. Census of Manufactures,* Vol. II, Industry Statistics, Part I, Major Groups 20 to 28, Washington, D.C., 1966, pp. 28A-8, 9, 28B-5; *Annual Survey of Manufactures: 1964 and 1965,* Washington, D.C., 1968, pp. 39, 41; *Annual Survey of Manufactures: 1966,* General Statistics for Industry Groups and Selected Industries (M66(AS)-1), Washington, D.C., 1967, pp. 12, 13; *1967 Census of Manufactures,* General Statistics for Industry Groups and Industries, Washington, D.C., April 1969, p. 7.

Value Added by Manufacture of Basic Chemicals,
by Major Product Groups, 1935-1967

	Alkalies and Chlorine	Industrial Gases	Cyclic (Coal-tar) Crudes	Inter-mediate Coal-tar Products	Inorganic Pig-ments	Organic Chemicals n.e.c.	Inorganic Chemicals n.e.c.
				(*millions*)			
1935	NA	$ 31	NA	NA	$ 31	NA	NA
1937	NA	42	NA	NA	37	NA	NA
1939	$ 68	40	$11	$ 79	38	$ 134	$ 166
1947	114	67	17	260	105	456	311
1949	145	76	22	NA	109	NA	NA
1950	185	86	23	NA	164	NA	NA
1951	228	103	NA	NA	179	NA	NA
1952	210	115	25	NA	141	NA	NA
1953	243	120	28	NA	159	NA	NA
1954	256	122	22	363	195	1,177	1,088
1955	284	138	25	447	233	1,481	1,338
1956	311	148	27	479	262	1,573	1,478
1957	314	157	27	511	244	1,625	1,435
1958	306	174	30	373	236	1,726	1,469
1959	348	197	34	480	293	2,040	1,683
1960	360	212	36	479	285	2,081	1,691
1961	363	222	37	493	296	2,199	1,688
1962	392	226	34	495	302	2,511	1,776
1963	389	260	35	570	286	2,727	1,903
1964	436	309	28	593	335	2,991	2,100
1965	443	347	27	655	331	3,472	2,022
1966	467	363	24	718	340	3,641	1,996
1967	437	376		708	329	3,637	2,204

NA - Not Available.

n.e.c. - not elsewhere classified.

Value added data since 1954 are adjusted and for previous years are unadjusted.

Data for 1949-1953, 1953-1957, 1959-1962, and 1964-1967 "represent estimates derived from a representative sample of manufacturing establishments canvassed in the Annual Survey of Manufactures. These estimates therefore, may differ from the results that would have been obtained from a complete canvass of all manufacturing establishments."

Sources: See Appendix Table 12.

APPENDIX TABLE 14

Value Added by Manufacture of Fibers, Plastics, Rubbers, by Major Product Groups, 1923-1967

	Plastics Materials	Synthetic Rubber	Cellulosic Man-Made Fibers	Organic Fibers Non-Cellulosic	Cellulosic Plus Organic Fibers, Non-Cellulosic
			(*millions*)		
1923	NA	NA	NA	NA	$ 12
1925	NA	NA	NA	NA	70
1927	NA	NA	NA	NA	84
1929	NA	NA	NA	NA	116
1931	NA	NA	NA	NA	97
1933	NA	NA	NA	NA	113
1935	NA	NA	NA	NA	121
1937	$ 31	NA	NA	NA	174
1939	40	NA	NA	NA	169
1947	198	$ 97	NA	NA	433
1949	267	65	NA	NA	519
1950	386	109	NA	NA	717
1951	473	138	NA	NA	711
1952	473	168	NA	NA	704
1953	563	151	NA	NA	708
1954	586	143	NA	NA	699
1955	723	201	NA	NA	905
1956	760	222	NA	NA	810
1957	835	230	NA	NA	851
1958	872	198	$390	$ 440	830
1959	1,111	282	445	558	1,003
1960	1,041	276	389	550	939
1961	969	292	358	668	1,027
1962	1,102	318	414	793	1,207
1963	1,202	330	412	922	1,334
1964	1,347	360	483	1,044	1,527
1965	1,480	392	516	1,215	1,731
1966	1,703	443	551	1,302	1,853
1967	1,722	411	420	1,334	1,754

NA - Not available.

Data for plastics materials for 1939 are not entirely comparable with 1937. Value added data since 1954 are adjusted and for previous years are unadjusted.

Data for 1949-1953, 1955-1957, 1959-1962, and 1964-1967 "represent estimates derived from a representative sample of manufacturing establishments canvassed in the Annual Survey of Manufactures. These estimates, therefore, may differ from the results that would have been obtained from a complete canvass of all manufacturing establishments."

Sources: See Appendix Table 12.

APPENDIX TABLE 15

Indexes of Industrial Production: Industrial Chemicals, Inorganic Chemicals, Organic Chemicals, Synthetic Materials, 1947-1968
(1957-59 = 100)

	Industrial Chemicals	Inorganic Chemicals	Organic Chemicals	Synthetic Materials
1947	34.8	32.0	36.0	31.8
1948	39.3	34.1	41.5	37.1
1949	38.8	35.4	40.3	37.4
1950	49.6	41.1	53.1	48.6
1951	57.9	48.6	61.8	59.0
1952	60.3	53.7	63.2	56.3
1953	69.6	64.2	71.9	63.9
1954	69.2	72.7	67.7	60.2
1955	84.5	85.0	84.3	78.0
1956	90.0	91.1	89.6	82.8
1957	94.8	96.3	94.1	90.8
1958	93.1	97.1	91.4	90.4
1959	112.2	106.7	114.4	118.8
1960	120.1	110.6	124.1	123.0
1961	129.6	113.7	136.3	136.5
1962	147.5	122.5	158.0	167.1
1963	162.5	135.6	173.9	192.1
1964	178.4	149.3	190.7	221.0
1965	196.3	159.7	211.7	257.0
1966	220.1	175.8	238.7	288.5
1967	236.0	190.9	254.9	299.9
1968	260.4	202.1	288.3	360.0

Sources: Board of Governors of the Federal Reserve System, *Industrial Production - 1957-59 Base,* Washington, D.C., pp. S-59, S-102, S-103; *Business Indexes,* passim.

APPENDIX TABLE 16

Production Worker Employment: All Manufacturing, Chemicals and Allied Products, and Chemicals, 1899-1967

	All Manufacturing	Chemicals and Allied Products	Chemicals	Per Cent of all Manufacturing Chemicals and Allied Products	Chemicals
	---------------(*thousands*)------------------				
1899	4,502	129	18	2.9	0.4
1904	5,182	130	22	2.5	0.4
1909	6,262	162	26	2.6	0.4
1914	6,602	179	35	2.7	0.5
1919	8,465	253	77	3.0	0.9
1929	8,370	285	105	3.4	1.3
1939	7,808	250	123	3.2	1.6
1947	11,918	432	214	3.6	1.8
1954	12,372	471	241	3.8	1.9
1958	11,666	453	244	3.9	2.1
1959	12,266	469	253	3.8	2.1
1960	12,186	468	255	3.8	2.1
1961	11,774	460	248	3.9	2.1
1962	12,139	471	255	3.9	2.1
1963	12,232	474	257	3.9	2.1
1967	13,975	544	285	3.9	2.0

Sources: See Appendix Table 1.

Employment: Chemicals and Chemicals and Allied Products, 1939-1968

	Chemicals*		Chemicals and Allied Products	
	All Workers	Production Workers	All Workers	Production Workers
		(thousands)		
1939	158	119	371	252
1940	178	136	399	274
1941	232	181	483	348
1942	317	254	571	435
1943	360	294	609	480
1944	351	286	650	512
1945	364	291	668	518
1946	288	226	633	482
1947	299	234	649	488
1948	309	239	655	485
1949	288	218	618	449
1950	301	226	640	461
1951	348	258	707	503
1952	370	266	730	506
1953	411	289	768	523
1954	400	275	753	503
1955	414	289	773	518
1956	427	292	797	526
1957	432	283	810	520
1958	422	263	794	494
1959	428	270	809	506
1960	439	272	828	510
1961	436	268	828	505
1962	447	277	849	519
1963	460	282	865	525
1964	470	288	879	529
1965	484	298	908	546
1966	509	308	961	574
1967	520	309	1,002	593
1968	532	317	1,031	610

*Data for 1939 to 1957 are for industrial inorganic and organic chemicals. Starting with 1958, the data cover a new series based on the 1957 Standard Industrial Classification; they include industrial chemicals and plastics and synthetics, except glass.

Sources: U.S. Department of Labor, Bureau of Labor Statistics, *Employment, Hours and Earnings* (for industrial inorganic and organic chemicals for the years 1939-1947) *passim; Employment and Earnings,* May 1954, pp. 54, 60; May 1959, pp. 67, 73; March 1964, p. 18; "Employment and Earnings Statistics for the United States, 1909-68," *Bulletin No. 1312-6,* Washington, D.C., 1968, pp. 639, 640, 643, 644, 649; January 1969, pp. 133-34.

APPENDIX TABLE 18

Wholesale Price Indexes: Chemicals and Chemicals and Allied Products, 1926-1968
(1957-59 = 100)

	All Commodities	Chemicals and Allied Products	Chemicals
1926	54.8	n.a.	68.3
1927	52.3	n.a.	67.9
1928	53.0	n.a.	67.4
1929	52.1	n.a.	68.1
1930	47.3	n.a.	66.2
1931	39.9	n.a.	61.6
1932	35.6	n.a.	60.7
1933	36.1	46.6	59.3
1934	41.0	48.8	59.3
1935	43.8	50.9	60.5
1936	44.2	51.2	60.1
1937	47.2	53.6	60.2
1938	43.0	51.0	59.0
1939	42.2	50.7	57.9
1940	43.0	51.6	58.1
1941	47.8	56.1	59.6
1942	54.0	62.3	65.8
1943	56.5	63.1	65.9
1944	56.9	63.8	65.7
1945	57.9	64.2	65.7
1946	66.1	69.4	68.1
1947	81.2	92.2	80.0
1948	87.9	94.4	84.9
1949	83.5	86.2	77.8
1950	86.8	87.5	81.8
1951	96.7	100.1	97.6
1952	94.0	95.0	93.1
1953	92.7	96.1	95.1
1954	92.9	97.3	95.1
1955	93.2	96.9	95.6
1956	96.2	97.5	98.2
1957	99.0	99.6	99.9
1958	100.4	100.4	99.9
1959	100.6	100.0	100.2
1960	100.7	100.2	100.5
1961	100.3	99.1	98.4
1962	100.6	97.5	96.3
1963	100.3	96.3	94.8
1964	100.5	96.7	94.2
1965	102.5	97.4	95.0
1966	105.9	97.8	95.7
1967	106.1	98.4	97.4
1968	108.7	98.2	98.4

NA - Not Available.

Sources: U.S. Department of Labor, Bureau of Labor Statistics, mimeographed sheets; U.S. Department of Commerce, Office of Business Economics, *Business Statistics,* 1967 edition, Washington, D.C., 1967, pp. 41, 42. *Monthly Labor Review,* May 1969, p. 117.

APPENDIX TABLE 19

Wholesale Price Indexes: Chemicals, Inorganic Chemicals, Organic Chemicals, and Plastic Materials, 1947-1968
(1957-59 = 100)

	Chemicals	Inorganic Chemicals	Organic Chemicals	Plastic Resins and Materials
1947	80.0	66.7	87.7	94.3
1948	84.9	72.3	92.5	93.8
1949	77.8	75.8	79.0	95.1
1950	81.8	78.1	83.9	95.7
1951	97.6	85.4	104.7	119.4
1952	93.1	85.5	97.7	118.7
1953	95.1	89.6	98.6	118.9
1954	95.1	93.3	96.0	118.0
1955	95.6	94.5	96.0	112.6
1956	98.2	97.2	98.6	102.3
1957	99.9	98.9	100.5	102.4
1958	99.9	100.2	99.8	101.0
1959	100.2	100.9	99.8	96.6
1960	100.5	101.8	99.6	96.3
1961	98.4	102.4	96.2	91.9
1962	96.3	102.4	92.6	91.7
1963	94.8	102.2	90.1	89.7
1964	94.2	103.0	88.7	89.0
1965	95.0	104.6	88.9	88.4
1966	95.7	106.0	89.1	89.0
1967	97.4	110.1	89.5	89.1
1968	98.4	114.4	88.6	82.0

Sources: U.S. Department of Labor, Bureau of Labor Statistics, mimeographed sheets, code 06-1, 06-11, 06-12, 06-73, *Wholesale Prices and Price Indexes,* various issues.

APPENDIX TABLE 20

**Productivity Indexes: Chemicals and Allied Products and All Manufacturing,
Selected Years, 1899-1957 (1929 = 100)**

Year	Output per Employee		Output per Manhour		Output per Unit of Capital Input		Total Factor Productivity	
	Chemicals and Allied Products	All Manu-facturing	Chemicals and Allied Products	All Manu-facturing	Chemicals and Allied Products	All Manu-facturing	Chemicals and Allied Products	All Manu-facturing
1899	49.1	54.1	41.1	45.5	72.4	93.9	49.2	53.9
1909	54.7	59.7	46.6	51.8	66.2	79.8	52.5	57.9
1919	48.6	60.8	45.4	58.0	55.8	65.7	48.9	59.6
1929	100.0	100.0	100.0	100.0	100.0	100.0	100.0	100.0
1937	113.7	102.1	127.2	116.9	126.9	121.0	127.1	116.7
1948	177.3	125.7	193.6	138.6	183.2	152.5	189.5	138.4
1953	231.6	147.6	259.7	163.9	194.4	158.4	232.1	156.8
1957	285.3	164.4	322.2	187.1	N.A.	N.A.	N.A.	N.A.
Per Cent Increase								
1899-1957....	481.1	203.9	683.9	311.2				
1899-1953....	371.7	172.8	531.9	260.2	168.5	68.7	371.7	190.9
1937-1957....	150.9	61.0	153.3	60.1				
1937-1953....	103.7	44.7	104.2	40.2	53.2	30.9	82.6	34.4

N.A.—Not available.

Source: John W. Kendrick, *Productivity Trends in the United States,* Princeton University Press, Princeton, N.J., 1961, pp. 464, 471.

APPENDIX TABLE 21

Man-Made Fibers, Output Per Employee and Per Manhour,
1939-1966

Year	Output Per Employee	Output Per Production Worker	Output Per All Employee Manhour	Output Per Production Worker Manhour
			(1957 - 59 = 100)	
1939	18.5	15.9	NA	16.1
1947	37.6	35.0	36.7	34.2
1949	43.9	42.0	39.9	39.2
1950	53.5	51.8	53.3	51.9
1951	56.6	54.9	56.8	55.5
1952	57.4	57.4	56.9	57.0
1953	57.2	57.3	57.9	58.3
1954	63.5	63.5	63.8	63.9
1955	81.7	77.5	81.4	77.3
1956	81.4	79.0	82.4	80.5
1957*	97.3	96.1	98.0	97.1
1958	94.2	97.0	94.0	96.5
1959	108.4	106.8	107.7	106.1
1960	101.9	102.0	103.0	103.4
1961	110.1	111.4	110.7	111.8
1962	121.8	121.0	121.5	120.3
1963	121.9	124.8	120.6	122.3
1964	131.1	133.3	128.3	129.3
1965	133.9	134.7	132.4	132.2
1966p	133.6	137.4	133.2	136.0

*New Series

p - Preliminary

Source: U.S. Department of Labor, Bureau of Labor Statistics, *Indexes of Output Per Manhour For Selected Industries, 1939 and 1947-61,* Washington, D.C., October 1962, p. 28 and *Ibid.,* "1939 and 1947-67," December 1968, pp. 57-59.

APPENDIX TABLE 22

Research and Development Expenditures: All Industry, Chemicals and Allied Products, and Chemicals, 1956-1967

Year	All Industry Total	All Industry Company Funds	Chemicals and Allied Products Total	Chemicals and Allied Products Company Funds	Chemicals Total	Chemicals Company Funds
			(millions of dollars)			
1956	6,605	3,277	641	NA	460	NA
1957	7,731	3,296	705	616	503	423
1958	8,389	3,630	792	666	553	443
1959	9,618	3,983	891	740	599	485
1960	10,509	4,428	986	804	666	538
1961	10,908	4,668	1,109	849	709	556
1962	11,464	5,029	1,190	894	748	572
1963	12,686	5,406	1,279	1,016	831	653
1964	13,353	5,753	1,284	1,054	856	684
1965	14,185	6,445	1,390	1,198	932	784
1966	15,548	7,216	1,461	1,271	955	796
1967	16,420	8,032	1,565	1,353	1,006	823

NA - Not Available

Sources: National Science Foundation, "Research and Development in the Chemicals and Allied Products Industry, 1956-1961," *Reviews of Data on Research and Development,* September 1963, p. 4; "Research and Development in American Industry, 1962," *Reviews of Data on Research and Development,* September 1963, p. 10; "Basic Research, Applied Research, and Development in American Industry, 1964," *Reviews of Data on Science Resources,* January 1966, pp. 6, 9, 10; "Research and Development in Industry, 1966," *Reviews of Data on Science Resources,* January 1968, p. 6; "Research and Development in Industry, 1967," *Reviews of Data on Science Resources,* February 1969, p. 3.

APPENDIX TABLE 23

Employment in Chemicals and Chemicals and Allied Products, 1939-1968

| Year | Chemicals | | Chemicals and Allied Products | |
| | All Workers | Production Workers | All Workers | Production Workers |
	(thousands)		(thousands)	
1939*	158.1	119.0	371.0	252.0
1940	177.9	135.7	399.0	274.0
1941	231.7	181.0	438.0	348.0
1942	316.8	253.6	571.0	435.0
1943	359.9	293.8	609.0	480.0
1944	350.9	286.3	650.0	512.0
1945	364.3	290.6	668.0	518.0
1946	287.8	226.3	633.0	482.0
1947	298.8	234.2	649.0	488.0
1948	308.6	239.2	655.0	485.0
1949	288.1	217.7	618.0	449.0
1950	301.1	226.4	640.0	461.0
1951	347.6	258.0	707.0	502.5
1952	370.0	266.1	730.1	506.1
1953	411.3	289.2	768.2	522.9
1954	399.7	275.2	752.7	503.0
1955	413.6	289.1	773.1	518.1
1956	426.7	292.0	796.5	525.7
1957	431.8	283.3	810.0	519.7
1958**	421.6	262.7	794.1	493.7
1959	428.0	269.6	809.2	505.6
1960	438.9	272.3	828.2	509.9
1961	436.2	267.6	827.2	504.3
1962	447.3	277.3	846.0	517.2
1963	460.0	282.3	865.3	524.2
1964	470.1	287.7	878.6	528.7
1965	483.8	297.5	906.4	546.0
1966	509.2	308.1	961.0	574.0
1967	519.7	308.6	1,002.0	592.0
1968	532.1	316.9	1,031.9	610.5

Notes: *Data for 1939 to 1957 are for industrial inorganic and organic chemicals.

**New series based on 1957 Standard Industrial Classification. Includes chemicals and plastics materials and synthetics.

Sources: U.S. Department of Labor, Bureau of Labor Statistics, *Employment and Earnings Statistics for the United States, 1909-68,* Bulletin No. 1312-6, Washington, D.C., 1968, pp. 639, 640, 643, 644, and 649. *Monthly Labor Review,* March 1969, pp. 92, 96.

APPENDIX TABLE 24

Average Hourly and Weekly Earnings, Chemicals, 1947-1968

Year	Average Hourly Earnings			Average Weekly Earnings		
	Inorganic	Organic	Weighted Average	Inorganic	Organic	Weighted Average
1947	$1.38	$1.31	$1.33	$ 55.65	$ 52.79	$ 53.46
1948	1.52	1.43	1.45	62.13	57.69	58.74
1949	1.57	1.54	1.55	63.90	60.83	61.58
1950	1.66	1.62	1.63	67.89	65.69	66.21
1951	1.80	1.75	1.76	74.88	71.40	72.21
1952	1.88	1.85	1.86	77.08	75.11	75.57
1953	2.01	1.97	1.98	82.81	80.18	80.79
1954	2.11	2.05	2.07	86.09	83.22	83.96
1955	2.20	2.13	2.15	89.98	87.33	88.01
1956	2.32	2.26	2.28	95.35	92.89	93.52
1957	2.44	2.37	2.39	100.04	96.93	97.73
1958	2.56	2.47	2.49	104.45	100.04	101.19
	Industrial	Synthetics	Weighted	Industrial	Synthetics	Weighted
1958	2.59	2.30	2.48	105.67	93.61	101.23
1959	2.72	2.41	2.60	113.15	100.50	108.34
1960	2.82	2.51	2.70	117.31	104.17	112.26
1961	2.90	2.58	2.78	120.93	107.07	115.55
1962	2.98	2.63	2.84	124.27	109.93	118.62
1963	3.07	2.71	2.92	128.02	113.01	121.83
1964	3.15	2.77	2.99	131.04	116.89	125.03
1965	3.24	2.84	3.06	136.08	120.70	129.31
1966	3.33	2.95	3.16	140.86	125.08	133.87
1967	3.45	3.07	3.28	144.56	128.33	137.53
1968	3.62	3.22	3.44	152.76	136.53	145.54
Dec. 1968	3.73	3.30	3.53	158.90	140.91	150.62

Sources: U.S. Department of Labor, Bureau of Labor Statistics, Employment, Hours, and Earnings (for industrial chemicals for the years 1947-1958), passim, "Employment and Earnings Statistics for the United States, 1909-68, *Bulletin No. 1312-6,* Washington, D.C., 1968, pp. 447, 449, 640-41, 644, 649-50. *Employment and Earnings,* March 1969, pp. 60, 94.

APPENDIX TABLE 25

Average Hourly Earnings: Chemicals, Chemicals and Allied Products, and All Manufacturing, 1947-1968

Year	Chemicals	Chemicals and Allied Products	All Manufacturing	Amount Greater than All Manufacturing	
				Chemicals	Chemicals and Allied Products
1947	$1.33	$1.22	$1.22	$.11	$.00
1948	1.45	1.34	1.33	.12	.01
1949	1.55	1.42	1.38	.17	.04
1950	1.63	1.50	1.44	.19	.06
1951	1.76	1.62	1.56	.20	.06
1952	1.86	1.69	1.65	.21	.04
1953	1.98	1.81	1.74	.24	.07
1954	2.07	1.89	1.78	.29	.11
1955	2.15	1.97	1.86	.29	.11
1956	2.28	2.09	1.95	.33	.14
1957	2.39	2.20	2.05	.34	.15
1958	2.49	2.29	2.11	.38	.18
1959	2.60*	2.40	2.19	.41	.21
1960	2.70	2.50	2.26	.44	.24
1961	2.78	2.58	2.32	.46	.26
1962	2.84	2.65	2.39	.45	.26
1963	2.92	2.72	2.46	.46	.26
1964	2.99	2.80	2.53	.46	.27
1965	3.06	2.89	2.61	.45	.28
1966	3.16	2.99	2.72	.44	.27
1967	3.28	3.10	2.83	.45	.27
1968 Dec.	3.44	3.26	3.01	.43	.25
1968	3.53	3.36	3.11	.41	.25

Note: *Beginning in 1959 new series for chemicals.

Sources: U.S. Department of Labor, Bureau of Labor Statistics, "Employment and Earnings Statistics for the United States, 1909-68," *Bulletin No. 1312-6,* Washington, D.C., 1968, pp. 50-51, 640-41, 644, 649-50; Employment, Hours and Earnings (for chemicals for the years 1947-1958), *passim. Employment and Earnings,* March 1969, p. 94.

APPENDIX TABLE 26

Average Weekly Earnings: Chemicals, Chemicals and Allied Products, and All Manufacturing, 1947-1968

Year	Chemicals	Chemicals and Allied Products	All Manufacturing	Amount Greater than All Manufacturing	
				Chemicals	Chemicals and Allied Products
1947	$ 53.46	$ 50.31	$ 49.17	$ 4.29	$ 1.14
1948	58.74	55.33	53.12	5.62	2.21
1949	61.58	57.67	53.88	7.70	3.79
1950	66.21	61.68	58.32	7.89	3.36
1951	72.21	66.91	63.34	8.87	3.57
1952	75.57	69.12	67.16	8.41	1.96
1953	80.79	74.21	70.47	10.32	3.74
1954	83.96	77.11	70.49	13.47	6.62
1955	88.01	80.97	75.70	12.31	5.27
1956	93.52	85.90	78.78	14.74	7.12
1957	97.73	89.98	81.59	16.14	8.39
1958	101.19	93.20	82.71	18.48	10.49
1959	108.34*	99.36	88.26	20.08	11.10
1960	112.26	103.25	89.72	22.54	13.53
1961	115.55	106.81	92.34	23.21	14.47
1962	118.62	110.24	96.56	22.06	13.42
1963	121.83	112.88	99.63	22.45	13.50
1964	125.03	116.48	102.97	22.06	13.51
1965	129.31	121.09	107.53	21.78	13.56
1966	133.87	125.58	112.34	21.53	13.24
1967	137.53	128.96	114.90	22.63	14.05
1968	145.44	136.27	122.51	22.93	13.76

Note: *Beginning in 1959 new series for chemicals.

Sources: U.S. Department of Labor, Bureau of Labor Statistics, "Employment and Earnings Statistics for the United States, 1909-1968," *Bulletin No. 1312-6,* Washington, D.C., 1968, pp. 50, 640, 644, 649; Employment, Hours, and Earnings (for chemicals for the years 1947-1958), *passim; Employment and Earnings,* March 1969, p. 98.

APPENDIX TABLE 27

Real Average Hourly Earnings: Chemicals, Chemicals and Allied Products, and All Manufacturing, 1947-1968

(in 1957-1959 dollars)

Year	Chemicals	Chemicals and Allied Products	All Manufacturing
1947	$1.71	$1.57	$1.57
1948	1.73	1.60	1.58
1949	1.87	1.71	1.66
1950	1.95	1.79	1.72
1951	1.94	1.79	1.72
1952	2.01	1.83	1.78
1953	2.12	1.94	1.87
1954	2.21	2.02	1.90
1955	2.30	2.11	1.99
1956	2.41	2.21	2.06
1957	2.44	2.24	2.09
1958	2.47	2.27	2.10
1959	2.56	2.36	2.16
1960	2.62	2.42	2.19
1961	2.67	2.48	2.23
1962	2.69	2.51	2.27
1963	2.74	2.55	2.31
1964	2.77	2.59	2.34
1965	2.78	2.63	2.37
1966	2.79	2.64	2.40
1967	2.82	2.67	2.43
1968	2.84	2.69	2.48
Dec. 1968	2.85	2.72	2.51

Sources: Economic Report of the President, February 1968, p. 261; U.S. Department of Labor, Bureau of Labor Statistics, "Employment and Earnings Statistics for the United States, 1909-68," *Bulletin No. 1312-6,* Washington, D.C., 1968, pp. 50-51, 640-41, 644, 649-50; *Employment, Hours, and Earnings* (for chemicals for the years 1947-1958), *passim. Employment and Earnings,* March 1969, p. 94.

APPENDIX TABLE 28

Wage Supplements for Chemicals and Allied Products, 1947-1967

Year	Total Wages and Salaries	Wage Supplements	Per Cent
	(millions)		
1947	$2,255	$ 139	6.2
1948	2,216	161	7.3
1949	2,207	170	7.7
1950	2,432	200	8.2
1951	2,930	270	9.2
1952	3,191	285	8.9
1953	3,575	305	8.5
1954	3,662	355	9.7
1955	3,931	369	9.4
1956	4,353	420	9.6
1957	4,667	494	10.6
1958	4,707	531	11.3
1959	5,050	610	12.1
1960	5,330	662	12.4
1961	5,534	699	12.6
1962	5,824	776	13.3
1963	6,111	828	13.5
1964	6,463	907	14.0
1965	6,872	991	14.4
1966	7,579	1,132	14.9
1967	8,144	1,288	15.8

Sources: U.S. Department of Commerce, Office of Business Economics, *The National Income and Product Accounts of the United States, 1929-1965,* Washington, D.C., August 1966, pp. 91-3, 95-7; *Survey of Current Business,* July 1968, p. 41.

APPENDIX TABLE 29

Output per Manhour, Average Hourly Labor Costs, and Unit Labor Costs, Chemicals, 1947-1968

	Average Hourly Labor Costs		Output per Manhour All Employees	Unit Labor Costs
	Dollars	Index		
		(1957-59 = 100)	*(1957-59 = 100)*	
1947	$1.40	50.7	50.7	100.0
1948	1.53	55.4	55.0	100.7
1949	1.63	59.1	59.1	100.0
1950	1.73	62.7	71.1	88.2
1951	1.89	68.5	71.0	96.5
1952	2.00	72.5	70.1	103.4
1953	2.13	77.2	72.7	106.2
1954	2.24	81.2	75.2	108.0
1955	2.33	84.4	87.5	96.5
1956	2.48	89.9	90.1	99.8
1957	2.63	95.3	94.2	101.2
1958	2.75	99.6	95.0	104.8
1959	2.89	104.7	112.0	93.3
1960	3.02	109.4	117.8	92.9
1961	3.12	113.0	128.0	88.3
1962	3.21	116.3	145.1	80.2
1963	3.32	120.3	159.0	75.7
1964	3.43	124.3	172.5	72.1
1965	3.54	128.3	186.8	68.7
1966	3.70	134.1	199.8	67.1
1967	3.90	141.3	207.8	68.0
1968	4.06*	147.1	226.9	64.8

* 1967 wage supplements.

Note: Average hourly labor costs combine BLS data for average hourly earnings of chemical production workers and wage supplements for all employees of chemicals and allied products.

Sources: Derived from U.S. Department of Labor, Bureau of Labor Statistics, "Employment and Earnings Statistics for the United States, 1909-68", *Bulletin No. 1312-6,* Washington, D.C., 1968, pp. 639, 641, 643, 644, 649, 650 and "Employment and Earnings Statistics for the United States, 1909-62", *Bulletin No. 1312-1,* Washington, D.C., 1963, pp. 447, 449; *Employment and Earnings,* March 1969, pp. 60, 94, 95; U.S. Department of Commerce, Office of Business Economics, *The National Income and Product Accounts of the United States,* Washington, D.C., August 1966, pp. 91-3, 95-7; *Survey of Current Business,* July 1968, p. 41; *Business Statistics,* 1967 Biennial Edition, Washington, D.C., September 1967, p. 16; *Federal Reserve Bulletin,* July 1968, p. A-57; *Business Indexes,* March 1969, p. 3.

Number of Returns, Total Compiled Receipts, and Profits of Chemicals and Allied Products Industry Group, 1963-1964

	Total Returns			Returns Without Net Income				
	Number	Total Compiled Receipts	Profits After Taxes	Number	Total Compiled Receipts	Deficit	% of Total Returns	% of Total Compiled Receipts
		(in millions)			*(in millions)*			
Chemicals and allied products	10,804	$33,728.1	$3,841.3	4,252	$1,495.2	$124.4	39.4	4.4
Basic chemicals	1,413	5,348.2	434.7	532	174.5	18.6	37.7	3.3
Plastics materials and synthetic resins, rubber, and man-made fibers, except glass	1,630	6,433.5	1,073.6	587	409.0	38.0	36.0	6.4
Drugs	1,325	4,659.1	723.6	604	163.8	10.9	45.6	3.5
Soap and related products except perfumes, cosmetics, and other toilet preparations	1,601	3,557.1	304.7	748	112.5	9.7	46.7	3.2
Perfumes, cosmetics, and other toilet preparations	821	1,376.6	169.6	445	104.2	10.0	54.2	7.6
Paints and allied products, including gum and wood chemicals	1,344	2,724.5	189.8	453	147.0	10.4	33.7	5.4
Fertilizers and other agricultural chemicals	1,162	1,611.6	50.6	395	309.6	18.6	34.0	19.2
Miscellaneous chemical products	1,355	2,982.1	290.1	423	74.2	8.0	31.2	2.5
Chemicals and allied products not allocable	153	5,035.4	604.6	65	0.4	13.7	42.5	*

*Less than 0.05 per cent.
Source: U.S. Department Internal Revenue Service, *Statistics of Income—1963, Corporation Income Tax Returns*, Washington, D.C., 1968, p. 55.

APPENDIX TABLE 31

Number of Returns, Total Compiled Receipts, and Net Income Before
Taxes, Chemicals and Allied Products Group, 1929-1966

	Returns With Net Income			Returns Without Net Income		
		Total	Income		Total	
		Compiled	Before		Compiled	
Year	Number	Receipts	Taxes	Number	Receipts	Deficit
		(in millions)			(in millions)	
1929	4,073	$ 9,578.7	$ 911.5	2,998	$ 737.3	$ 57.0
1930	3,287	9,643.6	534.1	3,727	2,352.3	175.5
1931	2,797	3,379.2	251.5	4,047	3,960.2	318.9
1932	1,741	2,770.3	167.8	5,315	3,702.1	223.3
1933	2,458	4,106.2	272.9	4,696	2,192.4	189.2
1934	3,049	3,329.4	324.0	4,559	3,327.9	178.5
1935	3,156	4,551.8	366.1	4,350	2,883.3	114.3
1936	3,303	3,653.2	479.3	3,508	275.8	18.8
1937	3,107	3,884.9	457.1	3,676	337.5	19.1
1938	2,799	3,232.2	339.1	4,002	479.9	30.7
1939	3,368	4,097.4	553.7	3,417	259.8	17.9
1940	3,484	4,641.0	683.2	3,350	228.3	17.0
1941	4,227	6,384.1	1,027.9	2,361	129.3	11.6
1942	4,258	7,203.3	1,140.4	2,098	121.9	13.3
1943	4,539	8,591.3	1,272.3	1,703	134.9	10.8
1944	4,408	9,795.9	1,302.0	1,636	156.7	10.9
1945	4,414	9,359.6	1,059.7	1,772	550.7	28.7
1946	4,608	10,558.9	1,524.7	2,229	270.9	27.3
1947	4,577	13,244.4	1,832.3	2,948	370.9	41.0
1948	4,323	13,696.1	1,728.5	3,088	558.5	46.6
1949	4,273	12,491.9	1,715.7	3,240	843.3	61.1
1950	4,847	16,217.5	2,794.0	2,540	250.1	22.0
1951	4,932	17,699.5	2,953.2	2,735	704.1	32.7
1952	4,655	17,451.5	2,297.8	2,973	616.6	55.6
1953	4,669	17,917.8	2,386.7	3,034	927.7	56.9
1954	4,588	17,976.9	2,289.2	2,768	1,123.6	63.9
1955-56	5,169	21,146.0	3,053.2	2,806	731.0	49.0
1956-57	5,074	22,364.5	3,016.9	2,842	715.6	49.4
1957-58	5,166	23,156.6	2,977.6	2,857	1,050.7	70.0
1958-59	5,571	22,189.8	2,651.5	2,504	1,097.8	58.1
1959-60	5,516	25,891.4	3,537.1	2,710	808.1	73.4
1960-61	5,668	25,695.1	3,283.0	3,347	1,276.6	89.7
1961-62	6,630	27,802.3	3,399.0	3,478	1,420.6	106.5
1962	6,992	29,270.8	3,552.0	4,040	1,239.0	127.5
1963	6,552	32,232.9	3,965.7	4,252	1,495.2	124.4
1964	7,049	34,347.6	4,607.5	3,908	1,398.2	120.7
1965	6,902	39,807.2	5,042.3	3,902	1,484.8	130.1
1966	7,040	43,403.4	5,374.7	3,529	1,120.7	92.5

Source: U.S. Treasury Department, Internal Revenue Service, Statistics of Income,
Corporation Income Tax Returns, 1929 to 1964, passim; Statistics of Income-1965,
Business Income Tax Returns, Washington, D.C., 1968, pp. 244, 252; Preliminary
Report, Statistics of Income-1966, Corporation Income Tax Return, Washington, D.C.,
1968, pp. 18, 26.

APPENDIX TABLE 32

Number of Returns, Total Compiled Receipts, and Net Income Before Taxes, Chemicals, 1948-1965

Year	Returns With Net Income			Returns Without Net Income		
	Number	Total Compiled Receipts	Income Before Taxes	Number	Total Compiled Receipts	Deficit
		(in millions)			*(in millions)*	
1948	400	$ 3,288.4	$ 643.6	254	$118.9	$ 8.9
1949	453	3,143.7	640.0	314	104.8	8.0
1950	551	3,932.3	1,017.2	227	20.7	3.4
1951	631	4,540.2	1,130.2	252	44.2	5.3
1952	504	4,536.8	924.6	334	100.9	12.8
1953	660	5,026.8	1,005.7	353	89.3	22.0
1954	587	5,444.3	998.5	294	187.7	22.8
1955-56	833	6,379.5	1,315.1	337	96.7	15.4
1956-57	722	6,810.0	1,195.9	309	85.6	11.1
1957-58	732	6,944.2	1,141.5	427	181.6	18.7
1958-59	943	6,690.0	949.1	410	622.9	22.3
1959-60	996	8,569.0	1,384.7	532	189.3	11.1
1960-61	1,006	8,290.0	1,220.7	439	353.0	39.8
1961-62	1,651	9,419.7	1,325.9	706	493.4	55.8
1962	1,729	10,212.9	1,415.2	927	622.6	72.2
1963	1,924	11,198.2	1,564.9	1,119	583.5	56.6
1964	2,025	15,222.4	2,266.2	1,068	406.7	55.9
1965	1,760	18,250.2	2,522.3	1,023	389.6	54.6

Note: Data for chemicals include industrial inorganic and organic chemicals and plastics materials and synthetic resins, synthetic rubber, synthetic and other man-made fibers, except glass.

Source: U.S. Treasury Department, Internal Revenue Service, *Statistics of Income, Corporation Income Tax Returns, 1948 to 1965.*

APPENDIX TABLE 33

Per Cent Margin on Sales for Chemicals and Allied Products and Chemicals, 1929-1968

| Year | Chemicals and Allied Products | | | Chemicals | | |
	FTC-SEC	Internal Revenue Service	Department of Commerce	First Nat'l. City Bank	FTC-SEC	Internal Revenue Service
1929		7.3	8.9			
1930		2.5	4.8			
1931		−1.3	5.7			
1932		−1.2	3.7			
1933		0.7	8.4			
1934		1.5	8.7	13.1		
1935		2.7	8.0	14.7		
1936		10.1	8.5	12.5		
1937		8.9	7.7	15.0		
1938		6.9	6.5	6.7		
1939		10.3	9.7	8.5		
1940		9.8	9.3	9.6		
1941		8.5	8.1	9.1		
1942		7.2	6.5	6.6		
1943		6.1	5.7	6.2		
1944		5.5	4.6	5.4		
1945		4.7	4.0	7.4		
1946		8.8	8.1	8.9		
1947	8.8	8.4	7.8	9.6		
1948	8.8	7.5	7.0	9.9		12.0
1949	8.2	7.9	7.3	10.3		12.9
1950	10.3	9.2	8.5	11.7		14.6
1951	6.4	6.5	6.0	9.9		9.8
1952	6.1	5.3	5.0	7.7		8.1
1953	6.1	5.3	4.9	7.6		7.7
1954	6.8	5.9	5.8	8.9		9.1
1955	8.3	7.0	6.9	10.0		10.8
1956	8.0	6.6	6.3	9.1	10.0	9.1
1957	7.7	6.1	5.9	8.5	9.5	8.4
1958	7.0	5.7	5.2	7.2	7.7	6.9
1959	7.9	6.6	6.1	8.9	9.4	8.4
1960	7.6	6.0	5.7	8.6	8.4	7.2
1961	7.3	5.8	5.2	7.3	8.1	6.8
1962	7.4	5.9	5.1	7.6	8.5	7.3
1963	7.5	6.3	5.1	7.7	8.4	7.2
1964	7.9	7.2	5.6	8.1	8.7	7.5
1965	7.9	7.0	6.2	8.6	8.3	7.0
1966	7.8	NA	6.1	8.0	8.0	NA
1967	6.9	NA	NA	6.5	6.5	NA
1968	6.8	NA	NA	6.3	6.3	NA

Notes: NA—Not available. FTC-SEC data on chemicals for 1956 includes last three quarters only. Internal Revenue Series is for the fiscal year beginning 1955-56.

Sources: U.S. Department of Commerce, Office of Business Economics, *The National Income and Product Accounts of the United States, 1929-1965,* Washington, D.C., 1966, pp. 126-129, 142-145; *Survey of Current Business,* July 1968, pp. 44, 46, and July 1969, pp. 42, 44; U.S. Federal Trade Commission-Securities and Exchange Commission, *Quarterly Financial Report for Manufacturing Corporations,* Washington, D.C., various issues; First National City Bank of New York, *Monthly Letter on Business and Economic Conditions,* April issue of each year, U.S. Treasury Department, Internal Revenue Service, *Statistics of Income, Corporation Income Tax Returns, 1929 to 1965, passim.*

APPENDIX TABLE 34

Per Cent Relationship of Profits Before and After Taxes and Depreciation to Sales in Chemicals and Allied Products, 1946-1966

	1	2	3	4	5	6	7	8
		Profits Before Taxes	Profits After Taxes	Depre-ciation	Profits Before Taxes To Sales	Profits After Taxes To Sales	Depre-ciation To Sales	Columns 5+7
Year	Sales							
		(in millions)			*(per cent)*			
1946	$10,594	$1,423	$ 860	$ 183	13.4	8.1	1.7	15.1
1947	13,333	1,714	1,038	228	12.9	7.8	1.7	14.6
1948	13,225	1,549	928	277	11.7	7.0	2.1	13.8
1949	12,405	1,525	904	327	12.3	7.3	2.6	14.9
1950	15,368	2,589	1,313	369	16.8	8.5	2.4	19.2
1951	17,217	2,782	1,039	432	16.2	6.0	2.5	18.7
1952	16,936	2,147	851	539	12.7	5.0	3.2	15.9
1953	17,682	2,198	860	660	12.4	4.9	3.7	16.1
1954	17,900	2,204	1,044	784	12.3	5.8	4.4	16.7
1955	20,661	2,912	1,419	916	14.1	6.9	4.4	18.5
1956	21,810	2,864	1,381	973	13.1	6.3	4.5	17.6
1957	22,938	2,846	1,364	1,045	12.4	5.9	4.6	17.0
1958	22,607	2,445	1,172	1,127	10.8	5.2	5.0	15.8
1959	26,136	3,377	1,606	1,228	12.9	6.1	4.7	17.6
1960	26,269	3,120	1,501	1,230	11.9	5.7	4.7	16.6
1961	28,424	3,134	1,471	1,342	11.0	5.2	4.7	15.7
1962	29,617	3,181	1,519	1,624	10.7	5.1	5.5	16.2
1963	32,706	3,497	1,655	1,725	10.7	5.1	5.3	16.0
1964	34,468	3,891	1,921	1,765	11.3	5.6	5.1	16.4
1965	40,222	4,619	2,479	1,905	11.5	6.2	4.7	16.2
1966	43,584	4,949	2,679	1,962	11.4	6.1	4.5	15.9

Sources: U.S. Department of Commerce, Office of Business Economics, *The National Income and Product Accounts of the United States, 1929-1965,* Washington, D.C., 1966, pp. 119-21, 127-29, 139-41, 143-45 and *Survey of Current Business,* July 1968, pp. 44, 45, 46 and July 1969, pp. 42, 43, 44.

Per Cent Return on Net Worth for Chemicals and Allied Products and Chemicals, 1925-1968

| Year | Chemicals and Allied Products | | Chemicals | |
	FTC-SEC	Internal Revenue Service	First National City Bank	FTC-SEC
1925			8.6	
1926			10.5	
1927			10.3	
1928			17.2	
1929			18.0	
1930			11.4	
1931			8.0	
1932			4.9	
1933			8.0	
1934			9.6	
1935			11.8	
1936			15.2	
1937			14.7	
1938		6.9	7.9	
1939		11.3	12.9	
1940		11.6	13.1	
1941		12.3	13.6	
1942		10.1	10.8	
1943		9.6	10.4	
1944		9.0	10.6	
1945		7.6	10.2	
1946		14.9	14.7	
1947	16.0	15.7	17.2	
1948	15.8	14.0	17.7	
1949	13.2	12.5	16.5	
1950	17.8	16.5	21.3	
1951	12.2	12.1	16.3	
1952	10.9	9.3	13.7	
1953	10.8	9.6	13.3	
1954	11.6	10.2	14.5	
1955	14.7	12.7	17.7	
1956	14.2	11.1	15.6	14.1
1957	13.2	10.8	14.0	13.0
1958	11.4	9.4	11.1	9.8
1959	13.6	11.3	14.4	12.9
1960	12.2	9.9	12.4	11.1
1961	11.8	9.6	11.8	10.6
1962	12.4	10.3	12.3	11.7
1963	12.9	11.6	13.0	12.3
1964	14.4	13.7	14.2	14.1
1965	15.3	13.9	15.4	14.3
1966	15.1	N.A.	14.6	14.0
1967	13.1	N.A.	11.5	10.9
1968	13.3	N.A.	11.4	11.0

Notes: N.A.—Not available. Internal Revenue Service series is for the fiscal year beginning 1955-56. First National City Bank series is return on net assets and that of FTC-SEC is return on stockholders equity. FTC-SEC data on chemicals for 1956 includes last three quarters.

Sources: First National City Bank of New York, *Monthly Letter on Business and Economic Conditions,* April issue of each year; U.S. Federal Trade Commission-Securities and Exchange Commission, *Quarterly Financial Report for Manufacturing Corporations,* Washington, D.C., various issues; U.S. Treasury Department, Internal Revenue Service, *Statistics of Income, Corporation Income Tax Retruns,* Washington, D.C., *passim.*

APPENDIX TABLE 36

Per Cent Returns on Net Worth for Leading Corporations in Chemical Products Industry and All Manufacturing Industries, 1925-1968

Year	Chemical Products	All Manufacturing	Excess for Chemical Products Over All Manufacturing
		(per cent)	
1925	8.6	10.7	-2.1
1926	10.5	10.8	-0.3
1927	10.3	9.0	1.3
1928	17.2	11.6	5.6
1929	18.0	12.8	5.2
1930	11.4	6.4	5.0
1931	8.0	2.3	5.7
1932	4.9	0.5	5.4
1933	8.0	2.5	5.5
1934	9.6	4.3	5.3
1935	11.8	6.7	5.1
1936	15.2	10.4	4.8
1937	14.7	10.8	3.9
1938	7.9	4.8	3.1
1939	12.9	8.5	4.4
1940	13.1	10.3	2.8
1941	13.6	12.4	1.2
1942	10.8	10.1	0.7
1943	10.4	9.9	0.5
1944	10.6	9.8	0.8
1945	10.2	9.1	1.1
1946	14.7	12.1	2.6
1947	17.2	17.0	0.2
1948	17.7	18.9	-1.2
1949	16.5	13.8	2.7
1950	21.3	17.1	4.2
1951	16.3	14.4	1.9
1952	13.7	12.3	1.4
1953	13.3	12.5	0.8
1954	14.5	12.4	2.1
1955	17.7	15.0	2.7
1956	15.6	13.9	1.7
1957	14.0	12.8	1.2
1958	11.1	9.8	1.3
1959	14.4	11.6	2.8
1960	12.4	10.6	1.8
1961	11.8	9.9	1.9
1962	12.3	10.9	1.4
1963	13.0	11.5	1.5
1963	13.2	11.6	1.6
1964	14.2	12.6	1.6
1965	15.4	13.9	1.5
1966	14.6	14.2	0.4
1967	11.5	12.6	-1.1
1968	11.4	13.1	-1.7

Source: First National City Bank of New York, *Monthly Letter on Business and Economic Conditions,* April issue of each year.

Large Foreign Chemical Companies, 1968

Rank	Company	Headquarters	Industry	Sales[a]	Assets[b]
				(millions)	
1	Royal Dutch/Shell	Netherlands-Britain	Petroleum products, natural gas, chemicals	$9,216	$14,303
2	Unilever	Britain-Netherlands	Food, detergents, chemicals, toiletries, feed	5,534	3,432
4	ICI (Imperial Chemical Industries)	Britain	Chemicals	2,970	4,388
6	Philips' Gloeilampenfabrieken	Netherlands	Electric equipment, electronics, chemicals	2,685[c]	3,407[c,d]
8	Montecatini Edison	Italy	Chemicals, textiles	2,316[c]	4,561[c]
16	Farbwerke Hoechst	Germany	Chemicals, pharmaceuticals	1,907	1,818[c]
20	Farbenfabriken Bayer	Germany	Chemicals, pharmaceuticals	1,731[c]	1,913[*]
28	ENI (Ente Nazionale Idrocarburi)[l]	Italy	Petroleum products, chem., eng., textiles	1,444[c]	4,026
30	BASF (Badische Anilin & Soda-Fabrik)	Germany	Chemicals	1,395[f]	1,700[*]
32	Courtaulds[g]	Britain	Fibers, textiles	1,383	1,369
34	Pechiney	France	Aluminum, chemicals	1,275	652
39	Rhone-Poulenc	France	Textiles, chemicals, pharmaceuticals	1,201	1,424
40	Nippon Kokan[g]	Japan	Iron & steel, shipbuilding, chemicals	1,194[c]	1,527
58	AKU (Algemene Kunstzijde Unie)	Netherlands	Textiles, chemicals	917	1,136
60	Ugine Kuhlmann	France	Chemicals, steel, nonferrous metals	908[i]	638[h]
62	Metallgesellschaft[j]	Germany	Nonferrous metals, chemicals, eng.	889[c]	565[c]
65	Pemex (Petroleos Mexicanos)	Mexico	Petroleum products, natural gas, petrochemicals	884	1,829
69	Saint-Gobain	France	Glass, chemicals, oil, paper, machinery	815[k]	1,133[k]
82	Hoffmann-La Roche	Switzerland	Pharmaceuticals	720[*]	189[k]
84	Rio Tinto-Zinc	Britain	Mining, chemicals, steel, aluminum	698	1,377
85	CSR (Colonial Sugar Refining)[g]	Australia	Sugar, bldg. materials, chemicals, mining	693	510
88	Toyo Rayon[g]	Japan	Synthetic fibers, plastics	678	718
89	Petroleo Brasileiro (Petrobras)[l]	Brazil	Petroleum products, petrochemicals	668	1,001
91	Solvay	Belgium	Chemicals	655[m]	979[m]
96	J. R. Geigy	Switzerland	Chemicals, dyestuffs, pharmaceuticals	624	874
98	Ciba	Switzerland	Chemicals, pharmaceuticals, plastics	607[n]	836[n]
102	Hibernia	Germany	Chemicals, petroleum products, mining	590	697
110	Degussa[j]	Germany	Chemicals, precious metals	539	234[c]
117	KZO (Koninklijke Zout-Organon)	Netherlands	Salt, chemicals, pharmaceuticals, food products	514	522
118	Mitsubishi Chemical Industries[o]	Japan	Chemicals, aluminum	514	835
123	Asahi Chemical Industry[g]	Japan	Synthetic fibers, chemicals, food products	502	581
124	Sandoz	Switzerland	Pharmaceuticals, dyestuffs, chemicals	502	584[p]
126	Kanegafuchi Spinning[u]	Japan	Textiles, cosmetics, food, pharmaceuticals	494	441
128	Teijin[g]	Japan	Synthetic fibers, textiles	475	547
133	Feldmuhle-Dynamit Nobel	Germany	Paper products, chemicals	455[c]	380[c]
134	Sumitomo Chemical	Japan	Chemicals	444	761
135	Snia Viscosa	Italy	Synthetic fibers, chemicals, machinery	442[c]	432[c]
138	Takeda Chemical Industries[g]	Japan	Pharmaceuticals, chemicals, food products	432	447
140	Klockner-Werke[j]	Germany	Iron & steel, cement, chemicals	423	397
145	Kubota Iron & Machinery Works[q]	Japan	Machinery, iron & steel, chemicals	410	409
147	Alusuisse (Swiss Aluminium)	Switzerland	Aluminum, plastics	406	409
151	Domtar	Canada	Pulp & paper, bldg. materials, chemicals	395	481
154	Mitsubishi Rayon[g]	Japan	Textiles, plastics	388	334
163	Ube Industries[g]	Japan	Chemicals, petrochemicals, cement, machinery	371	605
164	Maruzen Oil[g]	Japan	Petroleum products, petrochemicals	367	460
165	Norddeutsche Affinerie[j]	Germany	Metals, chemicals	363	91
169	Showa Denko	Japan	Chemicals, metals	353	618
171	DSM (Staatsmijnen)[l]	Netherlands	Chemicals, coal	350	453
172	L'Air Liquide	France	Industrial gases, chemicals, eng.	345[r]	247[h]
176	Saarbergwerke	Germany	Mining, petroleum products, chemicals	341[s]	512[s]
179	Glaxo Group[t]	Britain	Pharmaceuticals, food products	328	251
183	Beecham Group[g]	Britain	Pharmaceuticals, cosmetics, food products	321	320
187	Continental Gummi-Werke	Germany	Rubber products, plastics	312	221[c]
190	Bunge y Born	Argentina	Food products, textiles, chemicals	303[c]	217[c]
196	C.U.F. Group	Portugal	Chemicals, shipping, tobacco	299	720
197	Chemische Werke Huls	Germany	Chemicals	293	268[h]

Notes: [a] All companies on the list must have derived more than 50 per cent of their sales from manufacturing and/or mining. Sales do not include excise taxes or customs duties, so the figures for some corporations—most of them sell gasoline, liquor or tobacco—may be lower than those published by the corporations themselves. Unless otherwise noted: consolidated figures exclude intercompany transactions, include full figures of only those subsidiaries more than 50 per cent owned, and are for the year ending December 31, 1968. Figures have been converted into U.S. dollars at official exchange rates. In countries where devaluation occurred during a company's fiscal year, sales . . . have been converted using an exchange rate that represents an average for the whole fiscal year. Total assets . . . have been converted at the exchange rate prevailing at the company's year-end.
[b] Total assets employed in the business at the year's end, less depreciation.
[c] Includes full figures of subsidiaries owned 50 per cent or more.
[d] In a few cases, where the holding is 50 per cent, figures have been prorated.
[e] Excludes foreign subsidiaries.
[f] Includes prorated figures of companies 50 per cent owned.
[g] Figures for fiscal year ending March 31, 1969.

[h] Parent company only.
[i] Includes prorated figures of all companies more than 10 per cent owned.
[j] Fiscal year ending September 30, 1968.
[k] Not fully consolidated.
[l] Government owned.
[m] Includes full figures of subsidiaries owned 50 per cent or more and of one company less than 50 per cent owned.
[n] Fiscal year ending July 31, 1968.
[o] Fiscal year ending January 31, 1969.
[p] Comparable 1967 figures: Assets $527,555,000; invested capital $321,953,000.
[q] Fiscal year ending October 15, 1968. Name changed to Kubota, Ltd., in April, 1969.
[r] Includes prorated figures of all subsidiaries.
[s] Includes full figures of three companies 50 per cent or less owned.
[t] Fiscal year ending June 30, 1968.
[u] Fiscal year ending October 31, 1968.

[*] Fortune estimate.

Source: "The Fortune Directory of the 200 Largest Industrials Outside the U.S.," Fortune, August 15, 1969, pp. 107-110.

APPENDIX TABLE 38

Exports and Imports of Chemicals and Related Products, 1929-1955
(Old Series)

	Exports	Imports For Consumption	Excess of Exports
		(millions)	
1929	$ 152	$144	$ 8
1930	128	112	16
1931	100	83	17
1932	70	48	22
1933	77	59	18
1934	93	65	28
1935	103	69	34
1936	116	80	36
1937	138	103	35
1938	128	78	50
1939	163	80	83
1940	222	58	164
1941	292	61	231
1942	348	88	260
1943	474	204	270
1944	472	156	316
1945	413	145	268
1946	500	100	400
1947	783	105	678
1948	780	111	669
1949	774	107	667
1950	731	170	561
1951	977	300	677
1952	819	244	575
1953	819	293	526
1954	1,004	249	755
1955	1,091	255	836

Source: U.S. Department of Commerce, Bureau of the Census, *Foreign Commerce and Navigation,* Washington, D.C. (annual). *U.S. Exports of Domestic Merchandise,* FT 410 Series, Washington, D.C., (annual); *U.S. Imports of Merchandise for Consumption,* FT 110 Series, Washington, D.C., (annual).

Note: For New Series since 1956, see Appendix Table 39.

APPENDIX TABLE 39
Exports and Imports of Chemicals and Related Products, 1956-1968
(New Series)

	Exports	General Imports	Excess of Exports
		(millions)	
1956	$1,320	$ 541	$ 779
1957	1,457	668	789
1958	1,405	800	605
1959	1,543	874	669
1960	1,776	821	955
1961	1,789	726	1,063
1962	1,876	760	1,160
1963	2,009	701	1,308
1964	2,364	702	1,662
1965	2,402	769	1,633
1966	2,675	955	1,720
1967	2,803	963	1,840
1968	3,289	1,135	2,154

Source: U.S. Department of Commerce, Bureau of the Census, *Statistical Abstract of the United States: 1965,* Washington, D.C., 1965, pp. 871, 873, (for 1956-59 data): *Statistical Abstract of the United States: 1968,* Washington, D.C., 1958, pp. 805, 807 (for 1960-67 data): *U.S. Exports - Schedule B Commodity and Country,* Report FT 410, December, 1968, Washington, D.C., 1969, p. 1-5; *U.S. Imports - General and Consumption, Schedule A Commodity and Country,* Report FT 135, December 1968, Washington, D.C., 1969, p. 1-5.

APPENDIX TABLE 40

Chemicals and Allied Products: Per Cent Relationship of Exports and Imports (New Series) to Corporate Sales, 1956-1965

	Sales	Exports		General Imports	
		Total	Per Cent of Sales	Total	Per Cent of Sales
	(billions)	(millions)		(millions)	
1956	$21.8	$1,320	6.1	$541	2.5
1957	22.9	1,457	6.4	668	2.9
1958	22.6	1,405	6.2	800	3.5
1959	26.1	1,543	5.9	874	3.3
1960	26.3	1,776	6.8	821	3.1
1961	28.4	1,789	6.3	726	2.6
1962	29.6	1,876	6.3	760	2.6
1963	32.7	2,009	6.1	701	2.1
1964	34.5	2,364	6.9	702	2.0
1965	40.2	2,402	6.0	769	1.9

Source: U.S. Department of Commerce, Office of Business Economics, *The National Income and Product Accounts of the United States, 1929-1965,* Washington, D.C., August 1966, pp. 144-45; *Survey of Current Business,* July 1968, p. 46; U.S. Department of Commerce, Bureau of the Census, *Statistical Abstract of the United States: 1965,* Washington, D.C., 1965, pp. 871, 873; *Statistical Abstract of the United States: 1968,* Washington, D.C., 1968, pp. 805, 807.

APPENDIX TABLE 41

Exports and Imports of Chemicals and Related Products and Total Exports and Imports, 1929-1955

(Old Series)

Year	Exports			Imports For Consumption		
	Total	Chemicals and Related Products	Per Cent of Total	Total	Chemicals and Related Products	Per Cent of Total
	(millions)			*(millions)*		
1929	$ 5,347	$ 152	2.8	$ 4,463	$144	3.2
1930	3,929	128	3.3	3,104	112	3.6
1931	2,494	100	4.0	2,120	83	3.9
1932	1,667	70	4.2	1,343	48	3.6
1933	1,736	77	4.4	1,510	59	3.9
1934	2,238	93	4.2	1,763	65	3.7
1935	2,404	103	4.3	2,462	69	2.8
1936	2,590	116	4.5	2,546	80	3.1
1937	3,451	138	4.0	3,181	103	3.2
1938	3,243	128	3.9	2,173	78	3.6
1939	3,347	163	4.9	2,409	80	3.3
1940	4,124	222	5.4	2,698	58	2.1
1941	5,343	292	5.5	3,416	61	1.8
1942	9,187	348	3.8	3,499	88	2.5
1943	15,115	474	3.1	4,599	204	4.4
1944	16,696	472	2.8	5,043	156	3.1
1945	12,473	413	3.3	5,245	145	2.8
1946	11,707	500	4.3	5,073	100	2.0
1947	16,015	783	4.9	5,979	105	1.8
1948	13,193	780	5.9	7,563	111	1.5
1949	12,149	774	6.4	6,879	107	1.6
1950	10,117	731	7.2	9,108	170	1.9
1951	14,123	977	6.9	11,202	300	2.7
1952	13,319	819	6.1	10,838	244	2.3
1953	12,281	819	6.7	10,990	293	2.7
1954	12,799	1,004	7.8	10,354	249	2.4
1955	14,280	1,091	7.6	11,527	255	2.2

Source: U.S. Congress, Joint Economic Committee, *1962 Supplement to Economic Indicators,* Washington, D.C., 1962, p. 82; U.S. Department of Commerce, Bureau of the Census, *Foreign Commerce and Navigation,* Washington, D.C., (Annual); *U.S. Exports of Domestic Merchandise,* FT 410 Series, Washington, D.C., (Annual): *U.S. Imports of Merchandise for Consumption,* FT 110 Series, Washington, D.C., (Annual).

Note: For New Series since 1956, see Appendix Table 42.

APPENDIX TABLE 42

Exports and Imports of Chemicals and Related Products (New Series) and Total Exports and Imports, 1956-1968

Year	Exports Total	Chemicals and Related Products	Per Cent of Total	General Imports Total	Chemicals and Related Products	Per Cent of Total
	(millions)			(millions)		
1956	$17,379	$1,320	7.6	$12,804	$ 541	4.2
1957	19,390	1,457	7.5	13,291	668	5.0
1958	16,264	1,405	8.6	12,952	800	6.2
1959	16,295	1,543	9.5	15,310	874	5.7
1960	19,487	1,776	9.1	14,744	821	5.6
1961	19,944	1,789	9.0	14,522	726	5.0
1962	20,606	1,876	9.1	16,219	760	4.7
1963	22,071	2,009	9.1	17,014	701	4.1
1964	25,478	2,364	9.3	18,647	702	3.8
1965	26,447	2,402	9.1	21,496	769	3.6
1966	29,389	2,675	9.1	25,463	955	3.8
1967	30,681	2,803	9.1	26,821	963	3.6
1968	33,598	3,289	9.8	32,972	1,135	3.4

Sources: *Economic Report of the President,* January 1969, p. 324; U.S. Department of Commerce, Bureau of the Census, *Statistical Abstract of the United States: 1965,* Washington, D.C., 1965, pp. 871, 873; *Statistical Abstract of the United States: 1968,* Washington, D.C., 1968, pp. 805, 807; *Survey of Current Business,* March 1969, p. 32; *U.S. Exports - Schedule B Commodity and Country,* Report FT 410; December 1968, Washington, D.C., 1969, p. 1-5; *U.S. Imports - General and Consumption, Schedule A Commodity and Country,* Report FT 135, December 1968, Washington, D.C., 1969, p. 1-5; *Economic Indicators,* June 1969, p. 24.

APPENDIX TABLE 43

Per Cent Relationship of United States Exports to World Trade, 1956-1968

	Chemicals & Allied Products			Total Exports		
	World	United States*	Per Cent Relationship	World	United States	Per Cent Relationship
	(millions)			(millions)		
1956	$ 5,220	$1,320	25.3	$ 94,116	$17,379	18.5
1957	5,770	1,457	25.3	101,031	19,390	19.2
1958	5,900	1,405	23.8	95,400	16,264	17.0
1959	6,620	1,543	23.3	101,300	16,295	16.1
1960	7,450	1,776	23.8	113,400	19,487	17.2
1961	7,960	1,789	22.5	118,600	19,944	16.8
1962	8,500	1,876	22.1	124,700	20,606	16.5
1963	9,370	2,009	21.4	136,000	22,071	16.2
1964	10,910	2,364	21.7	152,500	25,478	16.7
1965	12,220	2,402	19.7	165,400	26,447	16.0
1966	13,700	2,675	19.5	181,400	29,389	16.2
1967	14,900	2,803	18.8	190,500	30,681	16.1
1968	NA	3,289		212,200	33,598	15.8

*New Series

NA - not available

Sources: Economic Report of the President, January 1969, p. 324 (for United States total export data): U.S. Department of Commerce, Bureau of the Census, Statistical Abstract of the United States: 1965, pp. 871, 873 (for 1956-59 United States chemical and allied products export data): Statistical Abstract of the United States: 1968, pp. 805, 807 (for 1960-67 United States chemical and allied products export data); International Monetary Fund, International Financial Statistics, July 1959, p. 20; August 1964, p. 34; March 1959, p. 32 (for world total export data); United Nations, Monthly Bulletin of Statistics, March 1961, p. xvi; March 1964, p. xxii; March 1969, p. xxvi (for world chemical and allied products export data); Survey of Current Business, March 1969, p. 32; U.S. Department of Commerce, Bureau of the Census, U.S. Exports - Schedule B Commodity and Country, Report FT 410, December 1968, Washington, D.C., 1969, p. 1-5; Economic Indicators, June 1969, p. 24.

APPENDIX TABLE 44

Export Surplus: Total Merchandise and Chemicals and Related Products, 1929-1968

	Total Merchandise	Chemicals and Related Products	Per Cent of Total
	(millions)		
1929	$ 884	$ 8	0.9
1930	825	16	1.9
1931	374	17	4.5
1932	324	22	6.8
1933	226	18	8.0
1934	475	28	5.9
1935	-58	34	-
1936	44	36	81.8
1937	270	35	13.0
1938	1,070	50	4.7
1939	938	83	8.8
1940	1,426	164	11.5
1941	1,927	231	12.0
1942	5,688	260	4.6
1943	10,516	270	2.6
1944	11,926	316	2.6
1945	7,228	268	3.7
1946	6,634	400	6.0
1947	10,036	678	6.8
1948	5,630	669	11.9
1949	5,270	667	12.7
1950	1,009	561	55.6
1951	2,921	677	23.2
1952	2,481	575	23.2
1953	1,291	526	40.7
1954	2,445	755	30.9
1955	2,753	836	30.4
1956	4,575	779	17.0
1957	6,099	789	12.9
1958	3,312	605	18.3
1959	985	669	67.9
1960	4,743	965	20.3
1961	5,422	1,063	19.6
1962	4,387	1,116	25.4
1963	5,057	1,308	25.9
1964	6,831	1,662	25.2
1965	4,951	1,633	33.0
1966	3,926	1,720	43.8
1967	3,860	1,840	47.7
1968	626	2,154	344.1

Note: New Series starts in 1956. Data from 1929 to 1955 based on "consumption imports" and from 1956 to 1968 on "general imports."

Source: See Appendix Table 42.

APPENDIX TABLE 45

Exports of Chemicals and Related Products,
Selected Years, 1958-1967

Standard International Tariff Classification	1958 Total (millions)	%	1962 Total (millions)	%	1967 Total (millions)	%
Organic chemicals	$ 166	11.7	$ 263	13.8	$ 748	26.7
Inorganic chemical elements, oxides, including hydroxides, peroxides, and halogen salts	108	7.6	115	6.1	191	6.8
Inorganic chemicals, except elements, oxides, hydroxides, peroxides, and halogen salts	40	2.8	50	2.7	108	3.9
Radioactive and stable isotopes; radioactive elements	2	0.1	2	0.1	51	1.8
Mineral, tar, tar oils, and crude chemicals from coal, petroleum, and natural gas	29	2.0	67	3.6	29	1.0
Synthetic organic dyes, natural indigo, color lakes, and toners	19	1.3	27	1.4	32	1.2
Dyeing and tanning extracts, including synthetic and artificial bates	2	0.1	3	0.2	3	0.1
Pigments, paints, varnishes, and related materials	46	3.2	47	2.5	74	2.6
Medicinal and pharmaceutical products	280	19.7	275	14.6	288	10.3
Essential oils, perfume, and flavor materials	35	2.5	48	2.5	44	1.6
Perfumery, cosmetics, and other toilet preparations, except soaps	15	1.0	18	1.0	26	0.9
Soaps, cleansing, polishing, and finishing preparations	52	3.7	60	3.2	70	2.5
Fertilizers, manufactured	82	5.8	103	5.5	231	8.2
Explosives and pyrotechnic products, sporting ammunition	21	1.5	14	0.7	18	0.6
Synthetic resins, regenerated cellulose, and plastic materials	219	15.4	306	16.3	473	16.9
Chemical products and materials, not elsewhere classified	307	21.6	485	25.8	416	14.9
Total	$1,423	100.0	$1,883	100.0	$2,802	100.0

Source: U.S. Department of Commerce, Bureau of the Census, *Foreign Commerce and Navigation of the United States, 1946-1963,* Washington, D.C., 1965, p. 8 and *Chemical and Engineering News,* February 10, 1969, p. 15.

Imports of Chemicals and Related Products, Selected Years, 1958-1967

Standard International Tariff Classification	1958		1962		1967	
	Total	%	Total	%	Total	%
	(millions)		(millions)		(millions)	
Organic chemicals	$ 42	11.5	$ 73	9.5	$219	22.8
Inorganic chemical elements, oxides, including hydroxides, peroxides, and halogen salts	67	18.3	60	7.8	167	17.3
Inorganic chemicals, except elements, oxides, hydroxides, peroxides, and halogen salts	48	13.1	64	8.4	49	5.1
Radioactive and stable isotopes; radioactive elements	2	0.5	258	33.7	16	1.7
Mineral, tar, tar oils, and crude chemicals from coal, petroleum, and natural gas	22	6.0	48	6.3	9	0.9
Synthetic organic dyes, natural indigo, color lakes, and toners	9	2.5	17	2.2	37	3.8
Dyeing and tanning extracts, including synthetic and artificial bates	13	3.5	9	1.2	10	1.0
Pigments, paints, varnishes, and related materials	3	0.8	5	0.7	6	0.6
Medicinal and pharmaceutical products	32	8.7	54	7.0	72	7.5
Essential oils, perfume, and flavor materials	20	5.4	29	3.8	49	5.1
Perfumery, cosmetics, and other toilet preparations, except soaps	4	1.1	8	1.0	13	1.3
Soaps, cleansing, polishing, and finishing preparations	2	0.5	2	0.3	6	0.6
Fertilizers, manufactured	65	17.7	88	11.5	142	14.8
Explosives and pyrotechnic products, sporting ammunition	3	0.8	7	0.9	41	4.3
Synthetic resins, regenerated cellulose, and plastic materials	8	2.2	13	1.7	60	6.2
Chemical products and materials, not elsewhere classified	27	7.4	31	4.0	67	7.0
Total	$367	100.0	$766	100.0	$963	100.0

Source: U.S. Department of Commerce, Bureau of the Census, *Foreign Commerce and Navigation of the United States, 1946-1963,* Washington, D.C., 1965, p. 13 and *Chemical and Engineering News,* February 10, 1969, p. 15.

APPENDIX TABLE 47

Export Prices In Terms of U.S. Dollars, Leading
Countries, Selected Years, 1937-1967
(1958 = 100)

	United Kingdom	United States	Germany	France	Japan	Italy
1937	51	48	56*	NA	36**	NA
1938	NA	NA	NA	41	NA	68
1948	103	92	NA	96	NA	123
1950	77	83	76	88	102	101
1951	91	95	95	101	145	123
1952	96	94	101	110	120	116
1953	92	94	97	103	113	110
1954	92	94	95	101	112	109
1955	93	94	96	98	109	104
1956	96	97	100	102	114	101
1957	101	100	102	104	110	105
1958	100	100	100	100	100	100
1959	99	100	99	93	104	92
1960	101	101	101	96	105	96
1961	101	103	106	96	100	92
1962	102	102	108	96	97	93
1963	105	102	108	98	100	94
1964	107	103	108	101	101	97
1965	109	106	110	102	100	94
1966	113	110	111	105	100	93
1967	115	112	110	105	101	95

*1936

**1934-1936.

Source: International Monetary Fund, *International Financial Statistics,* February 1949, p. 20; December 1950, p. XXIV; December 1957, p. 38; December 1959, p. 38; December 1960, p. 34; December 1961, p. 32; December 1962, pp. 36-7; June 1966, p. 30; August 1968, p. 30.